INSTRUCTOR'S MANUAL / TEST BANK to accompany

Understanding Human Communication

NINTH EDITION

RONALD B. ADLER
Santa Barbara City College

GEORGE RODMAN
Brooklyn College, City University of New York

Prepared by
T. J. Jenkins

New York   Oxford
OXFORD UNIVERSITY PRESS
2006

Oxford University Press

Oxford University Press, Inc., publishes works that further Oxford University's
objective of excellence in research, scholarship, and education.

Oxford New York
Auckland   Cape Town   Dar es Salaam   Hong Kong   Karachi
Kuala Lumpur   Madrid   Melbourne   Mexico City   Nairobi
New Delhi   Shanghai   Taipei   Toronto

With offices in
Argentina   Austria   Brazil   Chile   Czech Republic   France   Greece
Guatemala   Hungary   Italy   Japan Poland   Portugal   Singapore
South Korea   Switzerland   Thailand   Turkey   Ukraine   Vietnam

Copyright © 2006 by Oxford University Press, Inc.

Published by Oxford University Press, Inc.
198 Madison Avenue, New York, New York 10016
http://www.oup-usa.org

Oxford is a registered trademark of Oxford University Press

ISBN-13: 978-0-19-522194-7
ISBN: 0-19-522194-X

Printing number: 9 8 7 6 5 4 3 2 1

Printed in the United States of America
on acid-free paper

CONTENTS

STUDENT RESOURCE MANUAL (material on student CD ROM)

PLANNING YOUR COURSE

ORIENTATION OF THE TEXTBOOK

Understanding Human Communication is designed for use in a basic course in communication fundamentals. When designing your course you may choose to emphasize either the understanding of theory or the development of specific skills. The text can be adapted for use in either of these course types or in one which places an equal emphasis on both elements.

The authors present fundamental issues in communication by discussing theoretical foundations and research upon which practical communication principles are based. The text presents real-life vignettes, reports research findings, and describes basic assumptions about central concepts in the discipline of communication. Only after these theoretical underpinnings have been presented do the authors suggest strategies which can be used to improve communication effectiveness. Simply, the text is not an oversimplified "how to" manual. It is, instead, a theoretically grounded introductory text designed to orient novice students to key issues in the field of speech communication.

For those using the more theoretical approach, suggested activities interspersed throughout the text will encourage the discussion of concepts. They can also be used by students for their own personal understanding and integration of material. In-class use of the activities in the text and manual will encourage experiential learning important to those choosing to emphasize skill enhancement.

COURSE ARRANGEMENT

The text is divided into four units and an appendix which together present an overview of communication in general and an examination of three specific contexts in which communication occurs. Part 1: Elements of Communication includes consideration of the nature of communication, perception, self-concept, language, listening, and nonverbal communication, all of which have guiding principles which emerge throughout the remainder of the text. Part 11: Interpersonal Communication considers development of relationships, self-disclosure, conflict resolution, and interviewing. Part III: Communication in Groups presents an overview of the nature of groups and group problem solving. Part IV: Public Communication focuses on public speaking and suggests guidelines for topic selection, organization, use of supporting material, delivery, informative speaking, and persuasive speaking. The *Instructor's Manual* provides supplementary material on mass communication. This material may be used to provide additional scope to other units as the instructor desires, or to initiate a short unit introducing mass communication in the basic course. The supplementary material has the same structure as the text's chapters, including content, activities, and resources.

The following syllabus is adapted for a fifteen-week semester with classes that meet for 50-minute periods three times a week. It can be modified for those classes that meet twice a week for longer blocks of time.

SEMESTER SYLLABUS

Week One

Day #1   Introduction to the course, overview of syllabus and course policies. Assign dyad introductions (see First Day of Class, page 6). Allow class time for interviewing. *Assign Chapter 1.*

Day #2   Dyad interviews OR discuss importance of oral communication skills.

Day #3   Communication functions, models, components, misconceptions. *Assign Chapter 2.*

Week Two

Day #4   Perception: Discussion and activities.

Day #5   Self-Concept: Discuss nature of, importance of, and role in communication. Discuss empathy and self-fulfilling prophecy. *Assign Chapter 3.*

Day #6   Language: Discuss nature of language and language misunderstanding.

Week Three

Day #7   Language activity. *Assign Chapter 4.*

Day #8   Listening: Administer listening test and/or listening skills inventory. Discuss current listening abilities, misconceptions, components of the listening process, reasons for poor listening, and types of listening.

Day #9   Listening: Explore one of the types of listening. *Assign Chapter 5.*

Week Four

Day #10   Nonverbal communication: Discuss characteristics, differences between verbal and nonverbal communication, functions, and types.

Day #11   Nonverbal communication: Use activities to illustrate concepts. *Assign Chapter 6.*

Day #12   Interpersonal communication: Discuss characteristics of interpersonal relationships, self disclosure, and assertiveness. *Assign Chapter 7.*

Week Five

Day #13   Interpersonal communication: Discuss relational communication and conflict management.

Day #14   Use an activity or film to explore the concepts in Chapters Six and Seven. *Assign Chapter 8.*

Day #15   Explore the strategies of interviewing. *Assign Appendix.*

Week Six

Day #16   Communication in groups: Discuss nature, goals, types, and characteristics of groups. *Assign Chapter 10.*

Day #17   Problem solving: Discuss steps in problem solving. Use group problem-solving activity.

Day #18   Communication in groups: Discuss participant and leadership roles and dangers in group discussion.

Week Seven

Day #19   Group presentations.

Day #20   Group presentations.

Day #21   Group presentations. *Assign Chapter 11.*

Week Eight

Day #22   Mid-term exam.

Day #23   Public speaking: Discuss criteria for and process of choosing a topic.

Day #24   Discuss process of developing a topic. *Assign Chapter 12.*

Week Nine

Day #25   Organization: Discuss structuring ideas/outlines. Use a scrambled outline or other activity for practicing organizational skills. *Assign Chapter 13.*

Day #26   Supporting materials: Discuss research techniques, type and uses of supporting materials.

Day #27   Delivery: Discuss apprehension and delivery types.

Week Ten

Day #28 Delivery: Discuss vocal and visual delivery. Use an oral presentation activity. *Assign Chapter 14.*
Day #29 Informative speaking: Discuss informative techniques.
Day #30 Practice using informative strategies OR study a sample speech.

Week Eleven

Day #31 Informative speeches
Day #32 Informative speeches
Day #33 Informative speeches. *Assign Chapter 15.*

Week Twelve

Day #34 Persuasion: Discuss merits, types, and strategies of persuasion.
Day #35 Persuasion: Discuss organizing the persuasive speech.
Day #36 Persuasion: Discuss speaker credibility.

Week Thirteen

Day #37 Persuasion: Discuss logical appeals and fallacies.
Day #38 Persuasion: Discuss emotional appeals.
Day #39 Persuasion: Discuss audience analysis and adaptation.

Week Fourteen

Day #40 Persuasive speeches
Day #41 Persuasive speeches
Day #42 Persuasive speeches

Week Fifteen

Day #43 Persuasive speeches.
Day #44 Explore concepts of mass communication OR makeup speeches.
Day #45 Finish mass communication OR semester review.

Final Exam Period

Final Exam

SUGGESTED GRADING PROCEDURE

Class participation, attendance, minor written assignments	10%
Group project	15%
Informative speech	15%
Selected oral assignment (interview, report, demonstration, etc.)	10%
Persuasive speech	20%
Mid-term exam	15%
Final exam	15%
	100%

ALTERNATIVE APPROACHES TO THE COURSE

The overview and syllabus that are described in the preceding section represent a general approach that an instructor might take with this course. Alternative approaches are also possible.

1. The order in which the four basic sections are introduced may be altered. One popular sequence of coverage is to emphasize the first two theoretical sections at the beginning of the course and then to move to public speaking *before* treating small group communication. This order of coverage enables the class to develop rapport and a sense of safety before moving to public speaking. Moreover, it provides the additional benefit of avoiding the stress of presenting and grading public speeches at the end of the semester.

   If group assignments are selected and designed carefully, an instructor can greet the end of the semester without an enormous amount of time needed for grading. Moving the public-speaking section before the group section offers that possibility. In addition, students often appreciate class time available for group projects at the end of the semester more than at mid-semester.

2. Although the text is designed around contexts of communication, it is possible to structure the course around concepts. For instance, the concept of source credibility comes to bear in all contexts: interpersonal, group, and public address. An instructor can list those concepts which seem most essential and can stress their importance in all contexts. To do this, the instructor will need to be quite familiar with the book in order that relevant readings can be reorganized around the idea-oriented approach.

3. In order to staff more students economically, some colleges and universities have moved to a class format which involves a combination of mass lecture and small recitation sections. In the lecture/recitation format, a student meets once weekly in a mass lecture setting and meets the rest of the time in a class of approximately 20-25 students. The college save money in teaching because more students can be served by fewer faculty members. Material can be presented effectively in such a format if the lecture time is used primarily for presentation of theoretical issues as well as overview of relevant research. The recitation time, in order to complement the lecture, needs to involve much student participation and opportunities to practice skills.

4. Increasingly important to most educators is the writing ability (or lack of ability) of students. The course for which this text is designed may incorporate much additional writing in the assignments. Typically, fundamentals courses may require use of journals, either graded or ungraded; extensive reaction papers in which students respond cognitively and/or emotionally to assigned issues or events; and development of outlines, including bibliographies. It is not unusual for faculty members in all disciplines to require that papers be typed, that spelling be accurate, and that bibliographic entries be prepared according to standard form. The purpose of the assignment may determine how the instructor evaluates the writing.

5. A case study approach can be incorporated to a great extent in the classroom. This approach involves presentation of a "case" in which human interaction is described. The case may be from real life or may be fictional. Students meet in groups to discuss relevant issues present in the case and often make recommendations about how the case could be handled effectively. Case studies can be found in the newspaper, novels, personal experience, and books featuring case studies for educational use.

FIRST DAY OF CLASS

Many instructors using the manual will be first-year instructors, some of those graduate assistants or part-time teachers who do not know their teaching assignments until a day or two before classes begin. In order to provide some assistance, this section offers guidelines for preparation on the first several days of classes.

The first day of class sets a tone for the remainder of the semester. As research in impression formation demonstrates, the initial impression that students have of a class and of an instructor, may give students an overall view of the class which endures throughout the semester. Because the first class sessions do establish a tone, it is important that you arrive at the class giving the appearance of being knowledgeable and prepared.

This is, of course, most easily accomplished if you are genuinely prepared. *Before* the first day of class you should:

1. Read the entire text and manual. This will give you the overall perspective you need to plan the course and teach the component parts.

2. Write a day-by-day plan for the entire semester. If your department has a uniform syllabus, read that. Have copies of the syllabus ready to hand out to students. The syllabus should contain the following as appropriate for your course.

- Course name
- Course number
- Meeting times, and location
- Teacher name
- Office location
- Phone numbers
- Office hours
- Course description
- Catalogue description, including prerequisites
- Additional description as needed
- Course objectives

- Course policies
- Attendance
- Extra credit
- Assignment format information
- Make-up policy
- Class participation
- Plagiarism (reference to university policy)
- Grading Policy
- Statement of how final grade will be determined
- Topics and order of coverage

- Key dates
- Exams
- Assignment due dates
- Planned absences
- Assignments descriptions and relative weight
- Course materials
- Texts
- Supplies
- Supplemental readings
- Fees
- Lab Policy (if appropriate)

3. Plan in detail what you will do for the first class period. It will not take you 50 minutes to present the syllabus.

4. Learn department policy on students adding and dropping classes and the procedure for handling students in class who are not on your official class list.

During the first class period you should:

1. Write your name and the class name and number on the board so those who are in the wrong room will know immediately and be able to leave. Ask if anyone is in the wrong room. Introduce yourself. Tell students something about yourself, such as how long you've been at the school, where you were before that, other courses you teach, hobbies, etc.

2. Read the class list if you have one; it may not be available the first day of class. Tell students to correct your pronunciation of their names and notify you if they have a name they prefer to be called. If the list is not yet available, send around a sign-up sheet.

3. Write down the names of those who are on the list and are not present and those present who are not on the list. Follow department procedure.

4. Review with the class the course policies and syllabus. Ask if there are any questions.

5. Make the assignment for class #2.

6. Finish the class with an activity or discussion. Activities you might include:

- Assign students a partner. Tell them they are to introduce their partner to the class on day #2. Give them the remainder of class time to interview each other. Suggest things they would want to ask each other, encouraging them to go beyond name and major. Encourage them to be creative and make the introductions interesting. Emphasize that they will not be graded.

- Have students introduce themselves, giving them a time limit (1-2 minutes) and suggestions about what information to include.

- Have students sit in a circle and introduce themselves by saying their name and something they like to do which begins with the same letter. For example, "My name is Diane and I like to dance."

- As a follow-up to the introductory activity, ask students to write down each student's name as you point to them or ask a volunteer to try to orally name them all. You can refer back to this activity later when you discuss listening.

- Ask students, "Why are you here?" The most common answer is, "Because it's required." Follow up by asking, "Why do you think it's required?" Use these reasons and those offered by students taking the course as an elective to establish the importance of the class for students' present role as students and future role as professionals.

- For additional suggestions, see the index under "Icebreakers" in the *Speech Communication Teacher*, Fall 1990, Vol. 4, No. 1.

INSTRUCTOR EVALUATION

In order to gather feedback about teaching effectiveness, systematic evaluation procedures are needed. As you compare teaching evaluation results over a period of several semesters, you will be able to pinpoint areas of strengths and those needing improvement.

Most universities and colleges suggest some form of student evaluation of faculty teaching. One common form of evaluation is a list of statements describing the teaching methods of the instructor with instructions for students to respond to them with: strongly agree (1), agree (2), no opinion (3), disagree (4), and strongly disagree (5). If an instructor uses comparable statements over a period of time when gathering feedback about a particular course, the appraisals can be quite helpful for improving teaching effectiveness. Statements should ask for evaluation of both the instructor and the course. When designing your own evaluation form you would select statements such as the following and may also want to add more specific statements to match your course.

Instructor

1. My instructor displays a clear understanding of course topics.

2. My instructor seems well prepared for class.

3. My instructor uses many methods to involve me in learning.

4. My instructor stimulates interest in the course.

5. My instructor has stimulated my thinking.

6. My instructor teaches students to value the viewpoint of others.

7. My instructor emphasizes relationships between and among topics.

8. My instructor helps me apply theory to solve problems.

9. My instructor makes good use of examples and illustrations.

10. My instructor is actively helpful when students have problems.

11. My instructor is careful and precise when answering questions.

12. My instructor is readily available for consultation.

13. My instructor returns papers and critique sheets quickly enough to benefit me.

14. My instructor deals fairly and impartially with me.

15. My instructor develops classroom discussion skillfully.

16. My instructor motivates me to do my best work.

17. I would enjoy taking another course from this instructor.

18. Overall, this instructor is among the best teachers I have known.

Course

19. This course develops the creative ability of students.

20. The climate of this class is conducive to learning.

21. Exams accurately assess what I have learned in this course.

22. Exams are fair.

23. Exams stress important points of the lectures/text.

24. Grades are assigned fairly and impartially.

25. Length and difficulty of assigned readings are reasonable.

26. Assignments are related to goals of this course.

27. The format of this course is appropriate to course objectives.

28. Frequent attendance in this class is essential to good learning.

29. This course has clearly stated objectives.

30. I understand what is expected of me in this course.

31. The amount of material covered was reasonable.

32. I found this class challenging.

33. I highly recommend this course.

34. Overall, this course is among the best I have ever taken.

Sample Open Evaluation Statements

1. The one concept that I learned this semester (term) that was most helpful to me personally was . . .

2. The material that we covered that was least helpful was . . .

3. In relation to the difficulty level of other required courses, the difficulty level of this communication course was . . .

4. The exams were . . .

5. The speaking assignments were . . .

6. The written assignments were . . .

7. If the instructor were to change one thing about his/her teaching to make it more effective, it should be . . .

8. If I could come into class this semester (term) and find one thing different it would be . . .

9. All semester (term) I've been wanting to complain about . . .

10. All semester (term) I've wanted to compliment you on . . .

11. The textbook was . . .

12. If you change this course for next semester (term), be sure to change . . .

13. If you change this course for next semester (term), be sure to keep this one thing exactly the same . . .

14. My most vivid memory of class was when . . .

15. In addition . . .

Another form of evaluation which is of great help is *peer evaluation*. This evaluation involves peers, colleagues on the faculty, who visit your classes and give you feedback about your teaching. Usually such evaluation is done only after an invitation is extended. It provides an excellent opportunity to receive ideas from other teachers. The peers can be graduate assistants or regular full-time faculty. After a classroom visit, a conference is usually arranged at which time the visitor gives feed back to the instructor. It often helps for the visiting evaluator to provide a letter of feedback, particularly one which emphasizes the areas of strength, to the instructor. Criticisms are most helpful if presented in concrete behavioral terms. Unlike one instructor who was advised to "change your basic personality," it is most helpful if the suggestions can be made as specific as possible.

Before engaging in peer evaluation, it is important that both parties agree upon the purposes of the evaluation. If the evaluation visit is solely for the purpose of improving teaching effectiveness, then the suggestions may be more frank and more critical then if the purpose is evaluation on which salary recommendations or similar decisions are to be made. Be sure that you and your evaluator envision the same purpose for the visit. The feedback which you receive from colleagues is a powerful complement to that which you receive from students.

Confidentiality is essential in gathering student data. Not only should you guarantee that evaluation data will not be read before grades are posted, you should abide by that. If confidentially is not promised, students will likely be inhibited about giving negative feedback, even if it might be greatly constructive to you in improving your teaching. If possible, you might want to have another instructor come into the class to administer the evaluation. Another possibility is to have a student collect the forms and seal them into a large envelope. Students will appreciate knowing that they can be frank, and you will benefit more from their frankness than from incomplete feedback.

STRUCTURE OF THE INSTRUCTOR'S MANUAL

This *Instructor's Manual is* designed to provide a chapter-by-chapter summary of key concepts and suggested activities for use in the classroom. The manual provides the following materials for each of the fourteen chapters and appendix.

CHAPTER OVERVIEW A succinct summary of the major concepts from the chapter is provided. This will give the instructor an opportunity for cursory review of the chapter material.

CHAPTER OBJECTIVES The authors begin each chapter of the text with cognitive and behavioral objectives for students. The chapter objectives in the manual are for the instructor. They are both to help plan the instruction and act as a post-instruction checkup on the treatment of a given chapter. The materials in the manual are consistent with the authors' view of the importance of theory, research and skill development.

SUGGESTED INSTRUCTIONAL ACTIVITIES Each chapter guide includes two or three activities suitable for classroom use. These activities are presented with clear purposes, procedures, and a list of principles that the exercises illustrate. Moreover, an approximate time needed for the activity is noted, although that may vary from class to class. Some of these activities are original with this manual; others are tried-and-true classics that have been adapted from years of classroom use. All activities are adapted to different class sizes, generous or stringent budgets, and differing instructor's teaching styles.

An additional feature is the inclusion of a set of activities which are designed to encourage creative and critical thinking. While all activities require thinking, those labeled Activities to Promote Critical and Creative Thinking are specifically designed with that goal in mind. It is hoped they will facilitate the efforts of teachers who are concerned with teaching higher-level thinking skills.

Another unique feature of this manual is a reference to teaching activities published in *The Speech Communication Teacher* for each chapter. Special attention has been paid to updating these for this edition.

SUGGESTED EXAMINATION QUESTIONS This edition of the manual contains an expanded set of test items for each chapter. Many of the items have been used and statistically reviewed. Items are labeled according to cognitive level: recall (memory items), conceptual (requiring students to state knowledge in their own or different words), application (requiring students to connect learned information to novel settings), and syntheses (requiring students to see connections between concepts and to put ideas together to create insights).

BIBLIOGRAPHY Because many instructors of the basic course are not necessarily thoroughly familiar with the broad range of concepts covered in a survey course, a fairly extensive bibliography is provided for each chapter. The sources include textbooks, scholarly books, and periodical. The sources can be used in several ways:

1. To provide beginning instructors with a more in-depth knowledge of communication concepts.

2. To update the knowledge of experienced teachers.

3. As lecture materials.

4. As reading assignments for students.

5. As topics for student reports.

FILMS AND TAPES Information about films and tapes related to each chapter is provided at the end of each chapter guide. Whenever available, information is given about title, source, date of production, and length. Most of these films are available in the film libraries of major universities. Others, however, may be found with their original production source. An up-to-date film catalogue can be used to find addresses and costs.

STUDENT RESOURCE MANUAL The activities and quizzes from the Student Resource Manual have been reprinted in the Instructor's Manual for your ease of use. Students have these activities and quizzes on the CD ROM that accompanies every new copy of the text.

GENERAL RESOURCES FOR TEACHING THE BASIC SPEECH COURSE

The Communication Teacher is a quarterly publication by the National Communication Association. It contains teaching activities and resources for high school and college speech teachers. The website of www.natcom.org/pubs/ct/CT%20Index.htm includes a subject index for the last ten years of the publication. Relevant teaching activities are also cited as references in the "Supplementary Resources" section of each chapter in this manual. *The Communication Teacher* is available from NCA at: 1765 N. Street N.W. Washington, D.C. 20036. Back issues are available.

Communication Education is a journal published by the National Communication Association which presents current research and theory on issues in speech pedagogy and instructional communication. It is available with membership in NCA at the above address.

ERIC Resource. (Educational Resources Information Center, Clearinghouse on Reading and Communication Skills) is a vast network of educational material is available in most college libraries. The following may be particularly useful. They, and a complete list of offerings, are available from: ERIC

Clearinghouse on Reading, English and Communication, Indiana University, Smith Research Center, Suite 140, Bloomington, IN 47408-2698. Phone (800) 759-4723.

Minibibliographies

- Assessing Speech Communication
- Communication Apprehension
- Critical Thinking
- Decision-making
- Intercultural Communication
- Interpersonal Communication
- Listening
- Organizational Culture and Communication Research
- Problem Solving

ERIC/RCS Digests

- Planning, Implementing, Improving Work-based Resources (1997)
- Using Experiential Learning to Teach Group Communication (2001)
- Real Language Activities (1996)
- Dialogue Journals (Vol. 35, 1997)
- Communication Apprehension: The Quiet Student in Your Classroom
- Fostering Cognitive Development in College Students-The Perry and Toulmin Models
- Listening: Are We Teaching It, and If So, How?
- Semiotics
- ASHE-ERIC Higher Education Reports (ERIC Clearinghouse on Higher Education and the Association for the Study of Higher Education) Published by the George Washington University Graduate School of Education and Human Development, One Dupont Circle, Suite 630, Washington, DC 20036-1183. Phone: 1-800-773-ERIC.

Brochures

- ERIC/RCS: A Profile
- How to Search ERIC
- ERIC/RCS Publications List
- ERIC/RCS Newsletter (October 1988)
- ERIC Digests: A Listing from all Clearinghouses

Additional General Resources

C-Span
Professors' News
C-Span Educational Services
400 North Capital St., NW
Washington, DC 20001
Educators' Hotline (800) 523-7586

This network offers programs and tapes of a variety of political communication that can be used for anything from sample speeches to discussion starters to illustrations of specific concepts from the course. By writing to the above address you will receive a monthly newsletter informing you of new programs, suggestions for teaching strategies and faculty development workshops.

COMPETENCIES

Several publications are available that list expected competencies relevant to the basic speech course. You may want to use these to frame your course or to help in the development of student outcomes and assessment procedures.

- *Communication Education.* "Special Issue on the Communication Curriculum." Vol. 51, No. 1, January, 2002

- *Communication for Careers.* A brochure on oral competencies needed by community college graduates entering careers. Annandale, VA: SCA.

- *Latino Expectations of Communication Competence.* L. Bradford, Renee Meyers and Kristine Kane. *Communication Quarterly*, Winter 1999

Teaching Effectiveness

- National Library of Education. 400 Maryland Ave. SW, Washington, DC, 20020 Phone: (800) 424-1616. www.ed.gov/NLE/

- New Teacher Resource. 725 Front St., Suite 400, Santa Cruz, CA 95060. Phone : (831) 459-4323. www.newteachercenter.org

Speaking Across the Curriculum

Two resources that explain the structure and practices for implementing a "Speaking Across the Curriculum" program are:

- Communication across the Curriculum at Southern Illinois University in Carbondale. www.siu.edu/departments/cac/

- Speaking Across the Curriculum at Hamline University with an archive of the Speaking Across the Curriculum newsletter. www.hamline.edu/~ppalmert/sarchive/

Copyright Information

There is a growing concern with copyright issues of using video tapes, handouts, literature, etc. in the classroom. An authoritative resource which answers all your questions in easy to understand language is: *The Copyright Primer for Librarians and Educators.* Washington, DC: American Library Assoc., 1995.

Professional Associations

International Communication Association
1730 Rhode Island Ave. NW
Suite 300
Washington, DC, 20036
202-530-9855

International Listening Association
Jim Pratt, Executive Director
PO Box 744
Riverfalls, WI, 54022
800-425-4505

National Communication Association
1765 N. Street NW
Washington, DC 20036
202-464-4622

Southern States Communication Association
Hal Fulmer
Georgia Southern University
P.O. Box 8091-02
Statesboro, GA 30406
912-681-5502

Internet Addresses

Some of the voluminous resources on communication on the Internet that may prove to be useful are:

American Communication Association
www.americancomm.org/
A not-for-profit organization created to promote academic and professional research, criticism, and teaching of principles and theories of communication.

Canadian Communication Association
www.acc-cca.ca
A bilingual national organization devoted to integrating communication issues and research.

Communication Institute for Online Scholarship
www.cios.org
A not-for-profit organization that promotes the use of computer technologies in the service of communication scholarship and education.

Facial Analysis
http://mambo.ucsc.edu/psl/fanl.html
A web site with numerous articles and research perspectives on the study of facial expressions.

International Communication Association
www.icahdq.org
This organization focuses on communication research and scholarship from an international perspective.

International Listening Association
www.listening.org
A professional organization whose members are dedicated to learning more about the impact that listening has on all human activity.

National Communication Association
www.natcom.org
The oldest and largest communication association in the United States. It promotes all aspects of research and application in the field of communication.

Southern States Communication Association
http://ssca.net/
A not-for-profit communication association that encompasses researchers and academics from states in the southern regions of the U.S.

Western States Communication Association
www.westcomm.org
The purpose of WSCA is to "unite people in the western states who have an academic, lay or professional interest in communication."

QUOTATIONS ON COMMUNICATION

Speech is the image of life.
—Democritus, *Idylls*

Speech is the picture of the mind.
—John Ray, *English Proverbs*

Speech is the minor of action.
—Solon

All speech, written or spoken, is a dead language, until it finds a willing and prepared hearer.
—R. L. Stevenson, *Lay Morals*

His speeches are like cypress trees; they are tall and comely, but bear no fruit.
—Phocion

All speech is a hazard; oftener than not it is the most hazardous kind of deed.
—Miguel le Unamuna, *The Life of Lou Quixote*

For more than forty year…I have been speaking prose without knowing it.
—Moliere, *Le Bourgeois Gentilhomme*

Runs not this speech like iron through your blood?
—William Shakespeare, *Much Ado About Nothing*

Mend your speech a little, lest it may mar your fortunes.
—William Shakespeare, *King Lear*

The speaking in perpetual hyperbole is comely in nothing but in love.
—Francis Bacon, *Essays: Of Love*

Speak clearly, if you speak (it all; Carve every word before you let it fall.
—O. W. Holmes, *A Rhymed Lesson*

Every man, who can speak (it all, can speak elegantly and correctly if he pleases, by attending to the best authors and orators; and, indeed, I would advise those who do not speak elegantly, not to speak at all; for I am sure they will get more by their silence than by their speech.
—Lord Chesterfield, *Letters*

Let your speech be always with grace, seasoned with salt.
—New Testament, *Colossians*

To speak and to offend, with some people, are but one and the same thing.
—La Bruvere, *Les Caracteres: Du Coeur*

It is never more difficult to speak well than when one is ashamed to be silent.
—La Rochefoucauld, *Maximes Posthumes*

He will no, more speak fast, than he will run, for fear his tongue would go before his wit.
—Sir Roger L'Estrange, *Of Senecas's Epistles*

Grant me the power of saying things
Too simple and too sweet for words.
—Coventry Patmore, *The Angel in the House*

His speech was a fine sample, on the whole, Of rhetoric, which the learn'd call "rigamarole".
—Byron, *Don Juan*

He that speak lavishly shall hear as knavishly.
—Thomas Fuller, *Gnomologia*

He has a rage for saying something when there's nothing to be said.
—Samuel Johnson

And 'tis remarkable that they talk most who have the least to say.
—Matthew Prior, *Alma*

If your lips would keep from slips Five things observe with care; To whom you speak, of whom you speak, And how, and when, and where.
—W. E. Norris, *Thirlby Hall*

Discretion of speech is more than eloquence.
—Francis Bacon, *Essays: Of Discourse*

There is no man but speaketh more honestly than he can do or think.
—Francis Bacon, *Advancement of Learning*

Blessed is the man who having nothing to say, abstains from giving us wordy evidence of the fact.
—George Eliot, *Theophrastus Such*

He that speaks without care shall remember with sorrow.
—Thomas Fuller *Gnomologia*

Speaking without thinking is shooting without aiming.
—W. G. Benham, *Proverbs*

Think twice before you speak and then say it to yourself.
—Elbert I Hubbard, *The Philistine*

It is better to guard speech than to guard wealth.
—Lucian

CHAPTER 1 COMMUNICATION: WHAT AND WHY

OVERVIEW

This chapter provides an overview of human communication. The authors begin by discussing the important characteristics as well as several different types of communication. This chapter also explains how communication acts as a tool to satisfy a number of needs in our lives. Through explanation and illustration they provide two models of communication: the linear model, and the transactional model. Finally, this chapter discusses misconceptions of communication and the impact they have on our communication as a whole.

OBJECTIVES

1. To help students understand three important characteristics of communication such as:
    a. it occurs between humans
    b. it is a process
    c. it is symbolic
2. To explain to students that there are several different types of communication including:
    a. intrapersonal communication
    b. interpersonal (dyadic) communication
    c. small group communication
    d. public communication
    e. mass communication
3. To enable students to identify how communication helps satisfy needs in our lives by way of:
    a. physical needs
    b. identity needs
    c. social needs
    d. practical needs
4. To aid students in the understanding of the process of communication through two different models:
    a. the linear model
    b. the transactional model
5. To help students conceptualize how communication competence is a measure of a person's effectiveness by:
    a. defining the nature of competence and how it is acquired
    b. outlining the characteristics of competent communicators
6. To facilitate the understanding that there are certain misconceptions of communication through the clarification of common misconceptions such as:
    a. communication doesn't always require complete understanding
    b. communication isn't always a good thing
    c. no single person or event causes another's reactions
    d. meanings rest in people, not words
    e. communication isn't as simple as it often seems
    f. more communication isn't always better

SUGGESTED CLASSROOM ACTIVITIES

—COMMUNICATION MODELS

Approximate Time: 50 minutes

I. PURPOSE: to increase awareness of the complex process involved in creating a communication model and to heighten awareness of the components that are essential to a model of human communication.

II. PROCEDURE:

1. Review the concept of models, emphasizing models as representations of relevant elements of a process organized in relationship to each other. Note the strengths and deficiencies of models.
2. Divide the class into groups of five.
3. Assign each group the task of creating an accurate model of human communication. Provide the groups with large sheets of newsprint, magic makers, string, glue, and tape. If such materials are not available, ask each group to draw its model on the board. Give the groups 20-30 minutes to prepare their models of communication, encouraging them to note both components and relationships among the components.
4. Have a spokesperson from each group explain the model to the class. Solicit class feedback about strengths and weaknesses in the model. Encourage students to challenge the model's adequacy in areas such as motivation, changes over time, noise, and the other more complex components.
5. Select the model which best represents the complexities of human communication.

III. PRINCIPLES ILLUSTRATED:

1. Human communication is complex.
2. Models are oversimplifications of a complicated process.
3. Models must represent, in static form, a dynamic process.
4. Models must include components such as sender, encoding, channel, message, decoding, receiver, noise, environment, time as well as information about how they relate to one another.
5. Models have both advantages and disadvantages.
6. No model is perfect.

—WHAT IS COMMUNICATION?

Approximate Time: 30 minutes

I. PURPOSE: to familiarize the students with the definition of <u>communication</u> around which the entire text is structured.

II. PROCEDURE:

1. Ask the class to reread Chapter 1 with special attention given to the definition of communication.
2. When class meets, divide the class into groups of five.
3. Prepare a hand-out containing the following situations. Ask each group to decide whether communication (as defined in the text) has occurred in the situation. Provide about ten minutes.
    a. Maria Garcia boards a city bus, noticing a dirty, tired-looking man in one of the front seats. She decides to sit toward the rear of the bus. Is this communication?
    b. During a dramatic pause in her lecture, Professor Smart hears a student's stomach growling. Is this communication?
    c. Mike is studying in his apartment bedroom when he decides to fix himself a snack. He overhears his roommate talking on the phone saying "No I don't think he has any idea that I'm moving out." Is this communication?
    d. Mr. Putesky arrives home each evening and finds his dog, Spot, on the porch with his evening paper in its mouth. When he sits down, the dog fetches his slippers. Is this communication?
    e. A group of communication students meet to prepare for the midterm examination. They study for hours, yet they all fail the exam. Is this communication?
4. Meet once again in the large class group. Put the definition of communication on the board. Go through each situation deciding as a group whether the definition of communication is met. Encourage group members to raise issues which they considered in their discussions, especially if there was considerable controversy.
5. Review the essential components of human communication.

III. PRINCIPLES ILLUSTRATED:

1. Communication must involve human beings.
2. Communication must involve symbolism, verbal or nonverbal.
3. Communication can be intentional or unintentional.
4. Communication must include a response, direct or indirect, to symbolic behavior of another.
5. Communication must involve a sender and a receiver.

—WHAT TYPE OF POWER DO YOU WANT

Approximate Time: 20-30 minutes

I. PURPOSE: to get students acquainted with each other and illustrate that often times we communicate and disclose more information to others than we might realize.

II. PROCEDURE:

1. Pass out a note card to each student
2. Ask each student, if he or she could have any special power, or be any type of super hero, or X-Men, who would that be, or what power would that be, and why.
3. Have each student write their answers down on the note card.
4. Collect note cards
5. Hand out a new blank note card to each student
6. Write all the different listed, powers, heroes etc… on the board and have students try to match their classmates with the powers.
7. After the students have guessed whose power belongs to whom, have each student disclose what they had originally said along with their justification of why.

III. PRINCIPLES ILLUSTRATED:

1. Communication must involve humans.
2. Communication is transactional.
3. We cannot not communicate.
4. Communication is not reversible.
5. We communicate more about ourselves than we may be aware.
6. Sometimes what we say can cause misconceptions.
7. The way were learn about ourselves is through communication.

—INITIAL ENCOUNTER ACTIVITY

Approximate Time: 30 minutes

I. PURPOSE: to introduce students to the skills and issues surrounding "first encounters" or meeting someone for the first time.

II. PROCEDURE:

Students will work in groups for all the following items:

1. Initial encounters will often fail or succeed on the basis of small, subtle communication signals. In many instances these signals are unintentional. Think back to some of your first encounters with other people. Give examples of:
    a. At least three behaviors that subtly suggested the person was interested in speaking to you.
    b. At least three behaviors that subtly signaled the person was not very interested in further conversation.

2. One way of generating conversation with someone you don't know is to make reference to something in your immediate environment, i.e., someone or something that is right around you. Suppose you're meeting someone for the first time in this classroom. Give three examples of statements you could make that would illustrate this technique.

3. Anybody can talk about the weather, but 99% of the time it's really boring. People resort to talking about it because it's a familiar topic about which almost anyone will have something to say. Try to think of three other subject matters you could bring up which are still "universal" but that are not quite so bland. For each topic, indicate what statement you would make to initiate the subject.

4. Each of us has many interesting facets to our lives. It's often difficult, however, to bring these things up in an initial conversation. A main reason for this is that no one wants to appear to be bragging or self-absorbed. For instance, it would sound rather conceited to say, "Hi, my name's Jim. I sky dive." What is your recommendation for bringing up such subject matters about yourself without appearing to do so in a deliberate, self-serving manner? Give specific examples of the things you would say.

III. PRINCIPLES ILLUSTRATED:

1. Initial conversation-making can be a learned skill.
2. Initial conversations are based on finding common interests.
3. Initial conversations are based upon "reading" the other person.

ACTIVITY TO PROMOTE CRITICAL AND CREATIVE THINKING

Prepare a list of nouns and put each on a slip of paper. Ask students to draw slips and, after a short preparation period, explain orally how "Communication is like _____." A second student should be assigned to respond how "Communication is not like _____." The activity should encourage students to gain new insight into the nature of communication and to benefit from other students' insights as well.

SAMPLE NOUNS

apple	football game	doorknob
circus	file cabinet	egg
balloon	raspberry pie	lipstick
arrow	clouds	picnic

TEACHING ACTIVITIES IN THE SPEECH COMMUNICATION TEACHER

- Brown, D. S., Jr. (1997, Summer). *Increasing awareness of interpersonal communication patterns*, 11(4), p.4-5.
- Byrum-Robinson, B., & Alexander-Paul, J. (1998, Winter). *Teaching assertiveness, 12(2)*, pp. 4-7.
- Gschwend, L. (2000, Spring). *Every student deserves an assessment tool that works, 14(3)*, pp. 1-5.
- Hanna, M. S. (2000, Spring). *Design a role-playing case for study and practice, 14(3)*, pp. 12-14.
- Hemenway, P. T. M. (2000, Summer). *Motivating students to perform through individual goal objectives, 14(4)*, pp. 15-16.
- Presnell, S. (2000, Spring). *BINGO: An interactive exam review exercise, 14(3)*, pp. 11-12.
- Rumbough, T. B. (2000, Spring). *52 ways to break the ice, 14(3)*, pp. 6-8.
- Smith, R. E., Jr. (2000, Spring). *Communication images from art, 14(3)*, pp. 10-11.
- Spicer, Karin-Leigh and William E. Hanks. "Critical Thinking Activities for Communication Textbooks," (Summer 1993) 77 47 pp. 6-7.
- Stevens, S. R. (2000, Winter). *How to go into the lion's den and bring out a kitty cat: First day strategies for graduate teaching assistants, 14(2)*, pp. 10-12.
- Thameling, C. L. (1997, Winter). *The giving of gifts: An exercise in interpersonal communication theory, 11(2)*, pp. 8-9.

SUPPLEMENTARY RESOURCES

I.   BOOKS AND ARTICLES

- Beebe, Steven, Susan Beebe, and Diana Ivy, *Communication: Principles for a Lifetime,* Boston, MA: Allyn and Bacon/Longman, 2001.
- Dahnke, Gordon L. and Glen W. Clatterbuck (eds.). *Human Communication: Theory and Research.* Belmont, CA: Wadsworth, 1990.
- DeFleur, Melvin, Patricia Kearney, and Timothy Plax. *Fundamentals of Human Communication.* New York, NY: McGraw Hill, 1998.
- Hybels, Saundra and Weaver, *Communicating Effectively.* New York, NY: McGraw Hill, 2001.
- Littlejohn, Stephen. *Theories of Human Communication.* Belmont, CA: Wadsworth, 2002.
- McCroskey, James. *Introduction to Rhetorical Communication.* Boston, MA: Allyn and Bacon/Longman, 2001.
- Tubbs, Stewart and Sylvia Moss. *Human Communication: Principles and Contexts.* New York, NY: McGraw Hill, 2003.
- Woods, Julia. *Communication in our Lives.* Belmont, CA: Wadsworth. 2003.

II. FILMS/TAPES

- "Human Communication Theory." Insight Media, 1998, 24 minutes. This video examines verbal and nonverbal communication using the SMCR model. It also examines how cultural and socioeconomic biases can influence message sending and receiving.
- "Negotiating Cultural Communication." Media Insight, 2001, 60 minutes. This video describes a variety of intercultural communication encounters to illuminate numerous issues surrounding diversity in communication.
- "Speak Up: Skills of Oral Communication." Guidance Associates, 1989, 60 minutes, color, filmstrip on video. Uses exercises to provide students an opportunity for classroom participation in more effective oral communication. A series of audio-visual selections and exercises dramatize the four purposes of oral communication: narration, description, persuasion and argumentation.
- "The Uses of Media." Films for the Humanities, 1989, 26 minutes, color, VHS. This program examines the impact of television on the way we see ourselves as a society, exploring the subliminal messages television communicates and how they influence viewers.

CHAPTER 2 PERCEPTION, THE SELF, AND COMMUNICATION

OVERVIEW

This chapter focuses on perception of ourselves and how we view others. Through out this chapter we see how our perceptions of others shape the way we communicate with them. This chapter explains several factors that influence these perceptions. It also describes how communication depends on the way we perceive ourselves, as well as others. One of the principle differences between this chapter and chapter one is that this chapter discusses the differences between the perceived and presenting selves. This chapter helps give the reader a better grasp on how we as humans communicate to manage our identities, both through face-to-face and mediated channels.

OBJECTIVES

1. Help students understand that our perceptions of others shape the way we communicate with them by examining several factors that influence these perceptions such as:
    a. our success at constructing shared narratives through communication
    b. our tendency to make several perceptual errors
    c. factors arising from our own experience and from our prior relationship with that person
    d. our cultural background
    e. our ability to empathize
2. Facilitate the importance of how the skill of perception checking can help clarify mistaken perceptions, leading to a shared narrative and smoother communication.
3. To provide students the knowledge of how communication depends on the way we perceive ourselves, as well as others by appreciating the importance of the self as they read about:
    a. how communication shapes the self-concept
    b. the way culture shapes our self perception
    c. the role of personality in shaping our perceptions
    d. how self-fulfilling prophecies can lead to either more satisfying or less productive communication
4. To examine how the principle of identity management operates by explaining:
    a. the difference between perceived and presenting selves
    b. how we communicate to manage our identities, both via face-to-face and mediated channels
    c. reasons why we communicate to manage our identities

SUGGESTED CLASSROOM ACTIVITIES

—PERCEPTION OF AN EVENT

Approximate Time: varies according to length of film/lecture

I. PURPOSE: to demonstrate how different people can experience the same event in different ways.

II. PROCEDURE:

1. Before showing one of the films on communication or perception recommended in the manual or text, assign students one of the following roles:
    - small child
    - newlywed husband
    - senior citizen
    - professor in communication department
    - social worker
    - minister
2. Instruct students to watch the film from the perspective of their assigned role.

3.   After the film, ask for perceptions from each of the various roles. How were they different? What caused these differences? Is one of the perceptions more "correct" than the others?

—PERCEIVED SELF & PRESENTING SELF ACTIVITY

Approximate Time: 20 minutes

I.   PURPOSE: to allow students to personalize perceived self and presenting self

II.   PROCEDURE:

1.   Each student should examine Table 2-2. Men should select 2-3 of the Perceived Self adjectives for men, then think of examples for themselves. Women should select 2-3 for women, and think of examples for themselves. These may be personal and need not be discussed, unless the student wants to discuss them.
2.   Each student should then look at the Presenting Self list for 2-3 examples for themselves.
3.   Discussion questions:
     a.   Are there "gaps" between the perceived and presenting selves?
     b.   How might social norms cause any gaps?
     c.   Are these gaps potentially problems?

III. PRINCIPLES ILLUSTRATED:

1.   The Perceived Self is a reflection of the self-concept.
2.   The Presenting Self is a public image, the way we want to appear to others.

—PRIVILEDGES ACTIVITY

Approximate Time: 30-60 minutes

I.   PURPOSE: to illustrate the relationship between being a member of a "privileged" group and self-concept development.

II.   PROCEDURE:

1.   Instruct students to read handout.
2.   Place students in groups of 4 to 6.
3.   After groups have made their lists of privileges and expectations, discuss the lists as an entire class.

III. PRINCIPLES ILLUSTRATED:

1.   Self-concept formation.
2.   The perceived self is a reflection of self-concept.
3.   The role of stereotyping in perception.

Privileges Activity

There are certain privileges that go with being perceived as an attractive individual. Studies show, for instance, that attractive people are listened to more than are people who are perceived as being unattractive. Attractive people are also offered small favors more readily: "Do you need a ride home?" "Let me carry some of those books." There are dozens of small, and large, privileges that are available to attractive people which are not so readily available to those seen as less physically attractive. Clearly, these privileges are not given to all attractive people all the time. They are just tendencies that occur in our society on a fairly regular basis.

A. Your first task is to identify five such privileges. These privileges can be given to either men or women or to both. If you find yourself stuck on trying to think of examples, take the reverse approach of thinking of privileges that are denied to unattractive people.

   1.

   2.

   3.

   4.

   5.

B. Based on your experiences, identify which, if any, of the above privileges are so common that they seem to have become expectations on the part of the attractive person.

C. Just as there are privileges that come with attractiveness, there are also privileges associated with race. This is certainly true for individuals belonging to the majority Caucasian population in the United States. Your task is to identify five privileges that come from belonging to the white majority race in the U.S. Try to identify some of the more subtle everyday advantages that are just taken for granted by most Caucasians.

   1.

   2.

   3.

   4.

   5.

D. Based on your experiences, identify which, if any, of the above privileges are so common that they seem to have become expectations on the part of the Caucasian person.

—PERCEPTUAL DIFFERENCES I

Approximate Time: 20 minutes

I.   PURPOSE: to demonstrate how physical receptors can lead to perceptual differences.

II. PROCEDURE: (see also variation)

1.   From the biology department or a chemical supply house, obtain strips of litmus paper treated with PTO (phenyl-thio-caramide).
2.   Distribute the strips of paper to all members of the class. Have them taste the strips at the same time.
3.   How many found the paper to be salty? sweet? bitter? tasteless?
4.   Discuss these differences. Then ask students to think of other situations which people perceive differently because of physical influences. Relate these to the textbook discussion of physical influences on perception.

III. PRINCIPLES ILLUSTRATED:

1.   People perceive identical stimuli in vastly different ways.
2.   Physical differences in people can lead to perceptual differences.
3.   Not everyone perceives food, temperature, and interpersonal events in identical ways.

IV. VARIATION

1.   Have each student bring to class a bottle of perfume or after-shave cologne.
2.   Divide the class into groups of five.
3.   Each student smells the bottles brought by the others in their group.
4.   After smelling each, students write down their reaction and associations. For example, "Smells good, like fruit, reminds me of my Gramma's kitchen."
5.   Students compare and discuss differing perceptions and associations of same smells.

—PERCEPTUAL DIFFERENCES II

Approximate Time: 45 minutes

I.   PURPOSE: to illustrate how different perceptions of events may be and to identify reasons for the differences.

II. PROCEDURE:

1.   Divide into groups of five. If the class works better as a large unit with fairly good participation from all members, then this exercise can be done by the large group.
2.   Select one issue which affects everyone in the group, such as class assignments, testing, grading policy, room location, or scheduling. Note both the group's perception of the situation, then the perception of another party who might see it quite differently, e.g., the professor, the administrative person who schedules room assignments, or the person who schedules class times.
3.   Answer the following questions, keeping in mind the group perceptions and the perspective of the other person. Give the groups 20-25 minutes to do this.
     a.   What is the problem area?
     b.   How is information about the "problem" selected and organized by the other party?
     c.   What is the other party's interpretation of the situation?
     d.   How is information about the "problem" selected and organized by you?
     e.   What is your interpretation of the situation?
     f.   What physical filters affect the other party's perception? What social filters affect the other party's perception?

    g.   What physical filters affect your perception of the event? What social filters affect your perception of the situation?

    h.   What conclusion can you draw about different perceptions in this example?

    i.   What different approaches might be taken to address the problem?

4.   If you have divided into smaller groups, report to the class the basic problem on which you worked, the reasons for perceptual differences, and suggestions for action.

III. PRINCIPLES ILLUSTRATED:

1.   The same event can be perceived in vastly different ways by people involved in the event.

2.   Physical and social perspective influence one's selection and organization of an event.

3.   Some misunderstandings are more the result of differing perceptions than differences in opinion.

4.   Clear communication, perception checking, and extensive feedback can help clarify perceptual misunderstandings.

ACTIVITIES TO PROMOTE CRITICAL AND CREATIVE THINKING

Select a short poem which expresses a feeling or situation with which you can empathize. Prepare an oral reading of the poem for the class. Write a one-page paper in which you explain what feelings you feel the poem expresses and why you empathize with them.

Read the following Hayakawa quote.

There is an old joke about a man who was asked if he could play a violin and answered, "I don't know. I've never tried." This is psychologically a very wise reply. Those who have never tried to play a violin really do not know whether they can or not. Those who say too early in life and too firmly, "No, I'm not at all musical, " shut themselves off prematurely from whole areas of life that might have proved rewarding. In each of us there are unknown possibilities, undiscovered potentials--and one big advantage of having an open self-concept rather than a rigid one is that we shall continue to discover more and more about ourselves as we grow older — S. I. Hayakawa

Explore the concept of the self-fulfilling prophesy by selecting a behavior from your own life which you do not know if you can do because you never tried it. Explain:

    a.   what it is

    b.   why you never tried it

    c.   how your life might be different if you had

TEACHING ACTIVITIES IN THE COMMUNICATION TEACHER

- Aylor, B. A. (2000, Summer). *"Three theorists walk into a bar ...": Humanizing communication theory, 14(4),* pp. 13-14.
- Brunson, D. A. (2000, Winter). *Talking about race by talking about whiteness, 14(2),* pp. 1-4.
- Brunson, Deborah A. "A Perceptual Awareness Exercise in Interracial Communication," (Fall 1994) 9, 1, pp. 2-4.
- Faries, Liz. "The Upside-Down Exercise," (Summer 1992) 6, 4, p. 10.
- Finn, T. A. (1999, Winter). *Isolating interpersonal cues through student use of multiple media, 13(2),* pp. 6-7.
- Garrett, Roger L. "The Onion Concept of Self," (Summer 1992) 6, 4, pp. 6-7.
- Hankins, Gail Armstead. "Don't Judge a Book by Its Cover," (Summer 1991) 5, 4, p. 8.
- Hanna, M. S. (2000, Spring). *Design a role-playing case for study and practice, 14(3),* pp. 12-14.
- Hugenberg, B. S. (2000, Fall). *Teaching naturalistic inquiry with "Instinct," 15(1),* pp. 10-13.
- Kassing, Jeffrey W "The Color of Perception," (Summer 1994) 8, 4, pp. 4-5.
- Lane, S. D. (1997, Spring). *Communicating emotions, 11(3),* pp. 2-4.
- Patterson, B. R. (1994, Fall). *An experiential vehicle for instructors on human perception, 9(1),* pp. 7-8.
- Rivers, M. J. (2000, Summer). *For better or worse? Let's make it better, 14(4),* pp. 8-10.

- Ross, Roseanna. "What Is in the Show Box?" (Spring 1991) 5, 3, p. 12.
- Schnell, Jim. "The China Protests as a Perception Case Study," (Winter 1992) 6, 2, p. 13.

SUPPLEMENTARY RESOURCES

I.   BOOKS AND ARTICLES

- Anderson, Rob and Veronica Ross. *Questions of Communication.* Boston, MA: Bedford/St. Martin's, 2002.
- Carr, Jacquelyn. *Communicating With Myself. A Journal.* New York, NY: McGraw Hill, 1990.
- Cashmore, Ellis and James Jennings. *Racism: Essential Readings.* Thousand Oaks, CA: Sage, 2002
- Dyer, Wayne. *Your Erroneous Zones.* New York, NY: HarperCollins, 1991.
- Schiffman, Harvey. *Sensation and Perception: An Integrated Approach.* New York, NY: John Wiley & Sons, 2001.

II. FILMS/TAPES

- "Bill Cosby on Prejudice," Pyramid, 1972, 25 minutes, color. Cosby examines many common prejudices.
- "Frank Film," Pyramid Films, 9 minutes, color. Uses color cutouts that appear at a rate of one every ten seconds and a double soundtrack. Excellent stimulus for study of perception.
- "One Drop Rule," James Banks, Elixer Productions, California Newsreel, 2001, 45 minutes. This video examines the controversial issues surrounding skin color in the African American community..
- "Psychology of Winning in Action," Nightengale-Conant Corp., 1986, 58 minutes, color, VHS. Explores those characteristics common to winners in all walks of life. Discusses how to take the things we are born with and develop them in order to achieve excellence and live a winning lifestyle.
- "Self Awareness," Insight Media, 1997, 29 minutes. This video shows how self-concept affects both personal and public communication.
- "Shattering the Silences," Stanley Nelson, Gail Pellett, California Newsreel, 1997, 86 minutes. This video provides a perspective of American campuses through the eyes of minority faculty.
- "Tale of 'O'," Goodmeasure, Inc. 1980, 30 minutes, color, slide set, sound. Explores the consequences of being different. Focuses on a group of people in which there are "the main" referred to as the "X's" and "the few" referred to as the "O's." Emphasizes that differences can come from a wide variety of factors such as age, sex, race language, occupation, status, or even such things as hair style or length.

CHAPTER 3 LANGUAGE

OVERVIEW

This chapter describes the complexity of language and its many components. It explains the several characteristics of language such as how it is symbolic, meanings are in the people, and the governing rules. This chapter also explains how language can be very powerful, beyond simply expressing ideas. Not only does this chapter explain the wonderful components of language, but it also addresses how certain kinds of language can create certain types of problems. Beyond the positive and negative aspects of language within communication, this chapter illustrates the importance of gender and cultural factors within language.

OBJECTIVES

1. To show students the important aspects of communication:
    a. it is symbolic
    b. meanings reside in people, not in the words
    c. it is rule governed
    d. understanding rules help us understand one another
2. To help students understand the power of language beyond just expressing ideas:
    a. it can shape our attitudes towards thing and towards one another
    b. it can reflect the way we feel about things and people
3. To help students understand that some kinds of language can create problems unnecessarily by:
    a. disrupting relationships
    b. confusing others
    c. avoiding important information
4. To introduce students to the concept that gender has an important role in how language operates by:
    a. how the content of male and female speech varies
    b. men and women often have different reasons for communicating
    c. male and female conversational style varies
    d. gender is not always the most important factor in shaping language use
5. To introduce students to the concept that cultural factors shape the way we see and understand by:
    a. how different cultures have different notions of what language styles are and are not appropriate
    b. how the language we speak can shape the way we view the world

SUGGESTED CLASSROOM ACTIVITIES

—HOW OFTEN IS OFTEN?

Approximate Time: 20-30 minutes

I.   PURPOSE: to demonstrate that words can mean different things to different people.

II. PROCEDURE:

1. Distribute a handout similar to the following one. You could also read the directions and write the individual words on the chalkboard.
2. Discuss differences in responses. Even on words that sound fairly precise, people have diverse interpretations. Encourage students to give reasons for their choices.

III. PRINCIPLES ILLUSTRATED:

1. Meanings are in people, not in words.
2. Even words that sound precise may have vastly different interpretations for different people.
3. Use words as precisely as possible when clarity is your goal.

How Often is Often?

Below is a group of words often used to indicate degrees of frequency with which events tend to happen. The words mean different things to different people.   Beside each word indicate how many times out of 100 you think the word indicates an act is likely to happen.

For example, if "seldom" indicates to you that a thing would happen about 10 times out of 100, you should mark a 10 in the space after the expression. If it means about 2 times out of 100, then mark a 2.

1. almost never

2. very often

3. always

4. very seldom

5. about as often as not

6. usually not

7. frequently

8. usually

9. generally

10. sometimes

11. hardly ever

12. seldom

13. never

14. rather often

15. not often

16. rarely

17. now and then

18. once in a while

19. occasionally

20. often

How many are:

A. a few?

B. several?

C. many?

D. not many?

E. a lot?

Variation of How Often is Often

Respond to the following questions as best you can. There are no right or wrong answers to these.

How many are: _____ a few?   _____ several?   _____ many?   _____ a lot?
(Give quantities)

Which occurs the least? Seldom   Rarely   Hardly ever   Almost never

Which occurs the most? Usually   Frequently   Often

If someone tells you that a store is "not far away," what is the most amount of time it should take you to get there?

Your friend tells you he needs to buy a "cheap" car. How much do you estimate he wants to spend?

Who gets asked out for a date?

   A.   The person who is really cute.

   B.   The person who is just gorgeous.

   C.   The person who is quite attractive.

Write down a word (or phrase) you can define that you think some of your classmates will not be able to define.

Write down a word (or phrase) you can define that you think your instructor will not be able to define.

Suggestion: If you're stuck on the last two items, some possible areas to consider are slang words you know, terms from your job, or terms that are used in different parts of the country.

—"WHAT I REALLY MEAN IS"

Approximate Time: 30 minutes.

I.   PURPOSE: to discuss the nature of language and its role in human communication.

II. PROCEDURE:

1. Divide the class into groups of 4-5. This exercise may be done in the large class unit if desired.
2. Assign each group one of the following quotations:
    a.   "I know you believe you understand what you think I said, but I'm not sure you realize that what you heard is not what I meant."
    b.   "When I use a word, 'Humpty Dumpty,' said in a rather scornful tone, it means just what I choose it to mean-neither more nor less."
    c.   "Learn a new language and get a new soul." (Czech proverb)
    d.   "A rose by any other name would smell as sweet."
3. Each group should spend 15 minutes discussing the meaning of the quotation and coming up with a concrete example of the point that is made in the quotation.
4. Return to the larger group and report findings.

III. PRINCIPLES ILLUSTRATED:

1. Meanings are in people, not in words.
2. Language is arbitrary.
3. Language that is used habitually shapes perception
4. Meanings change.

—PRAGMATIC SQUARES

Approximate Time: 25 minutes

I.   PURPOSE: to better understand how pragmatic rules influence meaning.

II. PROCEDURE:

1. Prepare a handout for each student by copying Table 3-1 after you:
    a.   White out the content of situation columns 1, 2, and 3.
    b.   Fill in the content situation square with a new sentence such as, "You've got a great smile" or "That was a great pass!"
2. Divide the class into groups of 4-5.
3. Ask each group to fill in the empty squares in ways in which the meaning of the content will change.
4. Ask the groups to report on their decisions and to explain how the meaning of the sentence will be different for the three contexts they created.
5. It would enhance the discussion to have each group complete one Table on an overhead transparency that could be shown as the group reports.

III. PRINCIPLES ILLUSTRATED:

1. The meaning of a message is influence by pragmatic rules.
2. The interpretation of a message may be determined by the culture and gender of the participants.

IV. VARIATION

Use an overhead transparency of Table 3-1 with the situation content removed and a new content sentence. Let the class shout out the variables and fill them in. Then decide as a class what the sentence means in each situation.

ACTIVITIES TO PROMOTE CRITICAL AND CREATIVE THINKING

Brainstorm as a class or in a small group the meanings and associations of a word (color, test, rain, television, etc.). After generating a long list of associations, ask the group to classify them. Point out how the varied associations and ways of categorizing reflect personal meanings.

Examine a piece of writing by focusing on the choice of words. Ask why the author may have chosen a particular word and how a different word would affect the meaning. Articles from the Plain *Truth* or the *Enquirer* work well, as would poetry.

Have the class generate a short list of (4-5) words which will have special meanings for the class. Use made-up words and real words. Give each word a specific and common meaning and use them often. For example, a quiz could be called an egg. After frequent use, the meanings of these words will be different for this class than for other people, i.e., meaning is in people.

Ask each student to bring in an example of sexist language from a recent newspaper or magazine article or ad. Let students share their examples and explain what about it is not gender sensitive. Discuss how the author could have made the language more inclusive.

TEACHING ACTIVITIES IN THE COMMUNICATION TEACHER

- Bollinger, L., & Sandarg, J. (1998, Winter). *Dare to go where others fear to tread, 12(2)*, pp. 1-3.
- Hochel, S. (1990, Winter). *Language awareness and assessment, 4(2)*, pp. 4-5.
- Jensen, M. D. (1993, Fall). *Developing ways to confront hateful speech, 8(1)*, pp. 1-2.
- Jensen, K. K. (2000, Winter). *Teaching ideas for the basic communication course*, (Vols. 1 & 2), *14(2)*, pp. 14-15.
- Pawlowski, D. (1999, Winter). *Dialoguing the gender movements, 13(2)*, pp. 4-6.
- Phillips, T. G. (1997, Summer). *Introducing gender-biased language: Much ado about something, 11(4)*, pp. 3-4.
- Proctor, R. F., II. (2000, Winter). *Using "Swing Kids" to teach theories of persuasion, 14(2)*, pp. 5-6.
- Ringer, R. Jeffrey. "Simply Jargon" (Fall 1994) 9, 1, p. 11.
- Rowley, Edwin N. "More Than Mere Words," (Fall 1992), 7, 1, p. 5.
- Sprague, R. J. (2000, Winter). *Theory building in communication courses, 14(2)*, pp. 12-13.
- Young, Katherine. "Proving the Importance of Inclusive Language in the Basic Course" (Summer, 99) 13, 4, pp. 7-8

SUPPLEMENTARY RESOURCES

I. BOOKS AND ARTICLES

- Ellis, Donald. *From Language to Communication*. Mahwah, NJ: Lawrence Erlbaum Associates, 1999.
- Foss, Karen and Sonja Foss. *Women Speak: The Eloquence of Women's Lives*. Prospect Heights, IL: Waveland, 1991.
- Jones, Steve. *Cybersociety: Revisiting Computer Mediated Community and Technology*. Thousand Oaks, CA: Sage, 1999.
- Lewis, Jeff. *Cultural Studies: The Basics*. Thousand Oaks, CA: Sage, 2002.
- McCrum, Robert, William Cran, and Robert MacNeil. The Story *of English*. New York, NY: Viking Penguin, 1993.

- Tannen, Deborah. *You Just Don't Understand.* New York: Wm. Morrow and Co., 1990.
- Wodak, Ruth. *Methods of Critical Discourse Analysis.* Thousand Oaks, CA: Sage, 2002.

II. FILMS/TAPES

- "American Tongues," Facets Multimedia, 1980, 56 minutes, color, VHS. Examines the diversity of American culture by listening to the different ways Americans talk and investigating how we feel about each other's speech.
- "Communication Skills for the Workplace." Insight Media, 2000, 30 minutes. A video that examines the various communication skills that are needed to succeed on the job.
- "Introduction to Linguistics," Katrina Simmons, Michigan State University, 1980, 17 minutes, videotape.
- "Language," Insight Media, 1990, 30 minutes, VHS. This program identifies the essential characteristics of language, evaluates research into whether or not animals can acquire language skills, details the stages of language development in children, and discusses factors that influence language development.
- "The Accent Reduction Program: The Standard Edition." Insight Media, 2002, 100 minutes. This video targets 22 consonant and 10 vowels that are often confused or mispronounced.
- "The Mind Language," Public Broadcasting Service, 60 minutes, color, VHS. Discusses language development and focuses on how biology and environment interact to enable communication.
- "Speak Up: Skills of Oral Communication," The Center for Humanities, two VHS videotapes.
- "Style in Language," Films for the Humanities, 15 minutes, color.
- "Words and Meaning," Films for the Humanities, 15 minutes, color.

CHAPTER 4 LISTENING

OVERVIEW

This chapter examines the importance of listening. It explains the difference between hearing and listening. This chapter shows that listening is effort based and how messages are interpreted in different ways. After the authors define and explain listening, they provide two different approaches that can help to become a better listener. This chapter also highlights the different personal listening styles and the strengths and weaknesses. Finally this chapter discusses three ways to listen and respond.

OBJECTIVES

1. To emphasize to students that they need to think about listening is a new way by:
    a. understanding the difference between listening and hearing
    b. realizing that listening isn't a natural ability, and it takes effort and practice
    c. identifying how it's probable that people will hear the same message in different ways
2. To explain to students that there are two approaches that can help you become a better listener by:
    a. minimizing faulty listening behaviors
    b. understanding some of the reasons you listen poorly
3. To students understand that most people use one of four personal listening styles such as:
    a. content-oriented
    b. people-oriented
    c. action-oriented
    d. time-oriented
4. To help students conceptualize three different ways to listen and respond:
    a. for information
    b. to critically evaluate a speaker's ideas
    c. to help others with their problems

SUGGESTED CLASSROOM ACTIVITIES

—ONE-WAY AND TWO-WAY COMMUNICATION

Approximate Time: 30-45 minutes

I.   PURPOSE: to compare the effectiveness of communication exchanges that involve feedback with those that do not; to encourage students to use feedback to improve communication.

II. PROCEDURE:

1. Ask for a volunteer from the class.
2. Direct the volunteer to go to the rear of the classroom, facing the wall so that his or her back faces the backs of the class members. Then provide the volunteer with a diagram such as those on the next two pages. Instruct the class members that they may ask no questions, make no sounds, nor give any feedback to the volunteer as he/she describes the diagram. The volunteer should then describe the diagram so that the class members can replicate it on their papers. Instructor should record the amount of time needed. After the description is complete, the class members should NOT be shown the actual diagram.
3. On the board, the instructor should record the amount of time used. The instructor should ask class members to predict how many of the five shapes they copied correctly, both in terms of size and placement. Those totals should be placed on the board.
4. The volunteer should then display the diagram in order that the class members can assess their actual accuracy. Accuracy scores should also be recorded on the board.

5. The volunteer should then move to the front of the class and be given a similar diagram. In this instance, however, the class members may ask questions, seek clarification, and employ whatever feedback they desire. The only restriction it that the volunteer may not display the diagram directly.
6. After completing the procedure, the instructor should write the two-way time on the board, should seek student estimates of their accuracy, and should then have the volunteer display the diagram so that actual accuracy can be assessed.
7. Comparisons should then be made about:
    a. Audience feelings toward the speakers in both contexts
    b. Speaker feelings toward the audience in both contexts
    c. Merits of one-way communication (e.g., emergency situations)
    d. Problems of one-way communication (e.g., lecture in which instructor may overestimate understanding level of students)
    e. Merits of two-way communication (e.g., increased accuracy)
    f. Problems of two-way communication (e.g., time consuming)

III. PRINCIPLES ILLUSTRATED:

1. Communication without feedback (one-way communication) has the following general characteristics:
    a. It is fast.
    b. It is generally satisfying to the sender.
    c. It is generally frustrating to the receiver.
    d. It is not very accurate.
2. Two-way communication tends to be
    a. time consuming.
    b. frustrating to the sender.
    c. satisfying to the receiver.
    d. more accurate than communication without feedback.
3. When accuracy of communication is the goal, two-way communication, although time consuming, is preferable.
4. Two-way communication requires effective listening.

—LISTENING CHALLENGE

Approximate Time: 30 minutes

I.   PURPOSE: to illustrate how people fail to listen to others because they often prepare their next statements while the speaker is talking.

II. PROCEDURE:

1. Divide the class into groups of two.
2. Write several controversial topics on the board, such as abortion, drug testing, gun control, right to burn the flag. Ask the partners to take opposite sides on the issue, even if they disagree with the position they will have to argue.
3. Direct the dyads to begin debating the issues. After about 3-5 minutes of debate, tell them to switch sides. After a period of time, tell them to switch sides again.
4. Discuss what happened. What feelings were generated? Hostility? Frustration? Empathy?
5. Ask the same dyads to select a different topic. This time, each student should paraphrase the other's position before he or she can speak. That is, the person has to clearly report what was heard before proceeding to speak. Let this discussion proceed for 5-8 minutes.
6. Contrast the second situation with the first. Was it equally (or more) frustrating? What were the merits of each approach? Problems?

III. PRINCIPLES ILLUSTRATED:

1. We often fail to listen effectively because we are preparing our statements in advance.
2. Effective listening is difficult.
3. Effective listening is tiring.
4. Listening effectiveness can be improved with effort.

—FOUR AREAS OF LISTENING ACTIVITY

Approximate Time: 30 minutes

I. PURPOSE: To build an understanding of the communication behaviors and circumstances that surround effective and ineffective listening.

II. PROCEDURE:

1. Assign students to groups.
2. Instruct students to work on all items in the following handout as a group.
3. Instruct students to write down their answers.
4. Instruct students to be realistic, but also BE CREATIVE. If your group has totally unique examples in any one of these 4 areas (no other group has duplicated any one of your examples), your group will get five bonus points for the activity. Note: There is a maximum of 5 bonus points for the assignment.

III. PRINCIPLES ILLUSTRATED:

1. The influence of nonverbal behaviors on listening.
2. The influence on verbal communication habits on listening.
3. The influence of communication context on listening.
4. The interplay of sending and receiving skills in communication.

Four Areas of Listening

1. Identify five nonverbal behaviors on the part of a speaker that would likely result in that person NOT being listened to. Classify each behavior according to the type of nonverbal communication it illustrates.

2. Identify five nonverbal behaviors on the part of the speaker that would likely result in that person being listened to. (Do not write just the reverse of what you said in #1. Come up with totally different examples.) Classify by the type of nonverbal behavior it illustrates.

3. Identify five communication situations in which it is difficult to listen to another person.

4. Identify five verbal (speaking) behaviors or traits that are likely to result in the speaker not being listened to very well.

—**LISTENING AND PARAPHRASING**

Approximate Time: 20 minutes

I.   PURPOSE: to allow students to practice listening and paraphrasing.

II. PROCEDURE:

1. Form dyads (pairs).
2. Each student should think of a subject he or she can talk about for 3-5 minutes, such as vacations, movies, etc.   While one student talks, the other listens and tries his or her best to paraphrase back to the speaker as appropriate.
3. When the first student is finished talking, the other student takes his or her turn talking. Now, the first student is listening and paraphrasing as appropriate. In paraphrasing, students should:
    a.   try to change the speaker's wording
    b.   offer an example
    c.   reflect an underlying theme
4. Following the activity, class discussion questions:
    a.   Which of the above felt the most "natural"?
    b.   Which of the above seemed to help the speaker the most?
    c.   Which of the above do students seem to need to improve the most?

III. PRINCIPLES ILLUSTRATED:

1. Listening and paraphrasing require practice to improve.
2. Some students are using some of the techniques fairly well.
3. Some students will see areas of listening they can improve.

ACTIVITIES TO PROMOTE CRITICAL AND CREATIVE THINKING

Read a sample speech to the class. Stop at intervals and ask students what questions they could ask at this point. Questions should ask for clarification, details, and examples, and also for elaborations, such as "Why is this important?" "How are ideas one and two related?" "How do you know that?"

Present students with a character role (fifty-year-old firefighter) and a statement, "My job seems to be getting harder." Ask the class for implications of the statement. What does the speaker mean? What can be inferred? What questions and/or paraphrases could be used to test the accuracy of the inferences? Explore how the answers would change if a new role (a teacher) were used with the same statement.

Ask students to talk, in dyads, about any topics of interest, such as movies, places to eat, vacations, etc. Allow about five minutes for each to talk, a total of ten minutes. Then, ask the class to write down the two to three main points they think the other person talked about. Secondly, they should write why they think those were the other person's main points.

TEACHING ACTIVITIES IN THE COMMUNICATION TEACHER

- Adams, John C. "Earstorming," (Spring 1992) 6, 3. p. 3.
- Bohlken, B. (1996, Spring). *Think about listening, 10(3)*, pp. 5-6.
- Gutgold, N. D. (2000, Summer). *Meta communication in business communication means a rich learning experience that is truly a slice of life!, 14(4)*, pp. 14-15.
- Hanna, M. S. (2000, Spring). *Design a role-playing case for study and practice, 14(3)*, pp. 12-14.
- Hochel, S. (1999, Fall). *Analyzing how others see the dominant U.S. culture, 14(1)*, pp. 4-5.
- Kassing, J. W. (1996, Winter). *Can you hear what else I'm saying?, 10(2)*, pp. 4-5.
- Mallard, K. S. (1998, Winter). *The listening box, 12(2)*, p. 9.

- Mino, M. (1997, Fall). *Creating listening rules, 12(1)*, p. 8.
- Thameling, C. L. (2000, Summer). *Ethical communication in interpersonal relationships, 14(4)*, pp. 1-4.
- Thompson, Carol Lynn. "Fantasy Interviews," (Spring 1994) 8, 3, p. 7.
- Wirkus, T. E. (1993, Winter). *Creating student-centered listening activities, 7(2)*, pp. 3-4.

SUPPLEMENTARY RESOURCES

I.   BOOKS AND ARTICLES

- Barker, Larry Lee and Kittie Watson. *Listen Up: How to Improve Relationships, Reduce Stress, and Be More Productive by Using the Power of Listening*, New York, NY: St. Martin's Press, 2000.
- Borisoff, Deborah and Michael Purdy. *Listening in Everyday Life: A Personal and Professional Approach*. Lanham, MD: University Press of America, 1996.
- Bostrom, Robert. *Listening Behavior*. New York: Guilford Publications, 1990.
- Brownell, Judi. *Listening: Attitudes, Principles, Skills*. Needham Heights, MA: Allyn & Bacon/ Longman, 2002.
- Wolvin, Andrew and Carolyn Coakley. *Listening*. New York, NY: McGraw Hill, 1995.
- Wolvin, Andrew and Carolyn Coakley (eds.). *Perspectives on Listening*. Norwood, N.J: Ablex, 1993.

II.   FILMS/TAPES

- "Critical Listening" Insight Media, 1999, 20 minutes. A video that examines the components of critical listening. It looks at such message sending concepts as tone, pitch and volume.
- "Critical Thinking: How to Evaluate Information and Draw Conclusions." Center for the Humanities, 42 minutes, color, VHS. Begins with discussion of language in terms of "verbal maps" and continues to help students evaluate information and use reasoning to draw conclusions. Useful for teaching critical listening.
- "Effective Listening." Insight Media, 1986, 28 minutes, VHS. This program examines the four stages of listening: perception, comprehension, evaluation, and response—and analyzes the role of each in the overall listening process.
- "Just Between Us: Communication 101VideoActive." Insight Media, 2001, 29 minutes. An examination of effective listening techniques and tips that include perception checking, metacommunication and other basic listening tools.
- "Listening Assertively." Insight Media, 1986, 28 minutes, VHS. This program defines different types of listening: assertive, deliberative, apathetic, sympathetic, and empathic. It emphasizes the importance of deliberative and empathic listening in the listening process and looks at how preconceptions and biases about the speaker or the message can hinder assertive listening.
- "Listening for Results." Roundtable Films, 1980, 10 minutes, color. Disruptive listening behaviors are shown by an automobile dealer and his sales manager. Six rules for better listening are explained.
- "The Listening Process." Insight Media, 1986, 28 minutes, VI IS. Differentiating between hearing and listening, this program examines the listening process.
- "Listening—the Problem Solver." Barr Films, 1981, 20 minutes, color. In order to gain a complete understanding of another's meaning and intentions, one must learn to listen on two levels-the informational and the behavioral level.
- "Many Hear—Some Listen." Coronet, 12 minutes, color, VHS. Helps students understand what kind of listeners they are by using vignettes to illustrate the three types: the non-attender, the assumer, and the word-picker.
- "A Wild Goose Chase." Cally Curtis, 1986, 4½ minutes, black and white. This film uses classic film footage to create an entertaining, informative look at miscommunication. Highlights the problems caused by not really listening.
- "Why You Buy: I low Ads Persuade." Insight Media, 1989, 33 minutes, VHS. Using real advertisements to illustrate commonly used persuasion tactics, this program shows how companies create product involvement and appeal to emotions through advertising.

CHAPTER 5 NONVERBAL COMMUNICATION

OVERVIEW

This chapter defines nonverbal communication and explains the importance of its role within human communication. This chapter maps out several important characteristics of nonverbal communication such as its clarification of feelings, its conveyance of information about others, and its continual presence within encounters. The chapter continues by showing how culture shapes many nonverbal practices, and how gender plays a role in the way we communicate. In addition, this chapter explains how nonverbal communication serves many functions such as repeating, complementing and accenting spoken words, how it can be substituted for speech, how it can regulate spoken conversation, and conversely contradict spoken words. This chapter also covers many types of nonverbal communication such as: posture and gesture, face and eyes, voice, touch, physical appearance and attractiveness, distance and territory, and physical environment.

OBJECTIVES

1. To help students define nonverbal communication.
2. To help students understand the differences between verbal and nonverbal communication.
3. To aid students in identifying several important characteristics of nonverbal communication:
   a. It exists.
   b. One cannot not communicate.
   c. Nonverbal communication transmits feelings.
   d. It can be ambiguous.
   e. Nonverbal communication is primarily relational
   f. It varies from culture to culture.
4. To acquaint students with functions of nonverbal communication.
5. To introduce students to various ways that nonverbal messages can be sent, including:
   a. Posture and gesture
   b. Face and eyes
   c. Voice
   d. Touch
   e. Physical appearance and attractiveness
   f. Distance and territory
   g. Physical environment

SUGGESTED CLASSROOM ACTIVITIES

—VIOLATION OF NONVERBAL NORMS

Approximate Time: 20 minutes

I. PURPOSE: to increase awareness of the norms, which guide behavior.

II. PROCEDURE:

1. Review the concept of norms/rules that guide nonverbal communication behavior. Discuss the notion that people are often unaware of the norms until they are violated.
2. Assign each person in the class the task of violating a nonverbal norm on campus. Examples might include getting on an elevator and facing backward, maintaining eye contact with people in halls, walking close to someone on a sidewalk, sitting beside someone on an empty bus, engaging a stranger in conversation, etc.
3. Next class period students report what happened.

4. Instruct the students to note the response of the other person(s) and their own responses to the norm violation.
5. Focus on concepts such as:
    a. what feelings are generated by norm violation. (e.g., embarrassment, anger, feeling claustrophobic, etc.)
    b. what areas of nonverbal communication have norms. (They all do! space, objects, eye contact, and more)
    c. how nonverbal miscommunication can occur in seemingly harmless settings in which norms are violated unintentionally.

III. PRINCIPLES ILLUSTRATED:

1. Nonverbal behavior is guided by norms.
2. Norms vary among cultural, ethnic, geographic groups.
3. Nonverbal norms affect all areas of nonverbal communication, such as space, eye contact, dress.
4. Nonverbal norm violation, intentional and unintentional, can lead to communication problems that are difficult to detect.
5. Many people abide by norms without being aware of them.

—WE CANNOT NOT COMMUNICATE

Approximate Time: 30 minutes

I. PURPOSE: to increase students' awareness of physical appearance on nonverbal communication.

II. PROCEDURE:

1. Assign each student to a partner. (Preferably someone that they do not normally sit by)
2. Instruct partners to sit directly facing each other.
3. Instruct students that they are not allowed to talk to each other during the activity.
4. Have each student take one sheet of paper and pen and make two columns.
5. Have students write down everything they notice about that person in the left column. (i.e. jewelry, logos on t-shirt, type of shoes, name brands of clothes, how many articles on body, hair style, glasses)
6. Have students write down their assumption or impression of each item on the right column. (i.e. if wearing a wedding ring they are married, if wearing a t-shirt with a certain logo they could be conservative/liberal, if they are wearing cowboy boots they could have an agriculture background or major)
7. After each student has completed each column, have students share with their partner and identify how close or far off their assumptions or impressions were.
8. Discuss with the class how we draw conclusions about people on a daily basis by physical appearance and artifacts.

III. PRINCIPLES ILLUSTRATED:

1. Clothing has an impact on nonverbal communication.
2. We view people differently because of their artifacts.
3. We reveal more about ourselves in public than we might realize.
4. How we view physical attractiveness effects our perception of individuals.
5. We cannot not communicate.

—PROXEMIC INFLUENCE

Approximate Time: 16 minutes

1. PURPOSE: to increase students' awareness of spatial differences on communication.

II. PROCEDURE:

1. Assign students to a partner.
2. Instruct the partners to sit facing each other, four feet apart.
3. Have each dyad discuss a topic of their choice for one minute.
4. Now have students move one foot apart and continue the conversation.
5. Finally, have them sit with their knees touching and continue talking for one more minute.
6. Discuss as a class the differences between the three proxemic distances. What effect did each have on the conversation? How did each feel in the three settings?

III. PRINCIPLES ILLUSTRATED:

1. The use of space communicates.
2. The distance between speakers influences the nature of communication.
3. Appropriate use of space makes communication more effective and comfortable.

—NONVERBAL RULES ACTIVITY

Approximate Time: 30 minutes

I. PURPOSE: to demonstrate that specific circumstances can be regulated by unspoken nonverbal rules.

II. PROCEDURE:

Divide class into groups and ask them to follow the instructions of the assignment. Class discussion should follow all groups completing the written portion of the assignment.

III. PRINCIPLES ILLUSTRATED:

1. Communication is often driven by spoken and unspoken rules.
2. Nonverbal communication behaviors vary from situation to situation.
3. Individuals are assessed by their nonverbal behaviors.

Nonverbal Rules Activity

There are many "rules" of nonverbal behavior that are widely adhered to in our culture but rarely, if ever, verbalized. Here are some examples:

1. When entering an elevator with people you don't know, move to the farthest corner.
2. When receiving a gift, control your facial expressions and tone of voice to show approval rather than disappointment.
3. Don't wear house slippers to school.
4. When ending a conversation, decrease eye contact.
5. Don't brush your teeth in a drinking fountain.

Your group's task is to come up with two examples of other **unspoken** nonverbal rules that govern behavior in the following situations:

1. While visiting someone in the hospital.

    1.

    2.

2. While shopping at the mall.

    1.

    2.

3. While using a public restroom.

    1.

    2.

4. While eating in a restaurant.

    1.

    2.

5. While attending a funeral.

    1.

    2.

6. While watching television with your family at home.

    1.

    2.

7. While eating dinner at a relative's house on Thanksgiving Day.

    1.

    2.

ACTIVITIES TO PROMOTE CRITICAL AND CREATIVE THINKING

Invite a guest speaker who has recently come from a foreign culture. Ask him or her to talk about the differences in communication style and expectations between the "home" culture and U.S. culture. Ask him or her to use personal experiences to illustrate nonverbal communication differences. Allow them time for questions.

Bring several magazine ads to class. Divide the class up with females in one group and males in the other group. Ask each group to use all the nonverbal clues to make inferences about the person/people in the ad, paying specific attention to gender related issues. Then as a whole discuss how each group came to their conclusions about each ad. Also discuss how gender plays a role with nonverbal communication such as how each gender views the opposite sex and same sex.

Divide the class into groups of five. Each group is asked to review the major forms of nonverbal communication. Each group then selects three or four emotions, such as anger, hope, concern, etc. For each emotion, how do the media tend to show people displaying that emotion? Second, the group should consider whether people they know display the emotions in the same way as demonstrated in the media.

TEACHING ACTIVITIES IN THE SPEECH COMMUNICATION TEACHER

- Aylor, B. A. (2000, Summer). *"Three theorists walk into a bar ...": Humanizing communication theory, 14(4)*, pp. 13-14.
- Bozik, M. (1987, Winter). *A picture's worth a thousand words, 1(2)*, p. 5.
- Brunson, D. A. (1994, Fall). *A perceptual awareness exercise in interracial communication, 9(1)*, pp. 2-4.
- Coakley, C. (1991, Spring). *Getting acquainted nonverbally, 5(3)*, p. 15.
- Gschwend, L. (2000, Spring). *Every student deserves an assessment tool that works, 14(3)*, pp. 1-5.
- Hart, J. L. (Fall, 1999). *On parachutes and knapsacks: Exploring race and gender privilege, 14(1)*, pp. 16-17.
- May, S. T. (2000, Winter). *Proxemics: The hula hoop and use of personal space, 14(2)*, pp. 4-5.
- Myers Scott. "Classroom by Design" (Summer, 96) 10, 4, pp. 1-2
- Overton, Julia. "Look and Learn: Using Field Observation in the Nonverbal Course," (Summer 1993) 7, 4, p. 4.
- Parker, Rhonda G. and Dale (I. Leathers. "You Be the Judge: Impression Management in the Courtroom," (Fall 1992) 7, 1, p.4.
- Phillips, T. G. (1997, Summer). *Introducing gender-biased language: Much ado about something, 11(4)*, pp. 3-4.
- Siddens, P. J. (1996, Spring). *Touch, territoriality, and nonverbal communication, 10(3)*, pp. 2-4.
- Smith, K. A. (1999, Spring). *Identifying Knapp and Vangelisti's model in Nickelodeon's "Rugrats", 13(3)*, pp. 12-14.
- Spicer, K. (1995, Winter). *Stereotypes and appearances, 9(2)*, p. 10.
- Rowley, E. N. (1992, Fall). *More than mere words, 7(1)*, p. 5.
- Valentine, C. A. & Arnold, W. E. (1992, Winter). *Nonverbal scavenger hunt, 6(2)*, pp. 14-15.

SUPPLEMENTARY RESOURCES

I. BOOKS AND ARTICLES

- Burgoon, Judee, D. B. Buller, and W. G. Woodall. *Nonverbal Communication: The Unspoken Dialogue.* New York, NY: McGraw Hill, 1996.

- Ekman, Paul. *Telling Lies: Clues to Deceit in the Marketplace, Politics, and Marriage.* New York: Norton, 1994.
- Fisher, J.D. "Too Close for Comfort" *Journal of Personal and Social Psychology,* 32, 1995, pp. 15-21
- Guerrero, Laura, Joseph DeVito, and Michael Hecht (eds.). *The Nonverbal Communication Reader: Classic and Contemporary Readings, Second edition.* Prospect Heights, IL: Waveland, 1999.
- Hall, Edward. *The Silent Language.* Westport, CT: Greenwood Press, 1980.
- Hall, Edward. *The Hidden Dimension.* New York, NY: Anchor Books, 1990.
- Hickson, Mark and Don Stacks. *Nonverbal Communication: Studies and Applications, Fourth edition.* Los Angeles, CA: Roxbury Publishing Company, 2002.
- Jandt, Fred. *Intercultural Communication: An Introduction.* Thousand Oaks, CA: Sage, 2001
- Jones, Shirley. *The Right Touch: Understanding and Using the Language of Physical Contact.* Cresskill, NJ: Hampton Press, 1994.
- Knapp, Mark and Judith Hall. *Nonverbal Communication in Human Interaction, Fifth edition.* Belmont, CA: Wadsworth, 2002.
- Knapp, Mark and John Daly, (eds.). *Handbook of Interpersonal Communication, Third edition.* Thousand Oaks, CA: Sage, 2003.
- Leathers, Dale. *Successful Nonverbal Communication: Principles and Applications.* Needham Heights, MA: Allyn & Bacon/Longman, 1997.
- Lewis, Jeff. *Cultural Studies: The Basics.* Thousand Oaks, CA: Sage, 2002

II. FILMS/TAPES

- "Body Language." Insight Media, 1986, 30 minutes, VHS. In this clear, fast-paced introduction to the fascinating sciences of kinesics and proxemics, students learn how gestures mirror inner feelings and how posture can reveal opinions and send messages.
- "Codes." Media Insight. 2001. 50 minutes. This video examines the history of cryptology from the perspective of secret symbols and codes.
- "Eye Contact and Kinesics." Insight Media, 1986, 28 minutes, VHS. Examines the importance of eye contact and kinesics in nonverbal communication.
- "Legacy." California Newsreel. 2000. 90 minutes. A chronicles of three generations of African American women as they struggle to free themselves from welfare and poverty.
- "Man, the Symbol Maker." Biofilms, 1981, 25 minutes, color. Discusses nonverbal communication, the difference between animal signals and human symbols, and the potential dangers of the symbolic process and ways of transcending these dangers.
- "Nonverbal Communication." Insight Media, 1991, 27 minutes, VHS. Based on behavioral research and incorporating everyday examples, this program examines how nonverbal communication can be beneficial or detrimental to communication.
- "Paralanguage and Proxemics." Insight Media, 28 minutes, VHS. Examining the importance of nonverbal communication in creating first impressions and conveying the true meaning of a message, this program defines two nonverbal systems-- paralanguage and proxemics.
- "When You're Smilin'." Coronet, 6 minutes, color, VHS. Points out the importance and impact of the smile as a communication tool.

CHAPTER 6 UNDERSTANDING INTERPERSONAL RELATIONSHIPS

OVERVIEW

This chapter explores the dynamics of interpersonal relationships. It explains the characteristics that make interpersonal relationships distinctly different form other types of less personal relationships. This chapter examines how intimacy is a special dimension of interpersonal relationships, as well as explaining some forces that shape interpersonal relationships. Finally this chapter discusses the subject of self-disclosure as an important factor in interpersonal relationships and communication.

OBJECTIVES

1. To introduce to students how interpersonal communication has several characteristics such as:
   a. it is qualitatively different from less personal relationships
   b. interpersonal communication has both a content and relational dimension
   c. interpersonal communication can address relational matters explicitly through metacommunication
2. To provide students an understanding of how intimacy is a special dimension of interpersonal relationships through explaining:
   a. how it has several dimensions
   b. how men and women sometimes value and express intimacy differently
   c. how cultural background influences how we communicate intimacy
3. To aid students in the understanding of how communication scholars have explored some forces that shape personal relationships with:
   a. developmental models that describe how communication in relationships changes over time
   b. dialectical models that describe forces that always operates in relationships
   c. the concept that no matter which model is used, relationships are constantly changing
4. To help students understand the subject of self-disclosure is an important one in the study of interpersonal relationships by discussing:
   a. how people disclose (or withhold) personal information for a variety of reasons
   b. how models can help us understand how self-disclosure operates
   c. how regardless of the reason, self-disclosure in relationships possesses several characteristics
   d. how several guidelines can help you decide whether or not to disclose personal information

SUGGESTED CLASSROOM ACTIVITIES

—GENDER DIFFERENCES IN DISCLOSURE

Approximate time: 20 to 30 minutes

I. PURPOSE: To demonstrate to students that men and women value and express or self-disclose differently.

II. PROCEDURE:

1. Divide the class by gender (males in one group, females in another group)
2. Have one person from each group write down the comments for their group.
3. Ask each group to list what is appropriate to self-disclose on a first date.
4. Ask each group to list what is inappropriate to self-disclose on a first date.
5. Have the group discuss how inappropriate self-disclosure affects the communication for the rest of the date.
6. Ask each group if males or females are most likely to disclose more information on the first date.
7. Ask each group to list what is more typical for males to disclose verses females and vie versa

8. After each group has answered the questions, have them compare the similarities and contrast the differences among the class.

III. PRINICPLES ILLUSTRATED:

1. Men and women sometimes value and express intimacy differently.
2. Men and women view self-disclosure differently.
3. Self-concepts play a role in self-disclosure.
4. Depending on what we disclose, a disclosure can affect the communication encounter positively or negatively.

—SELF-DISCLOSURE ACTIVITIES

Approximate Time: 30 minutes.

I.   PURPOSE: to identify topics and contexts that are appropriate for self-disclosure.

II.   PROCEDURE:

1. Distribute a copy of the following form to each class member.
2. When you have completed this list for yourself, go back through it and label the items again, responding to each item with the label (L, M, H, or X) the you think represents the way "most people" (or "people in general") would respond to it.
3. Discuss the results as a class. Were most responses similar? Different? Why? Why is self-disclosure so risky? When is it appropriate? What can be gained by appropriate self-disclosure?

III. PRINCIPLES ILLUSTRATED:

1. Self-disclosure is risky.
2. Self-disclosure, when appropriate, can improve relationships.
3. Context, topic, and participants affect the appropriateness.
4. Appropriateness of self-disclosure varies from person to person.

Self-Disclosure Exercise

DIRECTIONS: Working alone, label each of the statements below.

L — (low risk), meaning you believe it is appropriate to disclose this information to almost anyone

M — (moderate risk), meaning you believe it is appropriate to disclose this information to those you know pretty well and have already established a friendship relationship with

H — (high risk), meaning you would disclose such information only to the few friends you have great trust in or to those you regard as your most intimate friends;

X — meaning you would disclose it to no one.

_____ 1. Your hobbies, how you like best to spend your spare time.

_____ 2. Your preferences and dislikes in music.

_____ 3. Your educational background and grades and your feelings about them.

_____ 4. Your personal views on politics.

_____ 5. Your personal habits that bother you.

_____ 6. Your personal characteristics that make you proud.

_____ 7. Your religious views and your religious participation.

_____ 8. The details of the unhappiest moments in your life.

_____ 9. The details of the happiest moments in your life.

_____ 10. The actions you have most regretted and why.

_____ 11. Your guiltiest secrets.

_____ 12. Your views on the way a husband and wife should live in their marriage.

_____ 13. The main unfulfilled dreams in your life.

_____ 14. What you do, if anything, to stay physically fit.

_____ 15. The aspects of your body you are most pleased with.

_____ 16. The features of your appearance you are most displeased with.

_____ 17. The person in your life whom you most resent and the reasons why.

_____ 18. The person in your life whom you most admire and the reasons why.

_____ 19. Your most significant fears.

_____ 20. The people with whom you have been sexually intimate and the circumstances of your relationship with each.

—LEVELS OF SELF-DISCLOSURE

Approximate Time: 15 minutes

I.   PURPOSE: to experience the differences in levels of self-disclosure.

II. PROCEDURE:

1. Divide the class into groups of five.
2. Instruct the groups to go around the circle, each giving his or her name.
3. After that is completed, do the same for the following. Assign each topic, one at a time, after each student has completed the previous one.
    a. major in school
    b. favorite song and the reason you like it
    c. one important quality you look for in a friend
    d. something you have in common with one other member of your group, other than physical characteristics, for example, "You have a good sense of humor and so do I," "Your major is math and I like it too."

III. PRINCIPLES ILLUSTRATED:

1. There are different levels of self-disclosure.
2. In a given setting, some levels seem more appropriate and comfortable than others.
3. The closer the topic of the self-disclosure is to a person, the greater the social penetration and risk.
4. Feelings about the appropriateness of self-disclosure vary from person to person.

—NEW RELATIONSHIPS

Approximate Time: 1 class period

I.   PURPOSE: to stimulate the development of a relationship between two strangers.

II. PROCEDURE:

1. Ask class members to pair off with someone in class they do not know.
2. Ask members to write down in 2-3 words their feelings about pairing off with a stranger.
3. Instruct the dyads to get to know each other as well as possible in twenty minutes. They may leave the classroom if they wish.
4. In twenty minutes, reconvene and ask students to write down what they were feeling at the beginning of the conversation and at the end of the conversation. They should also write down what they think their partners were feeling.
5. Allow dyads to compare notes briefly.
6. Discuss the exercise, emphasizing the commonality of anxiety and uncertainty about a new relationship. Note changes in the feelings throughout the twenty minutes. Did the discussion topics change? Ask students to identify their feelings about their partners now that the exercise is over. Note how this exercise was different from and similar to real-life relationship development.

III. PRINCIPLES ILLUSTRATED:

1. Relationships develop in fairly typical patterns.
2. Most people feel anxiety at the onset of a relationship.
3. Feelings about a relationship change during the course of the relationship.

—OBSERVING OTHERS ACTIVITY

Approximate Time: 20 to 30 minutes

I.   PURPOSE: to demonstrate the impact our communication behaviors have on the impressions others have of us.

II.   PROCEDURE:

1.   The class is divided into two large groups (Group A & Group B)
2.   Group A will conduct a 15 minute discussion in the middle of the classroom while Group B sits on the outside and observes.
3.   Next, Group B sits on the inside and conducts a 15 minute discussion while Group A sits on the outside and observes. (The topics for each discussion will be given on the day of the assignment.)
4.   Students are expected to make notes of their perceptions when they are in the role of observer.
5.   The types of observations to be made at this time can encompass almost any issue. Students may address who impressed or didn't impress them. They may note how someone dressed or how well and/or how poorly participants expressed themselves. They may describe the participant's hair, voice, mannerisms, jewelry or whatever else comes to mind.
6.   After each group has observed its counterpart, Groups A and B are then divided into smaller groups of 3 or 4 students. At this time the smaller groups are to share their observations of the larger group discussion that they watched. This discussion will last approximately 10 to 15 minutes. Honesty is very important in this portion of the assignment. All comments made in these smaller groups will be kept confidential.

III.   PRINCIPLES ILLUSTRATED:

1.   All communication behavior is subject to interpretation by others.
2.   Individuals have differing views of the same communication behavior.
3.   Our sense of self is largely influenced by how others perceive us.

ACTIVITIES TO PROMOTE CRITICAL AND CREATIVE THINKING

Have student role play a conversation between two partners in an interpersonal relationship. The first version should contain all, or nearly all, content messages. The second version should contain all, or nearly all, relational messages. Discuss the differences.

Have students examine one of their own interpersonal relationships in terms of the reasons for forming relationships stated in the text.

Show an appropriate segment of a soap opera tape that shows interpersonal communication between two people in a relationship. Use it as a stimulus for discussion. Frame the chapter objectives as questions. For example: Is the dialogue on the tape an example of interpersonal communication? Why or why not?

TEACHING ACTIVITIES IN THE SPEECH COMMUNICATION TEACHER

- Aylor, B. A. (2000, Summer). *"Three theorists walk into a bar ..."*: Humanizing communication theory, 14(4), pp. 13-14.
- Chowning, James. "Decision-Making Goes Interpersonal," (Winter 1995) 9, 2, p. 7.
- Hall, Donna. "Join the Breakfast Club," (Spring 1991) 5, 3, p. 3.
- Lane, Shelly. "Communicating Emotions" (Spring, 1999) 11, 3, pp. 2-4
- Lau, David. "Women and Men, Men and Women," (Winter 1991) 5, 2, pp. 9-10.
- Raftis, Scan. "Student Listening Tests," (Winter 1991) 5, 2, p. 5.
- Rivers, M. J. (2000, Summer). *For better or worse? Let's make it better*, 14(4), pp. 8-10.

- Samra, R. J. (2000, Summer). *Teaching public relations a la great American pastimes, 14(4),* pp. 12-13.
- Smithson, S. (1999, Summer). *Learning style perspectives: Impact in the classroom, 13(4),* pp. 15-16.
- Sprague, R. J. (2000, Winter). *Theory building in communication courses, 14(2),* pp. 12-13.
- Willer, L. R. (1999, Winter). *Ask the expert: Dialoguing with authors to learn about research, 13(2),* pp. 2-3.

SUPPLEMENTARY RESOURCES

I.   BOOKS AND ARTICLES

- Adler, Ronald, Russell Proctor, and Lawrence Rosenfeld. *Interplay: The Process of Interpersonal Communication.* New York, NY: Oxford University Press, 2001.
- Berko, Roy, Lawrence Rosenfeld, and Larry Samovar. *Connecting: A Culture-Sensitive Approach to Interpersonal Communication Competency.* Belmont, CA: Wadsworth, 1998.
- Daly, John and John Wiemann. *Strategic Interpersonal Communication.* Mahwah, NJ: Lawrence Erlbaum Associates, 1994.
- DeVito, Joseph. *The Interpersonal Communication Book.* Needham Heights, MA: Allyn & Bacon/Longman, 2001.
- Fisher, Roger, William Ury, and Bruce Patton. *Getting to Yes: Negotiating Without Giving In.* New York, NY: Penguin USA, 1992.
- Kim, Young Yun. *Becoming Intercultural: An Integrative Theory of Communication and Crosscultural Adaptation.* Thousand Oaks, CA: Sage. 2001.
- Lustig, Myron and Jolene Koester. *Intercultural Competence.* Needham Heights, MA: Allyn & Bacon/Longman, 2003.
- McCroskey, James and Virginia Richmond. *Fundamentals of Human Communication: An Interpersonal Perspective.* Prospect Heights, IL: Waveland, 2002.
- Samovar, Larry and Richard Porter. *Communication Between Cultures.* Belmont, CA: Wadsworth, 2000.
- Stewart, John. *Bridges Not Walls.* New York, NY: McGraw-Hill, 2002.
- Trenholm, Sarah and Arthur Jensen. *Interpersonal Communication.* New York, NY: Oxford University Press, 1992.
- Veenendall, Thomas and Marjorie Feinstein. *Let's Talk About Relationships: Cases in Study.* Prospect Heights, IL: Waveland. 2001.
- Verderber, Rudolph and Kathleen Verderber. *Inter-Act: Interpersonal Communication Concepts, Skills, and Contexts.* Belmont, CA: Wadsworth, 2001.
- Weaver, Richard. *Understanding Interpersonal Communication.* Needham Heights, MA: Allyn & Bacon/Longman, 1996.
- Woods, Julia. *Gendered Lives.* Belmont, CA: Wadsworth, 2003.

II.   FILMS/TAPES

- "Difficulties in Communication." Insight Media, 9 minutes, VHS. Underscoring the need to communicate clearly, yet sensitively, this program examines four dysfunctional methods of communication.
- "Interpersonal Communication Skills." Four Volume Set. 1995. 261 minutes. These videos discuss the values of small talk, entering and exiting conversation, body language, persuasive language and other important communication modalities.
- "Interpersonal Relationships." Insight Video. 1997. 30 minutes. This video looks at forms of defensive and supportive relationships as well as techniques for self-disclosure.
- "The Art of Communicating: Modern Myths." Films for the Humanities. 2001, 52 minutes. This video explores the role of myths in organizing communities.
- "The 90's Communication Series: Constructive Communications." Cambridge Educational Production. 1999. 30 minutes. This video demonstrates the E.A.S.Y. system for positive communication and understanding yourself.
- "Self-Awareness." Insight Media. 1997. 29 minutes. A videotape that examines the development of the self-concept, the evolution of self-awareness and describes self understanding.

CHAPTER 7 IMPROVING INTERPERSONAL RELATIONSHIPS

OVERVIEW

This chapter discusses the impact of interpersonal communication on our daily lives. Throughout this chapter the authors discuss how communication climates are intangible but critical ingredients in relational satisfaction. They go into explanation of what makes some messages confirming and other messages disconfirming, while explaining how the communication climate develops. The authors also give tips for creating positive communication climates. This chapter also focuses on conflict within relationships. The authors explain why conflict occurs, the different ways people express conflict, the influence of gender in conflict, and the methods of conflict resolution.

OBJECTIVES

1. To help students understand how communication climates are intangible but critical ingredients to relational satisfaction by discussing:
   a. what makes some messages confirming and other messages disconfirming
   b. how communication climates develop
   c. some tips for creating positive communication climates
2. To facilitate the understanding of the importance of looking at conflict in relationships by exploring:
   a. whey there is conflict
   b. how people express conflict
   c. the influence of gender and culture on conflict in relationships
   d. methods of conflict resolution, including the win-win approach

SUGGESTED CLASSROOM ACTIVITIES

—COMMUNICATION CLIMATE EXERCISE

Approximate Time: 30 minutes

I.   PURPOSE: to identify behaviors which demonstrate components of defensive and supportive climate.

II. PROCEDURE:

1. Put the following statements on the board or on a handout with the accompanying directions. Ask class members to work on them individually or in small groups.

III. PRINCIPLES ILLUSTRATED:

1. Certain behaviors create a defensive climate.
2. Certain behaviors create a more supportive climate.
3. Some statements can be easily altered to lessen their defensiveness.

Communication Climate Exercise

DIRECTIONS: Label the following statements as evaluation, certainty, control, strategy, neutrality, or superiority. After doing that, rephrase three of the statements so that they are descriptive, provisional, spontaneous, problem oriented, empathic, or equal.

1. Sue, turn that off! Nobody can study with all that noise! (Sue, I can't work with that radio on.)

2. Did you ever hear such a tacky idea as a formal reception with cheap paper plates?

3. That idea will never work.

4. Oh, Hank, you're so funny for wearing a printed shirt with those pants. Well, I guess that's a man for you.

5. Terry, you're acting like a child.

6. You have five minutes and not a second more. Get to work.

7. You man think you know how to handle the situation, but you really don't have the experience. I know when something's over your head.

8. Whatever you decide will be okay with me.

9. I think that the professor really wants us to figure out that there may be more than one right answer to these.

10. CLASS! BE QUIET!

Discuss as a large group. Be certain to relate the statements to Gibbs' categories. Note throughout that perceived threat can create defensiveness even when the speaker does not intend to threaten.

—PERCEPTIONS OF CONFLICT

Approximate Time: 20 minutes

I. PURPOSE: to identify common perceptions of conflict.

II. PROCEDURE:

1. Write the word "CONFLICT" on the chalkboard.
2. Ask students to name words that come into their minds when they see the word "conflict." Write their words on the chalkboard.
3. Discuss the implications of these perceptions on the study of conflict and conflict resolution. Note how many people have negative perceptions of conflict and how these perceptions might inhibit effective use of conflict. Discuss how conflict can be a beneficial force. Relate this discussion to the textbook identification of types of conflict resolution.

III. PRINCIPLES ILLUSTRATED:

1. Conflict has a negative connotation for many.
2. Negative perceptions of conflict make people reluctant to welcome it for its positive value.
3. Conflict is inevitable.
4. Conflict can be a helpful, dynamic force in communication.

—WIN-WIN CONFLICT RESOLUTION GROUP ACTIVITY

Approximate Time: 30 minutes

I. PURPOSE: to review the steps in win-win conflict resolution.

II. PROCEDURE:

1. Divide the class into an even number of groups.
2. Assign each group a "partner" group.
3. Instruct each group to write a brief description of a hypothetical problem and unmet need using the guidelines identifies in the Steps for Win-Win Problem Solving in Chapter 7.
4. Have each group exchange their description/problem statement with their "partner" group. Explain that they are to respond to their partner group's problem statement by paraphrasing the problem as they understand it.
5. Paraphrased messages are then exchanged between partner groups and checked for accuracy.
6. Each group then makes up a hypothetical description of Partner Needs based upon the partner group's original problem situation. This description is written out.
7. Partner Need Statements are exchanged and paraphrased by the partner groups.
8. Each group then works out its own problem situation through the four steps of negotiating a solution.
9. When a best solution has been decided upon, each group exchanges solutions with the partner group to gain final feedback.

III. PRINCIPLES ILLUSTRATED:

1. Conflict involves dealing with another person's perceptions of a situation.
2. Conflict can be a helpful, dynamic force in communication.
3. Conflict is inevitable.
4. Group pressures can influence the outcome of conflict.

—SELF-PERCEPTION STATEMENT ACTIVITY

Approximate Time: 30 minutes

1. PURPOSE: to demonstrate the relationship between a person's self-concept and the verbal utterances he/she makes.

II. PROCEDURE:

1. Students may work in pairs or groups to complete the statements requested in the instructions on the following handout.

III. PRINCIPLES ILLUSTRATED:

1. Self-concept influences all aspects of communication behavior.
2. Verbal communication directly and indirectly reveals relationship attitudes.
3. Application of the concepts of assertiveness, nonassertiveness, aggressiveness, supportiveness, and defensiveness.

Self Perceptions Statement Activity

Your assignment is to use the situation described below as a stimulus for writing a series of statements. Each statement is intended to illustrate a self-concept related behavior. When writing the statements, use complete sentences and avoid using the same statement more than once. You will have to speculate on what sort of things the individuals in the situation would actually say.

SITUATION: John and William have worked together at the same company for a long time. John has worked there for ten years; William for eleven. They have become very good friends during that time. They go bowling together on Fridays and their families often get together for picnics and parties. For the last month, John has made numerous comments to William about how excited he was about his own prospects for getting promoted to the new sales manager position. He, John, was the only one from the company to have applied and, as he explained it to William, he was sure he had the inside track. Whenever John talked about this, William would always give an encouraging smile and nod his head. So it came as quite a shock when this Monday morning John was told that William had just applied for the same position. John was stunned. He walked into his office and there sat William.

STATEMENTS:

1. What might John say to William that would illustrate NONASSERTIVENESS?

2. What might John say to William that would illustrate AGGRESSIVESS?

3. What might William say in response to John's preceding aggressive statement if William were feeling DEFENSIVE?

4. What might John say to William that would illustrate ASSERTIVENESS?

5. What might William say in response to John's preceding assertive statement if William were expressing SUPPORTIVENESS?

ACTIVITIES TO PROMOTE CRITICAL AND CREATIVE THINKING

Assign a piece of literature which focuses on a relationship. Discuss how the information in the text applies to the fictional relationship. "The Caretaker," by Susan Hill, is a short story which will work well. This could also be done with a TV show such as *The OC* or *ER*.

Have the class read "A Poison Tree," a poem by William Blake (in *Introduction to Literature*, Altenbernd and Lewis, 1975). Discuss the handling of conflict described there. Does it remind you of a situation from your own experience?

Present your class with the following. Use as a group project, journal entry, discussion topic, or written assignment. Assume that a creature from outer space arrived on Earth. It seeks you out as a consultant on how to establish good relationships with Earth people. Draw up a guide to "getting to know and getting along with Earthlings."

Have students compare the means of resolving conflict that are demonstrated in two different TV shows. Have students select one adult show and one children's show. Describe the possible target audiences for each show and explain what conflict resolution messages each audience receives.

TEACHING ACTIVITIES IN THE COMMUNICATION TEACHER

- Baldwin, J. R. (Fall, 1999). *Intercultural pals: A focused journal, 14(1)*, pp. 13-14.
- Brunson, D. A. (2000, Winter). *Talking about race by talking about whiteness, 14(2)*, pp. 1-4.
- Finn, T. A. (1999, Winter). *Isolating interpersonal cues through student use of multiple media, 13(2)*, pp. 6-7.
- Gutgold, N. D. (2000, Summer). *Meta communication in business communication means a rich learning experience that is truly a slice of life!, 14(4)*, pp. 14-15.
- Hanna, M. S. (2000, Spring). *Design a role-playing case for study and practice, 14(3)*, pp. 12-14.
- Myers, S. A. (1998, Summer). *Developing student awareness of interpersonal communication competence, 12(4)*, p, 6.
- Olaniran, B., Stalcup, K. A., & Jensen, K. K. (2000, Fall). *Incorporating computer-mediated technology to strategically serve pedagogy, 15(1)*, pp. 1-4.
- Pawlowski, D. (1999, Winter). *Dialoguing the gender movements, 13(2)*, pp. 4-6.
- Pawlowski, D. R. (2000, Winter). *Multiple method interviewing: Learning about performance appraisals through information-gathering phone interviews, 14(2)*, pp. 9-10.
- Plec, E. (1999, Winter). *The interview, 13(2)*, pp. 11-12.
- Roberto, A. (1999, Winter). *What's love got to do with it? Love, relationships and communication, 13(2)*, pp. 7-9.
- Thameling, C. L. (2000, Summer). *Ethical communication in interpersonal relationships, 14(4)*, pp. 1-4.

SUPPLEMENTARY RESOURCES

I. BOOKS AND ARTICLES

- Adler, Ronald and Neil Towne. *Looking Out, Looking In*. Belmont, CA: Wadsworth, 2002.
- Arliss, Laurie and Deborah Borisoff. *Women and Men Communicating*: Challenges and Changes. Prospect Heights, IL: Waveland Press, 2001.
- Cahn, Dudley. Conflict in Intimate *Relationships*. *New* York: Guilford, 1992.
- Carbaugh, Donal. Cultural Communication and Intercultural Contact. Mahwah, NJ: Lawrence Erlbaum Associates, 1990.
- Galvin, Kathleen and Bernard Brommel. *Family Communication: Cohesion and Change*. Needham Heights, MA: Allyn & Bacon/Longman, 2000.
- Goss, Blaine. *The Psychology of Human Communication*. Prospect Heights, IL: Waveland, 2002.

- Kalbfleisch, Pamela. *Interpersonal Communication: Evolving Interpersonal Relationships.* Mahwah, NJ: Lawrence Erlbaum Associates, 1993.
- Nardi, Peter. *Men's Friendships.* Thousand Oaks, CA: Sage, 1992.
- Samovar, Larry and Richard Porter. *Communication Between Cultures.* Belmont, CA: Wadsworth, 2001.
- Tannen, Deborah. *You Just Don't Understand.* New York, NY: Morrow, 1990.
- Veenedall, Thomas and Marjorie Feinstein. *Let's Talk About Relationships: Cases in Study.* Prospect Heights, IL: Waveland, 2002.
- Wood, Julia. *Communication Mosaics.* Belmont, CA: Wadsworth, 2001.

II. FILMS/TAPES

- "Communication Breakdown." Insight Media, 22 minutes, VHS. This program teaches how to improve communication skills and avoid misunderstandings. Viewers learn to identify personal barriers to communication and to change their behavior patterns.
- "Conflict: Causes and Resolutions." Roundtable Films, 34 minutes, color. How to turn potentially damaging conflicts into opportunities for creative solutions. flow to recognize the major causes of conflict: divergent goals, value differences, role pressure, status conflict, and perceptual differences. Three major approaches to conflict resolution: win-lose, negotiating, and problem solving (win-win).
- "Defensive/Supportive Communication." Insight Media, 28 minutes, VHS. This lesson shows defensive behaviors and explains how to replace them with supportive behaviors. It also offers an approach to productive conflict resolution.
- "Double Talk." Coronet, 9 minute, color, VHS. A satirical look at a "first date" situation provides a humorous and provocative look at the communication in this interpersonal setting.
- "I'd Rather Not Say." Roundtable Films, 30 minutes, color. Shows how to create an environment for more open communication. Demonstrates how to overcome defensive communication and how to gain acceptance necessary for revelation of potentially damaging facts.
- "Level With Me" Honest Communication." Insight Media, 1991, 29 minutes, VHS. Using entertaining dramatic sketches, this program examines five styles of manipulative communication.
- "Managing Conflict at Work." Insight Media, 2000. 20 Minutes. A video that prescribes techniques for using conflict to solve problems in the workplace.

CHAPTER 8 THE NATURE OF GROUPS

OVERVIEW

This chapter discusses the nature of groups and the complexity of groups. The authors explain several important characteristics of groups such as how groups have a variety of purposes for existing while each has its own operating style. This chapter discusses the difference between individuals and groups. It also examines how stated goal of groups and the personal goals of individual members interact in way that can affect success. The authors continue by explaining the various reasons groups exist in order to fulfill a variety of goals.

OBJECTIVES

1. To help students understand that groups have a variety of purposes for existing and each.has its own operating style.
2. To exemplify that a true group's interaction, interdependence, size, and length of time distinguish it from a less well-defined collection of individuals.
3. To provide students with the understanding of why different types of groups exist to fulfill a variety of goals such as:
    a. social reasons
    b. learning
    c. personal growth
    d. problem solving
4. To aid students in identifying group norms, rules, roles, patterns of interaction and methods of making decisions and show how they can shape the way members interact as well as their productivity and satisfaction.
5. To show students how cultural factors can shape the way groups operate.

SUGGESTED CLASSROOM ACTIVITIES

NOTE: For additional group activities that incorporate material on mass communication see Suggested Classroom Activities in the Guide to Mediated Communication section of this manual.

—TYPES OF GROUPS

Approximate Time: 20 minutes

I.   PURPOSE: to make students aware of the different types of groups in which they communicate.

II. PROCEDURE:

1. Put the textbook definition of small group on the board.
2. Divide the class into groups of 3-4.
3. Ask each group to list as many groups as possible in which the group members have participated.
4. Reconvene and list the groups by type (using categories from the textbook) on the board.

III. PRINCIPLES ILLUSTRATED:

1. Much communication time is spent in small groups.
2. Most people are members of many groups.
3. Most people are members of many types of groups.

—GROUP NORMS

Approximate Time: 20 minutes

I.   PURPOSE: to increase awareness of implicit norms that affect groups.

II.   PROCEDURE:

1. Define norms.
2. Brainstorm a list of norms that operate in this class. Put the norms on the board. Continue this for 10 minute.
3. Discuss by contrasting explicit with implicit norms. Note how many norms are implicit. Ask, "How do we know when we've broken a norm?" Ask students to share personal experiences in which they have broken norms. Ask students how they learn the norms.

III.   PRINCIPLES ILLUSTRATED:

1.   All groups have norms.
2.   Norms are both explicit and implicit.
3.   Norms are powerful but subtle.

—PHOBIA ACTIVITY:

Approximate Time: 15 to 20 minutes

I.   PURPOSE: A group discussion vehicle to be used to demonstrate a variety of group interaction principles.

II.   PROCEDURE:

1.   Students are assigned to groups and instructed to follow the directions on the following handout.
2.   Following the group discussion students are asked to analyze the discussion according to the concepts chosen by the instructor, i.e., norms, roles, patterns of interaction, etc.

ANSWER KEY: (in order listed) g, h, m, r, p, s, l, c, e, k

III.   PRINCIPLES ILLUSTRATED:

1.   This activity is used to demonstrate any number of concepts from the text. The specific concepts to be illustrated are to be chosen by the instructor.

Phobias Activity

Psychologists have coined numerous scientific terms to describe the many fears that plague people. Arachnophobia is a morbid fear of spiders. Ergophobia is a fear of work. Limnophobia is a fear of lakes.

Here are two lists. The first is a list of scientific terms that are used to describe specific fears or phobias. The second list describes the actual "thing" that is the focus of a person's fear. Your group's task is to match the phobia with the thing that is feared. Use **consensus** decision making in this activity, i.e., everyone in the group must agree with each decision.

NOTE: Some of the items listed in the second column do not match any of the phobias. There is only one correct match for each phobia.

PHOBIAS	WHAT IS FEARED
_____ batophobia	a. fire
	b. machines
_____ cryophobia	c. mice
	d. exercise
_____ demophobia	e. sex
	f. loud noises
_____ haptophobia	g. walking
	h. ice
_____ homichlophobia	i. slime
	j. deep water
_____ bibliophobia	k. monsters
	l. nudity
_____ gymnophobia	m. crowds
	n. marriage
_____ musophobia	o. mirrors
	p. fog
_____ genophobia	q. homosexuality
	r. touch
_____ teratophobia	s. books

ACTIVITY TO PROMOTE CRITICAL AND CREATIVE THINKING

Select a significant world or national problem. Assign the class the task of deciding whom to invite to participate in a problem-solving discussion of the problem. Participant selection should be based on each person's competence or position. Participants can include people from any time period and be fictional or real life. A rationale should be give for each participant selected. Predictions should be made about the role(s) each is most likely to play and why. This role mix should also be included in the selection process. The activity can be done as a class discussion or as an assigned paper or group project or a combination of written assignment and class discussion.

TEACHING ACTIVITIES IN THE SPEECH COMMUNICATION TEACHER

- Bello-Orgunu, J. O. (1997, Fall). *Questions and questioning in classroom discussions, 12(1)*, pp. 13-14.
- Benson, J. H. (1998, Summer). *Shaping attitudes: A role of the leader, 12(4)*, pp. 3-4
- Blomberg, D. L. (1998, Summer). *Group projects, A framework for success, 12(4)*, pp. 13-14.
- Bourhis, John. "Video Groups," (Summer 1992) 6, 4, p. 12.
- Chaudoin, Kristin. "The Reflective Thinking Method and Student Empowerment" (Winter, 1997) 11, 2, pp. 9-10.
- Dolphin, C. Z. (1998, Summer). *Using the Monroe Motivated Sequence: A group exercise, 12(4)*, p. 12.
- Hayward, P. A. (1997, Fall). *The 4x4 text analysis workshop, 12(1)*, pp. 8-10. [Goal: To analyze and present text readings in cooperative workgroups.]
- Johnson, Scott. "Exploring the Influence of Culture on Groups," (Winter 1995) 9, 2, p. 6.
- Martin, S. E. (2000, Winter). *Stock issues-based policy speech small group exercise, 14(2)*, pp. 13-14.
- Mitnick, A. D. (1999, Summer). *Put your money where your mouth is: Group communication classes go fundraising, 13(4)*, pp. 3-4.
- Scherer, Robert F. and Crystal L. Owen. "Demonstrating (Troup Dynamics in the Classroom: The Real Gorilla," (Fall 1992) 7, 1, p. 3.
- Watters, K. B. (1997, Fall). *Authentic and pseudo small groups, 12(1)*, pp. 6-7.

SUPPLEMENTARY RESOURCES

I.   BOOKS AND ARTICLES

- Brilhart, John and Gloria Galanes. *Effective Group Discussion*. New York, NY: McGraw Hill, 2001.
- Frey, Lawrence. *New Directions in Group Communication*. Thousand Oaks, CA: Sage. 2002.
- Johnson, David and Frank Johnson. *Joining Together*. Needham Heights, MA: Allyn & Bacon, 2003.
- Phillips, Gerald. *Teaching How to Work in Groups*. Norwood, NJ: Ablex, 1990.
- Rothwell, J. Dan. *In Mixed Company: Small Group Communication*. Belmont, CA: Wadsworth, 2001.
- Schultz, Beatrice. *Communicating in the Small Group: Theory and Practice*. Needham Heights, MA: Allyn & Bacon/Longman, 1996.
- Wilson, Gerald. *Groups in Context: Leadership and Participation in Small Groups*. New York: McGraw Hill, 2002.
- Young, Kathryn Sue, Julia Wood, Gerald Phillips, and Douglas Pedersen. *Group Discussion: A Practical Guide to Participation and Leadership,* Prospect Heights, IL: Waveland. 2002.

II.   FILMS/TAPES

- "Brain Power." Coronet, 12 minutes, color VHS. John Houseman explains the role of creativity, perception and communication in a group setting.
- "Business Communications." Films for the Humanities. 2001. A twenty part series on communication skills that are relevant to the workplace. Each video is 15 minutes in length and covers a designated topic: teamwork, conflict resolution, presentation skills, conducting a business meeting, and so on.

- "Communicate! Skills for School, Business, and Everyday Life." Cambridge Educational Production. 2002. CD-ROM (Windows only). An interactive tool for developing interpersonal and group communication skills at home or work.
- "Group Dynamics in the Electronic Environment." Media Insight. 1999. 30 minutes. A video that discusses unique qualities brought to group interaction with the advent of electronic communication.
- "How's Your New Friend?" McGraw-Hill, 1975, 12 minutes, color. A drama about high school students which deals with issues of group pressure and norms. Beau Bridges follows this open-ended drama with questions for consideration.
- "Managing Conflict at Work: The Art of Communication." Media Insight. 2000. 20 minutes. This video examines the forms that conflict takes with groups of people on the job and provides guidelines for dealing with it.

CHAPTER 9 SOLVING PROBLEMS IN GROUPS

OVERVIEW

This chapter discusses the importance of solving problems in groups. Throughout this chapter you will see when and when not to use groups for problem solving, what formats are best for different problem solving situations, and the pros and cons of computer-mediated groups. The authors also discuss the dynamics of successful problems solving groups who use a structured six-step approach. They also discuss how successful groups understand stages that groups experience while working on a problem and how to maintain positive relationships and an optimal level of cohesiveness. Next, this chapter explains that leadership and team member influence comes in many forms. It explores the six types of power group members can use, and how the effectiveness of leaders can be defined in different ways. They also explain how different leaderships styles are effective in different circumstances. Finally, this chapter looks into the dangers to effective problem-solving groups.

OBJECTIVES

1. To help students understand the dynamics of solving problems in groups by discussing:
    a.   when to use (and not use) groups for solving problems
    b.   what formats are best for different problem-solving situations
    c.   the pros and cons of computer-mediated groups
2. To aid students in understanding that while groups can solve problems in many different ways, the most successful groups:
    a.   tend to follow a structured six-step approach
    b.   understand the stages groups experience while working on a problem
    c.   maintain positive relationships and an optimal level of cohesiveness
3. To show students that leaderships and team member influence comes in many forms such as:
    a.   group members can use six types of power
    b.   the effectiveness of leaders can be defined in different ways
    c.   there are many different leadership styles, which are effective in different circumstances
4. To facilitate the understanding that there are dangers to effective problem solving in groups.

SUGGESTED CLASSROOM ACTIVITIES

—LEADERS' BASES OF POWER

Approximate Time: 30 minutes

1. PURPOSE: to identify the bases of power from which local leaders operate.

II. PROCEDURE:

1. Divide the class into groups of 4-5. Then review the bases of power from which leadership operates: legitimate, coercive, reward, expert, information, and referent.
2. Ask the groups to identify any campus leaders who operate from the different power bases. Allow 10-15 minutes for this activity. Groups should be able to defend their choices.
3. Reconvene to a large group and share information. Note similarities of selection. Emphasize the difference in the power bases for the leaders. Emphasize that this activity can be done in this class, in the larger society, and in any community.

III. PRINCIPLES ILLUSTRATED:

1. Institutions rarely have one clear leader.
2. Leaders operate from various bases of power: legitimate, coercive, reward, expert, and referent.

—GROUP PROJECT I

Approximate Time: 2-3 class periods

I.   PURPOSE: to enable each student to participate in a task group and experience the group behaviors discussed in Chapters 9 and 10.

II. PROCEDURE:

1. Three weeks before the assignment is due divide the class into groups of 5-7 members.
2. Have each group choose a product and develop a 20- to 30-minute presentation to sell it to the class.
    a. Groups may choose a real product (Hershey chocolate bar) or make one up (a new night club, toy, or health club).
    b. Groups may divide up the task as they choose, but all must participate in the oral presentation.
    c. Encourage the use of visual aids of all types, audio and videotapes, costumes, props, skits, samples, handouts, surveys, and audience participation.
3. On the day of the presentation each group will turn in a paper, including:
    a. names of group members
    b. group attendance record, including time and date of all meetings
    c. name of group product
    d. list of selling strategies in presentation

III. PRINCIPLES ILLUSTRATED:

1. Problem-solving strategies are required in task groups.
2. Group members adopt a variety of roles in a task group.
3. Working in a group can be fun.

—GROUP PROJECT II

Approximate Time: 30 minutes

I.   PURPOSE: to practice the techniques of brainstorming for possible solutions to a problem.

II. PROCEDURE:

1. Instruct the class on techniques of brainstorming, then divide the class into groups.
2. Have each group brainstorm as many possible solutions as they can for each of the three topics, which follow. Explain that the groups should not move on to the next topic until they have brainstormed at least ten solutions.
3. Instruct the groups to rotate the responsibility of being the recorder for the groups' solutions.
4. Reinforce the idea that no critical comments are allowed. Encourage piggybacking.

   TOPICS:

   1. How can the school get the student body more involved in recycling on campus?
   2. What can be done to get people to check the batteries in their smoke detectors on a regular basis?
   3. What can be done to reduce the dropout rate at this school?

III. PRINCIPLES ILLUSTRATED:

1. Procedures for brainstorming in a group.
2. Groups can be more productive than individuals acting alone.
3. Explicit norms (rules for brainstorming).

ACTIVITIES TO PROMOTE CRITICAL AND CREATIVE THINKING

Use the front page of *USA Today* to select a problem. This activity can be done as a class, in small groups, or as a written assignment.

1. Phrase the problem as a probative question.
2. Describe the information necessary to solve the problem. What would you need to know?
3. Identify impelling and restraining forces working for and against solving the problem.
4. Brainstorm possible solutions.
5. Describe how you would evaluate the solutions.

Watch a video movie and discuss the concepts in Chapter 10 as they relate to the group(s) in the movie. *The Breakfast Club, Stand by Me*, or *Twelve Angry Men* would work well.

TEACHING ACTIVITIES IN THE COMMUNICATION TEACHER

- Fernandes, J. J. (1998, Spring). *Creative problem solving -- from top to bottom, 12(3)*, pp. 1-2.
- Kassing, J. W. (1997, Fall). *Reframing creative problem solving, 12(1)*, pp. 5-6.
- Neumann, David. "Building and Destroying Groups," (Spring 1992) 6, 3, pp. 13-14.
- Rapone, Thomas. "Using History to Teach Small Group Communication," (Spring 1995) 9, 3, p. 1.
- Wilson, C. E. (2000, Spring). *Ending the public speaking course on a positive note, 14(3)*, pp. 5-6.

SUPPLEMENTARY RESOURCES

I. BOOKS AND ARTICLES

- Barker, Larry, Kathy Wahlers, and Kittie Watson. *Groups in Process: An Introduction to Small Group Communication*. Needham Heights, MA: Allyn & Bacon, 2001.
- Chadwick, S. A. (1998, Summer). *Using a conflict-driven simulation to teach the introductory organizational communication course, 12(4)*, 13.
- Chaudoin, K. F. (1997, Winter). *The reflective-thinking method and student empowerment, 11(2)*, 9-10.
- Frey-Hartel, C. (1996, Fall). *Taking the "ouch" out of a class discussion, 11(1)*, 5-6.
- Lumsden, Gay and Donald Lumsden. *Communicating in Groups and Teams: Sharing Leadership*. Belmont, CA: Wadsworth, 2000.
- Martin, S. E. (2000, Winter). *Stock issues-based policy speech small group exercise, 14(2)*, 13-14.
- Mitnick, A. D. (1999, Summer). *Put your money where your mouth is: Group communication classes go fundraising, 13(4)*, 3-4.
- Wilson, Gerald. *Groups in Context: Leadership and Participation in Small Groups*. New York, NY: McGraw Hill, 2002.

II. FILMS/TAPES

- "Guidelines for Groups." Films for the Humanities, 1982, 15 minutes, color. Presents guidelines for effective group discussion.
- "How to Conduct a Meeting." Coronet, 18 minutes, color, VHS. A neighborhood meeting runs into problems and a narrator intercedes to demonstrate how the use of parliamentary procedure allow the group to reach agreement.
- "Sharing the Leadership." Indiana University, 1963, 29 minutes, black and white. A dramatized incident is used to show how leadership arises in a group and what is involved in the concept of leadership."

CHAPTER 10 CHOOSING AND DEVELOPING A TOPIC

OVERVIEW

This chapter discusses the necessary steps to choosing and developing a topic. The chapter explains two guidelines in choosing a topic: 1) look for a topic early and 2) choose a topic that interests you. Along with choosing the appropriate topic it also explain how to develop your topic and define your general purpose, specific purpose, and central idea. After choosing and developing your topic this chapter continues by illustrating the importance analyzing the speaking situation. Finally the chapter explains how to gather the information for the speech.

OBJECTIVES

1. To help students understand the importance of choosing the right topic by following these guidelines:
    a. look for a topic early
    b. choose a topic that interests you
2. To explain to students how to develop on the chosen topic by developing:
    a. general purpose (to entertain, persuade, or inform)
    b. specific purpose (expressed in the form of a purpose statement)
    c. central idea (expressed in the form of a thesis statement)
3. To help students identify how analyzing the speaking situation by:
    a. analyzing the audience enables you to adapt your speech to your listeners
    b. analyzing the occasion enables you to customize your speech to its circumstances as a unique event.
4. To teach students how to gather information for their speech from sources such as:
    a. internet research
    b. library research
    c. interviewing
    d. personal observation
    e. survey research

SUGGESTED CLASSROOM ACTIVITIES

—AUDIENCE ANALYSIS

Approximate Time: 30 minutes

I.   PURPOSE: to practice adapting development of a speech topic to the audience being addressed.

II.   PROCEDURE:

1. Divide the class into groups of 4-5.
2. Write a controversial topic on the board, such as military spending, sex education, AIDS testing, education reform.
3. Assign the groups audiences such as those listed below. Each group should plan to speak to one of the audiences.
    a. A group of senior citizens
    b. The varsity football team
    c. High school students in a required junior English class.
    d. The monthly meeting of religious leaders in the city, representing all major religious groups
    e. The weekly meeting of a neighborhood association, a group that works to strengthen a deteriorating section of the community.

4. After the groups have been assigned their audiences, they should determine the following. Remind them to keep in mine their own knowledge, the audience, and the occasion.
    a. The position they would take on the topic.
    b. The general outline they would use.
    c. The ways they would make the outline relate directly to the audience.
    d. The evidence they might incorporate into the speech.
    e. The special considerations they might make about delivery, if any.
5. One member of each group should orally summarize the group's decisions for the class.

III. PRINCIPLES ILLUSTRATED:

1. The audience is the primary consideration in speech planning.
2. The speaker should make efforts to relate the speech directly to the audience at hand.
3. The make-up of the audience affects not only topic selection, but also organization, evidence, and delivery.
4. A topic can be developed in many different ways.

—WRITING A SPEECH PURPOSE STATEMENT

Approximate Time: 20-30 minutes

I. PURPOSE: to give the students an opportunity to write speech purpose statements that are effective.

II. PROCEDURE:

1. This exercise may be done individually or in small groups.
2. Give a brief overview of speech purpose statements, including the requirement that they describe the result desired, be specific and realistic.
3. Ask the class to prepare clear specific purpose statements for speeches which they might deliver to the class on the following topics. They should work individually or in groups of 2-3. Allow 10-12 minutes for the preparation.

    SPEECH TOPICS

    student eating patterns
    protest of military spending
    legalization of marijuana
    teacher evaluation

4. Reconvene in a large group and share different speech purpose statements. Note how different they are. Evaluate them on the basis of their describing results, being specific and realistic.

III. PRINCIPLES ILLUSTRATED:

1. Specific purpose statements should describe results, be specific and realistic.
2. Special purpose statements can be prepared for nearly any topic, no matter how general.
3. Writing purpose statements helps the speaker focus on the thesis which she or he wishes to develop.

—INTERNET RESEARCH ACTIVITY

Approximate Time: 30 minutes out of class, 20 minutes in class discussion

I. Purpose: to practice a search and share information about the search

II. PROCEDURE:

1. Students are asked to search "auto insurance" as a general topic.
2. Each student should develop his or her own "search string." Using their own or available computers, conduct the search out of class.
3. Each student is encouraged conduct their own search, anticipating they will be asked to describe the search in class.
4. In class groups, students are asked to present the information found in their own search, using their own search string.

III. PRINCIPLES ILLUSTRATED:

1. Specific development of "search strings"
2. General practice searching the internet
3. Topic information may differ, due to the search wording use.

ACTIVITIES TO PROMOTE CRITICAL AND CREATIVE THINKING

Hand out a copy of the front page of a newspaper. Ask students individually or in small groups to generate topics from the stories reported. After generating topics, move on to writing specific purpose statements.

Analyze a TV commercial in terms of the audience. At what type of audience is it aimed? What audience attitudes, beliefs, and values are assumed? How is the commercial adapted to the audience? What type of information is used?

TEACHING ACTIVITIES IN THE COMMUNICATION TEACHER

- Adams. J. C. (1992, Spring). *Earstorming, 6(3)*, p. 3.
- Bowers, A. A., Jr. (1994, Summer). *When we become they: Teaching audience awareness skills, 8(4)*, pp. 8-9.
- Downey, S. D. (1988, Winter). *Audience analysis exercise, 2(2)*, pp. 1-2
- Glaser, H. F. (1998, Summer). *Focusing the students on three speech topics, 12(4)*, p. 10.
- Gray-Briggs, A. (2000, Spring). *The gift of G. A. B.: The pro's and con's of ghostwriting, 14(3)*, pp. 14-16
- Gschwend, L. (2000, Spring). *Every student deserves an assessment tool that works, 14(3)*, pp. 1-5.
- Hanson, T. L. (2000, Winter). *So what if you found it on the Internet: An exercising in evaluating web-based information, 14(2)*, pp. 6-7.
- Herzog, R. L. (1996, Summer). *Library research assignment, 10(4)*, pp. 7-8.
- Kent, M. L. (2000, Fall). *Getting the most from your search engine, 15(1)*, pp. 4-7.
- Kent, M. L. (1999, Summer). *How to evaluate Web site validity and reliability, 13(4)*, pp. 8-9.
- Stem, Rick. "Audience Spinouts," (Spring 1991) 5, 3, pp. 7-8.
- Woodside, Daria. "Choosing Topics for Speeches: A Breath of Fresh Air (Earth, Water, and Fire)," (Fall 1992) 7, 1, pp. 1-2.

SUPPLEMENTARY RESOURCES

I. BOOKS AND ARTICLES

- DeVito, Joseph. *The Essential Elements of Public Speaking*. Needham Heights, MA: Allyn & Bacon/Longman, 2003.
- Koch, Arthur. *Speaking With a Purpose*, Sixth Edition. Needham Heights, MA: Allyn and Bacon, 2004.
- Lucas, Stephen. *The Art of Public Speaking*, Eighth Edition. New York, NY: McGraw-Hill, 2004.
- McCroskey, James. *Introduction to Rhetorical Communication*, Eighth Edition. Needham Heights, MA: Allyn & Bacon, 2001.

- Nelson, Paul and Judy Pearson. *Confidence in Public Speaking: Telecourse Version.* Los Angeles, CA: Roxbury Publishing, 2001.
- Osborn, Michael and Suzanne Osborn. *Public Speaking,* Seventh Edition. Boston: Houghton Mifflin Co., 2006.
- Samovar, Larry and Jack Mills. *Oral Communication: Speaking Across Cultures.* Los Angeles, CA: Roxbury Publishing, 2000.
- Vasile, Albert and Harold Mintz. *Speak With Confidence: A Practical Guide,* Ninth Edition. Needham Heights, MA: Allyn & Bacon/Longman, 2004.
- Verderber, Rudolph and Kathleen Verderber. *The Challenge of Effective Speaking,* Twelfth Edition. Belmont, CA: Wadsworth, 2003.

II. FILMS/TAPES

- "Communicating Successfully: Three-Part Series." Time-Life Films, Inc. Film #1. "How to Make a More Effective Speech," 25 minutes, color. This film discusses how to prepare and write a speech, analyze one's audience, prepare an objective, research the facts, organize one's material, and deliver the final parchment.
- "Contemporary American Speeches," The Educational Video Group, 120 minutes, VHS.
- "Critical Thinking: Making Sure of the Facts." Coronet Instructional Films, 1972, 11 minutes, color. Ways of evaluating the facts. How to determine whether information is primary or secondary, check sources of information, and assess the reliability of the sources.
- "Great Speeches, Volumes I, II, III, IV." The Educational Video Group, 1985-87, 138 minutes, VHS.
- "Planning Your Speech." Coronet, 1978, 13 minutes, color. Details the process of planning a speech.
- "Speakers and the Library." Films for the Humanities, 1982, 15 minutes, color. Discusses ways in which library research can be of help to public speakers.
- "The Speaker's Purpose and Occasion." Insight Media, 1986, 28 minutes, VHS. Identifying three basic purposes of communication-informing, persuading, and entertaining-this program explores the importance of the setting and the occasion for speaking in determining what to include in a speech and how to deliver it.
- "The Topic and the Audience." Films for the Humanities, 1982, 15 minutes, color. Suggests guidelines for topic selection and audience analysis.

CHAPTER 11 ORGANIZATION AND SUPPORT

OVERVIEW

This chapter explains the importance of organization within public speaking. There are several tools that are designed to make the important job of structuring a speech working outlines, formal outlines, and speaking notes. This chapter explains simple principles that will enable you to build an effective outline. In addition to explaining principles of an outline, the chapter also provides examples of effective introductions, conclusions, and transitions. The authors also discuss the functions, types, and style of supporting material and go into depth about visual aids as a supporting material.

OBJECTIVES

1. To help students identify different types of outlines for effectively structuring a speech by looking at:
    a. working outlines
    b. formal outlines
    c. speaking notes
2. To enable students to follow a few simple principles to building an effective outline by examining:
    a. standard symbols
    b. standard format
    c. the rule of division
    d. the rule of parallel wording
3. To provide students an understanding of:
    a. organizing your points in a logical order
    b. using transitions
4. To facilitate the understanding of effective:
    a. introductions
    b. conclusions
5. To encourage students to use supportive material by explaining the important aspects of:
    a. functions of supportive material
    b. types of supporting material
    c. style of support, including narration and citation
6. To help students see that visual aids are a unique type of supporting material by examining:
    a. types of visual aids
    b. media for the presentation of visual aids
    c. rules for using visual aids

SUGGESTED CLASSROOM ACTIVITIES

—ORGANIZING THE OUTLINE

Approximate Time: 15 minutes

I.   PURPOSE: to demonstrate how outlining can separate major points from minor ones.

II.   PROCEDURE:

1. Distribute copies of the following formal outline of an informative speech.
2. Instruct the students to indicate which items are major points and which items are subordinate points by fitting them into the outline form.
3. After students have taken 5-10 minutes to complete the outline, go through them as a class.

III. PRINCIPLE ILLUSTRATED:

1. Outlining helps identify main points from the minor points which support them.

Speech A: World War II

1. Events of the war
2. Causes of the war
3. Nazi policy of expansion
4. Japan seizes the Philippines
5. Germany attacks France
6. Germany attacks the Soviet Union
7. Japan desires an Eastern Empire
8. Effects of the war on America
9. Shortage of rubber tires
10. Sugar rationing

I.

   A.

   B.

II.

   A.

   B.

   C.

III.

Answer Key:

1. Events of the war
2. Causes of the war
3. Nazi policy of expansion
4. Japan seizes the Philippines
5. Germany attacks France
6. Germany attacks the Soviet Union
7. Japan desires an Eastern Empire
8. Effects of the war on America
9. Shortage of rubber tires
10. Sugar rationing

I. Causes of the war (2)

   A. Nazi policy of expansion (3)

   B. Japan desires an Eastern Empire (7)

II. Events of the war (1)

   A. Japan seizes the Philippines (4)

   B. Germany attacks France (5)

   C. Germany attacks the Soviet Union (6)

III. Effects of the war on America (8)

   A. Shortage of rubber tires (9)

   B. Sugar rationing (10)

---- OUTLINING: WHEN AND WHICH

Approximate Time: 45 minutes

I.   PURPOSE: To demonstrate how one speech needs more than just one outline.

II. PROCEDURE:

1. Provide the transcripts of a well-known speech, or a short story if appropriate. (Make sure the speech is relatively short for class time.)
2. Instruct the class that they will have to create various outlines based on the given speech
3. Have each student write a working outline, formal outline, and a key word outline.
4. After the students have written all the different outlines, ask students to identify the key differences among each outline.
5. Have students discuss when each and which outline would be appropriate

III. PRINICPLES ILLUSTRATED:

1. All prepared speeches come together in segments
2. All prepared speeches have more than one outline used
3. Identified the differences between outlines
4. There is not just a generic outline to use for everything

----ORGANIZATIONAL PATTERNS

Approximate Time: 30 minutes

I.   PURPOSE: to demonstrate how different organizational patterns are appropriate for different topics.

II. PROCEDURE:

1. Divide the class into groups of 3-4.
2. Review material from Chapter 12 about basic patterns of speech organization: time, space, topic, problem solution, motivated sequence, cause-effect, and climax.
3. Write the following speech topics on the board and have each group decide which type of pattern would be most appropriate for the topic. The groups should be able to defend their choices.

SAMPLE TOPICS:

A. The advantages of yogurt as a snack
B. Religious differences in the Middle East
C. Air safety
D. Preventing heart attacks
E. The making of a music video
F. Illiteracy in the United States
G. Graduation requirements at this college
H. Congressional funding for the military

4. Convene the large group and go through the decisions together. As differences emerge, note the arguments made to defend each. Stress ways in which topics can be organized to maximize speech effectiveness.
5. Note: This can be done as an individual take-home assignment.

III. PRINCIPLES ILLUSTRATED:

1. Basic types of outline patterns should be chosen to maximize speech effectiveness.
2. Different topics are better suited for some organization patterns than for others.
3. One topic may be suitable for organization in several different ways.

—SUPPORTING THE THESIS

Approximate Time: one class period

1. PURPOSE: to acquaint students with resources for finding supporting materials.

II. PROCEDURE:

1. On the day prior to this activity, list the following supportive materials on the board: definition, description, analogy, anecdote, example, statistics, visual aids, testimony. Encourage students to review the list so that they are familiar with each category.
2. Meet in the library for class.
3. Divide into groups of 3-4.
4. Give each group a speech thesis and tell them to use the class period to find as many strong supporting materials for the thesis as possible. Encourage each group to find at least one supporting item of each type. Some may be possible without library resources (e.g., analogy).
5. At the end of the hour or at the next class period, look at the material together. Evaluate its merits as supporting material.

   Sample theses:

   A. Abortion should be illegal.
   B. The United States should sell weapons to all countries that want to buy them.
   C. No more nuclear power plants should be built,
   D. There should be no gun control in the United States.
   E. Drunk drivers should be punished more severely than they are now.
   F. There should be mandatory AIDS testing.
   G. College tuition should be free.
   H. Foreign language study should be required for all university students.

III. PRINCIPLES ILLUSTRATED:

1. Supporting materials are necessary for a strong speech.
2. A wide variety of materials are available to support speech ideas.
3. The library is a good resource for speech preparation.

—SUPPORTING MATERIAL IN A RECENT SPEECH

Approximate Time: 30 minutes

I. PURPOSE: to demonstrate use of supporting material in an actual speech.

II. PROCEDURE:

1. Provide students with a copy of a recent speech in handout form, overhead transparency, or library reserve. The speech might be a recent political speech (e.g., Presidential inaugural speech) or one from Vital Speeches of the Day.
2. Review the basic types of supporting material.

3. Ask each student to go through the speech, noting each time that the speaker uses supporting material. Note the type of material used.
4. As a class, go through the speech. Ask students to identify supporting material for its variety, its credibility, and its effectiveness in supporting the thesis.

III. PRINCIPLES ILLUSTRATED:

1. Supporting material is essential in making a speech effective.
2. A variety of types of supporting material should be used.
3. Professional speakers use a variety of supporting materials.

—USING THE WEB FOR SOURCES

Approximate Time: 15 minutes out of class and 15 minutes in class

I. PURPOSE: to demonstrate how to use the World Wide Web for sources, and to correctly cite the sources.

II. PROCEDURE:

1. Students are asked to find three web sources for "television violence's influence on children." The searches are to be conducted out of class, at home or where computer access is available.
2. Students are asked to then correctly list the three web sources. The listing should follow the listing in chapter 11. Students are asked to bring the listings to class for discussion.
3. A small group of students (3-5) in class is asked to review the listings of its members, and correct any needing it. Each group is then asked to read aloud the listings – any number the instructor feels useful.

III. PRINCIPLES ILLUSTRATED:

1. Listing the sources should include the correct information, and in the correct order.
2. Students can help each other understand correct listing.
3. The listing helps the source of the information be viewed as important.

ACTIVITIES TO PROMOTE CRITICAL AND CREATIVE THINKING

Assign each student a "thing" label (book, movie, Fourth of July, etc.). Have them pin or tape the labels so they can be seen. Divide the class into two groups and instruct each group to "organize itself." You may want to limit the number of sub-groups/categories to 3-5. Students will be required to look for relationships between the objects and various ways of grouping things together. Allow the groups to trade members if they feel the need.

Divide the class into two groups. Tell them to "organize themselves." After the first plans, which will probably be by height (spatial) or age (time), request another organizational plan. Ask the other group to guess what the organizing principle is.

Divide the class into groups of 4-5. Assign each a topic from Chapter 12 (outlining, organizing patterns or a single pattern, introductions, etc.). Assign each group to introduce the topic in the most interesting way possible on the day you will cover the topic. You may want to include a time limit, such as 1-3 minutes.

TEACHING ACTIVITIES IN THE SPEECH COMMUNICATION TEACHER

- Bahti, C. L. (1993, Summer). *Building a joke, 7(4)*, p. 16.
- Brown, K. J. (1990, Spring). *"Spidergrams": An aid for teaching outlining and organization, 4(3)*, pp. 4-5.
- Hibben, Jean. "Eliminating the 'My Speech Is About' Introduction," (Fall 1992) 7, 1, p. 11.
- Kauffman, James. "Collecting and Evaluating Evidence," (Winter 1992) 6, 2, p. 12.
- Jones, J. A., & Jones, V. H. (2000, Summer). *A dynamic approach to the annual State of the Union Address (SUA), 14(4)*, pp. 10-11.
- Mino, Mary. "Structuring: An Alternative Approach for Developing Clear Organization," (Winter 1991) 3, 2, pp. 14-15.
- Muir, S. A. (1995, Spring). *Organizing and critiquing ideas, 9(3)*, pp. 8-10.
- Pasma, Kristen. "Transitional Stories," (Summer 1991) 5, 4, p. 15.
- Olsen, R. (1999, Summer). *Making sense of Lady Liberty: Using the Statue of Liberty to teach research methods, 13(4)*, pp. 13-15.
- Wilson, S. "The Little Speech That Could" (Spring, 1999) 13, 3, pp. 10-11

SUPPLEMENTARY RESOURCES

I. BOOKS AND ARTICLES

- Anderson, D. "How to Prepare for Presentations," Training, 20 (December 1983), p. 98.
- Brickman, Gayle and Lynn Fuller. *Organizing for Impact. A Practical Guide for the Public Speaker*. Dubuque, IA: Kendall/Hunt, 1994.
- *Business Week*. "The Serious Business of Using Jokes in Public Speaking," 93 (September 5, 1983), pp. 93-94.
- Campbell, Karlyn. *The Rhetorical Act*. Belmont, CA: Wadsworth, 1996.
- Gruner, Charles. "Advice to the Beginning Speaker on Using Humor — What the Research Tells Us," *Communication Education*, 34 (April 1995), pp. 142-147.
- Sprague, Jo and Douglas Stuart. *The Speaker's Handbook*, Seventh Edition. Belmont, CA: Wadsworth, 2005.

II. FILMS/TAPES

- "Bottom Line Communication: Get to the Point." Arthur Barr Productions, 1982, 18 minutes, color. Analyzes four structural approaches to communicating, each with the main point in a different location because each message has a different purpose.
- "Choosing the Audio-Visual Dimension." Films for the Humanities, 1982, 15 minutes, color. A visually interesting film which presents the advantages of using visuals and guidelines for doing so.
- "Choosing the Ideas and Words." Insight Media, 1986, 28 minutes, VHS. This program examines the internal controllable elements of a speech, including style, organization, and delivery, and explains how they should be shaped by external factors.
- "Communicating From the Lectern, Session 2: Let's Start at the Very Beginning." ACI Media, 1975, 6 minutes, color. Deals with the use of attention-getters.
- "Communicating From the Lectern, Session 6: And I quote..." ACI Media, 1975, 5 minutes, color. Illustrates the use of quotations from various types of sources when making a speech. Emphasizes using the library to find quotations.
- "Organizing the Speech." Insight Media, 1986, 12 minutes, VHS. Examines four types of speeches-impromptu, extemporaneous, memorized, and those read from a manuscript. It teaches how to gain the attention and involvement of the audience through such techniques as humor, suspense, and rhetorical questioning.
- "The Outline." Films for the Humanities, 1982, 15 minutes, color. Presents uses and strategies of outlining.

CHAPTER 12 PRESENTING YOUR MESSAGE

OVERVIEW

This chapter discusses the various aspects of presenting a message to an audience. This chapter explains the causes of stage fright and ways to overcome it. Beyond explaining barriers to presenting a message, the authors explain four types of delivery methods such as extemporaneous, impromptu, manuscript, and memorized. After understanding the barriers of presenting, and the different types of delivery methods, the authors presents guidelines for effective delivery and guidelines for presenting effective criticisms for speech delivery.

OBJECTIVES

1. To help students understand that stage fright is one of the most formidable barriers to effective speaking by looking at:
    a. the differences between facilitative and debilitative stage fright
    b. the sources of debilitative stage fright
    c. ways to overcome debilitative stage fright
2. To show the importance of choosing the right style of delivery for a speech by explaining the four types:
    a. extemporaneous
    b. impromptu
    c. manuscript
    d. memorized
3. To demonstrate to students the importance of practicing a speech by explaining guidelines:
    a. dealing with visual aspects of delivery
    b. dealing with the auditory aspects of delivery
4. To help students identify what constructive criticism is and how to appropriately give constructive criticism to fellow classmates.

SUGGESTED CLASSROOM ACTIVITIES

—IMPROMPTU SPEECH-MAKING

Approximate Time: 1-2 class periods

I.   PURPOSE: to introduce students to impromptu speaking strategies.

II.   PROCEDURE:

1. Introduce speakers to impromptu style of speaking. Emphasize the importance of thinking and organizing thoughts on the spot.
2. Have an envelope with quotations for students to choose from.
3. Each student needs to explain the quotation, decide whether they agree or disagree, and defend it.
4. Allow each student two minutes to prepare their speech, and allow them one note card to prepare with.
5. Allow each student to then speak up to five minutes on the topic.
6. Focus student feedback on positive aspects only.

POSSIBLE IMPROMPTU TOPICS

1. "Order leads to all the virtues, but what leads to order?"
    -- G.C. Lichienberg
2. "Research is an organized method of keeping you reasonably dissatisfied with what you have."
    -- Charles Kettering

3. "Many a glib talk has a lot of depth on the surface but way down deep is very shallow."
-- Author unknown
4. "It is discouraging to think how many people are shocked by honesty and how few by deceit."
-- Noel Coward
5. "We would all need introductions if we could see ourselves as others see us."
-- Author Unknown
6. "The trouble with many people is that they take so long to start to begin to get ready to commence."
--Author Unknown
7. "Cause and effect can be puzzling: for example, cold feet are often the result of burnt fingers."
-- Evan Esar
8. "A conclusion is the place where you got tired thinking."
--Martin H. Fischer
9. "Curiosity is lying in wait for every secret."
-- Emerson
10. "Men are generally more anxious to find out why things are so than whether things are so."
-- Montaigne
11. "The play was a success, but the audience was a failure."
-- William Collier
12. "If all the world's a stage, and men and women merely players, where is the audience to come from?"
-- Evan Esar
13. "A man who tells nothing or who tells all will equally have nothing told him."
--Chesterfield
14. "You can always tell a well-informed man: his views are the same as yours."
--Evan Esar
15. "There are three sides to every argument: your side, the other person's side, and to hell with it."
--Evan Esar

III. PRINCIPLES ILLUSTRATED:

1. Impromptu speaking requires energy and focus.
2. Quick preparation, a pause before speaking, and clear focus can create an effective impromptu speech.
3. Even impromptu speeches need to be organized.
4. Impromptu speeches should relate to the audience.

IV. VARIATION

Give the same quotation to two different students. Have one student present an impromptu speech on why the quotation is accurate, and have the other student argue the contrary.

—STAGE FRIGHT

Approximate Time: 1-2 class periods

I. PURPOSE: to give reticent students an opportunity to speak publicly with a minimum of debilitative stage fright.

II. PROCEDURE:

1. A week in advance of this activity, tell each student to select an object to explain to the class.
2. On the day of the activity, each participant should bring the object (e.g., calligraphy pen, model car, piece of cross-stitching). The object should be used in the explanation. The "speech" can be delivered sitting or standing, whichever seems best for the situation.
3. Feedback should emphasize only positive aspects of the explanation.

III. PRINCIPLES ILLUSTRATED:

1. Even anxious speakers can speak and survive.
2. An object which requires speaker attention can alleviate debilitative anxiety. (Students should note this when selecting appropriate visual aids for future speeches).
3. Moderate stage fright is an energizing force.

IV. VARIATION

A short oral reading of a selection of the student's choice can also be used as an early speaking experience. It gives students oral experience in front of the class yet frees them from concern with and responsibility for content. The readings often lead to interesting discussions about self-disclosure (through the choice of material), organization, language, and delivery.

ACTIVITY TO PROMOTE CRITICAL AND CREATIVE THINKING

Divide the class into four groups. Assign two groups to write a description of a bank robbery in an outline form. Assign the other groups to write a description of a bank robbery in manuscript form. Ask one student from each of the two outline groups to stand up and tell about the robbery using the outlines and two students from the manuscript groups to read their groups' descriptions. Discuss with the class how the two methods of delivery were different. You may want to tape the speeches to facilitate comparison.

Have the class watch two videos, one with a speaker giving a speech from a manuscript (i.e. state of the union address.) If possible, find the same speaker delivering a speech extemporaneously or impromptu. Have students discuss the similarities and differences and why each method was effective of ineffective for that occasion.

TEACHING ACTIVITIES IN THE COMMUNICATION TEACHER

- Bernum, B. (2000, Summer). *A drawing speech of introduction, 14(4)*, pp. 6-7
- Bollinger, L. (1995, Summer). *Tough self-evaluators, 9(4)*, p. 14.
- Crandall, H. (1999, Winter). *Practicing impromptu speeches, 13(2)*, pp. 3-4.
- Dobris, C. A. (1999, Spring). *Breaking the ice gently: A student-centered application for public speaking, 13(3)*, pp. 11-12.
- Gray-Briggs, A. (2000, Spring). *The gift of G. A. B.: The pro's and con's of ghostwriting, 14(3)*, pp. 14-16.
- Mills, D. D. (Winter 1991) *Tag Team Championship: Improving Delivery Skills, 5, 2*, pp. 10-11.
- Murphy, M. (Fall, 1996) *Case Study in Business and Professional Speaking, 11, 1*, pp. 1-2.
- Roubicek, H. L. (2000, Summer). *Presenting a personal narrative, 14(4)*, pp. 4-6.
- Sonandre, D. A., & Ayres, J. (1999, Winter). *Practice makes perfect, 13(2)*, pp. 14-15.
- Wilson, C. E. (2000, Spring). *Ending the public speaking course on a positive note, 14(3)*, pp. 5-6.
- Wilson, S. R. (1999, Spring). *The little speech that could, 13(3)*, pp. 10-11.

SUPPLEMENTARY RESOURCES

I. BOOKS AND ARTICLES

- Bianchi, Doris. *Easily Understood: A Basic Speech Text.* New York, NY: Avery/Penguin Putnam, 1980.
- Bytwerk, Randall. "Impromptu Speaking 11' xcrcises," *Communication Education,* 34 (April 1985), pp. 148-150.
- Communication Development Associates, Inc. *Fight the Fear. Reducing Speaker Nervousness.* Sherman Oaks, CA: Communication Development Associates, 1992.
- Daly, John, James McCroskey, and Joe Ayres. *Avoiding Communication: Shyness, Reticence, and Communication Apprehension.* Hampton Press, 1997.

- González, Alberto, Marsha Houston, and Victoria Chen. *Our Voices: Essays in Culture, Ethnicity, and Communication.* Los Angeles, CA: Roxbury, 2000
- McCroskey, James C. *Deep Muscular Relaxation Tape.* Annandale, VA: SCA, 1990.
- Nelson, Paul and Judy Pearson. *Confidence in Public Speaking: Telecourse Version.* Los Angeles, CA: Roxbury Publishing, 2001.
- Richmond, Virginia and James McCroskey. *Communication: Apprehension, Avoidance, and Effectiveness.* Needham Heights, MA: Allyn & Bacon/Longman, 1998.
- Stiggins, Richard, Philip Backlund, and Nancy Bridgeford. "Avoiding Bias in the Assessment of Communication Skills," *Communication Education,* 34 (April 1985, pp. 135-141.
- Wilder, L. *Professionally Speaking.* New York: Simon & Schuster, 1986.

II. FILMS/TAPES

- "Aids to Speaking." Coronet, 1979, 15 minutes, color. Examines the effective use of speaking aids, the lectern, visual aids, and the microphone.
- "Communicating From the Lectern, Session 8: Learning to Live With Fear" AC A Media, 1975, 5 minutes, color. Attempts to make the student aware of communication fears that are imaginary and those that are real, and explains how to handle these symptoms with beforehand preparation.
- "Communication by Voice and Action." Coronet, 1979, 14 minutes, color. Differentiates between the verbal and nonverbal aspects of communication. Stresses the importance of good posture and appearance for effective delivery.
- "Delivering the Speech." Insight Media, 1986, 28 minutes, VHS. Defining stage fright and presenting eight ways to overcome it, this video teaches how to deliver a speech effectively.
- "Fearless Public Speaking." Insight Media, 1989, 24 minutes, VHS. This video is designed to help the occasional speaker prepare and deliver a talk that will hold an audience's interest.
- "Making Your Point Without Saying a Word." Insight Media, 1990, 27 minutes, VHS. Focusing on practical tips and techniques, this video illustrates how to project messages with self-confidence, power, and authority.
- "The Public Speaker and the Audience." Insight Media, 1986, 28 minutes, VHS. This program explores how a speaker's image influences how a speech is received. It defines the terms ethos and explains how a speaker's reiteration, credibility, and image influence an audience.
- "Speak for Yourself: A Dynamic Vocal Workout." Insight Media, 1989, 25 minutes, VHS. Presents a series of vocal warm-up exercises that are divided into four categories: relaxation and stretching face preparation, pitch and resonance, and tongue twisters.
- "Speaking Effectively: To One or One Thousand." McGraw-Hill, 1979, 21 minutes, color. Examines the fear of public speaking and explores the major factors necessary for effective communication. Discusses all aspects of delivery
- "Stage Fright." Centron Corp., 1979, 14 minutes, color. Examines the psychological causes, physical symptoms, and effective control of stage fright.
- "Stage Fright." Learning Corp. Of America, 13 minutes color, VHS. Follows Bernie through the steps he uses to overcome his stage fright and give a successful speech.
- "Who Me? Make a Presentation?" EFN, 1980, 16 minutes, color. University of Illinois Film Center (217) 333-1360. Advises the speaker to match the style of delivery to his or her personality and rehearse in front of someone who can offer constructive criticism. Treats verbal and visual delivery.

CHAPTER 13 INFORMATIVE SPEAKING

OVERVIEW

This chapter begins by describing types of informative speaking based on content and purpose. Speakers are shown the major differences between informative speaking and persuasive speaking. This chapter explains the techniques of informative speaking by explaining how to define a specific informative purpose and create information hunger. It also illustrates the importance of how to emphasize important points along with clear organization and structure. Guidelines for use of clear language and generating audience involvement are also explained.

OBJECTIVES

1. To help students understand the nature and importance of informative speaking.
2. To help students identify the difference between informative and persuasive speaking.
3. To help students define a specific informative purpose.
4. To aid students in creating information hunger.
5. To help students learn how to use clear organization and structure.
6. To encourage students to: use clear language, use supporting materials, and emphasize main points effectively.

SUGGESTED CLASSROOM ACTIVITIES

—INFORMATIVE SPEECH

Approximate Time: 1 week

I.   PURPOSE: to prepare and present a 4-6 minute speech, which informs the audience about the topic.

II.   PROCEDURE:

Select one of the following options for your presentation.

a.   Conduct an interview outside of class with a person who is involved in a volunteer organization either on campus or in the community. Interview the person about his or her view of the organization, the need for the organization, and how the organization affects the campus or community. Review Chapter 8 and prepare a set of interview questions based on it.

After you conduct the interview, prepare an outline to be used in delivery of the 4- to 6-minute speech based on the interview. In the introduction, tell who you interviewed and why you selected her or him. In the body, discuss what major questions you asked and what major conclusions you drew. In the conclusion, summarize what you learned about the organization.

Attach the list of interview questions you used to your speech outline. Identify each question by type (e.g., open, closed, etc.).

b.   Select one word which characterizes your view of yourself. Think about personal experiences you have had which helped you conclude that the one word is appropriate. Prepare a 4- to 6-minute speech in which you elaborate on the experiences which led you to choose that word.

In the introduction, define the word. The body should include relevant experiences which have led you to choose this word as representative. In the conclusion, summarize and emphasize the word.

III. PRINCIPLES ILLUSTRATED:

1. How informative speeches are organized by content and purpose
2. Speech preparation can involve both library research and personal experience.
3. Interviewing is a helpful tool in speech preparation.
4. How to emphasize main points.
5. How to use supporting material effectively.

—WHY DO WE NEED THIS?

Approximate Time: 20-30 minutes

I. PURPOSE: to give students practice with developing information hunger in their audience.

II. PROCEDURE:

For each of the topics listed below discuss ways in which general and specific needs can be used to create information hunger in each of the audiences listed below. Ask specifically, why does the audience need to know about this topic? Some may require creativity; perhaps some audiences do not need to know about certain topics.

TOPIC	AUDIENCE
The Life of a Sponge	The Parent-Teacher Association
Vitamin A	Local Law Enforcement Officers
The Relationship Between the Moon and Tides	Navy Recruits
Jumping Rope	Parents of Children With Special Needs
Muscle Cramps and What to Do About Them	Fourth-Grade Class

III. PRINCIPLES ILLUSTRATED:

1. Each topic requires an examination of the audience's need for the information.
2. Some topics are more easily aimed at certain audiences.
3. Different audiences will need to know different things about a topic.
4. Use of clear language can enhance audience hunger
5. Use of supporting material can create a desire for the audience to listen

Sample Speech Critique Form

Speaker _____ Topic _____

Class Time _____ Critic _____

E=Excellent, G= Good, A= Average, F= Fair, P= Poor

Introduction

Establishment of importance of topic to audience	E	G	A	F	P
Preview of thesis	E	G	A	F	P
Preview of main points	E	G	A	F	P

Body

Clear main points	E	G	A	F	P
Clear sub points	E	G	A	F	P
Effective use of internal previews	E	G	A	F	P
Effective use of internal summaries	E	G	A	F	P

Conclusion

Review of main points	E	G	A	F	P
Reminder of importance of topic	E	G	A	F	P
Provided audience with memory aid	E	G	A	F	P

Supporting Materials

Appropriately used within speech	E	G	A	F	P
Effective in aiding within speech	E	G	A	F	P

Clear Language

Effectively used words within speech	E	G	A	F	P
Appropriate use of words within speech	E	G	A	F	P

Major Strengths:

Major Weaknesses:

ACTIVITY TO PROMOTE CRITICAL AND CREATIVE THINKING

Give students the following take-home assignment. "Make a list of all the pollutants in water and how they can affect the human body." Ask each student to explain his or her list. Note the variety of detail among each student. Ask each student to identify how he or she would create information hunger with this topic. Have each student identify how he or she would organize this speech to be purely informative. Ask students to identify what types of supporting materials and language would be most effective.

TEACHING ACTIVITIES IN THE SPEECH COMMUNICATION TEACHER

- Adams. J. C. (1992, Spring). *Earstorming, 6(3)*, p. 3.
- Auer, J. Jeffrey. "Creating an Extra and 'Real Life' Public Speaking Assignment," (Spring 1991) 5, 3, p. 3.
- Avyeryeva, T. "Practicing Delivery Skills" (Spring, 1999) 13, 3, pp. 9-10
- Bowers, A. A., Jr. (1994, Summer). *When we become they: Teaching audience awareness skills, 8(4)*, pp. 8-9.
- Danielson, M. A. (1996, Winter). *A critical thinking approach to the use of visual aids, 10(2)*, pp. 8-9.
- Fregoe, D. H. (1989, Winter). *Informative vs. Persuasive speaking: The objects game, 3(2)*, pp. 13-14.
- Glaser, H. F. (1998, Summer). *Focusing the students on three speech topics, 12(4)*, p. 10.
- Murray, Patricia. "The Objective Game," (Summer 1991) 5, 4, p. 15
- Nicosia, Gloria. "Establishing a Speakers' Bureau on a College Campus," (Summer 1992) 6, 4, pp. 13-14.
- O'Neill, Daniel J. "Researching National Issues Forum Topics," (Fall 1991) 6, 1, pp. 1-2.
- Rifkind Lawrence. "The Outstanding Speaker Contest," (Spring 1992) 6, 3, pp. 14-15.
- Roubicek, H. L. (2000, Summer). *Presenting a personal narrative, 14(4)*, pp. 4-6.
- Schneider, Valerie. "Pointers for Polished Public Speaking," (Fall 1991) 6, 1, pp. 5-6.
- Thompson, Carol and Christina Standerfer. "Interactive Public-Speaking Activities," (Summer 1992) 6, 4, pp. 2-3.
- Wilson, Susan and Mark H. Wright. "From 'Animism' to 'Zeitgeist': Culturally Literate Assigned Topics," (Winter 1991) 5, 2, pp. 8-9.

SUPPLEMENTARY RESOURCES

I.   BOOKS AND ARTICLES

- Fletcher, Leon. *How to Design & Deliver Speeches*, Eighth Edition. Needham Heights, MA: Allyn & Bacon/Longman, 2004.
- Koch, Arthur. *Speaking With a Purpose*. Needham Heights, MA: Allyn & Bacon/Longman, 2004.
- McKerrow, Raymie, Bruce Gronbeck, Douglas Ehninger, and Alan Monroe. *Principles and Types of Public Speaking*, Fifteenth Edition. Needham Heights, MA: Allyn & Bacon/Longman, 2003.
- Osborn, Michael and Suzanne Osborn. *Public Speaking*. Boston: Houghton Mifflin, 2006.
- Petrie, Charles. "Informative Speaking: A Summary and Bibliography of Related Research," *Speech Monographs, 30* (1963), pp. 79-91.
- Sprague, Jo and Douglas Stuart. *The Speakers Handbook*. Belmont, CA: Wadsworth, 2005.
- Verderber, Ralph and Kathleen Verderber. *The Challenge of Effective Speaking*, Twelfth Edition. Belmont, CA: Wadsworth, 2003.

II.   FILMS/TAPES

- "Oral Communications." McGraw-Hill, 1968, 16 minutes, color. Demonstrates the preparations of a speech to inform.
- "Reporting and Briefing." Centron, 1979, 16 minutes, color. Shows how a speaker can add clarity, interest, and accuracy to an oral report. Demonstrates the importance of organizing materials, using examples and appropriate humor, and working with visual aids.
- "Types of Information." Films for the Humanities, 1982, 15 minutes, color.

CHAPTER 14 PERSUASIVE SPEAKING

OVERVIEW

This chapter deals with the various aspects of persuasion. Throughout this chapter persuasion is defined as the process of motivating someone, through communication, to change a belief, attitude, or behavior. The authors also explain the characteristics of persuasion. They also categorize the types of persuasion by type of proposition, desired outcome, and directness of approach. This chapter describes how to prepare an effective persuasive speech by following a few simple rules set by the authors. Lastly, the chapter discusses how to adapt your message to appeal to your audience and the importance of speaker credibility.

OBJECTIVES

1. To help students understand the definition of persuasion by explaining that persuasion is the process of motivating someone through communication to change a behavior, attitude, or behavior.
2. To provide students an understanding of important characteristics of persuasion such as:
   a. persuasion is not coercive
   b. persuasion is usually incremental
   c. persuasion is interactive
   d. persuasion can be ethical
3. To explain to students the different categories of persuasion of the following types:
   a. by type of proposition
   b. by desired outcome
   c. by directness of approach
4. To enable student to prepare an effective speech by following a few simple rules:
   a. setting a clear purpose
   b. structuring the message carefully
   c. using solid evidence
   d. avoiding fallacies
5. To emphasize the importance of adapting to your audience as an important part of persuasive strategy by:
   a. establishing common ground
   b. organizing according to the expected response
   c. neutralizing potential hostility
6. To show the importance of how speaker credibility is an essential component of persuasiveness, and the characteristics that include:
   a. competence
   b. character
   c. charisma

SUGGESTED CLASSROOM ACTIVITIES

—PERSUASIVE SPEECH

Approximate Time: 1 week

I.   PURPOSE: to prepare and present a 4- to 6- minute speech which persuades the audience either a) to buy something or b) to do something.

II. PROCEDURE:

Select one of the following options for your presentation.

a.   Choose a real product that you will "sell" to the audience. In 4-6 minutes, deliver a speech that will persuade the audience that this is a product worth buying. Take into account: audience analysis, the needs of the audience to whom you will be making the appeal, the best evidence you can use to persuade the audience, and the actual response you want from the audience.

b.   Choose a tourist attraction within 150 miles of the university and persuade the audience to visit it. Choose a place that you have some familiarity with. Emphasize the audience needs to which you will be appealing, the supporting materials that will be most convincing to the audience, and the actual behavior that you would like to see audience members show after the speech.

c.   Choose a political candidate and persuade the audience to vote for him or her in an election. You can also use a referendum as a subject if there is one of merit. Establish your credibility at the outset of the speech, than be aware of which audience needs you will be addressing, what evidence will best make your case, and what actual response you would life from the audience.

III. PRINCIPLES ILLUSTRATED:

1.   Persuasive speeches need to take into account audience needs.
2.   Persuasive speeches should be organized, well supported with evidence, and clear about desired audience response.

—REASON GIVING

Approximate Time: 15 minutes

I.   PURPOSE: to help students become aware of the possible arguments for and against their purpose statement.

II.   PROCEDURE:

1.   After assigning a persuasive speech such as the one in the previous activity, instruct students to make a list of all the possible reasons for the audience responding in the desired way. For example, list every possible reason someone would want to visit the Statue of Liberty, vote for candidate A, etc.
2.   Instruct students to list every possible reason that could be given not to do the recommended action. For example, list all the possible reasons why someone would not want to (or be able to) visit the Statue of Liberty, vote for candidate A, etc. These lists should be completed at home.
3.   Have the students bring the lists to class. Divide the class into groups of 4-5. Each student should in turn tell the others why they should do the desired behavior. The other students should react to these reasons by stating whether they are viable reasons for them, what they would say in response, etc.
4.   Students should write down all the responses and reactions and compare these with their anticipated negative reasons.
5.   At home students should review the lists and choose which reasons to use their speeches. They should then turn to the lists, and in addition, list the reasons (the main ideas) they have chosen to develop in their speech and how they will answer negative responses and objections.

III. PRINCIPLES ILLUSTRATED:

1.   A clear purpose is important in planning a speech.
2.   It is necessary to consider the reasons for and against the purpose.
3.   It is helpful but difficult to anticipate how the audience will respond.
4.   Knowing how a part of your audience will respond to an argument can help you adapt a speech to a particular audience.

-----**GARAGE SALE**

Approximate Time: One full class period

I.   PURPOSE: To help students understand how to effectively appeal to their audience and use successful strategies.

II.   PROCEDURE:

1.   Have each student bring in an unwanted item from their home. (Can be anything elaborate to something as simple as a role of toilet paper)
2.   Each student needs to prepare a 3-5 minute persuasive pitch to the class on the item and persuade the audience that they need the item for themselves.
3.   Have each student identify its uses that would be relevant to that particular audience
4.   The student should identify the target audience and their plan to establish their credibility and how they will adapt their delivery to their intended audience

III. PRINCIPLES ILLUSTRATED

1.   Persuasive speaking requires successful adaptation to the target audience.
2.   Credibility is an essential component of persuasion.
3.   How to prepare and effective persuasive speech by following the simple rules.
4.   Persuasion has several characteristics.

Sample Speech Critique Form

Speaker _____   Topic _____

Time _____   Critic _____

Each criterion rates as follows: 1 = superior
2 = above average
3 = average
4 = needs special attention

CRITERIA					COMMENTS
INTRODUCTION					
gained attention and interest	1	2	3	4	
previewed topic	1	2	3	4	
demonstrated importance of topic	1	2	3	4	
CONTENT					
focus on theses	1	2	3	4	
developed ideas	1	2	3	4	
use of evidence	1	2	3	4	
quality of supporting material	1	2	3	4	
PURPOSE					
purpose was clear	1	2	3	4	
subject was appropriate to this audience	1	2	3	4	
ORGANIZATION					
main ideas clearly presented	1	2	3	4	
relationship of ideas clear to audience	1	2	3	4	
effective transitions	1	2	3	4	
outline	1	2	3	4	
VOICE					
conversational manner	1	2	3	4	
OTHER NONVERBAL FACTORS					
use of notes	1	2	3	4	
posture	1	2	3	4	
movement and gestures	1	2	3	4	
eye contact	1	2	3	4	
CONCLUSION					
provided closure	1	2	3	4	

ACTIVITIES TO PROMOTE CRITICAL AND CREATIVE THINKING

Bring a collection of persuasive appeals to class. Ads or claims from editorials or letters to the editor work well. Ask students, "What would it take to get you to buy/believe this?" Explore both the appeals which would be needed and how those are different for each student as well as what appeals are actually used.

"What Ever Happened to Ethics," Time, May 25, 1987, pp. 14-29, relates ethics to contemporary issues. Use the article as a springboard to discussion of the implications of ethics and ethical communication for society.

View the video, *Tin Men,* which details the selling strategies used by aluminum salesmen in the 1950s. Discuss the strategies in terms of both ethics and reasoning fallacies. Discuss how these practices led to the passage of consumer protection laws.

TEACHING ACTIVITIES IN THE COMMUNICATION TEACHER

- Dittus, James K. "Grade Begging as an 14' xcrcise in Argumentation," (Summer 1992) 6, 4, p. 5.
- Garrett, Roger L. "The Premises of Persuasion," (Spring 1991) 5, 3, p. 13.
- Gray-Briggs, A. (2000, Spring). *The gift of G. A. B.: The pro's and con's of ghostwriting, 14(3),* pp. 14-16. [Goal: To improve students' speechwriting and speechmaking skills while teaching persuasive public speaking.]
- Norris, Kathy. "The Speech Shopping Channel," (Winter 1992) 6, 2, p. 16.
- Pendelton, S. "Using Figurative Language in Persuasive Speeches" (Summer 1999) 13, 4, pp. 5-7
- Proctor, R. F., II. (2000, Winter). *Using "Swing Kids" to teach theories of persuasion, 14(2),* pp. 5-6.
- Schumer, Allison. "To Tell the Truth," (Fall 1992) 7, 1, pp. 4-5.
- Schreier, H. N. (2000, Winter). *Experiencing persuasion and the persuader, 14(2),* pp. 7-9.
- Stoebig, Joe. "Speech Logs With a Twist," (Spring 1992) 6, 3, p. 13.

SUPPLEMENTARY RESOURCES

I.   BOOKS AND ARTICLES

- Bettinghouse, Erwin P. and Michael J. Cody. *Persuasive Communication.* Belmont, CA: Wadsworth, 1994.
- Blake, K. (1995, Fall). *Just for fun, 10(1),* pp. 1-3.
- Bozik, Mary. "An Exercise in Inference Making," *Communication Education,* 33 (October 1984), pp. 41-42.
- Cammilleri, S. (1995, Winter). *Creating persuasive commercials, 9(2),* pp. 10-11.
- Greenberg, Karen and Brenda Dervin. *Conversations on Communication Ethics.* Norwood, NJ: Ablex, 1991.
- Johannesen, Richard, Ron Allen, Wilmer Linkugel, and Ferald Bryan. *Contemporary American Speeches.* Dubuque, IA: Kendall/Hunt, 2000.
- Johannesen, Richard. *Ethics in Human Communication.* Prospect Heights, IL: Waveland, 2002.
- Kahane, Howard. *Logic and Contemporary Rhetoric: The Use of Reason in Everyday Life.* Belmont, CA: Wadsworth, 2002.
- Larson, Charles. *Persuasion: Reception and Responsibility.* Belmont, CA: Wadsworth, 2001.
- Mauro, John. *Statistical Deception at Work.* Mahwah, NJ: Lawrence Erlbaum Associates, 1992
- Murfield, L. O. (1997, Spring). *Generating interest and community involvement in student speeches, 11(3),* pp. 5-6.
- Nelsen, L. A. (1995, Spring). *Sell us Monroe's Motivated Sequence, 9(3),* p. 13.
- Neumann, D. (1990, Summer). *Selecting messages: An exercise In audience analysis, 4(4),* p. 9.
- Pendleton, S. C. (1999, Summer). *Using figurative language in persuasive speeches, 13(4),* pp. 5-7.

- Perloff, Richard. *The Dynamics* of *Persuasion*. Mahwah, NJ: Lawrence Erlbaum Associates, 1993.
- Proctor, R. F., II. (2000, Winter). *Using "Swing Kids" to teach theories of persuasion, 14(2)*, pp. 5-6.
- Zurakowski, M. M. (1997, Winter). *Modeling rhetorical criticism, 11(2)*, pp. 10-11.

II.   FILMS/TAPES

- "Communicating Successfully: How to Give a More Persuasive Presentation." Time-Life Films., *1973*, 23 minutes, color.
- "How to Give a Persuasive Speech." Time-Life Films, *1973*, 25 minutes, color.
- "Oral Communications: The Power of Emotion in Speech." McGraw-Hill, *1968*, 16 minutes, color. Marc Anthony's funeral oration from Shakespeare's Julius *Caesar is* analyzed as a model of a persuasive speech.
- "Persuasion Gone Awry." Insight Media, *1977*, 30 minutes, VHS. This lesson identifies some of the ways that persuasion can be misused. The program then explains test-, to distinguish persuasion fallacies from legitimate appeals.
- "Persuasive Appeals." Insight Media, *1977*, 30 minutes, VHS. Distinguishing among beliefs, attitudes, and values, this program examines what can motivate people.
- "Power Packed Selling." Creative Media, 32 minutes, color. Presents an extensive study of customer relations to various sales approaches. Show-, how trust can often make the difference.
- "Psycho-Sell: Advertising and Persuasion." Insight Media, *1991*, 25 minutes, WIS. Using soap as an example, it shows how advertising is tailored to fit emotional needs. It demonstrates how to make consumers believe one brand is different from its competitors, and shows how the advertiser can position a product to appeal to a particular segment of the market.
- "Reason and Emotion." Films for the Humanities, *1982*, 15 minutes, color.
- "Truth and the Dragon." McGraw-Hill, *1969,* 10 minutes, color. Uses an animated dragon to describe and symbolize seven propaganda systems: name calling, glittering generalities, testimonial, transfer, plain folks, card stacking, and bandwagon.
- "Understanding Persuasion." Films for the Humanities, *1982*, 15 minutes, color.
- "What You Are Is Where You Were When." Magnet Video Corp., 90 minutes, color. Examines value systems. Explores influence factors by decades of age groups.

APPENDIX: INTERVIEWING

OVERVIEW

Interviewing is defined as a form of oral communication involving two parties who both speak and listen and at least one of whom has a preconceived and serious purpose. It differs from conversation in purpose, structure, control, and balance. To be effective, an interview must be planned. The interviewer must clarify the purpose, develop tentative questions, and arrange the setting. The interviewee must clarify personal goals, gather necessary information, and anticipate probable questions. The chapter concludes by describing the responsibilities for both persons and describing several types of interviews.

OBJECTIVES

1. To explain how interviewing differs from conversation.
2. To give advice on planning and conducting an interview.
3. To explore types and strategies for asking questions.
4. To clarify the roles of interviewer and interviewee.
5. To acquaint students with a variety of interview types.
6. To describe the major stages of an interview.

SUGGESTED CLASSROOM ACTIVITIES

—INTERVIEW QUESTIONS

Approximate Time: 30 minutes

I. PURPOSE: to practice preparing various types of questions for use in an interview.

II. PROCEDURE:

1. On the board, list the following categories of questions for use in an interview: factual, opinion, open, closed, direct, indirect, primary, and secondary.
2. Ask each student to write a series of questions that will be asked publicly of the instructor or of another student in the class. Allow 10-15 minutes for preparation of questions.
3. Ask for all factual questions, then opinions, etc. Allow 15 minutes for students to ask the questions. This will provide practice in question preparation as well as an enjoyable opportunity for class members to get to know each other better.

III. PRINCIPLES ILLUSTRATED:

1. There are many different types of questions appropriate for use in an interview.
2. In an interview, it is best to have a variety of types of questions.

—ROLE PLAYING AN INTERVIEW

Approximate Time: 15 minutes per interview, and 20 minutes for discussion per interview

I. PURPOSE: to provide a simulation of an actual interview for students to experience behavior in interviews that they may have in the future.

II. PROCEDURE:

1. Recruit volunteers from the community who hold a professional position:
2. Select a location that will provide a real interview atmosphere (such as your office or an empty room with a table)

3. Have the volunteer devise an interview schedule with questions such as:

    ➤ Tell me about a time when you had to deal with a difficult person.
    ➤ Tell me about a time when you had to pull a team together.
    ➤ What is your definition of success?
    ➤ What do you consider your greatest accomplishment to be?

4. Place a video camera in the room to record the interview. Just allow the tape to run, so the interview will not be interrupted with turning on and off the camera. (to make the scenario feel more real)
5. Have the student arrive at the location as if it were a real interview
6. After the interview schedule a time for you and the student to view the tape together, and discuss the encounter. (For a shorter process, you can have the student watch the tape on his/her time and do a self analysis of the project.)

III. PRINCIPLES ILLUSTRATED:

1. To show students the structure of an interview
2. To provide students an understanding of the dyadic structure of an interview
3. To allow students the opportunity to practice the appropriate levels of self disclosure

ACTIVITIES TO PROMOTE CRITICAL AND CREATIVE THINKING

Use role playing to stimulate students' imaginations and develop interviewing skills. Divide the class into groups of five. Select a volunteer from each group to play the role of a famous person. The roles can be selected by you or by the groups from a list of possibilities, or by the groups themselves. They can be real-life or fictional, dead or alive, whimsical or serious. Planning should include setting specific content objectives, framing questions, and doing research to obtain necessary background information. Have each group conduct the interview of the famous person in front of the class.

Have students watch two different television talk shows, with the instructions that they should keep track of the types of questions asked by the host: open/closed, leading/neutral, etc. Ask students to use the results of their observations to make comparisons about the agendas of the different shows. For instance, is the host's main intention to entertain? To inform? To pass judgment? To make himself or herself look good at the expense of the guest? Do the questions reveal that the shows may have different audiences? Also consider how responsive the show's guests are to the different types of questions.

TEACHING ACTIVITIES IN THE COMMUNICATION TEACHER

- Ellis, B. G. "Using the Interview as a Teaching Dynamic," (Fall 1991) 6, 1, pp. 2-3.
- Gutgold, N. D. (2000, Summer). *Meta communication in business communication means a rich learning experience that is truly a slice of life!, 14(4)*, pp. 14-15.
- Hanna, M. S. (2000, Spring). *Design a role-playing case for study and practice, 14(3)*, pp. 12-14.
- Hardins, David. "Group Feud: Reinforcing Interviewing Skills," (Summer 1995) 9, 3, p. 6.
- Pawlowski, D. R. (2000, Winter). *Multiple method interviewing: Learning about performance appraisals through information-gathering phone interviews, 14(2)*, pp. 9-10.
- Plec, Emily. "The Interview" (Winter 1999) 13, 2, pp. 11-12
- Renz, May Ann. "Job Specific Interviews," (Winter 1992) 6, 2, pp. 4-5.
- Sellnow, Timothy L. "An Oral History Exercise for the Self-Evaluation of Interview Skills," (Winter 1992) 6, 2, p. 11.
- Sharp, S. (1994, Winter). *Varied approaches to teaching job interviewing, 8(2)*, pp. 6-7.
- Wallenstein, Martin. "The Investigative Interview" (Fall 1996) 11, 1, pp. 2-4
- Willer, Lynda. "An Interdisciplinary Approach to Teaching Interviewing," (Summer 1995) 9, 4, p. 10.

SUPPLEMENTARY RESOURCES

I.   BOOKS AND ARTICLES

- Adler, Ronald and Jeanne Marquardt Elmhorst. *Communicating at Work.* New York, NY: McGraw Hill, 2002.
- Andrews, Patricia and John Baird. *Communication for Business and the Professions.* New York, NY: McGraw Hill, 2000.
- Arnold, William and Lynne McClure. *Communication Training and Development.* Prospect Heights, IL: Waveland, 1996.
- Donaghy, William. *The Interview: Skills and Applications.* Salem, WI: Sheffield Publishing. 1989.
- Goldhaber, Gerald. *Organizational Communication.* New York, NY: McGraw Hill, 1993.
- Hamilton, Cheryl and Cordell Parker. *Communicating for Results: A Guide for Business and the Professions.* Belmont, CA: Wadsworth, 2001.
- Hanna, Michael and Gerald Wilson. *Communicating in Business and Professional Settings.* New York: McGraw-Hill, 1998.
- Jackson, P. "A Day in the Life of an Interviewer," *Personnel Management,* 15 (November 1983), pp. 54-55.
- Siebold, David and Renee Meyers. "Co-Participant Perception of Information-Gathering Interviews: Implications for Teaching Interviewing Skills," *Communication Education,* 34 (April 1985), 106-118.
- Stewart, Charles. *Teaching Interviewing for Career Preparation.* Annandale, VA: SCA, 1991.
- Stewart, Charles and William Cash. *Interviewing: Principles and Practices.* New York, NY: McGraw Hill, 2003.
- "What You Should Know About Interviewing," Pamphlet available free from General Electric Company, Educational Communications, Room 901, 570 Lexington Ave., New York, NY 10022.
- Wilson, Gerald L. and Lloyd H. Goodall. *Interviewing in Context.* New York: McGraw-Hill, 1991.
- Yeager, Neil and Lee Hough. *Power Interviews: Job-Winning Tactics from Fortune 500 Recruiters.* New York, NY: John Wiley & Sons, 1998.

II. FILMS/TAPES

- "Constructive Communications: Talking Your Way to Success." Insight Media, 1991, 30 minutes, VHS. This program teaches the "EASY" Method-Effect, Audience, Subject, Yourself--for developing effective communication skills, and demonstrates how to apply this method during job interviews and to everyday situations in the workplace.
- "The Interview." Learning Corp. of America, 1960, 5 minutes, color. Portrays a satirical interview between a "square" announcer and a "hip" horn player. Also good for language.
- "Interview: Ready or Not." Dimension Films, 1975, 25 minutes, color. Shows a job interview in a role-play situation with a professional interviewer from a large corporation. A group of students then discusses what happened. The interviewer also gives her opinion.
- "Interview Techniques." Insight Media, 1992, 25 minutes, VHS. From putting the interviewee at ease to getting enough film for the edit, this program demonstrates techniques for conducting a successful television news interview.
- "Job Interview: Whom Would You Hire? Large Business." Dimension Films, 1980, 20 minutes, color. Presents candid interviews by a corporation personnel officer of three young applicants for trainee positions. Viewers are asked to rate each applicant.
- "Job Interview: Whom Would You Hire? Small Business." Dimension Films, 1980, 20 minute, color. Four applicants for jobs in a coffee shop are interviewed by the manager. Viewers rate each one.
- "Job Interview: Whom Would You Hire? (Three Young Men)." Dimension Films, 1967, 17 minutes, color. Views actual job interviews with three young men for trainee positions. Gives viewers a chance to evaluate the applicants as an employer would.

GUIDE TO MEDIATED COMMUNICATION

OVERVIEW

This chapter discusses the types of mediated communication, such as mass communication, mediated interpersonal communication and converging communication media. The authors also discuss theories of media effects. The theories discussed in this appendix are flow theories, social learning theory, individual differences theory, cultivation theory, agenda setting-theory, and cumulative effects theory. Beyond theories, this chapter explains different approaches to analyzing mediated communication through looking and gender and political and economic views. Finally the authors discuss how we use media through the types of uses and through media consumers.

OBJECTIVES

1. To help students distinguish between mass communication and other forms of communication.
2. To increase students' awareness of the social, political, and economic importance of mass media.
3. To offer students information on theories and cultural studies in mass media.
4. To sensitize students to the ethical and legal issues related to mass communication.
5. To help students become more informed observers and consumers of mass communication.
6. To introduce students to possible media-related careers.

SUGGESTED CLASSROOM ACTIVITIES

—WHAT'S SO IMPORTANT?

Approximate Time: 30-50 minutes

I. PURPOSE: to understand the social, political and economic importance of selected pieces of mass media.

II. PROCEDURE:

1. Divide the class into four groups.
2. Assign each group a different type of media, giving them the actual printed copy or video or audio tape.

    Sample types and selections:

    a. advertising-magazine ad or video taped commercial
    b. editorial-newspaper editorial or TV station editorial, political cartoon
    c. news-radio or TV news broadcast
    d. entertainment-soap opera, TV sitcom, or newspaper cartoon

3. Have students work in groups to examine their selection in terms of its social, political, and economic importance.
4. Tell the groups to prepare to share their analyses with the class in a 5- to 10-minute presentation that incorporates what they have learned about visual aids, audience analysis, etc.
5. Discuss with the entire class the concepts presented.

III. PRINCIPLES ILLUSTRATED:

1. Media are important for their social, economic, and political impact.
2. Perception plays a major role in how a piece of media is viewed.
3. Different forms of media function differently in terms of impact.

—I'M AN INDIVIDUAL AND I'M DIFFERENT

Approximate Time: 50 minutes

I.   PURPOSE: to explore the individual differences theory of media effects.

II. PROCEDURE:

1.   On slips of paper write the names of the five types of people identified by Everett Rogers who have different levels of willingness to accept new ideas from the media: innovators, early adopters, early majority, late majority, and laggards. Make enough slips for every student to get one.
2.   Put the students with each of the types into groups.
3.   Play a video or hand out a printed selection that introduces a new idea. For example: a commercial for a new (or improved) product or calls for change in an editorial or a political commercial. Another possibility is for the teacher to make a taped commercial for an innovative product he or she designed.
4.   Ask each group to analyze how their type of person would respond. They should consider what factors (age, sex, geographic region, intelligence, education level, and wealth) would help explain their response.
5.   Have students role play their type of person's reaction.

III. PRINCIPLES ILLUSTRATED:

1.   Individual differences affect the impact of media.
2.   Different types of people have different levels of acceptance of new ideas.
3.   Predicting the effect of media is difficult and complex.
4.   How we each respond to a media event is influenced by our age, education, etc.

ACTIVITIES TO PROMOTE CRITICAL AND CREATIVE THINKING

Ask students what their favorite TV show is. Have them use that show to examine one of the theories of media effects.

Put students into small groups and ask them to decide which of the ten media milestones they feel is most important. Have them prepare to explain and defend their choice for the class.

Play a segment from Cheers and examine the gender role research by Deming and Jenkins as it relates to the viewed segment.

Play a brief segment of a soap opera without sound. Examine it in terms of a semiological analysis. Relate what you find to the material on nonverbal communication.

Explore the Peter Wood analogy between TV and dreams by brainstorming a list of ways in which they are dissimilar. Compare the similarities and differences.

TEACHING ACTIVITIES IN THE SPEECH COMMUNICATION TEACHER

- Gullickson-Tolman, Liz. "Court Television Programs" (Summer 1999) 13, 4, p. 12
- Haefner, Margaret J. and C . Sue Strohkirch. "A Day Without Mass Media," (Winter 1992) 6, 2, pp. 1-2.
- Kaye, Tom. "Video Scavenger Hunt," (Fall 1991) 6, 1, p. 13.
- Modaff, J. V. (1998, Summer). *The radio commentary speech, 12(4)*, pp. 1-3.
- Shelley, D. B. (1996, Fall). *Propaganda use in advertising, 11(1)*, pp. 4-5.

- Strohkirch, C. Sue and Margaret J. Hefner. "Conflict on TV: How Real Is It?" (Summer 1990) 4, 4, p. 14.
- Tolar, Debra Olson. "My Favorite News Team: Comparative Analysis of the Nightly News," (Fall 1992) 7, 1, p. 9.

SUPPLEMENTARY RESOURCES

I.   BOOKS AND ARTICLES

- Avery, Robert and David Eason. *Critical Perspectives on Media and Society*. New York: Guilford Publications, 1991.
- Biagi, Shirley. *Media/Impact: An Introduction to Mass Media*. Belmont, CA: Wadsworth, 2003.
- Bryant, Jennings and J. Allison Bryant. *Television and the American Family* Hillsdale, NJ: Lawrence Erlbaum Associates, 2001.
- Kubey, Robert and Mihaly Csikszentmihlyi. *Television and the Quality of Life: How Viewing Shapes Everyday Experience*. Hillsdale, NJ: Lawrence Erlbaum Associates, 1990.
- Whetmore, Edward Jay. *Mediamerica, Mediaworld*. Belmont, CA: Wadsworth, 1996.

II.   FILMS/TAPES

- "Being on TV: The Crash Course. " Insight Media, 1990, 30 minutes, VHS. Gwenn Kelly, a successful television skills trainer, teaches viewers what to expect when they appear on television and demonstrates how to handle oneself in front of the camera. She shows how to shape a message to appeal to a television audience.
- "The Making of a Newspaper." Insight Media, 1988, 28 minutes, VHS. This introductory-level program explores the process of producing a daily newspaper in a metropolitan market.
- "News Gathering." Insight Media, 1991, 12 minutes, VHS. Show the interlocking roles performed by assignment editors, producers, news directors, reporters, writers, and photographers.
- "Psychology of Advertising." (Part 1) Insight Media, 1989, 22 minutes, VHS. Focuses on print advertising, looking at critical advertising assumptions, social trends, and consumer life cycles.
- "Psychology of Advertising." (Part 2) Insight Media, 1991, 17 minutes, VHS. Explains how to design an advertisement to fit a target market.

CHAPTER 1 HUMAN COMMUNICATION: WHAT AND WHY

MULTIPLE CHOICE

1. One characteristic of human communication is that it is symbolic. In this symbolic communication meanings are located in:

    a. words
    b. events
    c. people
    d. objects

    Answer: c   Key 1: R

2. _____ means communicating with oneself.

    a. Interpersonal communication
    b. Intrapersonal communication
    c. Dyadic communication
    d. Intradyadic communication

    Answer: b   Key 1: R

3. We satisfy our _____ by communicating pleasure, affection, and inclusion.

    a. social needs
    b. physical needs
    c. practical needs
    d. identity needs

    Answer: a   Key 1: R

4. Shonda was sitting in a crowded room that was very warm and stuffy. This was making it difficult for her to listen to the speaker's message. What type of noise was Shonda suffering from?

    a. psychological noise
    b. physiological noise
    c. environmental noise
    d. external noise

    Answer: d   Key 1: A

5. A _____ is the method by which a message is conveyed between people.

    a. channel
    b. receiver
    c. sender
    d. medium

    Answer: a   Key 1: R

6. A sender _____ ideas and feelings into some sort of message.

    a. decodes
    b. encodes
    c. mediates
    d. channels

    Answer: b   Key 1: R

7. All of the following are examples of an environment EXCEPT:

    a. personal experience
    b. cultural background
    c. choice of medium
    d. physical location

    Answer: c   Key 1: R

8. All of the following are characteristics of the transactional model of communication EXCEPT:

    a. it reflects the fact that we send and receive messages simultaneously
    b. the sender only encodes and the receiver only decodes
    c. it reflects the fact that there is feedback
    d. noise can occur with the encoding and decoding process

    Answer: b   Key 1: C

9. All of the following are characteristics of communication competence EXCEPT:

    a. communication cannot be learned
    b. there is no ideal way to communicate
    c. competence is situational
    d. competence is relational

    Answer: a   Key 1: R

10. _____ is the ability to construct a variety of frameworks for viewing an issue.

    a. Perspective taking
    b. Self-monitoring
    c. Skill performing
    d. Cognitive complexity

    Answer: d   Key 1: R

11. Julia told Kacie that Taylor was "loaded." Kacie took this to mean that Taylor had too much to drink, when Julia meant that he was very wealthy. This is an example of:

    a. meaning is in people not words
    b. communication is simple
    c. communication does not always require complete understanding
    d. communication is not always a good thing

    Answer: a   Key 1: A

12. All of the following are misconceptions of communication EXCEPT:

    a. More communication is better
    b. Communication always requires complete understanding
    c. Communication won't solve all problems
    d. Meanings are in words

    Answer: c   Key 1: R

Answer Key Code: R = Recall   C= Conceptual   A = Application   S = Synthesis

13. When we are searching for words to express an idea, we are involved in the process of:

    a. assigning meaning
    b. transmitting
    c. decoding
    d. encoding

    Answer: d   Key 1: C

14. _____ is the discernible response of a receiver to a sender's message.

    a. Feedback
    b. Noise
    c. Encoding
    d. Decoding

    Answer: a   Key 1: R

15. All of the following are examples of mediated communication EXCEPT:

    a. instant messages
    b. face-to-face interaction
    c. voice mail
    d. videoconferencing

    Answer: b   Key 1: R

16. John is trying to listen to a speech but his headache interferes. He's experiencing:

    a. external noise
    b. physiological noise
    c. psychological noise
    d. a distraction not classified as noise

    Answer: b   Key 1: A

17. The type of communication most often characterized by an unequal distribution of speaking time is:

    a. intrapersonal
    b. dyadic
    c. small group
    d. public

    Answer: d   Key 1: R

18. Perspective taking is associated with:

    a. psychological noise
    b. physiological noise
    c. empathy
    d. channels

    Answer: c   Key 1: R

19. A(n)_____ is the communication channel that the sender has the highest control over how the message is composed.

   a. Instant message
   b. Face to face conversation
   c. Telephone conversation
   d. Hard copy message

Answer: d   Key 1: C

TRUE/FALSE

20. Because communication is transactional, when communication failure occurs it is a fairly simple task to figure how which party is to blame.

Answer: F   Key 1: C
The text states that from the transactional perspective it is a mistake to suggest that just one party is responsible for a relationship.

21. Interpersonal communication, dyadic communication, small group communication, and public communication all occur in different contexts.

Answer: T   Key 1: R
The number of participants frames a different context for each.

22. A receiver's act of assigning meaning to a symbol is called encoding.

Answer: F   Key 1: R
This refers to decoding.

23. Communication helps satisfy most of our human needs.

Answer: T   Key 1: R
The text says this directly and describes the needs as physical, social, identity, and practical.

24. Noise can be internal and/or external.

Answer: T   Key 1: R
External noise is physical noise. Internal noise is either physiological noise, involving biological factors, or psychological noise which refers to "forces within the communicator that interfere with the ability to express or understand a message accurately."

25. Skillful communication can solve most of the world's problems.

Answer: F   Key 1: R
Clear and accurate communication can help solve some problems but it can also identify irresolvable differences.

26. Skilled communicators can quickly pick out which party is to blame when communication fails.

Answer: F   Key 1: C
Skilled communicators see communication as transactional, where assigning blame is fruitless and counterproductive.

27. Meanings rest in people, not in words.

Answer: T   Key 1: R
Communication is symbolic and the words we use to communicate are arbitrary and personal.

Answer Key Code: R = Recall C= Conceptual A = Application S = Synthesis

28. Communication is something done to listeners by speakers.

Answer: F   Key 1: R
Communication is a transaction between speakers and listeners and is a process in which those roles are shared.

29. Symbols can be either verbal or nonverbal.

Answer: T   Key 1: R
Both can be given symbolic meaning.

30. Research shows that communication is related to physical health.

Answer: T   Key 1: R
Medical researchers have identified health hazards which result from a lack of interpersonal relationships.

31. Communication is the only way we learn who we are.

Answer: T   Key 1: R
Our sense of identity comes from the way we interact with others.

32. There is no ideal way to communicate.

Answer: T   Key 1: R
A variety of communication styles can be effective depending upon the situation.

33. The authors of your textbook define the ideal way to communicate as using humor, honesty, and intelligence.

Answer: F   Key 1: R
There is no 'ideal" way to communicate.

34. Communication always requires complete understanding.

Answer: F   Key 1: R
Although some understanding is necessary as the book states, understanding does not have to always be the primary goal, for example having social rituals, deliberate ambiguity, and coordinate action.

35. Communication competence is a trait that individuals either possess or lack.

Answer: F   Key 1: R
It is situational, rather than a trait a person either possesses or doesn't possess.

36. Socially isolated people are four times more susceptible to the common cold than those who have active social networks.

Answer: T   Key 1: R
One of the primary functions of communication is through fulfilling physical needs.

37. The channel you choose does not make a big difference in the effect of a message.

Answer: F   Key 1: R
Actually the opposite is true. The medium has a large effect on how the message is received.

38. The linear communication model proves that communication is relational not individual.

Answer: F   Key 1: C
The transactional model shows that communication isn't something we do to people, but with people, whereas the linear shows communication to be one way.

39. Communication is individual.

    Answer: F   Key 1: C
    Communication is relational not individual.

SHORT ANSWER

40. Describe an experience where you have found communication satisfying, but you have also realized that you did not fully understand all the things being said.

    Answer: Key 1: A

41. It has been said that "communication is more important than understanding." Do you agree or not? Use a specific example to justify your answer.

    Answer: Key 1: S

42. What makes communication interactive?

    Answer: Key 1: A

43. Communication competence is situational. Give three examples of this situational nature.

    Answer: Key 1: A

44. List four channels you have used for communication in the past week.

    Answer: Key 1: A

45. Describe five elements of the environment that affected a recent conversation.

    Answer: Key 1: A

46. Describe a conversation you have had in which "the world was a different place for the sender and for the receiver." What cause(s) were there for this difference?

    Answer: Key 1: A

47. Describe an event which fulfills your text's definition of communication. Explain how it satisfies the three characteristics of communication used to form its working definition.

    Answer: Key 1: S

48. Communication scholars argue that we are attracted to people who confirm our identity, whether positive or negative. Does your own experience conform to this perspective? Explain why you think this is so.

    Answer: Key 1: A

49. Define and explain the concept of "coordination" in communication. Illustrate your answer with personal examples.

    Answer: Key 1: S

50. List three characteristics of communication competence and give one example of each.

    Answer: Key 1: A

51. Describe someone you know who is a competent communicator. Do they possess the characteristics listed in your text? Do they possess other qualities not on the list?

    Answer: Key 1: A

Answer Key Code: R = Recall C= Conceptual A = Application S = Synthesis

52. List five practical needs you fulfilled or attempted to fulfill today by using communication.

    Answer: Key 1: A

53. Does the statement by your authors that "communication will not solve all problems" imply that communication training is pointless? Why or why not?

    Answer: Key 1: S

MATCHING

54. Match the behavior with the characteristic of communication competence. Each answer may be used once, more than once, or not at all.

    ____ Asking, "How am I doing?

    ____ Using humor in an appropriate situation

    ____ Using your voice effectively

    ____ Knowing how to communicate in many situations

    ____ Showing concern for your communication partner

    ____ Thinking about an issue from various perspectives

    A. a wide range of behaviors

    B. an ability to choose the appropriate behavior

    C. skill at performing behaviors

    D. empathy

    E. cognitive complexity

    F. self-monitoring

    G. commitment to the relationship

    Answer: F, B, C, A, G, E   Key 1: A

OTHER

55. Place a "yes" or "no" in front of each statement to indicate which of the following fit your authors' definition of feedback.

    _____   The listener smiles.

    _____   The listener thinks, "This is boring."

    _____   The listener walks away.

    _____   The listener asks, "What do you mean?"

    _____   The listener is confused.

    _____   The listener wishes the speaker would stop talking.

    _____   The listener raises his/her hand.

    Answer: Yes, No, Yes, Yes, No, No, Yes   Key 1: A

CHAPTER 2 PERCEPTION, THE SELF, AND COMMUNICATION

MULTIPLE CHOICE

1. _____ are personal stories that we and others create to make sense of our personal world.

    a. Narratives
    b. Perceptions
    c. Social constructs
    d. Social phenomenons

    Answer: a   Key 1: R

2. _____ is the process of attaching meaning to behavior.

    a. Perception checking
    b. Self-serving bias
    c. Attribution
    d. Assimilation

    Answer: c   Key 1: R

3. Judy did not correctly complete a task that her supervisor had given her. Judy's supervisor thought that the reason she didn't complete the task correctly was because she did not listen well or try hard enough. Judy felt that it was because the directions were not clear and her supervisor did not provide her enough time to complete it. Judy's explanation is an example of:

    a. self-fulfilling prophecy
    b. self-serving bias
    c. perception checking
    d. attribution error

    Answer: b   Key 1: A

4. All of the following are common perceptual tendencies EXCEPT:

    a. We often judge ourselves more harshly than we judge others
    b. We are influenced by what is most obvious
    c. We tend to assume that others are similar to us
    d. We tend to favor negative impressions over positive ones

    Answer: a   Key 1: R

5. _____ is the ability to re-create another person's perspective, to experience the world from the other's point of view.

    a. Sympathy
    b. Assimilation
    c. Perception
    d. Empathy

    Answer: d   Key 1: R

Answer Key Code: R = Recall   C= Conceptual   A = Application   S = Synthesis

6. All of the following are dimensions of empathy EXCEPT:

    a. perspective taking
    b. understanding the emotional dimension
    c. having sympathy
    d. having genuine concern

    Answer: c   Key 1: R

7. _____ is like a mental mirror that reflects how we view ourselves.

    a. self-worth
    b. self-concept
    c. self-perception
    d. self-analysis

    Answer: b   Key 1: R

8. All of the following are ways we generate our self-concept EXCEPT:

    a. through self-esteem
    b. through reflected appraisal
    c. through empathy
    d. through significant others' views

    Answer: c   Key 1: R

9. _____ is the communication strategy people use to influence how others view them.

    a. Impression management
    b. Social identity
    c. Perception checking
    d. Self analysis

    Answer: a   Key 1: R

10. _____ is the reflection of the self concept.

    a. Presenting self
    b. Managed self
    c. External self
    d. Perceived self

    Answer: d   Key 1: R

11. Your friend gave you confusing directions to a party that caused you to be late. When you arrived you stated "Sorry I am late, I am a terrible navigator." By using this sort of mild self-depreciating humor to defuse a potentially unpleasant situation you are engaging in:

    a. cultural identity
    b. perception checking
    c. framework
    d. facework

    Answer: d   Key 1: A

12. All of the following are characteristics of identity management EXCEPT:

    a. We strive to construct a single identity
    b. Identity management is collaborative
    c. Identity management can be conscious
    d. Identity management can be unconscious

    Answer: a   Key 1: R

13. All of the following are factors that influence our perceptions EXCEPT:

    a. Our cultural background
    b. Our ability to sympathize
    c. Our ability to empathize
    d. Our success at constructing shared narrative through communication

    Answer: b   Key 1: C

14. All of the following are disadvantages to being an extremely high self-monitor EXCEPT

    a. They are often viewing the situation from a detached position, not being able to experience it fully
    b. They make it hard for others to tell how they are really feeling
    c. They are not good "People readers"
    d. They have a hard time knowing themselves how they really feel

    Answer: c   Key 1: R

15. In face-to-face impression management, all of the following are ways to manage communication EXCEPT:

    a. through manner
    b. through appearance
    c. through intellect
    d. through setting

    Answer: c   Key 1: R

16. In impression management through mediated communication, all of the following are advantages of using a medium for communication management EXCEPT:

    a. you can choose the level of ambiguity of your message
    b. it forces the receiver to have to respond to the message
    c. it allows the sender to control his or her emotions in a message
    d. it gives the sender much greater control of information they want to hide

    Answer: b   Key 1: R

17. All of the following are characteristics of self-concept EXCEPT:

    a. It is innate, rather than learned.
    b. It aids in predicting the person's effectiveness as a communicator.
    c. It influences interactions with others.
    d. It can change over time.

    Answer: a   Key 1: R

Answer Key Code: R = Recall   C= Conceptual   A = Application   S = Synthesis

18. A person's self-concept is a set of:

    a. constantly changing perceptions of others
    b. stable perceptions of others
    c. uniquely changing perceptions of ourselves
    d. relatively stable perceptions of ourselves

    Answer: d   Key 1: R

19. Math is your weakest subject. On the first day of college algebra you tell the student next to you, "I bet I'll get a D in this course." At the end of the semester you get a D. This result could be an example of:

    a. self-denial
    b. self-disclosure
    c. self-fulfilling prophecy
    d. self-motivation

    Answer: c   Key 1: A

20. In the study of communication, the term "narrative" refers to:

    a. stories made up by experts to explain general human behavior
    b. stories we and others make up to make sense of our personal worlds
    c. stories told to teach a lesson
    d. none of the above

    Answer: b   Key 1: R

21. Several factors influence the selection of perceived stimuli. Which of the following is not one of those factors?

    a. repetition
    b. contrast
    c. correctness
    d. intensity

    Answer: c   Key 1: R

22. Which statement best captures the connection between self-concept and communication?

    a. The self-concept shapes communication behavior.
    b. Communication behavior affects the self-concept.
    c. Self-concept shapes communication behavior, but communication behavior has little impact on self-concept.
    d. Self-concept shapes communication behavior and is affected by the response to the behavior.

    Answer: d   Key 1: C

23. Attribution refers to:

    a. judging the personal qualities of another
    b. heredity
    c. the reflective self concept
    d. the process of attaching meaning to behavior

    Answer: d   Key 1: R

24. If you have left only the night before a test to study, and then explain it by saying you were just too busy, but when your friends do the same thing you label them "procrastinators," you are exhibiting:

    a. an attributional error
    b. the effect of repeated stimuli
    c. empathy
    d. the self-serving bias

    Answer: d   Key 1: A

25. All of the following are parts to perception checking EXCEPT:

    a. a description of your personal narrative
    b. a description of the behavior you noticed
    c. At least two possible interpretations of the behavior
    d. A request for clarification about how to interpret the behavior

    Answer: a   Key 1: R

TRUE/FALSE

26. The self-concept is a set of relatively stable perceptions that other people hold about us.

    Answer: F   Key 1: R
    It is the internalized set of relatively stable perceptions that we hold about ourselves.

27. People constantly receive stimuli from the environment, but they do not always perceive all of these stimuli.

    Answer: T   Key 1: R
    People do not attaching meaning to experiences for all the stimuli to which they are exposed.

28. When you answer the question, "Who am I?" you are describing your self-concept.

    Answer: T   Key 1: R
    The self-concept is your definition of yourself including the ways in which you identify who you are.

29. First impressions are often dangerous and should be avoided.

    Answer: F   Key 1: R
    They are inevitable parts of the perception process; clinging to them should be avoided.

30. It is easy for people with empathy to quickly discard inaccurate first impressions.

    Answer: F   Key 1: C
    Most people cling to first impressions and change later information to fit them. Empathy has no relevance.

31. People are more influenced by negative than positive characteristics of others.

    Answer: T   Key 1: R
    Research shows that when people are aware of both the positive and negative characteristics of others, they tend to be more influenced by the undesirable traits.

32. The self-concept includes both what we think is unique about us and what we think makes us similar to others.

    Answer: T   Key 1: R
    The self-concept includes our conception of what makes us both similar to, and different from, others.

Answer Key Code: R = Recall   C= Conceptual   A = Application   S = Synthesis

33. There is little relation between others' evaluations of us and our self-concept.

    Answer: F   Key 1: R
    There is a relationship between the two which persists from childhood to adulthood.

34. Empathy requires sympathy.

    Answer: F   Key 1: C
    We only sympathize with people whom we pity; it is possible to empathize without feeling sympathy.

35. A skilled communicator is able to remove the perceptual filters caused by culture.

    Answer: F   Key 1: C
    Perceptual filters from one's culture are not removable, but if made aware of them, communicators can prevent them from causing misunderstanding.

36. Empathy has both a cognitive and an emotional dimension.

    Answer: T   Key 1: R
    It requires a setting aside of one's own opinions and feelings and attempting to view things as the other person does.

37. The tendency to judge ourselves more charitably than others is called the self-serving bias.

    Answer: T   Key 1: R
    This is the definition in the text.

38. Our culture is an example of a perceptual filter.

    Answer: T   Key 1: R
    Culture is a filter that influences the way we interpret events.

39. Satisfied couples blame outside forces for problems, rather than each other.

    Answer: T   Key 1: R
    They tend to not attribute responsibility to one another.

40. When you speak in public your audience sees your presenting self.

    Answer: T   Key 1: A
    The presenting self is your public self.

41. The perceived self is maintained by facework.

    Answer: F   Key 1: R
    The presenting self is maintained by facework.

42. High self-monitors tend to be socially skillful.

    Answer: T   Key 1: R
    They are good actors who can handle social situations smoothly, putting others at ease.

43. The degree of interdependence is lower in collective cultures compared to individualistic cultures.

    Answer: F   Key 1: R
    One characteristic of collective cultures is their high degree of interdependence.

44. The United States is primarily an individualistic culture.

    Answer: T   Key 1: R
    The U.S. and Australia are the two examples used in the text.

45. Personality describes a relatively consistent set of traits people exhibit in a specific context.

    Answer: F   Key 1: R
    It is exhibited across a variety of situations.

46. Narratives offer a framework for explaining behavior and shaping future communication.

    Answer: T   Key 1: R
    Narratives help us make sense of our personal world.

47. Shared narratives may be desirable and easy to achieve.

    Answer: F   Key 1: R
    Shared narratives are often hard to achieve because of attribution error.

48. We tend to assume that others are similar to us.

    Answer: T   Key 1: R
    This is a common perceptual tendency.

49. Total empathy is impossible to achieve.

    Answer: T   Key 1: R
    Different backgrounds and limited communication skills makes it too difficult to achieve total empathy.

50. Reflected appraisal is how we develop an image of ourselves from the way we think others view us.

    Answer: T   Key 1: R
    This is the notion of the "looking-glass self."

51. Facework involves managing other's identity of ourselves and communicating in ways that reinforce the identities that others are trying to present.

    Answer: F   Key 1: R
    Facework actually involves managing our own identity rather than other's identity of ourselves.

SHORT ANSWER

52. George Bernard Shaw said: "The only person who behaves sensibly is my tailor. He makes new measurements every time he sees me. All the rest go on with the old measurements." Explain how this quotation relates to self-concept, reflected appraisal, and self-fulfilling prophecy.

    Answer: Key 1: S

53. Explain how the self-fulfilling prophecy works. Use the self-fulfilling prophecy to explain your performance in this course up to this point.

    Answer: Key 1: A

54. Identify two filters that affect the perceptual process. Give examples of situations in which these filters were at work.

    Answer: Key 1: A

Answer Key Code: R = Recall   C= Conceptual   A = Application   S = Synthesis

55. Give an example of a "significant other" in your life. Explain why this person fits that description. How does this person affect your self-concept?

    Answer: Key 1: A

56. Name, explain, and justify each step in the perception checking process.

    Answer: Key 1: R

57. Define the self-fulfilling prophecy. Give an example of a personal experience with this concept.

    Answer: Key 1: A

58. You're attending a family reunion. A cousin with whom you were once good friends comes over and says, "I hear you're a big-time college student now!" Explain how 2-3 of the situational factors influencing perception relate to how you would interpret this message.

    Answer: Key 1: A

59. Using your family as a culture, describe how your perceptions have been influenced by it. Include at least one example.

    Answer: Key 1: A

60. Explain how spending a day in a wheelchair could promote empathy by the participants.

    Answer: Key 1: A

61. Describe both your perceived self and your presenting self in this class.

    Answer: Key 1: A

62. According to impression management, we have communication strategies that we use to influence how others see us. Discuss the difference between the perceived self and the presenting self. Explain and provide examples of how your perceived self is different from your presenting self.

    Answer: Key 1: A

63. Explain the following: I am not what I think I am. I am not what you think I am. I am what I think you think I am.

    Answer: Key 1: A

64. Give examples from your own experience to match the statement that the one big advantage of having an open self-concept rather than a rigid one is that we shall continue to discover more and more about ourselves as we grow older.

    Answer: Key 1: A

65. Discuss the advantages and disadvantages of managing our identities through both face-to-face communication and mediated communication.

    Answer: Key 1: C

66. What are the major differences between high self-monitors and low self monitors? What are some advantages and disadvantages of each?

    Answer: Key 1: C

CHAPTER 3 LANGUAGE

MULTIPLE CHOICE

1. A speaker just said the word "dog." If you apply Ogden and Richards' triangle of meaning to this message, which of the following would go on the bottom right point?

    a. a semantic rule to determine the word's meaning
    b. a syntactic rule to determine the word's usage
    c. the actual dog
    d. the listener

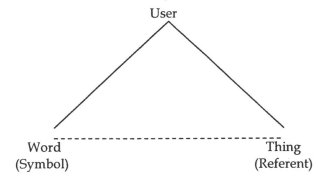

Answer: c   Key 1: A

2. Ogden and Richards' triangle of meaning demonstrates visually that meanings are in:

    a. words
    b. minds
    c. vocabularies
    d. nonverbals

    Answer: b   Key 1: R

3. _____ govern how words sound when pronounced.

    a. Semantic rules
    b. Phonological rules
    c. Syntactic rules
    d. Pragmatic rules

    Answer: b   Key 1: R

4. _____ govern the structure of language.

    a. Semantic rules
    b. Phonological rules
    c. Syntactic rules
    d. Pragmatic rules

    Answer: c   Key 1: R

Answer Key Code: R = Recall   C= Conceptual   A = Application   S = Synthesis

5. When entering a public restroom, which language rule makes it possible for us to know whether to enter through the "Men's" or "Women's" door?

    a. semantic rules
    b. phonological rules
    c. syntactic rules
    d. pragmatic rules

    Answer: a   Key 1: C

6. You tell your best friend that you have won the lottery. Her response is "Shut Up!!" Based on your relationship, this is a saying that the two of you use as an expression of excitement. Which of the following would explain this type of language?

    a. semantic rules
    b. phonological rules
    c. syntactic rules
    d. pragmatic rules

    Answer: d   Key 1: A

7. Language use can reflect the speaker's willingness to take responsibility for his/her statements. Which of the following categories of statements reflects the highest amount of speaker responsibility?

    a. "it" statements
    b. "you" statements
    c. "they" statements
    d. "I" statements

    Answer: d   Key 1: C

8. You are at the pizza restaurant ordering pizza with several friends. Suzanne says, "Don't order one with anchovies. Just hearing the word 'anchovies' about makes me sick!" Suzanne is responding to:

    a. equivocal meaning
    b. relative meaning
    c. emotive meaning
    d. fictional meaning

    Answer: c   Key 1: A

9. All of the following can affect the status of a person EXCEPT:

    a. their accent
    b. their choice of words
    c. their speech rate
    d. the volume of their voice

    Answer: d   Key 1: R

10. Using the word "salesman" rather than "sales representative" is an example of:

    a. status language
    b. racist language
    c. pragmatic language
    d. sexist language

    Answer: d   Key 1: R

11. "Don't you think we should give it another try?" This is an example of a:

    a. tag question
    b. hedge
    c. disclaimer
    d. hesitation

    Answer: a   Key 1: R

12. Communicators who want to set themselves apart from others adopt the strategy of _____.

    a. convergence
    b. divergence
    c. negation
    d. sequential placement

    Answer: b   Key 1: R

13. Meanings are in people, not in words. Which of the following rules best relates to this statement?

    a. semantic rules
    b. syntactic rules
    c. pragmatic rules
    d. phonological rules

    Answer: a   Key 1: C

14. _____ words have more than one correct dictionary definition.

    a. Relative
    b. Overly abstract
    c. Jargon
    d. Equivocal

    Answer: d   Key 1: R

15. Fast or slow, small or large, smart or stupid, and short or long are examples of what type of words?

    a. relative
    b. slang
    c. jargon
    d. equivocal

    Answer: a   Key 1: C

16. "He was daydreaming when he hit the desk" is an example of:

    a. fact
    b. opinion
    c. inference
    d. language

    Answer: c   Key 1: C

Answer Key Code: R = Recall   C= Conceptual   A = Application   S = Synthesis

17. _____ contains words that sound as if they are describing something when they are really announcing the speaker's attitude toward something.

   a. Pragmatic language
   b. Syntactic language
   c. Semantic language
   d. Emotive language

   Answer: d   Key 1: R

18. "He strategizes — she manipulates" is an example of:

   a. emotive language
   b. abstract language
   c. equivocal language
   d. evasive language

   Answer: a   Key 1: C

19. _____ are pleasant terms substituted for a more direct but potentially less pleasant terms.

   a. Slang words
   b. Euphemisms
   c. Abstractions
   d. Emotive words

   Answer: b   Key 1: R

20. The CEO of a company tells her employees that "the organization is going to be restructuring each department" rather than saying "there are going to be layoffs in each department." This is an example of:

   a. jargon
   b. abstractions
   c. euphemisms
   d. equivocations

   Answer: c   Key 1: A

21. Roger has reported to your study group that he plans to improve his study habits this semester. In fact he said, "I will study two hours outside of class for each hour in class." His statement is an example of:

   a. abstract description
   b. syntactic description
   c. behavioral description
   d. emotive description

   Answer: c   Key 1: A

22. Human communication is symbolic. Why?

   a. A particular word means the same thing to any two people.
   b. There are logical reasons why certain words stand for certain ideas.
   c. Words are arbitrary and open to individual interpretation.
   d. We are emotionally connected to others.

   Answer: c   Key 1: C

23. Syntactic rules determine:

    a.   the meaning of a particular symbol
    b.   the pronunciation of a particular symbol
    c.   the hierarchy of meaning in symbols
    d.   the sequence of a set of symbols

    Answer: d   Key 1: R

24. Which one of the following types of words gains its meaning by comparison?

    a.   equivocal
    b.   relative
    c.   emotive
    d.   abstract

    Answer: b   Key 1: R

25. A conclusion based on an interpretation of evidence is called a(an):

    a.   fact
    b.   opinion
    c.   inference
    d.   connotation

    Answer: c   Key 1: R

26. All of the following are examples of how women use language differently than men EXCEPT:

    a.   women ask more questions in mixed sex conversations
    b.   women interrupt others more frequently in mixed sex conversations
    c.   women use talk to maintain harmony
    d.   women use conversation to pursue social needs

    Answer: b   Key 1: C

27. A behavioral description describes behavior that is:

    a.   positive
    b.   negative
    c.   abstract
    d.   observable

    Answer: d   Key 1: R

28. Which of the following is valued most highly in communication by women in all-female talk?

    a.   humor
    b.   new ways to solve problems
    c.   empathy
    d.   rapid pace

    Answer: c   Key 1: C

Answer Key Code: R = Recall   C= Conceptual   A = Application   S = Synthesis

29. Which of the following is more typical of men in same-sex conversations?

    a. use of filler words to begin sentences
    b. questions
    c. justifiers
    d. personal pronouns

    Answer: a   Key 1: C

30. Cultures that value straight talk are said to be:

    a. empathic
    b. elaborate
    c. high context
    d. low context

    Answer: d   Key 1: R

31. Which of the following are types of evasive language?

    a. inferences
    b. euphemisms
    c. equivocation
    d. b and c

    Answer: d   Key 1: C

32. Which of the following statements would researchers classify as being the most powerfully

    expressed?

    a. "I guess I have a question."
    b. "Excuse me, but I have a question."
    c. "I think I have a question."
    d. "I have a question."

    Answer: d   Key 1: A

33. Linguistic relativism means that:

    a. the world view of a culture is shaped by the language its members speak
    b. the world view of a culture is reflected by the language its members speak
    c. language is determined by the physical structure of vocal apparatus of its speakers
    d. a & b

    Answer: d   Key 1: R

TRUE/FALSE

34. Gender and non-gender factors characterize the speech of men and women.

    Answer: T   Key 1: R
    There are instinctual differences and similarities among how men and women use language.

35. The type of accent you have can affect how people perceive your status.

    Answer: T   Key 1: R
    Several factors combine to create negative or positive impressions of status.

36. The relationship between a symbol and its referent is arbitrary.

    Answer: T   Key 1: R
    The triangle of meaning demonstrates that meaning is arbitrary and that it exists in the minds of the users.

37. Syntactic rules organize words for comprehension.

    Answer: T   Key 1: R
    Syntax deals with the structure of language.

38. When a stock trader refers to the "NASDAQ," that person is using jargon.

    Answer: T   Key 1: A
    Jargon is technical language used within a trade and often times the word is also an acronym.

39. Behavioral descriptions are high on the abstraction ladder.

    Answer: F   Key 1: R
    They are low on the ladder. More abstract terms are at the top of the ladder.

40. A language is a collection of symbols.

    Answer: T   Key 1: R
    Symbols make up a language.

41. In order to speak a language fluently, a speaker should be able to describe the rules that govern that language.

    Answer: F   Key 1: C
    Most people cannot articulate all the rules of language; most rules are learned unconsciously.

42. Semantic rules make communication possible.

    Answer: T   Key 1: C
    Without semantic rules we would each use symbols in unique ways and communication would be impossible.

43. "I'm kinda disappointed" is an example of an intensifier.

    Answer: F   Key 1: A
    This would be an example of a hedge.

44. A professional who wants to establish credibility by using unfamiliar words to an audience is using a strategy known as convergence.

    Answer: F   Key 1: C
    This would be known as divergence.

45. Relative language contains words that sound as if they're describing something when they are really expressing the speaker's attitude toward something.

    Answer: F   Key 1: R
    This describes emotive language.

46. "The climate in Portland is better than in Seattle." This is an example of a fact.

    Answer: F   Key 1: A
    This is a description of opinion statements.

Answer Key Code: R = Recall   C= Conceptual   A = Application   S = Synthesis

47. "He sticks to his guns—she's stubborn." This is an example of emotive language.

    Answer: T   Key 1: A
    This example is from the list of examples of emotive language.

48. Using the word "policeman" is a form of sexist language.

    Answer: T   Key 1: A
    The correct term would be police officer, because the position is not limited to males.

49. Recent changes in male and female roles are reflected in gender differences in choice of conversational topics.

    Answer: F   Key 1: C
    Research has shown that over years and changes within males and females roles, language patterns and conversational topics have remained consistent.

50. Social harmony is an important goal of speakers in a high context culture.

    Answer: T   Key 1: R
    These speakers use context to discover meanings.

51. Euphemisms are used to avoid clear communication.

    Answer: T   Key 1: R
    They are one type of evasive language.

52. When your friend asks your opinion on a paper that you think is poorly written and you reply, "You've chosen a really different topic," you are using equivocation.

    Answer: T   Key 1: A
    You are giving an indirect answer to be tactful.

53. Common names are likely to be viewed as more active and likeable than unusual names.

    Answer: T   Key 1: C
    Research shows this to be true.

54. When people adapt their vocabulary and rate of speaking to each other it is termed convergence.

    Answer: T   Key 1: R
    Convergence is conversational adaptation.

SHORT ANSWER

55. Give an example of the following language rules:

    - Phonological
    - Syntactic
    - Semantic
    - Pragmatic

    Answer: Key 1: A

56. Discuss how language might differ among high context cultures and low context cultures.

    Answer: Key 1: A

57. Attack or defend the statement "language shapes a person's perception of reality." Provide evidence from experts and from your own experience to support your position.

    Answer: Key 1: S

58. Explain and give an example of how overly abstract language can lead to stereotyping.

    Answer: Key 1: A

59. Discuss in detail several important characteristics of language.

    Answer: Key 1: C

60. Discuss in detail and provide examples of how language can be very powerful.

    Answer: Key 1: A

61. Explain why you think a course entitled "Home Economics for Boys" had a small enrollment, but a course entitled "Bachelor Living" attracted 120 students. Give an example of a course you've taken which either could attract more students by changing its name or one which you think was not accurately titled.

    Answer: Key 1: A

62. Imagine you work as a sales clerk at a local music store. Your friend holds the same position at a competitor's store. Your boss gives you the title "Customer Consultant." Your friend remains a clerk. Discuss what impact this new title might have on you and how it might result in differences between you and your friend.

    Answer: Key 1: A

63. Rewrite the following paragraph to make it nonsexist.

    Mankind has long been intrigued by the concept of time. Ever since the first cave dweller drew a picture of the moon on the cave wall for his wife to admire, he has been conscious of the seasons. It wasn't long before man-
    made objects were used to help keep track of time.

    Answer: Key 1: A

64. Change the following statements to reflect more speaker responsibility.

    1. It's too cold for a picnic.
    2. You make me mad when you act like that.
    3. That's an interesting plan, but it's too expensive.
    4. Do you really think that's wise?

    Answer: Key 1: A

65. What are the dangers in discussing gender differences in communication?

    Answer: Key 1: C

Answer Key Code: R = Recall   C = Conceptual   A = Application   S = Synthesis

66. The authors of your text claim that the power of language to shape attitudes influences how we perceive entire groups of people. Do you agree? Why or why not?

    Answer: Key 1: S

67. Give an example from your own experience in which you attempted to achieve linguistic convergence and one aimed at divergence.

    Answer: Key 1: A

68. Imagine you just met your sister's new boyfriend. You are not impressed. Write an equivocation you could use as a response to her question, "What do you think of him?"

    Answer: Key 1: A

69. Discuss some cultural factors that can shape the way we see and understand language.

    Answer: Key 1: A

70. Discuss the difference of how male and female conversational styles vary.

    Answer: Key 1: C

71. Discuss and provide examples of the difference between equivocation and euphemisms.

    Answer: Key 1: C

72. Discuss in detail the ways, according to your text, that certain types of language can cause problems.

    Answer: Key 1: A

MATCHING

73. Match each example with the appropriate language characteristic or problem.

    ____ I'm glad we found these inexpensive mugs.   A. overly abstract words

    ____ People say Frank is eccentric. I think he's   B. emotive words
    crazy.
                                                            C. equivocal words
    ____ That's an interesting hat you have.
                                                            D. relative words
    ____ College students are irresponsible.

    Answer: D, B, C, A   Key 1: A

74. Match the appropriate statement with the appropriate term.

    ____ Disclaimers   A. "I think we should…"

    ____ Tag questions   B. "I'm not very hungry."

    ____ Intensifiers   C. "I probably shouldn't say this but…"

    ____ Hedges   D. "It's about time, isn't it?"

    Answer: C, D, B, A   Key 1: R

75. Match the following language rule to the appropriate example.

____ "You look pretty today" interpreted different ways

____ Pronouncing "champagne"

____ Knowing which public restroom to walk into based on what's listed on the door

____ Saying "have you the cookies bought" or saying "have you bought the cookies"

A. Phonological

B. Semantic

C. Syntactic

D. Pragmatic

Answer: D, A, B, C   Key 1: A

OTHER

76. State one inference you could make based on each of the following facts.

a. Benny works full time and takes college classes.
b. Angela has a 3.7 GPA.
c. The population of Ocean City goes from 2,000 to 20,000 in summer.
d. The average temperature last month was 5 degrees below average.
e. Three of my friends read *Death on Campus* and said I'd like it.

Answer: Key 1: A

77. For each of the following sexist terms provide a non-sexist alternative.

Mankind   _____

Manhood   _____

Fireman   _____

Congressman   _____

Manpower   _____

Answer: Key 1: A

78. Identify the following as either a fact (F) or opinion (0).

____ The English language has too many rules.
____ Male and female conversational styles vary.
____ All words are symbols.
____ Ryan studies a lot of hours.
____ The authors of your textbook are Adler and Rodman.

Answer: 0, F, F, 0, F   Key 1: A

79. Place the correct phrase by the commonly used acronyms used in emails.

_____ Also known as
_____ Good for you
_____ Pretty darn quick
_____ Laughing out loud
_____ Need your opinion
_____ Got to go

Answer: AKA, GFY, PDQ, LOL, NYO, G2G Key 1: R

Answer Key Code: R = Recall   C= Conceptual   A = Application   S = Synthesis

CHAPTER 4 LISTENING

MULTIPLE CHOICE

1. _____ is the process in which sound waves strike the eardrum and cause vibrations that are transmitted to the brain.

   a. Hearing
   b. Listening
   c. Attending
   d. Understanding

   Answer: a   Key 1: R

2. _____ occurs when the brain interprets sound and gives meaning to the sound.

   a. Hearing
   b. Listening
   c. Attending
   d. Understanding

   Answer: b   Key 1: R

3. Which of the following is the act of paying attention to a signal?

   a. hearing
   b. listening
   c. attending
   d. understanding

   Answer: c   Key 1: R

4. Researchers have revealed that on average people remember about _____ of what they hear immediately after hearing it.

   a. 25%
   b. 50%
   c. 75%
   d. 100%

   Answer: b   Key 1: R

5. Listening is _____ while hearing is _____.

   a. passive/ active
   b. understanding/attending
   c. attending/ understanding
   d. active/ passive

   Answer: d   Key 1: R

6. John and Cynthia were on a date. During dinner John kept nodding his head as Cynthia was talking. However, John was really thinking about the game that he was missing while Cynthia was talking. Which type of faulty listening behavior was John having?

    a. pseudolistening
    b. selective listening
    c. defensive listening
    d. insulated listening

    Answer: a   Key 1: A

7. _____ listeners respond only to the parts of a speaker's remarks that interest them, rejecting everything else.

    a. Pseudo
    b. Selective
    c. Defensive
    d. Insulated

    Answer: b   Key 1: R

8. Adriana had been on the telephone for a while talking with a friend. When she came out of her room her mom had asked her what she had been doing. Adriana perceived this question as an invasion of her privacy. Which type of faulty listening behavior was Adriana guilty of?

    a. pseudo listening
    b. selective listening
    c. defensive listening
    d. insulated listening

    Answer: c   Key 1: A

9. _____ listeners listen carefully, but only because they are collecting information to attack what you have to say.

    a. Pseudo
    b. Selective
    c. Defensive
    d. Ambush

    Answer: d   Key 1: R

10. Chris is watching a football game. His wife tells him that she has to go out of town on business for the next weekend. He acts surprised to see her packing for her trip. Which type of faulty listening behavior was Chris suffering from?

    a. selective listening
    b. defensive listening
    c. pseudolistening
    d. insulated listening

    Answer: d   Key 1: A

Answer Key Code: R = Recall   C= Conceptual   A = Application   S = Synthesis

11. You are at a noisy wedding reception. Suddenly you notice your name mentioned in the group of people near the refreshment table. Which component of the listening process best describes what occurred in this situation?

    a. hearing
    b. attending
    c. understanding
    d. remembering

    Answer: b   Key 1: A

12. What is the relationship between the rate that people speak and the speed at which people listen?

    a. People can understand speech at rates much greater than people can speak.
    b. People can speak at rates much greater than they can understand speech.
    c. People speak and listen at approximately the same rate.
    d. No predictable relationship exists between speech rate and rate of understanding.

    Answer: a   Key 1: R

13. Which component of the listening process most makes it a transactional event?

    a. hearing
    b. attending
    c. understanding
    d. responding

    Answer: d   Key 1: R

14. _____ listeners do not look beyond the words and behavior to understand what the speaker has said. Instead, they tend to take a speaker's remarks at face value.

    a. Pseudo
    b. Insulated
    c. Insensitive
    d. Defensive

    Answer: c   Key 1: R

15. _____ try to turn the topic of conversations to themselves instead of showing interest in the speaker.

    a. Stage hogs
    b. Defensive listeners
    c. Insensitive listeners
    d. Selective listeners

    Answer: a   Key 1: R

16. All of the following are reasons for poor listening EXCEPT:

    a. message overload
    b. effort
    c. psychological noise
    d. message underload

    Answer: d   Key 1: R

17. The average listener can understand up to how many words per minute?

    a. 140
    b. 600
    c. 1,000
    d. 300

    Answer: b   Key 1: R

18. Anita had just received some upsetting news before her shift as a waitress at a restaurant. All evening long, Anita kept taking people's orders incorrectly. What reason did Anita have for this listening problem?

    a. effort
    b. message overload
    c. psychological noise
    d. physical noise

    Answer: c   Key 1: A

19. Even though speakers can speak 100 to 140 words per minute, listeners can understand up to 600 words per minute. This can cause what type of reason for poor listening?

    a. rapid thought
    b. effort
    c. physical noise
    d. hearing problems

    Answer: a   Key 1: R

20. During class, many students were having difficulty listening to the lecture because it was very warm and stuffy inside the classroom. What was the reason for the distraction?

    a. lack of effort
    b. psychological noise
    c. physical noise
    d. hearing problems

    Answer: c   Key 1: A

21. _____ listening style is valuable when the goal is to evaluate the quality of ideas and when the value in looking at issues from a wide range of perspectives.

    a. People-oriented
    b. Content-oriented
    c. Action-oriented
    d. Time-oriented

    Answer: b   Key 1: R

22. _____ listening is the approach to take when you want to understand another person.

    a. Persuasive
    b. Informational
    c. Content-oriented
    d. Action-oriented

    Answer: b   Key 1: R

Answer Key Code: R = Recall   C= Conceptual   A = Application   S = Synthesis

23. All of the following are ways to become a more effective informational listener EXCEPT:

    a. separate the message from the speaker
    b. look for specific points
    c. be opportunistic
    d. look for key ideas

    Answer: b   Key 1: R

24. All of the following are examples of counterfeit questions EXCEPT:

    a. questions that paraphrase the speaker's statement
    b. questions that make statements
    c. questions that carry hidden agendas
    d. questions that are based on unchecked assumptions

    Answer: a   Key 1: R

25. All of the following are guidelines for critical listening EXCEPT:

    a. listen for information before evaluating
    b. examine the speaker's evidence and reasoning
    c. evaluate the speaker's speaking style
    d. evaluate the speakers' credibility

    Answer: c   Key 1: R

26. When examining the speaker's evidence and reasoning, you should ask all of the following questions EXCEPT:

    a. Is the evidence recent enough?
    b. Is the evidence from a reliable source?
    c. Is enough evidence presented?
    d. Is the evidence from a well-known person?

    Answer: d   Key 1: R

27. Before offering advice you need to make sure all of the following conditions are present EXCEPT:

    a. being confident that the advice is correct
    b. being certain the receiver will not blame himself or herself
    c. asking yourself whether the person seeking your advice seems willing to accept it
    d. delivering your advice supportively

    Answer: b   Key 1: R

28. Alicia listens intently to student debates in class, but often finds herself voting for the people she likes best rather than the team with the best information. Alicia most likely has a listening style that is

    a. action-oriented
    b. people-oriented
    c. time-oriented
    d. content-oriented

    Answer: b   Key 1: A

29. In a question and answer period a speaker responded to a question saying, "If I understood your question correctly, you are asking how I interpret the legal battle. Am I correct?" This speaker's response is an example of:

    a. paraphrasing
    b. evasion of the question
    c. an open question
    d. passive listening

    Answer: a   Key 1: A

30. Shaniqua was having difficulty deciding which university she wanted to attend. She was accepted to three different universities across the county. Maria listened intently trying to help Shaniqua solve her dilemma. What type of listening was Maria using?

    a. informative
    b. evaluative
    c. empathic
    d. active

    Answer: c   Key 1: A

31. _____ involves using silences and brief statements of encouragement to draw others out, and in so doing to help them solve their own problems.

    a. Paraphrasing
    b. Prompting
    c. Advising
    d. Supporting

    Answer: b   Key 1: R

32. "Let me try to explain it to him" is an example of:

    a. paraphrasing
    b. prompting
    c. advising
    d. supporting

    Answer: d   Key 1: R

TRUE/FALSE

33. Listening and hearing are the same thing.

    Answer: F   Key 1: R
    Hearing is the physical portion of listening.

34. People should try to listen to everything in all situations.

    Answer: F   Key 1: R
    People couldn't tolerate the "message overload" of constant good listening.

35. One valuable type of verbal feedback is the use of questions.

    Answer: T   Key 1: R
    Questions can gather additional information about the speaker's message, and assist the speaker in understanding your reaction.

Answer Key Code: R = Recall   C= Conceptual   A = Application   S = Synthesis

36. Understanding often depends on the ability to organize the information we hear into recognizable form.

    Answer: T   Key 1: R
    Understanding includes putting what we hear into a meaningful structure.

37. While people may speak differently from one culture to the next, the process of listening remains the same across cultures.

    Answer: F   Key 1: R
    Research suggests that young adults from different cultures often have different listening styles.

38. When taking notes, your goal is to get as close to the word-for-word original message of a speaker as possible.

    Answer: F   Key 1: R
    Write down what you will need to remember since writing a transcript will be impossible.

39. When you are listening to a salesperson list the reasons you should buy a particular car, you are doing critical listening.

    Answer: T   Key 1: A
    Critical or evaluative listening involves testing ideas for acceptance or rejection.

40. Attending is the process of making sense of a message.

    Answer: F   Key 1: R
    This is the definition of understanding. Attending is the act of paying attention to a signal.

41. Understanding is the act of paying attention to a signal.

    Answer: F   Key 1: R
    This is the definition of attending. Understanding is the process of making sense of a message.

42. The final step in the listening process in remembering.

    Answer: T   Key 1: R
    Remember is the final process in interpreting what was just heard.

43. Studies have proven that the more children watch television, the more their attention spans are shortened because of the rapid-fire visual images.

    Answer: T   Key 1: R
    Study mentioned in text states that it is not due to the type of programming but the rapid-fired visual images is what causes the loss of attention span. The study also shows that those who watch more have increased loss of attention.

44. The residual message is the part of the message that we actually remember.

    Answer: T   Key 1: R
    The residual message is a small fraction of what we hear, and is the long term of what we remember.

45. Research suggests that children listen more poorly than adults.

    Answer: F   Key 1: R
    Actually, results show the opposite; the older we get, the worse we become at listening.

46. "If I don't interrupt them, I'll never get to say my idea" is an example of a faulty assumption.

    Answer: T   Key 1: R
    Often, individuals look at communication as a competition.

47. The goal of informational listening is to judge the quality of a message in order to decide whether to accept or reject it.

    Answer: F   Key 1: R
    This is the definition of critical listening.

48. Empathetic listening is the approach to use when others seek help for personal dilemmas.

    Answer: T   Key 1: R
    This is part of the definition of empathetic listening

49. In a judging response, the listener offers an interpretation of a speaker's message.

    Answer: F   Key 1: R
    This is the definition of analyzing. Judging evaluates the sender's thoughts or behaviors in some way.

50. As a group, men are more likely than women to give supportive responses when presented with another person's problem.

    Answer: F   Key 1: R
    The opposite is true. Men tend to respond to others' problems by offering advice or by diverting the topic.

SHORT ANSWER

51. Your text cites reasons for poor listening. Explain how four of them might have applied to your listening and to the oral directions given for this exam.

    Answer: Key 1: A

52. In informational listening, what is the effect of premature judgment or argument? Discuss in detail.

    Answer: Key 1: S

53. What factors determine to what we attend? Give an example of something you heard to which you attended and how these factors caused you to pay attention.

    Answer: Key 1: A

54. List and discuss the four types of listening styles. Provide examples of when each style would be most appropriately used.

    Answer: Key 1: A

55. Discuss the implications of the Chinese characters for "to listen." How do the four elements relate to what you have learned about listening?

    Answer: Key 1: S

56. Discuss in detail the differences between hearing and listening. Provide examples of each.

    Answer: Key 1: A

Answer Key Code: R = Recall   C= Conceptual   A = Application   S = Synthesis

57. List and describe two approaches suggested by your text that can help you become a better listener. Provide examples for each.

    Answer: Key 1: A

58. Why is it probable that people will hear the same message in different ways? Provide examples.

    Answer: Key 1: A

59. List and describe at least three types of faulty listening behaviors, and provide personal examples of when you have suffered from each.

    Answer: Key 1: A

60. Think of three recent incidents when trying to understand the other person would have been the most appropriate style of listening. Then think of three different situations when an evaluative approach would have been the most appropriate way to listen. Based on your conclusions, develop a set of guidelines describing when it is best to listen purely for information, and then describe the circumstances when it is more appropriate to listen evaluatively.

    Answer: Key 1: A (comes directly from the text as an exercise)

CHAPTER 5 NONVERBAL COMMUNICATION

MULTIPLE CHOICE

1. All of the following are important characteristics of nonverbal communication EXCEPT:

    a. nonverbal communication is always present when people encounter one another
    b. nonverbal communication has great value in conveying information about others intentionally and unintentionally
    c. nonverbal communication is useful in suggesting how others feel about you and the relationship
    d. nonverbal communication is less ambiguous than verbal communication

    Answer: d   Key 1: R

2. All of the following are examples of nonverbal communication in relational context EXCEPT:

    a. yawning during a conversation with a friend
    b. smiling a lot at a party
    c. discussing last night's party
    d. patting your friend on the back

    Answer: c   Key 1: A

3. The study of the way people and animals use space is called:

    a. paralanguage
    b. proxemics
    c. pixation
    d. kinesics

    Answer: b   Key 1: R

4. Using words such as "uh uh" and "I see" or nodding your head in agreement are examples of using which function of nonverbal communication?

    a. substituting
    b. regulating
    c. accepting
    d. contradicting

    Answer: b   Key 1: A

5. Carla and Jorge made plans to have a quiet weekend in their apartment. Promptly at 9 p.m. Saturday night, Carla's parents arrive for a surprise weekend visit. Startled, Carla stares at her parents, and says in a monotone, "Hi, it's sure great to see you." This is an example of which function of nonverbal communication?

    a. substituting
    b. regulating
    c. accenting
    d. contradicting

    Answer: d   Key 1: A

Answer Key Code: R = Recall   C= Conceptual   A = Application   S = Synthesis

6. Hall identifies four main "distance zones" which many North Americans use for their relationships. Which is the most common spacing for two persons who work together in an office but who do not know each other well at all?

    a. intimate
    b. public
    c. social
    d. personal

    Answer: c   Key 1: C

7. All of the following are functions of nonverbal communication EXCEPT:

    a. nonverbal communication can repeat, complement, and accent spoken words
    b. nonverbal communication can sometimes be substituted for speech
    c. nonverbal communication can regulate spoken conversation
    d. nonverbal communication cannot contradict spoken words

    Answer: d   Key 1: R

8. Artifacts and appearance can most effectively communicate which of the following:

    a. emotional state of mind of that moment
    b. intelligence
    c. attitude towards any given subject
    d. status

    Answer: d   Key 1: R

9. Public distance is described in your text as:

    a. 0 to 18 inches
    b. 18 inches to 4 feet
    c. 4 feet to 12 feet
    d. 12 feet and beyond

    Answer: d   Key 1: R

10. Which nonverbal behavior is least likely to be misinterpreted cross-culturally?

    a. a direct gaze at another person
    b. the "okay" gesture made by joining thumb and forefinger to form a circle
    c. maintaining "social distance" while conducting business
    d. a smile

    Answer: d   Key 1: C

11. All of the following are typically more female nonverbal characteristics than male EXCEPT:

    a. women are more vocally expressive than men with conversational partners
    b. women are more likely to lean forward in conversations than men
    c. women interact at closer distances than men in same sex conversations
    d. women are more likely to face conversational partners head on

    Answer: b   Key 1: C

12. All of the following are typically more male nonverbal characteristics than female EXCEPT:

    a. men typically use more expansive gestures than women
    b. men express less facial expressions than women
    c. men are more vocally more expressive than women
    d. men typically stand at an angle rather than face conversational partners head on

    Answer: c   Key 1: C

13. Nonverbal sensitivity is also defined as:

    a. affect blends
    b. behavioral manipulators
    c. identity management
    d. emotional intelligence

    Answer: d   Key 1: R

14. When you say, "The margin should be one inch," and hold your thumb and index finger one inch apart, you are using the nonverbal function of:

    a. repeating
    b. substituting
    c. complementing
    d. accenting

    Answer: a   Key 1: A

15. Julio asked Dolores how her day at work was. She answered him by shrugging her shoulders. This is an example of using which of the following functions of nonverbal communication?

    a. repeating
    b. substituting
    c. complementing
    d. accenting

    Answer: b   Key 1: A

16. All of the following are nonverbal clues that indicate deception EXCEPT:

    a. raising vocal pitch
    b. less shifting in posture
    c. blinking eyes more rapidly
    d. stammering, stuttering, or having false starts

    Answer: b   Key 1: R

17. Adriana always sits next to the window in French class. One day Andrew sits in the seat that is next to the window. Adriana gets upset with Andrew for taking the seat that she normally sits in. Which nonverbal concept is this situation dealing with?

    a. kinesics
    b. proxemics
    c. environment
    d. territory

    Answer: d   Key 1: A

Answer Key Code: R = Recall   C= Conceptual   A = Application   S = Synthesis

18. The study of body movement, gesture, and posture is called:

    a. proxemics
    b. kinesics
    c. artifacts
    d. single channels

    Answer: b   Key 1: R

19. Jamie was awakened by her roommate at 5:30 am when she did not have to wake up until 8:00 am. Jamie blurted to her roommate, "Thanks for waking me up!" This is an example of using:

    a. emotional intelligence
    b. disfluencies
    c. vocal echoes
    d. paralanguage

    Answer: d   Key 1: A

20. All of the following are examples of manipulators EXCEPT:

    a. playing with an earlobe
    b. picking at your fingernails
    c. winking at a friend
    d. twirling a strand of hair

    Answer: c   Key 1: A

21. Skilled communicators adapting their behavior to those from other cultures during a conversation is called:

    a. nonverbal convergence
    b. nonverbal divergence
    c. sympathetic responsiveness
    d. cultural diversity

    Answer: a   Key 1: R

22. Touch is also known as:

    a. haptics
    b. kinesics
    c. proxemics
    d. chronemics

    Answer: a   Key 1: R

23. _____ are deliberate nonverbal behaviors that have precise meanings known to everyone within a cultural group.

    a. Illustrators
    b. Identifiers
    c. Manipulators
    d. Emblems

    Answer: d   Key 1: R

24. _____ are nonverbal behaviors that accompany and support spoken words.

   a. Illustrators
   b. Identifiers
   c. Manipulators
   d. Emblems

   Answer: a   Key 1: R

25. _____ are probably the most powerful in communicating nonverbal messages.

   a. Posture and gestures
   b. Face and eyes
   c. Voice and eyes
   d. Touch and face

   Answer: b   Key 1: R

26. _____ is/are the combination of two or more expressions showing different emotions.

   a. Identify management
   b. Behavioral manipulators
   c. Affect blends
   d. Emotional Intelligence

   Answer: c   Key 1: R

TRUE/FALSE

27. Despite cultural differences, some nonverbal behaviors are universal.

   Answer: T   Key 1: R
   The book mentions smiles and laughter as examples.

28. Career counselors who use "posture echoes" to copy their clients' positions would be rated as less empathic than those who did not.

   Answer: F   Key 1: C
   They would be rated more favorably.

29. Saying something sarcastically is an example of paralanguage.

   Answer: T   Key 1: R
   It is one instance in which both emphasis and tone of voice help change a statement's meaning to the opposite of its verbal message.

30. One cannot not communicate.

   Answer: T   Key 1: R
   Because of the nature of nonverbal communication, all behaviors, intentional or unintentional, are potentially communicative.

31. Culture shapes many nonverbal practices.

   Answer: T   Key 1: R
   Nonverbal codes vary from one culture to another.

Answer Key Code: R = Recall   C= Conceptual   A = Application   S = Synthesis

32. The face can express six basic emotions which seem to be recognizable in all cultures.

Answer: T   Key 1: R
Ekman and Friesen's research supports this claim.

33. Personal space is a stationary bubble; territoriality is a movable bubble.

Answer: F   Key 1: R
These are exactly the opposite; territoriality is a stationary type of bubble while personal space is movable.

34. Vocal communication and verbal communication are synonymous.

Answer: F   Key 1: R
Vocal means by mouth, verbal means with words.

35. When a receiver observes an inconsistency between verbal and nonverbal messages, the verbal message carries more weight.

Answer: F   Key 1: C
The unspoken message is more likely to be believed.

36. Nonverbal behaviors often contribute more to the relational message than to the content message of any given communication.

Answer: T   Key 1: C
Nonverbal communication serves a common series of social functions, such as identity management, relational definition, and emotional expression.

37. Women seem to be better at decoding nonverbal messages than men.

Answer: T   Key 1: C
Over 95 per cent of the studies showed women to be more accurate.

38. While we can't control all nonverbal behaviors, most nonverbal messages are conscious.

Answer: F   Key 1: R
Most nonverbal messages are unconscious.

39. Emblems are nonverbal behaviors that accompany and support spoken words.

Answer: F   Key 1: R
That description fits illustrators.

40. Illustrators substitute for verbal messages.

Answer: F   Key 1: R
That description fits emblems.

41. Nonverbal behaviors that contradict the speaker's verbal message are usually unintentional and should be avoided if possible.

Answer: F   Key 1: C
Deliberately sending mixed messages can be an effective way of handling difficult communication situations.

42. Clothing is more important in the early stages of a relationship than in the later stages.

Answer: T   Key 1: C
It is most important to first impressions.

43. When we substitute nonverbal for verbal symbols we sometimes make the message more ambiguous.

    Answer: T   Key 1: C
    At time we take advantage of the vague nature of nonverbal communication.

44. Research shows that men are more accurate at detecting lying than women.

    Answer: F   Key 1: C
    Women are better at this.

45. People who speak more slowly are judged as having more conversation control than fast talkers.

    Answer: T   Key 1: R
    This was demonstrated in the recent research of Tusing and Dillard.

46. Since deceivers make more speech errors than truth-tellers, it is safe to suspect that people who are tongue-tied, fidgeting, and blinking a lot are not telling the truth.

    Answer: F   Key 1: A
    While it is true that deceivers make more speech errors, concluding that such errors indicate deceit is incorrect.

47. Communication scholars agree that biological factors have more influence than social factors in shaping how men and women behave.

    Answer: F   Key 1: C
    It's the complete opposite.

48. Nonverbal communication is the oral and nonoral messages expressed by other than linguistic means.

    Answer: T   Key 1: R
    This is the text's definition of nonverbal communication.

49. Communicating with disfluencies is a characteristic of paralanguage.

    Answer: T   Key 1: R
    Tone of voice, pitch, volume, length of pause, and disfluencies are all part of paralanguage.

50. Touch can increase a child's mental functioning as well as physical health.

    Answer: T   Key 1: C
    The text explains the importance of touch within communication.

51. Culture shapes many nonverbal practices.

    Answer: T   Key 1: C
    Not all nonverbal cues are universal; many nonverbal behaviors are bound by culture.

52. Personal distance begins with skin contact and ranges out to about eighteen inches.

    Answer: F   Key 1: R
    Personal distance ranges from 18 inches to 4 feet. Intimate contact begins with skin and ranges to 18 inches.

SHORT ANSWER

53. List five types of nonverbal communication. Explain how each type can aid in successful communication.

    Answer: Key 1: A

            Answer Key Code: R = Recall   C= Conceptual   A = Application   S = Synthesis

54. Researchers of touch have suggested a number of factors that determine the intensity of a message. Use four of the eight factors given in your text to analyze a specific example of touch in terms of its intensity.

    Answer: Key 1: A

55. Differentiate between Hall's concept of personal space and the concept of territoriality. Note similarities and differences.

    Answer: Key 1: S

56. Provide three examples of accenting your instructor has used when teaching in class. Explain why each of these is an example of accenting.

    Answer: Key 1: A

57. Describe a situation in which the ambiguity of nonverbal communication caused you difficulty.

    Answer: Key 1: A

58. What does the author mean in the statement that nonverbal communication is relational? Provide detailed support and examples to back your claims.

    Answer: Key 1: A

59. Explain how gender affects nonverbal communication. Provide specific examples of how men and women differ in their nonverbal communication.

    Answer: Key 1: A

60. List three examples of how culture affects nonverbal communication. Provide specific examples of nonverbal behavior that could be misinterpreted.

    Answer: Key 1: A

61. How is nonverbal sensitivity a major part of emotional intelligence? Explain the connection between spoken language and nonverbal dimensions.

    Answer: Key 1: A

62. What is NVLD? How cans this effect successful transmition of nonverbal communication? Be specific.

    Answer: Key 1: A

MATCHING

63. Match the term with the definition.

    ____ The study of the use of space   A. Chronemics

    ____ The study of the use and structure of   B. Kinesics
         time
                                                     C. Paralanguage
    ____ The study of body movements
                                                     D. Proxemics
    ____ Nonverbal, vocal messages

    Answer: D, A, B, C   Key 1: R

64. Match the descriptions with the appropriate type of space use described by Hall.

____ An employer behind a desk talks with an employee seated in front of the desk.

____ A child sits on your lap.

____ A teacher lectures to a large class.

____ Couples stand in line at a movie theater.

A. intimate distance

B. personal distance

C. social distance

D. public distance

Answer: C, A, D, B   Key 1: A

65. Match the behavioral example with the function of nonverbal communication. Each function may be used once, more than once, or not at all.

____ Pointing your finger at someone while saying "It was all your fault!"

____ Snapping your fingers when you state "I've got it!"

____ Shrugging your shoulders when asked a question rather than replying verbally

____ Giving instructions on how to get to the drugstore and pointing in the direction with your hands

____ Yelling "No, I'm not angry!"

____ Indicating that you're yielding the floor by raising your vocal intonation pattern

A. repeating

B. substituting

C. complementing

D. accenting

E. regulating

F. contradicting

Answer: D, C, B, A, F, E,   Key 1: A

OTHER

66. Fill in the correct answer in each box.

	Verbal Communication	*Nonverbal Communication*
Complexity	_____	_____
Flow	_____	_____
Clarity	_____	_____
Impact	_____	_____
Intenationality	_____	_____

A. One dimension
B. Multiple dimensions
C. Usually deliberate
D. Often unintentional
E. Less subject to misinterpretation
F. More ambiguous
G. Intermittent
H. Continuous
I. Has less impact when verbal and nonverbal cues are contradictory
J. Has stronger impact when verbal and nonverbal cues are contradictory

Answer: Verbal: A, G, E, I, C Nonverbal: B, H, F, J, D   Key 1: R

Answer Key Code: R = Recall   C= Conceptual   A = Application   S = Synthesis

CHAPTER 6 UNDERSTANDING INTERPERSONAL RELATIONSHIPS

MULTIPLE CHOICE

1. _____ occurs when people treat one another as unique individuals, regardless of the context in which the interaction occurs or the number of people involved.

   a. Qualitatively impersonal communication
   b. Qualitatively interpersonal communication
   c. Quantitatively interpersonal communication
   d. Quantitatively impersonal communication

   Answer: b   Key 1: R

2. _____ is the degree to which people like or appreciate one another.

   a. Affinity
   b. Respect
   c. Immediacy
   d. Control

   Answer: a   Key 1: R

3. _____ describes the degree of interest and attraction we feel toward and communicate to others.

   a. Affinity
   b. Respect
   c. Immediacy
   d. Control

   Answer: c   Key 1: R

4. _____ is the degree to which we admire others and hold them in esteem.

   a. Affinity
   b. Respect
   c. Immediacy
   d. Control

   Answer: b

5. _____ is the amount of influence communicators seek.

   a. Affinity
   b. Respect
   c. Immediacy
   d. Control

   Answer: d   Key 1: R

6. All of the following are qualities of intimacy EXCEPT:

   a. Physiological
   b. Physical
   c. Intellectual
   d. Emotional

   Answer: a   Key 1: R

7. _____ to _____ relationships have the highest disclosure rate.

   a. Male to male
   b. Male to female
   c. Female to female
   d. Female to male

   Answer: c   Key 1: R

8. Which culture expects more intimacy from their friendships?

   a. Hispanic
   b. Japanese
   c. American
   d. British

   Answer: b   Key 1: R

9. In the developmental model, which stage does the conversation develop as people get acquainted by making "small talk?"

   a. initiating stage
   b. experimenting stage
   c. intensifying stage
   d. integrating stage

   Answer: b   Key 1: R

10. Asif was having difficulty conversing with Janie in person. He found that making contact with her via the Internet helpful in starting a conversation with her. According to the developmental model, which stage is Asif at?

    a. initiating stage
    b. intensifying stage
    c. integrating stage
    d. bonding stage

    Answer: a   Key 1: A

11. All of the following are strategies for managing dialectical tensions EXCEPT:

    a. Admittance
    b. Denial
    c. Segmentation
    d. Alternation

    Answer: a   Key 1: R

Answer Key Code: R = Recall   C= Conceptual   A = Application   S = Synthesis

12. According to Richard Conville, relationships constantly change, evolving as a cycle in which partners move through a series of stages, returning to ones they previously encountered. Which of the following is the correct cycle of stages?

    a. disintegration, resynthesis, alienation, security
    b. security, alienation, disintegration, resynthesis
    c. alienation, security, resynthesis, disintegration
    d. security, disintegration, alienation, resynthesis

    Answer: d   Key 1: R

13. _____ is the process of deliberately revealing information about oneself that is significant and that would not be normally known by others.

    a. Self discovery
    b. Self disclosure
    c. Self dialect
    d. Self analysis

    Answer: b   Key 1: R

14. Patrice is giving a speech in front of her class. She keeps shifting nervously back and forth. Patrice is not aware of her shifting but her classmates are. According to Johari's Window, which window or area would this fall under?

    a. the open area
    b. the hidden area
    c. the blind area
    d. the unknown area

    Answer: c   Key 1: R

15. All of the following are characteristics of effective self-disclosure EXCEPT:

    a. Self-disclosure is influenced by culture
    b. Self-disclosure usually occurs in dyads
    c. Self-disclosure occurs at once
    d. Self-disclosure is usually symmetrical

    Answer: c   Key 1: R

16. _____ has two or more equally plausible meanings.

    a. Equivocal language
    b. Denotative language
    c. Altruistic language
    d. Ambiguous language

    Answer: a   Key 1: R

17. In which of the following countries is social harmony valued over truthfulness?

    a. America
    b. Germany
    c. Japan
    d. Great Britain

    Answer: c   Key 1: R

18. According to Altman and Taylor, the degree of intimacy in a relationship depends on the:

    a. depth of information shared
    b. breadth of information shared
    c. depth and breadth of information shared
    d. The nature of the information shared does not affect intimacy.

    Answer: c   Key 1: R

19. Your partner tells you, "You look nice in that outfit." The implication that he or she likes you and is proud of the way you look is the _____ of the message.

    a. content
    b. relational dimension
    c. dialectical intensifier
    d. equivocation

    Answer: b   Key 1: A

20. Recent research shows that women often build friendships through shared positive feelings, whereas men often build friendships through:

    a. metacommunication
    b. catharsis
    c. impression management
    d. shared activities

    Answer: d   Key 1: R

21. Which of the following is an example of metacommunication?

    a. "I hate it when you yell at me."
    b. "Let's go to the movies."
    c. "Please bring me a paper."
    d. "Stop doing that!"

    Answer: a   Key 1: A

22. Which type of gender related self-disclosure tends to produce the greatest amount and depth of information exchanged?

    a. female to female
    b. male to female
    c. male to male
    d. none of the above

    Answer: a   Key 1: R

Answer Key Code: R = Recall   C= Conceptual   A = Application   S = Synthesis

23. If you tell a friend you don't have any money to lend him when in reality you do, you're demonstrating which of the "reasons for lying?"

    a. presenting a competent image
    b. increasing social desirability
    c. protecting resources
    d. acquiring resources

    Answer: c   Key 1: R

24. The characteristic of the relationship development model that states movement is always to a new place refers to the concept of communication as:

    a. dynamic
    b. fulfilling
    c. irreversible
    d. manageable

    Answer: c   Key 1: R

25. Which of the following is NOT one of the guidelines for self-disclosure:

    a. Is the other person important to you?
    b. Will the effect be constructive?
    c. Will the self-disclosure increase your power?
    d. Is the disclosure reciprocated?

    Answer: c   Key 1: R

TRUE/FALSE

26. Mark Knapp's model of relationship stages is a dialectical model.

    Answer: F   Key 1: R
    Knapp's model is a developmental one.

27. Self-disclosure is usually reciprocal.

    Answer: T   Key 1: R
    Research demonstrates that as one person self-discloses, the other person is likely to do the same.

28. The results of self-disclosure are nearly all positive in terms of helping the relationship.

    Answer: F   Key 1: R
    Self-disclosure can result in rejection, alienation, loss of control, and hurt to others.

29. Relational messages are usually expressed nonverbally.

    Answer: T   Key 1: R
    They are often never discussed and we may not even be conscious of them.

30. The higher your level of self-disclosure, the more you are apt to be liked.

    Answer: F   Key 1: R
    The self-disclosure must be appropriate.

31. Explicitness is important in self-disclosure.

    Answer: T   Key 1: R
    It is important that your self-disclosure be clear and understandable.

32. Catharsis is listed in the text as one of the good reasons for disclosing family secrets.

    Answer: F   Key 1: R
    Disclosure of family secrets requires even more stringent criteria than simple self-disclosure. Their criteria include permission, urgency, and relational security, among others.

33. In general, as the amount of information partners know about each other increases, so does their attraction.

    Answer: T   Key 1: R
    We generally like people better as we get to know them.

34. Research shows that emotional expression is the only way to develop close relationships.

    Answer: F   Key 1: R
    Men often grow close to one another by doing things together.

35. The ideal self-disclosure between partners in an intimate relationship is total, sharing of everything.

    Answer: F   Key 1: R
    Even in close relationships it is not necessarily advisable to tell all. It is usually better to focus on "here and now" as opposed to "there and then."

36. Affinity is the degree of interest and attraction we feel toward and communicate to others.

    Answer: F   Key 1: R
    Affinity is the degree to which people like or appreciate one another.

37. Research confirms that mediated communication can enhance the quantity and quality of interpersonal communication.

    Answer: T   Key 1: R
    While some surveys have disconfirming results, the current research supports that email and other mediums serve as a useful tool in maintaining interpersonal relationships.

38. Most research shows that men are more willing to share their thoughts and feelings than women.

    Answer: F   Key 1: R
    Actually most research indicates the opposite is true.

39. Although both sexes are equally likely to reveal negative information, men are less likely to share positive feelings.

    Answer: T   Key 1: R
    Women typically disclose more than men, and are more comfortable discussing items that bother them more.

40. People from the United States are less likely to self-disclose than other countries.

    Answer: F   Key 1: R
    Actually people from US disclose more than most people from other countries.

Answer Key Code: R = Recall   C= Conceptual   A = Application   S = Synthesis

41. One of the least functional strategies for managing dialectical tension is denial.

    Answer: T   Key 1: R
    People will deny that there are problems to avoid conflict or tension, but it often perpetuates the problem.

42. Self-disclosure must be deliberate and significant.

    Answer: T   Key 1: R
    According to the text, accidentally disclosing trivial information does not constitute self-disclosure because the information must be significant.

43. With strangers, reciprocity becomes the most common reason for disclosing.

    Answer: T   Key 1: R
    People offer information in hopes that the other person will disclose as well, thus allowing us to learn more about them.

44. Jenae had an argument with her husband on the phone before she had to give a sales presentation to a group of clients. This caused her to be mentally disorganized and not give a good presentation. None of her co-workers knew why she was upset. According to Johari's Window this would be in Janae's blind area.

    Answer: F   Key 1: A
    This would actually be in her hidden area.

45. Effective self-disclosure occurs incrementally.

    Answer: T   Key 1: R
    If you disclose too much too soon to a person, it can alter the communication encounter because effective disclosure relies on reciprocity.

46. Altruistic lies are lies we tell that are intended to be helpful or spare others feelings for the sake of maintaining harmony.

    Answer: T   Key 1: R
    Altruistic lies are also known as "white lies."

47. The demand for honesty is contextual.

    Answer: T   Key 1: R
    In some countries lying is expected in order to keep social harmony. It depends on what the truth concerns.

48. Equivocal language has one distinct meaning.

    Answer: F   Key 1: R
    Equivocal language has two or more equally plausible meanings.

49. Hints are less direct than equivocal language.

    Answer: F   Key 1: R
    Hints are actually more direct.

50. In interpersonal relationships, the relational part of the message is the most important.

    Answer: F   Key 1: R
    In interpersonal relationships there are content and relational messages both of which are important within successful communication.

SHORT ANSWER

51. Explain how an obsession with intimacy can lead to <u>less</u> satisfying relationships.

    Answer: Key 1: C

52. Select an interpersonal relationship and describe it in terms of the qualities your text offers as those distinguishing personal from less personal relationships.

    Answer: Key 1: A

53. List and define the two benefits your text claims can result from sending a positive piece of metacommunication?

    Answer: Key 1: R

54. Using the Altman/Taylor theory of relationship development and social penetration, describe the breadth and depth factors that might be present in the following two relationships:

    casual acquaintances
    husband/wife

    Answer: Key 1: R

55. According to your text, there are guidelines for appropriate self-disclosure. List and discuss four of the guidelines in detail. Provide examples for each.

    Answer: Key 1: R

56. Psychologist George Bach claims that all of us have a psychological "belt line." Describe what this means and give an example of the belt line of someone you know.

    Answer: Key 1: S

57. Describe a piece of self-disclosure from your personal experience. Explain how it fits your authors' three requirements for self-disclosure.

    Answer: Key 1: A

58. Describe the communication pattern of a couple who is in the integrating stage of a relationship.

    Answer: Key 1: A

59. Your authors present seven questions you should ask in order to determine the appropriateness of self-disclosure. List and explain three of them.

    Answer: Key 1: R

60. Define and provide examples of perception checking and relational messages.

    Answer: Key 1: A

61. Desmond Morris suggests three stages of interpersonal relationships: "Hold me tight," "Put me down," and "Leave me alone." Relate these to what you know about the development of interpersonal relationships.

    Answer: Key 1: S

Answer Key Code: R = Recall   C= Conceptual   A = Application   S = Synthesis

62. What are the four areas to Johari's Window? Provide examples of each area.

    Answer: Key 1: A

MATCHING

63. Match the researcher with the concept for which he/she is known.

    ____ George Bach   A. 10 stages of relationship development

    ____ Mark Knapp   B. psychological belt line

    ____ Sissela Bok   C. "hold me tight"

    ____ Altman and Taylor   D. model of social penetration

    ____ Desmond Morris   E. ethics of deception

    Answer: B, A, E, D, C   Key 1: R

OTHER

64. Identify the ten stages of a relationship listed below according to the sequence in which they are said to occur.

    ____ stagnating

    ____ bonding

    ____ intensifying

    ____ terminating

    ____ experimenting

    ____ avoiding

    ____ initiating

    ____ differentiating

    ____ circumscribing

    ____ integrating

    Answer: 8, 5, 3, 10, 2, 9, 1, 6, 7, 4   Key 1: R

CHAPTER 7 IMPROVING INTERPERSONAL RELATIONSHIPS

MULTIPLE CHOICE

1. _____ refers to the emotional tone of a relationship.

   a. Communication climate
   b. Relational component
   c. Emotional climate
   d. Interpersonal component

   Answer: a   Key 1: R

2. All of the following are the positive levels of confirming communication EXCEPT:

   a. recognition
   b. acknowledgement
   c. endorsement
   d. inattention

   Answer: d   Key 1: R

3. All of the following are distancing tactics EXCEPT:

   a. humoring
   b. endorsement
   c. deception
   d. discounting

   Answer: b   Key 1: R

4. _____ is displaying verbal or nonverbal clues that minimize interest, closeness or availability.

   a. Discounting
   b. Deception
   c. Nonimmediacy
   d. Restraint

   Answer: c   Key 1: R

5. According to the Gibb categories, _____ is often described as "You Language."

   a. evaluative language
   b. control language
   c. certainty language
   d. superiority language

   Answer: a   Key 1: R

6. According to the Gibb categories, _____ communication focuses on the speaker's thoughts and feelings instead of judging the listener.

   a. evaluative
   b. certainty
   c. descriptive
   d. neutral

   Answer: c   Key 1: R

Answer Key Code: R = Recall   C= Conceptual   A = Application   S = Synthesis

7. In _____ orientation, communicators focus on finding a solution that satisfies both their needs and those of the others involved.

    a. spiral
    b. problem
    c. control
    d. conflict

    Answer: b   Key 1: R

8. According to Gibb, spontaneity can also be termed as:

    a. honesty
    b. strategy
    c. neutrality
    d. indifference

    Answer: a   Key 1: R

9. According to Gibb, all of the following can create a defensive climate EXCEPT:

    a. neutrality
    b. equality
    c. superiority
    d. strategy

    Answer: b   Key 1: C

10. All of the following is true about conflict EXCEPT:

    a. There does not have to be expressed struggle
    b. There does not have to be perceived compatible goals
    c. There are perceived scarce rewards
    d. There is a sense of interdependence

    Answer: a   Key 1: R

11. _____ is the inability or unwillingness to express thoughts or feelings in a conflict.

    a. Direct aggression
    b. Nonassertion
    c. Passive aggression
    d. Indirect communication

    Answer: b   Key 1: R

12. Lee was having a conflict with a colleague at work. He tried to gain control by making her feel responsible for changing and accommodating in order to suit him better, by making little statements such as, "Well, I will do this job task, but it's really your place to do it." This is an example of:

    a. direct aggression
    b. indirect communication
    c. passive aggression
    d. nonassertion

    Answer: c   Key 1: A

13. Yelling "Shut up!" or "Get it yourself!" is an example of:

    a. direct aggression
    b. indirect communication
    c. passive aggression
    d. nonassertion

    Answer: a   Key 1: A

14. All of the following are parts to an assertive message EXCEPT:

    a. a behavioral description
    b. the person's interpretation of your behavior
    c. a description of your feelings
    d. a description of the consequences

    Answer: b   Key 1: R

15. "You asked me to tell you what I really thought about your idea, and then when I gave it to you, you told me I was too critical." This is an example of:

    a. behavioral description
    b. a description of your feelings
    c. a description of the consequences
    d. your interpretation of the other person's behavior

    Answer: a   Key 1: A

16. Intention statements can communicate all of the following kinds of messages EXCEPT

    a. where you stand on an issue
    b. descriptions of how you plan to act in the future
    c. requests of others
    d. what happens to others

    Answer: d   Key 1: R

17. _____ is the distinguishing characteristic in win-lose problem solving.

    a. Struggle
    b. Collaboration
    c. Conflict
    d. Power

    Answer: d   Key 1: R

18. A nation that gains a military victory at the cost of thousands of lives is an example of:

    a. compromise problem solving
    b. lose-lose problem solving
    c. win-lose problem solving
    d. win-win problem solving

    Answer: b   Key 1: R

Answer Key Code: R = Recall   C= Conceptual   A = Application   S = Synthesis

19. All of the following are steps in win-win problem solving EXCEPT:

    a. identify their problem and met needs
    b. make a date to discuss
    c. describe your problem and needs
    d. your partner checks back to clarify what you have said

    Answer: a   Key 1: R

20. All of the following are steps in negotiating a solution EXCEPT:

    a. Generate a number of possible solutions
    b. Evaluate the alternative solutions
    c. Identify and define the solution
    d. Decide on the best solution

    Answer: c   Key 1: R

21. When conflict exists in an interpersonal relationship and you ignore it, you are exhibiting:

    a. indirect aggression
    b. assertion
    c. self-sufficiency
    d. nonassertive behavior

    Answer: d   Key 1: R

22. Descriptive communication is characterized by:

    a. evaluation
    b. its disconfirming effect
    c. "I" messages
    d. "You" messages

    Answer: c   Key 1: R

23. Cynthia states to John, "I don't care what you want for dinner! I want Mexican food tonight!" This is an example of what type of message?

    a. controlling message
    b. descriptive message
    c. evaluative message
    d. problem orientation message

    Answer: c   Key 1: R

24. Which of the following is a difference between males' behavior in mixed-sex groups and in all-male groups? In mixed-sex groups, males:

    a. use less volume.
    b. are less aggressive.
    c. listen more carefully.
    d. ask more theoretical questions.

    Answer: b   Key 1: R

25. The text describes the need for providing "consequence statements" when delivering assertive messages. If Marco says to Darma, "I'm angry because you didn't tell me about the annual report deadline. Now my boss is irritated with me for turning it in late." Which part of Marco's statement illustrates the consequence statement?

    a. "I'm angry..."
    b. "...you didn't tell me about the deadline..."
    c. "Now my boss is irritated with me..."
    d. none of the above

Answer: c   Key 1: A

TRUE/FALSE

26. Relational structure refers to the emotional tone of a relationship.

Answer: F   Key 1: R
Emotional tone of a relationship refers to communication climate.

27. Messages that show you are valued are known as confirming responses.

Answer: T   Key 1: R
Confirming messages say that you matter, you exist, or you are important.

28. All disconfirming behavior is unintentional.

Answer: F   Key 1: R
Not all disconfirming behavior is unintentional; there are some deliberate tactics to create distance in an undesired relationship.

29. Treating the other person like a stranger or interacting with him/her as a role rather than a unique individual is known as the distancing tactic of nonimmediacy.

Answer: F   Key 1: R
This describes the distancing tactic of impersonality.

30. Unlike confirming messages, disconfirming messages are a matter of perception

Answer: F   Key 1: R
Confirming messages and disconfirming messages are both a matter of perception.

31. Escalatory conflict spirals are the least visible way that disconfirming messages reinforce one another.

Answer: F   Key 1: R
Actually escalatory conflict spirals are the most visible.

32. Spirals rarely go on indefinitely.

Answer: T   Key 1: R
Most relationships pass through cycles of progression and regression.

33. Passive aggressiveness is the inability or unwillingness to express thoughts or feelings in a conflict.

Answer: F   Key 1: R
Nonassertion is the inability to express thoughts or feelings.

Answer Key Code: R = Recall   C= Conceptual   A = Application   S = Synthesis

34. As long as people perceive their goals mutually exclusive, they create self-fulfilling prophecy in which the conflict is very real.

    Answer: T   Key 1: R
    This is also known as perceived incompatible goals

35. With direct aggression, it can be hurtful at the time, but the consequences for the relationship are usually only short-lasting.

    Answer: F   Key 1: R
    The consequences of direct aggression are can in fact be long lasting.

36. When girls have conflicts and disagreements, they are less likely to handle them via indirect aggression.

    Answer: F   Key 1: R
    Studies have proven that girls are more likely to handle conflict through indirect aggression. It is usually the boys who handle aggression directly.

37. According to Gibb, provisionalism is a supportive behavior.

    Answer: T   Key   1: R
    Provisionalism is a blend of strong beliefs with a willingness to listen to others.

38. In Gibb's defensive and supportive climate research, "neutrality" is best defined as fairness.

    Answer: F   Key 1: R
    Neutrality implies disinterest and lack of concern.

39. Compromise is the most effective approach to conflict.

    Answer: F   Key 1: R
    While compromise may be effective, it may result in a situation in which everyone ends up a loser.

40. Whether communication is perceived as confirming or disconfirming depends almost completely on the content of the message.

    Answer: F   Key 1: R
    Relational climate is determined more by how we convey a message than by the content of what we say.

41. "I" language is used in evaluative communication.

    Answer: F   Key 1: R
    "I" language is used in descriptive communication.

42. Strategic communication, as defined by Gibb, is thoughtful, well planned, and never manipulative.

    Answer: F   Key 1: R
    The authors state that a more accurate term for strategic communication is manipulation.

43. The win-lose method of conflict resolution should be avoided at all times.

    Answer: F   Key 1: R
    There are some circumstances when the win-lose method may be necessary.

44. When delivering an assertive message it is important to describe the behavior before stating your feelings.

    Answer: F   Key 1: R
    The order of the parts may vary; sometimes it is best to begin by stating your feelings or intentions.

45. Using competitive communication never contributes to forming good relationships.

    Answer: F   Key 1: R
    Many strong male relationships are built around competition, particularly at work or in athletics.

46. A low-context society places a premium on being direct and literal.

    Answer: T   Key 1: R
    In contrast, high-context cultures value self-restraint and avoidance of confrontation.

47. "Making a date" to discuss a conflict tends to increase defensiveness.

    Answer: F   Key 1: R
    It is advisable to set up a time that is agreeable for both parties.

48. A de-escalatory conflict spiral occurs when one partner uses empathy.

    Answer: F   Key 1: R
    De-escalatory conflict spirals occur when the parties lessen their dependence on each other and withdraw.

49. A person who uses dogmatic communication illustrates the defensive behavior of certainty.

    Answer: T   Key 1: R
    People who speak as though they know everything are indicating certainty rather than provisionalism.

50. After a relational conflict begins, women are often more likely than men to withdraw if they become uncomfortable or fail to get their way.

    Answer: F   Key 1: R
    Men are often more likely than women withdraw if they become uncomfortable or fail to get their way.

SHORT ANSWER

51. What is communication climate? Explain how communication climate plays an essential role in interpersonal relationships. Provide some tips for creating a positive communication climate.

    Answer: Key 1: A

52. List and describe four of the distancing tactics in disconfirming messages. How can these tactics negatively affect communication patterns?

    Answer: Key 1: C

53. Discuss the difference between control verses problem orientation. Which one is more likely to create a positive communication climate? Be specific and give examples.

    Answer: Key 1: A

54. What is the nature of conflict? Explain in detail how conflicts operate.

    Answer: Key 1: C

Answer Key Code: R = Recall   C= Conceptual   A = Application   S = Synthesis

55. Explain in detail the five different styles of expressing conflict. Provide specific examples of each.

Answer: Key 1: A

56. Explain in detail the five parts a complete assertive message. Give examples of each.

Answer: Key 1: A

57. How do men and women handle conflict differently? Explain who is more likely to use indirect aggression and who is more likely to use direct aggression. Provide specific examples.

Answer: Key 1: A

58. How does culture influence conflict? Discuss two different cultures and how each culture handles conflict differently from your culture. How would this affect your communication climate if you were dealing with a conflict with someone from each of these cultures?

Answer: Key 1: A

59. Discuss in detail the difference between a compromise conflict resolution and a win-win resolution. What are the distinct differences? Be specific and provide examples of each.

Answer: Key 1: A

60. Discuss in detail the steps in a win-win problem solving approach. Provide examples of each step.

Answer: Key 1: A

MATCHING

61. Match the style of conflict with the description.

_____ Expressing hostility in an obscure way

_____ Expressing aggression overtly by attacking the other party

_____ Inability to express thoughts or feelings

_____ Explaining to someone why you are angry

A.   Nonassertive

B.   Direct aggressive

C.   Passive aggressive

D.   Assertive

Answer: C, B, A, D   Key 1: R

CHAPTER 8 THE NATURE OF GROUPS

MULTIPLE CHOICE

1. All of the following are factors that help form a group EXCEPT:

    a. interaction
    b. independence
    c. time
    d. size

    Answer: b   Key 1: R

2. _____ is the most obvious type of individual motive for belonging to a group.

    a. Task orientation
    b. Group orientation
    c. Social orientation
    d. Goal orientation

    Answer: a   Key 1: R

3. A bible study group would be best classified as which type of group?

    a. Growth group
    b. Problem-solving group
    c. Learning group
    d. Social group

    Answer: c   Key 1: C

4. A committee deciding on the best candidate to hire for a position would be considered which type of group?

    a. Growth group
    b. Problem-solving group
    c. Learning group
    d. Social group

    Answer: b   Key 1: R

5. _____ outline how the group should operate.

    a. Social norms
    b. Task norms
    c. Formal norms
    d. Procedural norms

    Answer: d   Key 1: R

6. _____ focus on how the job itself should be handled.

    a. Social norms
    b. Task norms
    c. Formal norms
    d. Procedural norms

    Answer: b   Key 1: R

Answer Key Code: R = Recall   C= Conceptual   A = Application   S = Synthesis

7. _____ govern the relationship of members to each other.

   a. Social norms
   b. Task norms
   c. Formal norms
   d. Procedural norms

   Answer: a   Key 1: R

8. All of the following are examples of task roles EXCEPT:

   a. initiator
   b. information seeker
   c. opinion seeker
   d. gatekeeper

   Answer: d   Key 1: R

9. A _____ reconciles disagreements, mediates differences, and reduces tensions by giving group members a chance to explore their differences.

   a. conciliator
   b. harmonizer
   c. gatekeeper
   d. feeling expresser

   Answer: b   Key 1: R

10. A _____ is a communication pattern in which one person acts as a clearinghouse, receiving and relaying messages to all other members.

   a. chain network
   b. gate keeping network
   c. wheel network
   d. spiral network

   Answer: c   Key 1: R

11. Which of the following decision-making methods call for the greatest need of communication skill?

   a. majority control
   b. consensus
   c. expert opinion
   d. authority rule

   Answer: b   Key 1: R

12. _____ is the approach most often used by autocratic leaders.

   a. Minority control
   b. Expert opinion
   c. Consensus
   d. Authority rule

   Answer: d   Key 1: R

13. _____ refers to the degree to which members are willing to accept a difference in power between members of a group.

    a. Power influx
    b. Power distance
    c. Authority control
    d. Power avoidance

Answer: b   Key 1: R

14. All of the following countries are considered to be concerned more with high task orientation EXCEPT:

    a. Portugal
    b. Japan
    c. Austria
    d. Mexico

Answer: a   Key 1: R

15. All of the following are countries considered to have a low uncertainty avoidance EXCEPT:

    a. U.S.A
    b. India
    c. Japan
    d. Singapore

Answer: c   Key 1: R

16. _____ societies are characterized by a focus on making the team more competent through training and the use of up-to-date methods.

    a. Task-oriented
    b. Social-oriented
    c. Short-term-oriented
    d. Long-term-oriented

Answer: a   Key 1: R

17. An all-channel communication network will be more efficient than a wheel network in:

    a. providing the leader with more information than other members
    b. solving simple, routine tasks
    c. solving complex, ambiguous tasks
    d. finding one member to serve as a clearinghouse for information

Answer: c   Key 1: C

18. A sense of belonging and being liked by others are related to:

    a. group task orientation
    b. group social orientation
    c. individual task orientation
    d. individual social orientation

Answer: d   Key 1: R

Answer Key Code: R = Recall   C= Conceptual   A = Application   S = Synthesis

19. "Deserter," "Dominator," "Recognition Seeker," and "Aggressor" are all examples of:

    a. task roles
    b. social roles
    c. dysfunctional roles
    d. all the above

    Answer: c   Key 1: R

20. The role of gatekeeper is most influential in the _____ network.

    a. circular
    b. all-channel
    c. chain
    d. wheel

    Answer: d   Key 1: R

21. Members of collectivistic cultures are more likely to:

    a. tolerate conflict
    b. be team players
    c. use a solution-oriented approach
    d. gain their identity from their accomplishments

    Answer: b   Key 1: R

22. Which of the following are advantages of "virtual groups"?

    a. meet whenever necessary, even if members are widely separated
    b. fast and easy getting together
    c. leveling of status differences
    d. all of the above

    Answer: d   Key 1: R

23. An all channel network, a wheel network, and a chain network are all examples of:

    a. a matrix caliper
    b. a total mode
    c. a sociogram
    d. a group regenerator

    Answer: c   Key 1: R

24. Every Sunday evening Lana's family hashes out their schedules, their conflicts, whose turn it is to handle which chores, and so on. This group best illustrates:

    a. a problem-solving group
    b. a dysfunctional group
    c. a chain network
    d. all the above

    Answer: a   Key 1: A

25. Rochelle is secretly resentful that the group did not choose her as their leader, but instead selected Joachim. As a result she is overly critical of the suggestions made by Joachim during their discussions. Rochelle's behavior illustrates:

    a. social role
    b. hidden agenda
    c. a virtual group
    d. a chain network

    Answer: b   Key 1: A

TRUE/FALSE

26. Without interaction, a collection of people could not be a group.

    Answer: T   Key 1: R
    You must have interaction to have a group.

27. Members of a group are interdependent of each other.

    Answer: T   Key 1: R
    The behavior of one person affects all the others in a group causing a ripple effect.

28. A learning group focuses on teaching the members more about themselves.

    Answer: F   Key 1: R
    This would be a growth group.

29. All social groups are considered informal types of groups.

    Answer: F   Key 1: R
    Social groups can be formal or informal.

30. Procedural norms focus on how the job itself should be handled.

    Answer: F   Key 1: R
    This would be the definition of task norms.

31. Norms define acceptable group standards; roles define patterns of behavior expected of members.

    Answer: T   Key 1: R
    Norms allow the group to know what is acceptable or not, while roles allow the group to know how to function within those norms.

32. A person who plays the aggressor role interferes with progress by rejecting ideas or taking a negative stand on any and all issues.

    Answer: F   Key 1: R
    This would be what the role of a blocker would do. An aggressor struggles for status by deflating the status of others.

33. The presence of positive social roles and the absence of dysfunctional roles are key ingredients in the effectiveness of groups.

    Answer: T   Key 1: R
    Research suggests that the more positive roles group members play the more productivity you will have within the group.

Answer Key Code: R = Recall   C= Conceptual   A = Application   S = Synthesis

34. The majority control decision-making method is most often the superior method to use.

    Answer: F   Key 1: R
    Even though majority control is sometimes a good method, it is not superior to others in all situations.

35. When time is of the essence, the consensus decision-making method is the best method to use.

    Answer: F   Key 1: R
    This method usually takes the most time because everyone in the group has to agree upon it.

36. Expert opinion is the approach most often used by autocratic leaders.

    Answer: F   Key 1: R
    Authority rule is the approach most often used by autocratic leaders.

37. Homogenous groups are less cohesive than diverse groups.

    Answer: F   Key 1: R
    Homogenous groups are usually more cohesive than diverse groups.

38. Diverse group often develop better solutions to problems and enjoy themselves more while working together than homogenous groups.

    Answer: T   Key 1: R
    Diverse groups provide more perspectives and different ideas because of the diversity they bring to the group.

39. Members of collectivistic cultures are less likely to be team players.

    Answer: F   Key 1: R
    Actually they are more likely to be team players than people from individualistic cultures.

40. Members of individualist cultures are far more likely than collectivistic cultures to produce and reward stars.

    Answer: T   Key 1: R
    Individualistic culture focuses more on the "me" rather than the "we" so they value individual effort more than group effort.

41. Power distance refers to the degree to which members are willing to accept a difference in power and status between members of a group.

    Answer: T   Key 1: R
    This is the definition of power distance.

42. Countries such as Japan and China have more of a short-term focus than USA and Canada.

    Answer: F   Key 1: R
    Japan and China are more long-term focus whereas USA and Canada are more short-term focused.

43. A collection of people who interact for a short while would not qualify as a group.

    Answer: T   Key 1: R
    One qualifier of a group is time. Onlookers at the scene of an accident would not qualify as a group.

44. Groups are influenced by individual goals and group goals.

    Answer: T   Key 1: R
    Both individual goals (task and social) and group goals influence group development and interaction.

45. Informal roles are sometimes determined by personality characteristics.

    Answer: T   Key 1: R
    Some individuals simply feel more comfortable performing a certain function because of their nature.

46. Norms must be explicit to be effective.

    Answer: F   Key 1: R
    Norms are unstated rules and thus not effective or ineffective. Both explicit and implicit norms function in all groups.

47. Maintenance roles and social roles refer to the same thing.

    Answer: T   Key 1: R
    The two terms are synonyms.

48. Role fixation occurs when a group member acts out a role whether or not the situation requires it.

    Answer: T   Key 1: R
    That is the definition of role fixation.

49. Group members in high power distance cultures expect leaders to be considerate of their needs.

    Answer: F   Key 1: R
    This is true of low power distance cultures.

50. Chain networks work well for complex verbal messages.

    Answer: F   Key 1: R
    The inaccessibility of all members to all other members makes communication difficult.

SHORT ANSWER

51. Discuss the differences between individual goals and group goals. How can individual goals positively or negatively affect group goals? Provide a detailed example of a time when you were in a group of how your individual goals affected the group goal.

    Answer: Key 1: A

52. Discuss the difference between an all-channel network, a wheel network, and a chain network. Explain what types of messages would work best for each type of network. Be specific.

    Answer: Key 1: C

53. Bormann claims that in groups people make bids for roles. Explain and provide detailed examples.

    Answer: Key 1: A

54. List and explain the five cultural forces that shape the attitudes and behaviors of groups.

    Answer: Key 1: R

55. Where do you feel the U.S. falls on a continuum between task and social orientations? Defend your answer by describing each orientation and by using examples.

    Answer: Key 1: S

Answer Key Code: R = Recall   C= Conceptual   A = Application   S = Synthesis

56. What is a group? explain how interaction, interdependence, time, size and goals play major factors in groups. Be specific with examples.

    Answer: Key 1: A

57. What are the four types of groups listed by your text? Explain each one in detail and give an example.

    Answer: Key 1: A

58. Explain the difference between social norms, procedural norms, and task norms. How do these different types of norm affect a group? Be specific using examples.

    Answer: Key 1: A

59. Discuss the difference between task roles and social roles. Provide examples of each type of roles.

    Answer: Key 1: A

60. Discuss the five different styles of decision-making methods. Explain when each method would be the most appropriate method to use. Be specific.

    Answer: Key 1: A

OTHER

61. Label the following behaviors as Task (T) or Social/Maintenance (S).

    _____ Prods the group to action

    _____ Summarizes what has taken place

    _____ Keeps communication channels open

    _____ Contributes ideas and suggestions

    _____ Reconciles disagreements

    _____ Reduces tension, relaxes group members

    Answer: T, T, S, T, S, S   Key 1: C

CHAPTER 9 SOLVING PROBLEMS IN GROUPS

MULTIPLE CHOICE

1. All of the following are advantages to solving problems in groups EXCEPT:

    a. They provide more accuracy
    b. They provide more resources
    c. They create a stronger sense of commitment
    d. They solve problems faster

    Answer: d   Key 1: R

2. A _____ is used as a market research tool to enable sponsoring organizations to learn how potential users or the public at large regards a new product or idea.

    a. focus group
    b. buzz group
    c. problem census
    d. symposium

    Answer: a   Key 1: R

3. In a _____ participants divide the topic in a manner that allows each member to deliver in-depth information without interruption.

    a. focus group
    b. panel discussion
    c. symposium
    d. buzz group

    Answer: c   Key 1: R

4. A _____ allows nonmembers to add their opinions to the group's deliberations before the group makes a decision.

    a. focus group
    b. forum
    c. panel discussion
    d. symposium

    Answer: b   Key 1: R

5. All of the following are steps to John Dewey's "reflective thinking" model EXCEPT:

    a. Identify the problem
    b. Analyze the solution
    c. Develop possible creative solutions through brainstorming
    d. Evaluate solutions

    Answer: b   Key 1: R

Answer Key Code: R = Recall   C= Conceptual   A = Application S = Synthesis

6. According to Dewey's "reflective thinking" model, in the second step, analyzing the problem, you should do all of the following EXCEPT:

    a. identify specific tasks
    b. word the problem as a probative question
    c. gather relevant information
    d. identify impelling and restraining forces

    Answer: a   Key 1: R

7. All of the following are criteria of brainstorming EXCEPT:

    a. freewheeling is encouraged
    b. combination and improvement are desirable
    c. criticism is forbidden
    d. quality is better than quantity of ideas

    Answer: d   Key 1: R

8. According to the Nominal Group Technique, all of the following steps should be followed to enhance the brainstorming phase EXCEPT:

    a. members work together to develop a list of possible solutions
    b. in a round-robin fashion, each member lists one of the possible solutions
    c. each member privately ranks his or her choice of the ideas in order
    d. have a free discussion of the top ideas held

    Answer: a   Key 1: R

9. According to Fisher, in the _____ stage members approach the problem and one another tentatively.

    a. conflict
    b. orientation
    c. emergence
    d. reinforcement

    Answer: b   Key 1: R

10. All of the following are factors that increase the goal of cohesiveness EXCEPT:

    a. Shared or compatible goals
    b. Lack of perceived threat between members
    c. Independence between members
    d. Mutual perceived attractiveness and friendship

    Answer: c   Key 1: R

11. _____ power is also known as position power.

    a. Nominal
    b. Reward
    c. Referent
    d. Legitimate

    Answer: d   Key 1: R

12. DeShawn is the captain of the scholastic team. The team was at tournament when one of team members went into a seizure. Nyia was certified in first aid, so she became the leader of the group during this crisis. Even though DeShawn was the group leader, what type of power was Nyia exhibiting?

    a. Referent power
    b. Information power
    c. Coercive power
    d. Expert power

    Answer: d   Key 1: A

13. _____ leadership style relies on legitimate, coercive, and reward power to influence others.

    a. Laissez-faire
    b. Democratic
    c. Authoritarian
    d. Situational

    Answer: c   Key 1: R

14. According to the Leadership Grid, which type of management style has a very high concern for people and a very low concern for production?

    a. team management
    b. country club management
    c. impoverished management
    d. authority obedience

    Answer: b   Key 1: R

15. According to the Leadership Grid, which type of management style is the best management style to strive for?

    a. team management
    b. country club management
    c. impoverished management
    d. authority obedience

    Answer: a   Key 1: R

16. "Reflective thinking" refers to:

    a. systematic problem solving
    b. communication patterns
    c. brainstorming
    d. a leadership strategy

    Answer: a   Key 1: R

17. Which of the following is not part of the "develop creative solutions" phase of problem solving?

    a. Encourage "freewheeling" ideas.
    b. Develop a large number of ideas.
    c. Combine two or more individual ideas.
    d. Relate group goals to possible solutions.

    Answer: d   Key 1: R

Answer Key Code: R = Recall   C= Conceptual   A = Application   S = Synthesis

18. In a panel discussion the leader is called a (an):

    a. moderator
    b. organizer
    c. manager
    d. facilitator

    Answer: a   Key 1: R

19. Fiedler's theory of leadership that recommends a leader's style should change with the circumstances is labeled:

    a. emergent
    b. situational
    c. fluid
    d. laissez-faire

    Answer: b   Key 1: R

20. Fisher's four-stage group decision-making process shows that the stages of a problem-solving group are:

    a. confusing
    b. preplanned
    c. linear
    d. cyclical

    Answer: d   Key 1: R

21. Robert actually is enjoying his group project in speech class. Everyone seems to listen to everyone else, and they all take part in finding solutions to the problem they are working on. Robert is surprised at how committed he is to these solutions. His commitment demonstrates the principle of:

    a. reactive decision making
    b. proactive decision making
    c. interdependent decision making
    d. participative decision making

    Answer: d   Key 1: A

22. When your group has too much information it experiences:

    a. information overload
    b. information underload
    c. lack of cohesion
    d. group think

    Answer: a   Key 1: R

23. Group think occurs when:

    a. there is little dissent
    b. the group strives for unanimity
    c. members do not voice ideas that deviate from the consensus
    d. all of the above

    Answer: d   Key 1: R

24. Which of the following should be the first task of a problem-solving group?

    a. define the problem
    b. analyze the problem
    c. decide upon all the group's norms
    d. offer solutions to the problem

    Answer: a   Key 1: R

25. Which of the following would NOT be included in the structured problem solving process?

    a. the reflective thinking technique
    b. the nominal group technique
    c. the ideal-solution technique
    d. none of the above

    Answer: c   Key 1: R

TRUE/FALSE

26. Groups are best suited to tackling problems that have a single cut-and dry answer.

    Answer: F   Key 1: R
    Individuals work better in this situation, but groups work better if they do not have a clear-cut answer.

27. When the number of members is too large for effective discussion, focus groups can be used to maximize effective participation.

    Answer: F   Key 1: R
    Buzz groups would be the correct group to use. Focus groups are used as a market research tool.

28. For best productivity, groups should never rely on computer mediated meetings, or virtual meetings.

    Answer: F   Key 1: R
    There are an abundance of affordable tools that make virtual meetings successful, and it saves time from group members actually having to be physically present in a room when not necessary.

29. A panel discussion format is where participants talk over the topic informally, much as they would in ordinary conversation.

    Answer: T   Key 1: R
    Panel discussion encourages everyone to participate because of its casual nature.

30. The reflective-thinking model is a systematic method of solving problems.

    Answer: T   Key 1: R
    John Dewey created the reflective thinking model to help with the systematic organization of problem solving.

31. The first step in the reflective thinking model is to analyze the problem.

    Answer: F   Key 1: R
    This would be the second step; the first step is to identify the problem.

32. According to the developmental stages in problem solving, during the orientation stage members approach the problem and one anther tentatively.

    Answer: T   Key 1: R
    Since some people may not know each other or their positions, this allows them to get acquainted with both.

Answer Key Code: R = Recall   C= Conceptual   A = Application   S = Synthesis

33. Highly cohesive groups communicate differently than less cohesive groups.

    Answer: T   Key 1: R
    Since cohesive groups spend more time with each other interacting, there are more expressions of positive feelings for one another.

34. Social groups are not considered cohesive because they only stay together because they enjoy one another's company.

    Answer: F   Key 1: R
    Actually social groups are a good example of a group with a high level of cohesion because they stay together because they enjoy one another's company.

35. Legitimate power is not the same thing as position power.

    Answer: F   Key 1: R
    Legitimate power is sometimes called position power.

36. All legitimate power resides with nominal leaders.

    Answer: F   Key 1: R
    Actually not all legitimate power resides with nominal leaders. For example, the person with an orange cap may direct traffic at a road repair site is unlikely to be in charge of the entire project, but possesses legitimate power in the eyes of the motorist who go and stop at their command.

37. A drill sergeant is an example of someone who holds coercive power.

    Answer: T   Key 1: A
    Coercive power occurs when influences come from threat or actual imposition of some unpleasant consequences.

38. Power is considered an either-or concept.

    Answer: F   Key 1: R
    Power isn't an either-or concept because members don't either have it or not, it's a matter of degree.

39. According to the Leadership Grid, the management style with the highest concern for productivity and people is known as the middle of the road management style.

    Answer: F   Key 1: R
    This would be team management.

40. According to the Leadership Grid, the management style with highest concern for production and the lowest concern for people is known as impoverished management.

    Answer: F   Key 1: R
    This would be authority obedience

41. The quality of ideas is tested during the emergence stage of problem-solving groups.

    Answer: F   Key 1: R
    This occurs during the conflict stage.

42. An effective way to begin understanding a group's problem is to identify the concerns of each member.

    Answer: T   Key 1: R
    This approach helps with the first step of identifying the problem.

43. The research of Aubrey Fisher indicates that the most successful groups can by-pass the conflict stage of development.

    Answer: F   Key 1: R
    Fisher discovered that successful groups engage in a conflict stage where members take strong positions while retaining their respect for each other.

44. The principle of participative decision making implies that students who have input into the assignments required in a course would work harder to carry them out.

    Answer: T   Key 1: A
    This concept means group members are most likely to accept solutions they help create.

45. Dewey's method of problem solving suggests that groups begin by brainstorming possible solutions to the problem.

    Answer: F   Key 1: R
    Dewey begins with identification of the problem.

46. Force field analysis notes that some forces prevent a group from reaching its goal while other forces support the group's efforts.

    Answer: T   Key 1: R
    Force field analysis describes this process by noting also that some forces are stronger than others.

47. Cohesiveness refers to the rules by which group members abide.

    Answer: F   Key 1: R
    Cohesiveness is the totality of forces that cause group members to feel a part of the group and to want to remain in the group.

48. Most problem-solving groups meet privately because an audience hinders group functioning.

    Answer: F   Key 1: C
    Many groups are designed to function before audiences. Those that don't, function in private for reasons of efficiency, confidentiality, or limited interest.

49. Research indicates that a structured procedure produces better results than discussions using no pattern.

    Answer: T   Key 1: R
    While research shows that no single approach is best for all situations, the use of structure is related to effectiveness.

50. A leader exercising referent power in a group gains that power based on the respect, liking, and trust others have for the leader.

    Answer: T   Key 1: R
    That is the definition of referent power.

SHORT ANSWER

51. What are the advantages of group problem solving? Provide specific examples of each advantage.

    Answer: Key 1: A

Answer Key Code: R = Recall   C= Conceptual   A = Application   S = Synthesis

52. Discuss the difference between a panel discussion group and a forum. When would it be best to implement each one of these? Be specific.

    Answer: Key 1: A

53. List and discuss in detail the six steps in problem solving.

    Answer: Key 1: C

54. Why is group cohesiveness so important? Explain the eight factors that can achieve the goals of cohesiveness, giving examples of each.

    Answer: Key 1: A

55. What is legitimate power? How can legitimate power be an important power to have within a group? Provide examples of when you have had legitimate power within a group.

    Answer: Key 1: A

56. Discuss the difference between a buzz group and a focus group. Provide a detailed example of when each would be most appropriately used.

    Answer: Key 1: A

57. List and discuss the five styles of management according to the leadership grid. Provide examples of the characteristics that each type of manager would have.

    Answer: Key 1: A

58. Brainstorming is an important aspect of developing creative solutions. According to your text, what are the five rules of brainstorming? Provide examples for each.

    Answer: Key 1: A

59. Cite three reasons why groups are effective and give an example of how each advantage operates.

    Answer: Key 1: A

60. Your text discusses overcoming certain dangers in group discussion. List and explain in detail three of the dangers a groups can face.

    Answer: Key 1: C

MATCHING

61. Match developmental stages with the description. Each answer may be used once, more than once, or not at all.

    ____ Members are cautious and polite.   A. orientation

    ____ Members take strong positions.   B. conflict

    ____ Members back off from dogmatic   C. emergence
         positions.
                                                       D. reinforcement
    ____ Members are reluctant to take a stand.

    ____ Members endorse the group's decision.

    Answer: A, B, C, A, D   Key 1: R

62. Match the format with the description.

_____ Each member delivers in-depth information.

_____ Group uses rules about how topics may be discussed.

_____ Nonmembers add their opinions to the group's deliberations.

_____ Participants talk over the topic informally.

A. parliamentary procedure

B. panel discussion

C. symposium

D. forum

Answer: C, A, D, B   Key 1: R

63. Match the form of power with examples. Each answer may be used once, more than once, or not at all.

_____ An efficiency expert at a corporation meeting on plan efficiency

_____ A chairperson of a committee

_____ A manager of a movie theater you are attending

_____ A group member with a pleasing personality

_____ A parent who gives spankings

_____ A friend with two tickets to a rock concert you'd like to attend

A. Legitimate power

B. Coercive power

C. Reward power

D. Expert power

E. Referent power

Answer: D, A, A, E, B, C   Key 1: A

OTHER

64. Use the figure below to comply with the following:

   A. Draw an "X" on the grid to represent the most effective leader.
   B. Draw an "0" on the grid to represent a leader who is highly task-oriented.
   C. Assume you are the leader of a study group for this class. Draw an "I" to indicate what type of a leader you think you would be. Explain why you placed it where you did.
   D. This grid is two-dimensional. What other dimensions of leadership exist that are not represented here?

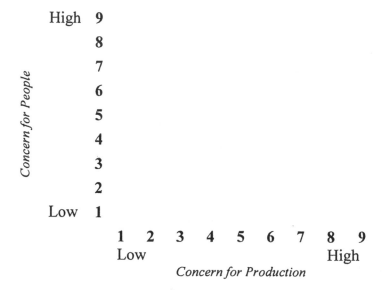

Answer: Key 1: S

CHAPTER 10 CHOOSING AND DEVELOPING A TOPIC

MULTIPLE CHOICE

1. Which of the following statements fits the description of a thesis statement as defined in the text?

    a. The audience will vote for Joanne Miller in the upcoming election.
    b. This speech is about abortion, its causes, abuses, and ethical implications.
    c. Foreign language courses should be required for business majors.
    d. I will convince the audience to buy an American-made car the next time they purchase a car.

    Answer: c   Key 1: A

2. All of the following are types of general purposes EXCEPT:

    a. to entertain
    b. to explain
    c. to inform
    d. to persuade.

    Answer: b   Key 1: R

3. _____ is the general purpose of relaxing your audience by providing it with a pleasant listening experience.

    a. Speaking to entertain
    b. Speaking to explain
    c. Speaking to inform
    d. Speaking to persuade

    Answer: a   Key 1: R

4. _____ is the general purpose of enlightening your audience by teaching it something.

    a. Speaking to entertain
    b. Speaking to explain
    c. Speaking to inform
    d. Speaking to persuade

    Answer: c   Key 1: R

5. _____ is the general purpose of moving your audience toward a new attitude or behavior.

    a. Speaking to entertain
    b. Speaking to explain
    c. Speaking to inform
    d. Speaking to persuade

    Answer: d   Key 1: R

6. All of the following are criteria for a good purpose statement EXCEPT:

    a. a purpose statement should be speaker oriented
    b. a purpose statement should be receiver oriented
    c. a purpose statement should be specific
    d. a purpose statement should be realistic

    Answer: a   Key 1: R

Answer Key Code: R = Recall   C= Conceptual   A = Application   S = Synthesis

7. "After listening to my speech, my audience will be able to list the five steps for preparing a small claims case" is an example of a:

    a. thesis statement
    b. purpose statement
    c. preview statement
    d. general purpose

    Answer: b   Key 1: A

8. _____ tells you the central idea of your speech.

    a. The thesis statement
    b. The preview statement
    c. The purpose statement
    d. The general purpose

    Answer: a   Key 1: R

9. Which of the following are components to analyzing any speaking situation?

    a. the audience and occasion
    b. the occasion and speaker
    c. the audience and speaker
    d. the topic and occasion

    Answer: a   Key 1: R

10. _____ is the purest form of receiver orientation.

    a. Speaking to inform
    b. Developing a topic
    c. Audience analysis
    d. Speaking to persuade

    Answer: c   Key 1: R

11. Which of the following is not a demographic characteristic?

    a. group membership
    b. purposes for gathering
    c. age
    d. sex

    Answer: b   Key 1: R

12. _____ are audience members who have gathered because of common interests.

    a. Captives
    b. Passersby
    c. Observers
    d. Volunteers

    Answer: d   Key 1: R

13. _____ are audience members who have gathered for some reason besides the joy of hearing you speak.

    a. Captives
    b. Passersby
    c. Observers
    d. Volunteers

    Answer: a   Key 1: R

14. Which of the following is not a concern of audience analysis?

    a. the reason the audience is present
    b. audience characteristics
    c. audience values
    d. All are concerns of audience analysis.

    Answer: d   Key 1: R

15. Psychological Abstracts can be used to locate information in:

    a. nonprint materials
    b. reference works
    c. periodicals
    d. the card catalogue

    Answer: c   Key 1: R

16. A purpose statement should tell:

    a. what you will do in your speech
    b. what your audience will know after the speech
    c. what your audience will be able to do after the speech
    d. b or c

    Answer: d   Key 1: R

17. A(n)_____ is a predisposition to respond to something in a favorable or unfavorable way.

    a. thought
    b. value
    c. attitude
    d. belief

    Answer: c   Key 1: R

18. A(n)_____ is an underlying conviction about the truth of something, often based on cultural training.

    a. thought
    b. value
    c. attitude
    d. belief

    Answer: d   Key 1: R

Answer Key Code: R = Recall   C= Conceptual   A = Application   S = Synthesis

19. A(n)_____ is a deeply rooted belief about a concept's inherent worth or worthiness.

    a. thought
    b. value
    c. attitude
    d. belief

    Answer: b   Key 1: R

20. "Because not enough of us choose to become organ donors, thousands of us needlessly die every year. You can help stop this needless dying." This is an example of:

    a. the topic
    b. the general purpose
    c. the specific purpose
    d. the thesis statement

    Answer: d   Key 1: A

21. Audience analysis should include consideration about how the audience feels about the speaker, the subject, and the speaker's intentions. Those feelings of the audience that lie closest to the surface, that have the least depth, are labeled:

    a. attitudes
    b. beliefs
    c. values
    d. opinions

    Answer: a   Key 1: R

22. Which of the following is not a part of the occasion of a speech?

    a. 7 p.m.
    b. North Hall
    c. a political debate
    d. an audience of college students

    Answer: d   Key 1: A

23. The occasion of the speech is determined by the circumstances surrounding it. All of the following are circumstances EXCEPT:

    a. audience size
    b. audience expectations
    c. the place
    d. the time

    Answer: a   Key 1: R

23. The best place to obtain definitions is in:

    a. the library catalogue
    b. reference works
    c. periodicals
    d. interviews

    Answer: b   Key 1: R

24. The American work ethic is an example of a(n):

    a. value
    b. belief
    c. opinion
    d. attitude

    Answer: a   Key 1: A

25. Infotrac Academic Index is a(n):

    a. card catalogue
    b. periodical
    c. on-line database
    d. vertical file

    Answer: c   Key 1: R

26. All of the following are criteria for evaluating websites EXCEPT:

    a. the credibility of the creator of the website
    b. the objectivity of the author
    c. the currency of the website
    d. the search engine used to find the website

    Answer: d   Key 1: R

27. Which of the following is not one of the three criteria for an appropriate purpose statement?

    30. A purpose statement must avoid revealing any degree of audience orientation.
    31. A purpose statement must describe the results you are seeking.
    32. A purpose statement must be specific.
    33. A purpose statement must be realistic.

    Answer: a   Key 1: R

28. Before developing his speech Paul paused to take into account that he'd be speaking to a large group of middle-aged women who had been long-time members of the Riverside Aquatic Recreational Club. Paul's reflection best illustrates:

    a. the thesis statement
    b. self analysis
    c. demographics
    d. purpose statement

    Answer: c   Key 1: A

29. _____ enables you to use current, local, first-hand research that you have done yourself.

    a. Survey research
    b. Personal observation
    c. Periodicals
    d. Nonprint materials

    Answer: b   Kay 1: R

Answer Key Code: R = Recall   C= Conceptual   A = Application   S = Synthesis

TRUE/FALSE

30. A speech purpose and a speech thesis are the same.

Answer: F   Key 1: R
A speech purpose tells what the speaker wants the audience members to do after hearing the speech, while a speech thesis is a more subtly worded statement that is aimed at the audience in order to convey the central idea of the speech.

31. A speech to inform has the primary function of expanding audience knowledge on a topic.

Answer: T   Key 1: R
By definition.

32. A specific purpose sentence tells what the speaker plans to do in a speech.

Answer: F   Key 1: R
It should indicate what the audience will know or do as a result of the speech.

33. Listeners in a communication class with required attendance are described as "captives."

Answer: T   Key 1: R
As compared to "volunteers" who choose to listen to a speech, "captives" are people who have no choice but to attend the speaking occasion.

34. A belief is a predisposition to respond to something in a favorable or unfavorable way.

Answer: F   Key 1: R
This is the definition of an attitude. A belief is a deeper, more basic conviction about the truth of some situation.

35. Often the difference between a successful and an unsuccessful speech is the choice of topic.

Answer: T   Key 1: C
Directly stated in text as such.

36. No one speech can have more than one general purpose.

Answer: F   Key 1: C
The general purposes are interrelated because a speech designed for one purpose will almost always accomplish a little of the other purposes.

37. You should use information from personal observation, interviewing, surveys, and the library in all of your speeches.

Answer: F   Key 1: C
Not necessarily; the amount and type of evidence you need depends upon your topic, purpose, and audience.

38. No one gives a speech without having a reason to do so.

Answer: T   Key 1: C
Speaking is purposeful.

39. Most speeches have an equal emphasis on the three general speech purposes.

Answer: F   Key 1: R
Most speeches have a primary speech purpose.

40. A key word in purpose statements is "audience" or "listeners."

    Answer: T   Key 1: A
    A purpose statement should be phrased in terms of what the audience will know or do.

41. A purpose statement tells what the speaker plans to tell the audience.

    Answer: F   Key 1: R
    A purpose statement describes the audience response the speaker hopes to achieve.

42. Both the thesis statement and purpose statement should be part of your introduction.

    Answer: F   Key 1: R
    The purpose statement is often unstated in the speech.

43. Beliefs and values underlie attitudes.

    Answer: T   Key 1: R
    Attitudes are predispositions to act, which are based on beliefs and values.

44. If an article on a web site is current and has an author listed it usually is considered credible.

    Answer: F   Key 1: R
    Web sites must be evaluated for credibility and objectivity, as well as currency.

45. A purpose statement should be speaker oriented.

    Answer: F   Key 1: R
    A purpose statement should be receiver oriented.

46. Not all purpose statements should be specific.

    Answer: F   Key 1: R
    Purpose statements should be specific in order to be effective.

47. The thesis statement and purpose statement are synonymous.

    Answer: F   Key 1: R
    The thesis statement tells you what the central idea of the speech is and the purpose statement explains what you plan to accomplish within the speech.

48. Audience analysis is the purest form of receiver orientation.

    Answer: T   Key 1: R
    Taken straight from the text

49. The time when the speech is presented is a circumstance of the occasion.

    Answer: T   Key 1: R
    Time is one of the listed circumstances listed under occasion.

50. The location of your speech is an irrelevant factor to the occasion of the speech.

    Answer: F   Key 1: R
    Actually the opposite is true. The physical location can be a circumstance to the occasion.

Answer Key Code: R = Recall   C= Conceptual   A = Application   S = Synthesis

51. Google is a recommend website by your text as a first step in your hunt on the Internet.

    Answer: T   Key 1: C
    The text provides a lengthy explanation of the benefits of using Google as a search engine.

SHORT ANSWER

52. Describe various categories of demographic information that a speaker might want to note. Explain how you would use the data on two of the following speech topics.

    1. sex education
    2. drunken driving
    3. manufacturing safer cars

    Answer: Key 1: A

53. Distinguish between attitudes, beliefs, and values. Give an example of each that you hold. How would each affect your interpretation of a communication event?

    Answer: Key 1: A

54. It has been said that your experiences, your thoughts, and your investigation of a topic will be, by definition, unique. Explain why this is so.

    Answer: Key 1: S

55. List the three types of audiences and give an example of when you were a member of each type.

    Answer: Key 1: A

56. The Learning Skills Center is offering a workshop on successful test taking. List five different audience purposes that might be present in those attending.

    Answer: Key 1: A

57. Explain the difference between "analyzing" and "stereotyping" an audience. What are the implications of these differences?

    Answer: Key 1: S

58. Your authors claim, "Older people...tend to have more practical interests." Is this audience analysis, which they recommend, or stereotyping? Defend your answer.

    Answer: Key 1: S

59. List five of your own demographic characteristics.

    Answer: Key 1: A

60. Explain how the occasion of a speech is influenced by time, place, and audience expectations.

    Answer: Key 1: C

61. Assume your audience holds the following two attitudes: a positive attitude toward environmental protection, a negative attitude toward littering. Make an inference about another attitude they probably hold based on your knowledge of these two.

    Answer: Key 1: A

62. You've been asked to speak to a high school class about your college experiences. If you had the opportunity to survey the class the week before your speech, what would you ask them? How would you use the answers in your speech?

    Answer: Key 1: A

63. Use the topic, "Reading for Fun" and explain how two demographic characteristics of your audience would be variables in planning your speech.

    Answer: Key 1: A

OTHER

64. Age can be a demographic variable that is crucial for your audience analysis. Match the generation labels to the ages they represent.

    ____ Generation X   A. born 1922-1946

    ____ Baby Boomers   B. born 1946-1964

    ____ Generation Y   C. born 1965-1978

    ____ Traditionalists   D. born 1979-present

    Answer: C, B, D, A   Key 1: R

65. Make the following purpose statements more specific:

    After listening to my speech, my audience will:

    a.   know how to carve wood
    b.   know more about Europe
    c.   give a successful dinner party
    d.   become an intelligent consumer

    Answer: Key 1: A

66. Place the following speech preparation steps in the order in which they should occur. Place a 1 next to the first step, etc.

    ____ Gather information
    ____ Determine your interests
    ____ Determine your knowledge
    ____ Define your purpose

    Answer: 4, 1, 2, 3   Key 1: R

67. Label the following as attitudes (A), beliefs (B), or values (V).

    ____ School spirit is important.
    ____ Students should support their school.
    ____ Being involved in school activities is good for students; I'm going to join the Key Club.

    Answer: V, B, A   Key 1: A

Answer Key Code: R = Recall   C= Conceptual   A = Application   S = Synthesis

68. Place the appropriate term with each statement.

_____ "After listening to my speech, audience members will recognize the importance of organ donation and will sign an organ donor's card for themselves."

_____ Organ Donation

_____ To Persuade

_____ "Because not enough of us choose to become organ donors, thousands of us needlessly die every year. You can help stop this needless dying."

A. Topic

B. General Purpose

C. Specific Purpose

D. Thesis Statement

Answer: C, A, B, D   Key 1: A

CHAPTER 11 ORGANIZATION AND SUPPORT

MULTIPLE CHOICE

1. A _____ is a construction tool used to map out your speech.

    a. working outline
    b. formal outline
    c. delivery outline
    d. written outline

    Answer: a   Key 1: R

2. All of the following could be purposes of a formal outline EXCEPT:

    a. it can serve as a visual aid
    b. it can serve as a record of a speech that was delivered
    c. it can serve as a guide to keep the speaker on track while delivering
    d. it can serve as a tool to analyze the speech

    Answer: c   Key 1: R

3. Tammica was giving a speech on history of the high-heeled shoe. Which type of organizational pattern should Tammica use?

    a. space pattern
    b. time pattern
    c. topic pattern
    d. cause-effect pattern

    Answer: b   Key 1: A

4. Masha was giving a speech about three different countries that border Russia. She discussed Georgia, Estonia and Kazakhstan. What type of pattern would you expect her to use?

    a. space pattern
    b. time pattern
    c. topic pattern
    d. cause-effect pattern

    Answer: a   Key 1: A

5. A _____ pattern is based on types or categories.

    a. space
    b. time
    c. topic
    d. cause-effect

    Answer: c   Key 1: R

Answer Key Code: R = Recall   C= Conceptual   A = Application   S = Synthesis

6. Brenda was giving a speech about skin cancer. Her first main point discussed that overexposure to sunlight creates skin cancer. Her second main point discussed the different types of skin cancer as a result of overexposure to the sun. What pattern of organization was Brenda using?

    a. time pattern
    b. topic pattern
    c. problem-solution pattern
    d. cause-effect pattern

    Answer: d   Key 1: A

7. Which step in the Motivated Sequence proposes a solution?

    a. attention step
    b. visualization step
    c. action step
    d. satisfaction step

    Answer: d   Key 1: R

8. All of the following are functions of a transition EXCEPT:

    a. they tell how the conclusion relates to the body of the speech
    b. they tell how one main point relates to the next main point
    c. they tell how your subpoints relate to the points they are a part of
    d. they tell how your supporting points relate to the points they support

    Answer: a   Key 1: R

9. All of the following are ways to capture your audience's attention in the attention step EXCEPT:

    a. ask a question
    b. state the thesis
    c. cite a startling fact or opinion
    d. refer to the occasion

    Answer: b   Key 1: R

10. Motivated sequence is most closely related to what other organizing pattern?

    a. topic
    b. cause-effect
    c. climax
    d. problem-solution

    Answer: d   Key 1: C

11. What type of supporting material is represented in the following excerpt from a speech?
    "Your own preventive checkups are like automobile checkups. While most of us are responsible for, even proud of, how we maintain our vehicles, we don't feel the same sense of accomplishment with our own bodies."

    a. description
    b. definition
    c. analogy
    d. anecdote

    Answer: c   Key 1: A

12. All of the following are functions of supporting material EXCEPT:

    a. to disprove
    b. to clarify
    c. to make interesting
    d. to make memorable

    Answer: a   Key 1: R

13. A(n)_____ is a specific case that is used to demonstrate a general idea.

    a. definition
    b. analogy
    c. example
    d. statistic

    Answer: c   Key 1: R

14. Officer Rader was giving a speech to college freshmen about drinking responsibly. In his speech he stated, "one out of seven students will be arrested or cited for an alcohol-related violation." According to this statement, what rule did Officer Rader forget when using a statistic?

    a. citing the source of the statistic
    b. reducing the statistic to a concrete image
    c. not making it vivid enough
    d. making sure he sounded credible stating it

    Answer: a   Key 1: A

15. The outline which is most changeable is the:

    a. working outline
    b. formal outline
    c. manuscript outline
    d. speaking notes outline

    Answer: a   Key 1: C

16. _____ involves telling a story with your information.

    a. Testimony
    b. Narration
    c. Citation
    d. Analogies

    Answer: b   Key 1: R

17. "According to the July 25, 2005 edition of Time Magazine" is an example of a:

    a. testimony
    b. narration
    c. citation
    d. explanation

    Answer: c   Key 1: A

Answer Key Code: R = Recall   C= Conceptual   A = Application   S = Synthesis

18. All of the following are rules for effectively using a visual aid EXCEPT:

    a. Make visual aids large enough for entire audience to view
    b. Make visual aids visually interesting
    c. Make visual aids appropriate for occasion
    d. Make visual aids complex and involved

    Answer: d   Key 1: R

19. All of the following should be included in a conclusion EXCEPT:

    a. an apology for any uncovered points
    b. a review of the thesis
    c. a review of main points
    d. a memorable final remark

    Answer: a   Key 1: R

20. Katya started her speech off with saying "According to Mother Theresa, we cannot all do great things, but we can all do small things with great love." In what way was Katya capturing her audience's attention?

    a. by using an anecdote
    b. by using a quotation
    c. by citing a fact or opinion
    d. by referring to the occasion

    Answer: b   Key 1: R

21. A key-word outline is:

    a. formal
    b. brief
    c. most useful if displayed as a visual aid
    d. about one-third as long as your speech

    Answer: b   Key 1: R

22. I.   Capital punishment is not effective
    II. Capital punishment is not constitutional
    III. Capital punishment is not civilized

    According to the above organization of points, which of the following best represents this structure?

    a. parallel wording
    b. sequential structuring
    c. chronological structuring
    d. anticlimactic structuring

    Answer: a   Key 1: A

TRUE/FALSE

23. Telling your audience what you are going to tell them is called a preview and should be part of your introduction.

    Answer: T   Key 1: R
    It is part of an effective introduction.

24. Attention getters tend to be amusing and slightly outrageous and should not be part of a serious presentation.

Answer: F   Key 1: R
If the introduction fails to capture the audience's attention, what follows will not be heard. It is also essential to prepare the listener for the ideas to come.

25. The cause-effect pattern of organization describes a situation that is wrong and then proposes a way to improve the situation.

Answer: F   Key 1: R
A problem-solution format does this.

26. Speeches should have no more than five main points.

Answer: T   Key 1: R
The text recommends 3-4 main points, with five as a maximum.

27. "Let me repeat that one more time," is an example of a transition.

Answer: F   Key 1: A
A transition ties ideas together and shows how they are related.

28. Examples can be used to prove a position.

Answer: F   Key 1: R
They can be used to clarify information and make it memorable, but they do not prove a point since they refer to isolated instances which may, or may not, be representative.

29. Analogies are brief stories with a particular point.

Answer: F   Key 1: R
Analogies are comparisons in the form of extended similes and metaphors.

30. Statistics are more valuable as proof than are examples.

Answer: T   Key 1: R
Statistics are actually a collection of examples.

31. An effective speech uses a repetitive structure.

Answer: T   Key 1: R
The "preview-develop-review" structure builds in the redundancy necessary for listeners.

32. When you have given a speech on a topic which required more research than you had time to do, you should indicate that in your conclusion by saying, "Unfortunately I wasn't able to spend the necessary time researching."

Answer: F   Key 1: A
You should not apologize in the conclusion.

33. When a quotation is used to prove a point, it is called a testimony.

Answer: T   Key 1: R
Testimony allows the speaker to use the support of someone who is more authoritative and experienced.

Answer Key Code: R = Recall   C= Conceptual   A = Application   S = Synthesis

34. The anticlimax organizational pattern is a good choice for an uninterested audience.

   Answer: T   Key 1: R
   With an uninterested audience you need to build interest early to get them to listen to the rest of the speech.

35. In formal outline, main points and subpoints always represent a division of a whole.

   Answer: T   Key 1: R
   This is the rule of division.

36. A formal outline can serve as a visual aid.

   Answer: T   Key 1: C
   The formal outline can be displayed while the speaker speaks, or handed out.

37. The action step in the Motivated Sequence describes the results of the solution.

   Answer: F   Key 1: R
   This is the definition of the visualization step.

38. When concluding your speech, it is important to end abruptly.

   Answer: F   Key 1: R
   The opposite is true.

39. A good definition is simple and concise.

   Answer: T   Key 1: R
   Simple and concise answers make it easier for retention.

40. A hypothetical example can be more powerful than a factual example.

   Answer: T   Key 1: R
   This is because a hypothetical example asks the audience to imagine something causing them to become an active participant.

41. An anecdote is a brief story that can be based on personal experience.

   Answer: T   Key 1: R
   Not all anecdotes have a point, but often do and mostly come from personal experience.

42. One advantage of using Power Point is that it forces otherwise befuddled speakers to organize their thoughts in advance.

   Answer: T   Key 1: C
   Power point has pros and cons, but it does force the speaker to have prepared in advance.

SHORT ANSWER

43. Select three organizational patterns. Illustrate each by indicating an appropriate topic and set of main ideas.

   Answer: Key 1: A

44. What is the function of a speech introduction? Discuss how the credibility of the speaker and the characteristics of the audience affect the success of an introduction in achieving its purpose.

   Answer: Key 1: C

45. Explain how statistics can function effectively in a speech. Note also how statistics can be abused in speechmaking.

    Answer: Key 1: C

46. Describe the purposes of supporting materials in speech presentations. Give a brief example of a type of supporting material that illustrates each purpose.

    Answer: Key 1: A

47. Select one of the following speech topics. List and describe three different types of visual aids you might use in a speech on that topic.

    Topic #1 - The causes and effects of skin cancer
    Topic #2 - How trees become paper

    Answer: Key 1: A

48. Discuss the value of parallel wording in an outline. Support your discussion with an example.

    Answer: Key 1: A

49. Explain how analyzing your audience will help you demonstrate the importance of a topic to your audience.

    Answer: Key 1: S

50. Is it always necessary to demonstrate the importance of your topic to your audience? If yes, why? If not, when is it not necessary?

    Answer: Key 1: S

51. Your authors advise you to end your speech effectively. What does that mean? Why is it important? How can you do it?

    Answer: Key 1: S

52. Explain how the rule of division operates in outlining.

    Answer: Key 1: C

53. What is the difference between a working and a formal outline? What are the strengths and weakness of each? When should each outline be used?

    Answer: Key 1: C

Answer Key Code: R = Recall   C = Conceptual   A = Application   S = Synthesis

54. Answer the following questions based on the accompanying visual aid.

    What type of visual aid is illustrated?
    What does this aid show? Describe the content in words.
    How could a speaker use this aid?
    What concerns or considerations should the speaker take into account when using this aid?

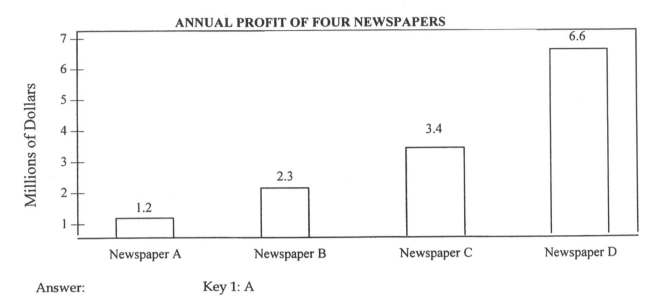

ANNUAL PROFIT OF FOUR NEWSPAPERS

Answer: Key 1: A

55. The text offers advice on effective conclusions. Discuss what your text means by the statement "Do not end abruptly but don't ramble either." Explain how this statement is not a contradiction.

    Answer: Key 1: C

OTHER

56. Match the following steps of the Motivated Sequence to the correct definition.

    _____ establishes the problem   A. Attention Step

    _____ creates interest   B. Need Step

    _____ appeals directly to the audience   C. Satisfaction Step

    _____ proposes a solution   D. Visualization Step

    _____ describes the results of the   E. Action Step
               solution

    Answer: B, A, E, C, D   Key 1: R

CHAPTER 12 PRESENTING YOUR MESSAGE

MULTIPLE CHOICE

1. _____ is the type of stage fright that inhibits effective self-expression.

   a. facilitative
   b. irrational
   c. articulative
   d. debilitative

   Answer: d   Key 1: R

2. Irrational thinking is a cause of:

   a. previous negative experience
   b. debilitative stage fright
   c. facilitative stage fright
   d. destructive stage fright

   Answer: b   Key 1: R

3. Before Jacob gets up to deliver his speech, he says "Somebody will probably laugh at me." This is an example of which type of fallacy?

   a. catastrophic failure
   b. perfection
   c. approval
   d. overgeneralization

   Answer: a   Key 1: A

4. The fallacy of _____ might also be labeled as the fallacy of exaggeration.

   a. catastrophic failure
   b. perfection
   c. approval
   d. overgeneralization

   Answer: d   Key 1: R

5. The fallacy of _____ is the irrational belief that you must gain acceptance from everyone in the audience.

   a. catastrophic failure
   b. perfection
   c. approval
   d. overgeneralization

   Answer: c   Key 1: R

6. All of the following are strategies that can help you manage debilitative stage fright EXCEPT:

   a. using nervousness to your advantage
   b. being rational about your fears
   c. maintaining speaker orientation
   d. keeping a positive attitude

   Answer: c   Key: R

Answer Key Code: R = Recall   C= Conceptual   A = Application   S = Synthesis

7. A(n)_____ speech is planned in advance but presented in direct, spontaneous manner.

    a. manuscript
    b. memorized
    c. impromptu
    d. extemporaneous

    Answer: d   Key 1: R

8. All of the following are helpful tips for impromptu speaking EXCEPT:

    a. make sure to remember what every other expert says about your topic
    b. don't be afraid to be original
    c. keep your comments brief
    d. keep a positive attitude

    Answer: a   Key 1: R

9. All of the following are guidelines for preparing a n.......script speech EXCEPT:

    a. recognize the difference between written messages and speeches
    b. use long paragraphs to help establish eye contact with your audience
    c. print out the manuscript triple spaced, in capital letters
    d. rehearse until you can "read" whole lines without looking at the manuscript

    Answer: b   Key 1: R

10. Often times, _____ speeches are the most difficult to deliver effectively and overall the least effective style of delivery.

    a. manuscript
    b. impromptu
    c. memorized
    d. extemporaneous

    Answer: c   Key 1: R

11. All of the following are visual aspects of delivery EXCEPT:

    a. appearance
    b. pitch
    c. movement
    d. facial expression

    Answer: b   Key 1: R

12. _____ is perhaps the most important nonverbal facet of delivery.

    a. Movement
    b. Posture
    c. Appearance
    d. Eye contact

    Answer: d   Key 1: R

13. On average, the normal speaking speed is between _____ words per minute.

    a. 170 to 190
    b. 250 to 270
    c. 120 to 150
    d. 110 to 130

    Answer: c   Key 1: R

14. Carla kept falling asleep during Caleb's speech because he was very monotone. Which of the following nonverbal vocal cues was Caleb having difficulty with?

    a. pitch
    b. volume
    c. articulation
    d. rate

    Answer: a   Key 1: A

15. During Brent's speech he kept slurring his words together. Which of the following nonverbal vocal cues was Brent having difficulty with?

    a. pitch
    b. volume
    c. articulation
    d. rate

    Answer: c   Key 1: A

16. The use of tag questions is a form of:

    a. deletion
    b. substitution
    c. slurring
    d. addition

    Answer: d   Key 1: R

17. _____ is the most common mistake in articulation of words.

    a. Substitution
    b. Deletion
    c. Addition
    d. Slurring

    Answer: b   Key 1: R

18. In Ellen's speech she said "dat" instead of "that." Ellen was having a problem with which aspect of articulation?

    a. deletion
    b. addition
    c. substitution
    d. slurring

    Answer: c   Key 1: A

Answer Key Code: R = Recall   C= Conceptual   A = Application   S = Synthesis

19. Appropriate eye contact in a classroom setting would be to:

    a. look just slightly over the audience members' heads
    b. look at the front and back rows
    c. look at each member of the audience at least once
    d. focus on those who look supportive

    Answer: c   Key 1: R

20. When speakers expect themselves to perform flawlessly, they exhibit the fallacy of:

    a. perfection
    b. approval
    c. overgeneralization
    d. all the above

    Answer: a   Key 1: R

21. A dialect affects:

    a. pitch
    b. volume
    c. articulation
    d. emphasis

    Answer: c   Key 1: R

22. When you picture yourself presenting a successful speech before you give it, you are using:

    a. rationality
    b. a received-oriented approach
    c. substitution
    d. visualization

    Answer: d   Key 1: R

TRUE/FALSE

23. Stage fright is always harmful.

    Answer: F   Key 1: R
    Stage fright can facilitate performance. Only when it becomes debilitative does it become harmful.

24. One effective way to alleviate communication apprehension is to concentrate so hard on what you are saying that the audience becomes a minor concern.

    Answer: F   Key 1: R
    It is important to be receiver-oriented and concentrate on your audience.

25. Speeches use more repetition than written messages.

    Answer: T   Key 1: R
    Repetition helps speakers and listeners remember ideas and information.

26. Movement by the speaker can extend the "action zone" of the audience.

    Answer: T   Key 1: R
    The normal "action zone" (front and center) may be enlarged by a speaker who uses appropriate movement and thus maintains contact with all members of the audience.

27. The ideal eye contact for a classroom speaker is to catch the eye of only listeners seated in the "action zone."

    Answer: F   Key 1: R
    Ideally the speaker maintains brief eye contact with every member of the audience.

28. An impromptu speech allows the dual advantage of careful planning and spontaneity.

    Answer: F   Key 1: R
    This is true of an extemporaneous speech.

29. When you practice a speech you risk losing that "freshness" required for an effective speech.

    Answer: F   Key 1: R
    Practice is essential to a successful speech and familiarity should free you to use more eye contact and gestures which help "freshness."

30. Appearance is considered an aspect of speech delivery.

    Answer: T   Key 1: R
    It is one of the visual aspects.

31. Voluntary movement is preferred over involuntary movement in speech delivery.

    Answer: T   Key 1: R
    Involuntary movement occurs as shaking or twitching and is distracting.

32. Researchers have determined that the highest level of speech anxiety occurs during the time you spend preparing your speech.

    Answer: F   Key 1: R
    Researchers have determined that the highest level of speech anxiety occurs just before speaking, the second highest level at the time the assignment is announced and explained, and the lowest level during the time you spend preparing your speech.

33. Rapid rate is associated with speaker competence.

    Answer: T   Key 1: R
    Studies indicate this is true.

34. Facilitative stage fright is a factor that can help improve your performance.

    Answer: T   Key 1: R
    Facilitative stage fright is a positive energy that can be channeled into your speech.

35. Being completely calm can take away the passion that is one element of a good speech.

    Answer: T   Key 1: R
    It helps to use nervousness to your advantage in your speech.

Answer Key Code: R = Recall   C= Conceptual   A = Application   S = Synthesis

36. It is realistic to expect that you'll deliver a perfect speech.

    Answer: F   Key 1: R
    One way of overcoming debilitative stage fright is to be rational about your fears.

37. Another technique for building a positive attitude is known as visualization.

    Answer: T   Key 1: R
    Keeping a positive attitude is an aspect of overcoming debilitative stage fright.

38. Preparation is the most important key to controlling speech anxiety.

    Answer: T   Key 1: R
    Preparation is the most important aspect of overcoming debilitative stage fright.

39. Extemporaneous speaking tends to create a more formal and less casual atmosphere.

    Answer: F   Key 1: C
    Actually the opposite is true. Extemporaneous requires a more conversational tone thus creating a more casual atmosphere.

40. One way to control involuntary movement is to move voluntarily when you feel the need to move.

    Answer: T   Key 1: R
    Being aware of your movements makes them become voluntary, whereas involuntary movements the speaker is usually blind to.

SHORT ANSWER

41. Compare and contrast facilitative with debilitative stage fright. Suggest approaches with which to decrease excessive anxiety about speechmaking.

    Answer: Key 1: C

42. Describe the four types of speech delivery. Explain the advantages and disadvantages of each.

    Answer: Key 1: R

43. Relate what you know about paralanguage to auditory delivery.

    Answer: Key 1: S

44. Explain the connection between the self-fulfilling prophecy and giving a speech.

    Answer: Key 1: S

45. Relate the following statement by Leonard Zunin to giving a speech. "Courage is seeing your fear in a realistic perspective, defining it, considering the alternatives, and choosing to function in spite of the risk."

    Answer: Key 1: S

46. Communication consultants recommend you concentrate on the following three statements before you speak. "I'm glad I'm here." "I know my topic." "I care about you." (meaning the audience) What if one or more were not true?

    Answer: Key 1: S

47. Critique the following piece of criticism in terms of the three criteria for constructive criticism.

    "I liked your speech, but it was hard to hear."

    Answer: Key 1: A

48. Describe your own presentation skills. What would you most like to improve? How would you develop those skills?

    Answer: Key 1: A

49. Discuss in detail some important guidelines for the visual aspects of delivery. How can each of the guidelines enhance the delivery of your speech?

    Answer: Key 1: A

MATCHING

50. Match the following events with the most appropriate type of delivery.

    _____ Presidential State of the Union   A. Memorized
          Address
                                                  B. Manuscript
    _____ Class lecture on stage fright
                                                  C. Impromptu
    _____ A speech used in an oratory contest
                                                  D. Extemporaneous
    _____ An unplanned speech given on the
          same day assigned

    Answer: B, D, A, C   Key 1: A

Answer Key Code: R = Recall   C= Conceptual   A = Application   S = Synthesis

CHAPTER 13 INFORMATIVE SPEAKING

MULTIPLE CHOICE

1. "After listening to my speech the audience will be able to explain the problems with punch card ballots." This purpose statement is:

    a. good because it tells what the audience will be able to do
    b. good because it explains what the speaker will do
    c. bad because it does not tell what the speaker will do
    d. bad because it is not adapted to the audience

    Answer: a   Key 1: A

2. Which of the following are effective ways to emphasize important points?

    a. repetition
    b. signposts
    c. strong organization
    d. all of the above

    Answer: d   Key 1: R

3. Audience involvement with a speech by use of participation or volunteers will generally have the effect of:

    a. distracting some listeners
    b. decreasing topic relevance
    c. increasing audience comprehension
    d. decreasing information hunger

    Answer: c   Key 1: R

4. In a question and answer period, a speaker may respond to a question by saying, "If I understand your question correctly, I think you are asking how I interpret the legal battle. Am I correct?" This speaker's response is an example of:

    a. defensive reaction to a question
    b. evasion of the question
    c. brief answer to the question
    d. paraphrasing

    Answer: d   Key 1: A

5. Information overload is also commonly known as:

    a. redundancy
    b. information anxiety
    c. information phenomenon
    d. information hunger

    Answer: b   Key 1: R

Answer Key Code: R = Recall   C= Conceptual   A = Application   S = Synthesis

6. Informative speeches are generally categorized according to their content, including the following types EXCEPT:

    a. speeches about objects
    b. speeches about instructions
    c. speeches about processes
    d. speeches about events

    Answer: b   Key 1: R

7. An informative specific purpose statement will usually be worded to stress:

    a. knowledge
    b. ability
    c. attitude
    d. a & b

    Answer: d   Key 1: R

8. A sentence that states, "After listening to my speech my audience will be able to..." is an example of a:

    a. thesis
    b. briefing
    c. central idea
    d. specific purpose

    Answer: d   Key 1: R

9. The ideal number of main points in an informative speech is:

    a. 3-5
    b. 1 or 2
    c. 6-7
    d. 3-7

    Answer: a   Key 1: R

10. Which of the following patterns is recommended for presenting information?

    a. vague to clear
    b. simple to complex
    c. complex to simple
    d. central to superficial

    Answer: b   Key 1: R

11. Which of the following is not essential in the introduction of an informative speech?

    a. establish the importance of your topic
    b. preview the thesis
    c. state your specific purposes
    d. preview the main points

    Answer: c   Key 1: R

12. In informative speaking supporting material is used to:

 a. clarify
 b. make interesting
 c. make memorable
 d. all of the above

Answer: d   Key 1: R

13. A speech of _____ is the most straightforward type of informative speech.

 a. description
 b. explanation
 c. instruction
 d. persuasion

Answer: a   Key 1: R

14. Creating a reason for your audience to want to listen and learn from your speech is known as:

 a. a thesis statement
 b. a specific purpose
 c. information hunger
 d. a central idea

Answer: c   Key 1: R

15. All of the following are ways to make it easy for your audience to listen EXCEPT:

 a. Speak loud enough to be heard by your listeners
 b. Limit the amount of information you present
 c. Use unfamiliar information to increase understanding of the familiar
 d. Use simple information to build up the understanding of complex information

Answer: c   Key 1: R

16. In Jordan's speech about the negative effects of using tanning beds, she states "What I am about to say about UVB rays is important." This is an example of a:

 a. signpost
 b. internal summary
 c. statement of preview
 d. statement of emphasis

Answer: a   Key 1: A

17. All of the following are ways to generate audience involvement EXCEPT:

 a. personalizing your speech
 b. using clear language
 c. using volunteers
 d. having a question-and-answer period

Answer: b   Key 1: R

Answer Key Code: R = Recall   C= Conceptual   A = Application   S = Synthesis

18. Which of the following are organizational principles that are important to address in the conclusion of an informative speech?

    a.   review of main points
    b.   establish importance of thesis
    c.   provide audience with a memory aid
    d.   a and c only

Answer: d   Key 1: R

TRUE/FALSE

19. Signposts can be used to warn your audience that something important is coming up.

Answer: T   Key 1: R
By definition, signposts serve this function.

20. Audience involvement, such as the members raising their hands, increases comprehension.

Answer: T   Key 1: R
As noted in the text, audience involvement increases comprehension..

21. A speaker who reacts to a threatening question by cutting down the questioner is reacting defensively.

Answer: T   Key 1: A
A speaker is defensive when he or she reacts to a question as a personal attack.

22. A speaker should avoid repetition.

Answer: F   Key 1: R
Repetition is necessary for listeners, but should not be used with trivial or boring points or to run an important point into the ground.

23. Information overload is also known as information anxiety.

Answer: T   Key 1: R
Speakers need to know how much in formation to provide their listeners that will not cause psychological stress.

24. Personal information and personal anecdotes do not belong in formal public presentations and can detract from the impact.

Answer: F   Key 1: R
One way to encourage audience involvement in a serious presentation is to give the audience a human being to connect to.

25. "All novels contain three basic elements" is a thesis statement.

Answer: T   Key 1: A
A thesis statement presents the central idea.

26. Giving your audience a reason to listen is creating information hunger.

Answer: T   Key 1: R
This is the definition of the phrase.

27. In an informative speech it is important to remind your audience of the importance of your topic to them.

    Answer: T   Key 1: R
    This is one of the three things a conclusion should do, along with reviewing main points and providing a memory aid.

28. A clear purpose statement will lead to a clear thesis statement.

    Answer: T   Key 1: R
    Having a clear purpose statement helps with the clarity of the speech and thesis statement.

SHORT ANSWER

29. List the four suggestions your text offers for answering audience questions after your speech. Explain what might happen if the advice is not followed.

    Answer: Key 1: A

30. Explain what the term "information hunger" means. Discuss why a speaker wants to create information hunger and how a speaker can achieve this aim.

    Answer: Key 1: R

31. Discuss three ways to generate audience involvement. Provide examples for each.

    Answer: Key 1: A

32. Discuss the similarities and differences between informative speaking and persuasive speaking.

    Answer: Key 1: R

33. How does the following quotation by Anatole France relate to "information hunger"? "The whole art of informing is only the art of awakening the natural curiosity of a mind for the purpose of satisfying it afterwards."

    Answer: Key 1: S

34. Assume you are to speak on a complex topic. Which forms of supporting material will be most helpful? Explain how each will be helpful.

    Answer: Key 1: A

35. Critique the following sentences in terms of the three qualities of clear language presented in Chapter Thirteen.

    "With regard to the big problem we face today, we must get going. We must not fool around anymore."

    Answer: Key 1: A

36. Explain three ways to create information hunger within your audience and give an example of each.

    Answer: Key 1: A

37. Explain what effect, if any, using a single audience volunteer has on the rest of the audience.

    Answer: Key 1: R

Answer Key Code: R = Recall   C= Conceptual   A = Application   S = Synthesis

38. For the topic of "Low Calorie Cooking," write three different purpose sentences using three of the verbs listed below.

   Compare   Explain   Apply
   Describe   List   Analyze

   Answer: Key 1: A

39. Discuss the differences between speeches about objects and events. How would each type of speech be structured differently? Provide examples of each.

   Answer: Key 1: A

40. Write a specific purpose sentence and a thesis sentence for an informative speech on baseball.

   Answer: Key 1: A

41. E.M. Forester said, "Knowledge is power they say. Knowledge is not only power, it is good fun." What are the implications of this for informative speakers? What can be done to make information "good fun?"

   Answer: Key 1: S

42. How is what is taught in school an example of how cultural background is always a part of informative speaking?

   Answer: Key 1: S

MATCHING

43. Match the speech topic with the type of informative speech content.

   _____ The role of conservation on the   A. Objects
         modern farm
                                                 B. Processes
   _____ Preparing the field for harvest   C. Events

   _____ The invention of the cotton gin and its D. Concepts
         impact on farming

   _____ Types of fertilizer

   Answer: D, B, C, A   Key 1: A

44. Match the speech topic with the type of informative speech purpose.

   _____ A new product for cleaning toilet   A. Explanations
         bowls
                                                  B. Instructions
   _____ Why the national debt is so large
                                                  C. Descriptions
   _____ Discussing the perfect golf swing

   Answer: C, A, B   Key 1: A

CHAPTER 14 PERSUASIVE SPEAKING

MULTIPLE CHOICE

1. _____ tells us that when members of an audience hear a persuasive appeal, they compare it to opinions that they already hold.

   a.   Social penetration theory
   b.   Social judgment theory
   c.   Sapir-Worf theory
   d.   Dialectical judgment theory

   Answer: b   Key 1: R

2. In a persuasive presentation the _____ best represents the listener's point of view.

   a.   latitude of acceptance
   b.   latitude of rejection
   c.   latitude of noncommitment
   d.   anchor

   Answer: d   Key 1: R

3. All of the following are examples of unethical behavior in persuasion EXCEPT:

   a.   stating your personal opinion
   b.   faking enthusiasm about a speech topic
   c.   plagiarizing material from another source
   d.   making up statistics to support your case

   Answer: a   Key 1: R

4. All of the following should be done when creating a persuasive message EXCEPT:

   a.   set a clear, persuasive purpose
   b.   structure the message carefully
   c.   create multiple solutions
   d.   use solid evidence

   Answer: c   Key 1: R

5. _____ fallacy is when the speaker attacks a person's integrity in order to weaken the argument.

   a.   Ad hominem
   b.   Reductio ad absurdum
   c.   Post hoc
   d.   Argumentum ad populum

   Answer: a   Key 1: R

6. Lee was giving a persuasive speech on saving wild life when he said "If we allow developers to build homes in one section, soon we will have no open spaces left." This is an example of which fallacy?

   a.   ad hominem
   b.   reductio ad absurdum
   c.   post hoc
   d.   argumentum ad populum

   Answer: b   Key 1: A

7. _____ fallacy mistakenly assumes that one event causes another because they occur sequentially.

   a. Ad hominem
   b. Reductio ad absurdum
   c. Post hoc
   d. Argumentum ad populum

   Answer: c   Key 1: R

8. All of the following are ways to adapt to your audience EXCEPT:

   a. establish common ground
   b. organize according to your personal persuasive needs
   c. neutralize potential hostility
   d. organize according to expected response

   Answer: b   Key 1: R

9. All of the following are components of credibility EXCEPT:

   a. appearance
   b. competence
   c. character
   d. charisma

   Answer: a   Key 1: R

10. All of the following are rules for preparing an effective persuasive speech EXCEPT:

    a. set a clear, persuasive purpose
    b. use solid evidence
    c. use appeals that appeal to authority
    d. structure the message carefully

    Answer: b   Key 1: R

11. All of the following are characteristics of persuasion EXCEPT:

    a. persuasion is not coercive
    b. persuasion is not usually incremental
    c. persuasion is interactive
    d. persuasion can be ethical

    Answer: b   Key 1: R

12. A speaker who begins a speech by stating the desired audience response is using:

    a. direct persuasion
    b. indirect persuasion
    c. reasoning by sign
    d. an attention-getter

    Answer: a   Key 1: R

Answer Key Code: R = Recall   C= Conceptual   A = Application   S = Synthesis

13. President Lyndon Johnson began most of his speeches with the phrase, "My fellow Americans." This is an example of:

    a. building credibility
    b. using an ad hominem argument
    c. developing a "yes" response
    d. establishing common ground

    Answer: d   Key 1: A

14. Listeners are required to determine the truth when there is a proposition of:

    a. fact
    b. value
    c. policy
    d. b and c

    Answer: a   Key 1: R

15. "California is the best place to live" is a proposition of:

    a. fact
    b. value
    c. policy
    d. actuation

    Answer: b   Key 1: A

16. "Tobacco companies should be abolished" is a proposition of:

    a. fact
    b. value
    c. policy
    d. actuation

    Answer: c   Key 1: A

17. Changing the way an audience thinks refers to:

    a. convincing
    b. actuating
    c. stimulating
    d. intellectualizing

    Answer: a   Key 1: R

18. Action is to actuating as _____ is to convincing.

    a. theory
    b. belief
    c. value
    d. fact

    Answer: b   Key 1: C

19. When facing a hostile audience the speaker should use:

    a. direct persuasion
    b. indirect persuasion
    c. redirect persuasion
    d. bipolar directed persuasion

    Answer: b   Key 1: R

20. Honesty and impartiality are most closely related to:

    a. congeniality
    b. competence
    c. character
    d. charisma

    Answer: c   Key 1: R

21. Enthusiasm is most closely related to:

    a. common ground
    b. competence
    c. character
    d. charisma

    Answer: d   Key 1: R

22. "Either we outlaw alcohol in city parks, or there will be no way to get rid of drunks!" This is an example of:

    a. Either-or fallacy
    b. Reductio ad absurdum fallacy
    c. Post hoc fallacy
    d. Argumentum ad populum fallacy

    Answer: a   Key 1: R

23. Dynamism is another word for:

    a. enthusiasm
    b. competence
    c. character
    d. strength of impression

    Answer: a   Key 1: R

24. A speaker who uses the phrase "we all care about the environment we live in" is attempting to:

    a. show that he or she likes the audience
    b. increase his or her credibility
    c. emphasize similarities between speaker and audience
    d. indicate competence

    Answer: c   Key 1: A

Answer Key Code: R = Recall   C= Conceptual   A = Application   S = Synthesis

25. Because attitudes do not change instantly or dramatically, persuasion is usually:

    a. ethical
    b. incremental
    c. direct
    d. charismatic

    Answer: b   Key 1: R

26. When you are "highly ego-involved" with a topic you:

    a. are apathetic
    b. are concerned, but not motivated to change
    c. care very strongly
    d. are deceiving yourself about something

    Answer: c   Key 1: R

27. According to Motivated Sequence, the last step in a sequence designed to motivate others is:

    a. the need step
    b. the action step
    c. the satisfaction step
    d. the visualization step

    Answer: b   Key 1: R

TRUE/FALSE

28. Persuasion and coercion are synonymous.

    Answer: F   Key 1: R
    Persuasion is not coercive; the listener has free will.

29. Successful persuasion is usually incremental.

    Answer: T   Key 1: R
    Most attitudes are not normally changed instantly or dramatically.

30. The view point of the speaker is known as the anchor.

    Answer: F   Key 1: R
    The anchor is the view point of the listener.

31. Propositions of value recommend a specific course of action.

    Answer: F   Key 1: R
    This would be a proposition of policy.

32. "Cheerleaders are not as important as the athletes on the field" is an example of proposition of fact.

    Answer: F   Key 1: A
    This would be an example of proposition of value.

33. When you set about to actuate an audience, you want to move its members to a specific behavior.

    Answer: T   Key 1: R
    Actuating is changing behavior and convincing is changing the way the audience thinks.

34. Indirect persuasion is sometimes easy to spot.

   Answer: T   Key 1: R
   Even though direct persuasion is the most obvious, indirect persuasion can sometimes be spotted.

35. Emotional evidence is an ethical fault only when it used to obscure the truth.

   Answer: T   Key 1: R
   Using emotional evidence is useful and ethical in persuasion if used correctly.

36. In Chris's speech he stated "How could we believe Michael Moore's documentary Fahrenheit 9/11 because he is such a fat slob!" This is an example of an ad hominem fallacy.

   Answer: T   Key 1: A
   Ad hominem is when a speaker attacks the integrity of a person in order to weak the argument.

37. An appeal to authority fallacy involves relying on testimony of someone who is an authority in the case being argued.

   Answer: F   Key 1: R
   An appeal to authority fallacy would involve the testimony of someone who is not an authority in that case, like a movie star endorsing a certain political candidate.

38. The target audience is the subgroup you must persuade, and you aim your speech mostly at them.

   Answer: T   Key 1: R
   This is the definition of target audience.

39. One possible way of neutralizing potential hostility is show that you understand their point of view.

   Answer: T   Key 1: R
   This helps establish a common ground.

40. Credibility does not refer to the believability of a speaker.

   Answer: F   Key 1: R
   Credibility does refer to believability, and the audience must perceive the speaker as believable to trust and view as credible.

41. Charisma is not the same thing as dynamism.

   Answer: F   Key 1: R
   Dynamism is another term for charisma.

42. The social penetration theory tells us that when members of an audience hear a persuasive appeal, they compare it to opinions that they already hold.

   Answer: F   Key 1: R
   This is the definition of the social judgment theory.

43. The social judgment theory suggest that the best chance of changing a person's attitude would come by presenting an argument based on a position that fell somewhere within the listener's latitude of noncommitment.

   Answer: T   Key 1: R
   The closer to the latitude of rejection or acceptance it is, the more their minds are already set prior to the encounter.

Answer Key Code: R = Recall   C= Conceptual   A = Application   S = Synthesis

44. Faking enthusiasm would be an example of unethical persuasion.

    Answer: T   Key 1: R
    Enthusiasm that is not genuine would be misleading the audience and thus would be unethical.

45. Direct persuasion is most effective with a friendly audience.

    Answer: T   Key 1: R
    In contrast, indirect persuasion is most useful with a hostile audience.

46. Withholding information can be considered an unethical communication practice.

    Answer: T   Key 1: R
    It is considered suppressing information to the audience.

47. Persuasion differs from coercion because persuasion makes a listener want to change.

    Answer: T   Key 1: R
    The absence of force is a major distinction between the two.

48. Emotional appeals sometimes can be considered evidence that strongly supports a claim.

    Answer: T   Key 1: R
    Supporting factual material that evokes emotions can also establish the truth of a claim.

49. Personal interviews do not require as careful a citation as printed forms of evidence.

    Answer: F   Key 1: R
    Careful citations are important no matter what the source of your evidence.

SHORT ANSWER

50. Define ethical persuasion. Based on your definition, are the following situations examples of ethical or unethical persuasion? Explain your decision.

    Situation #1 — You are a sales clerk and the customer is trying on an outfit which you do not think is flattering. He or she seems to really feel good about how it looks and feels. He/she asks, "What do you think?" You say, "It looks like you enjoy that outfit. It is really contemporary looking."

    Situation #2 — The same situation as above, but you say, "I think that style isn't as flattering as some of the others, but you should buy what you like."

    Situation #3 — You're a little league coach and one little boy is not a good hitter. Just before he goes to the plate you say, "Hit it out of the park! I know you can do it!"

    Situation #4 — You believe you are the better of two candidates running for mayor. You point out to your audience that your opponent is a practicing attorney who has said previously he would like to work part-time at each job. Recently, however, he has added that he would be a full-time mayor if necessary. You don't mention this more recent statement.

    Answer: Key 1: A

51. Assume you are planning a speech in which your goal is to get the audience to give blood. Explain what you would do at each step of the Motivated Sequence to accomplish your purpose.

    Answer: Key 1: A

52. Explain why the following are considered unethical communication behaviors.

    Insufficient evidence
    Not revealing the source of information
    Using fallacious reasoning to misrepresent the truth
    Failing to use balanced appeals
    Plagiarism

    Answer: Key 1: C

53. Explain the connections between informative and persuasive speaking.

    Answer: Key 1: C

54. In what ways could persuasive speaking be viewed as problem solving?

    Answer: Key 1: C

55. Do emotions play a role in the problem-solving sequence used in persuasive speaking? How?

    Answer: Key 1: C

56. List the "Three C's" of credibility and define each.

    Answer: Key 1: R

57. List and discuss the rules for preparing an effective persuasive speech. Provide examples for each.

    Answer: Key 1: A

58. Explain how persuasion can be interactive in a public speaking situation.

    Answer: Key 1: R

MATCHING

59. Match the following statements to the appropriate fallacy.

    _____ I don't agree with that speaker, he looks   A. Reduction to the absurd
          like an idiot!
                                                             B. Either-or
    _____ If we allow one person to leave the
          meeting early, no one will come to the   C. Ad hominem
          meeting at all!
                                                             D. Bandwagon appeal
    _____ America, Love it or Leave it!
                                                             E. Appeal to authority
    _____ You should buy this sports car because
          Tiger Woods says it's a good car.

    _____ If you buy this brand of clothes, you will
          be cool like the rest of us!

    Answer: C, A, B, E, D   Key 1: A

Answer Key Code: R = Recall   C= Conceptual   A = Application   S = Synthesis

OTHER

60. Label the following as propositions of fact (F), value (V), or policy (P).

    _____ Corporal punishment is harmful to children.

    _____ Inflation is caused by consumers overspending.

    _____ Men talk more than women.

    _____ States should provide a free college education to all who want it.

    _____ Freedom of speech is our most precious freedom.

    Answer: V, F, F, P, V   Key 1: A

APPENDIX: INTERVIEWING

MULTIPLE CHOICE

1. A good introduction for an interview should:

    a. give a preview of the subjects to be covered.
    b. avoid giving away all the subjects that will be covered.
    c. indicate some subjects that will be covered, but keep some as fresh topics for later.
    d. determine mutually what topics will be covered.

    Answer: a   Key 1: R

2. If an interviewer misinterprets your ideas you should:

    a. talk more slowly
    b. remember "the interviewer is always right"
    c. correct the mistaken impression
    d. ask the interviewer a question

    Answer: c   Key 1: R

3. The longest stage of the interview is the:

    a. opening
    b. body
    c. closing
    d. Ideally all are equal.

    Answer: b   Key 1: R

4. An interview in which an employer screens job applicants to determine their suitability for employment is called a (an):

    a. selection interview
    b. information-gathering interview
    c. appraisal interview
    d. counseling interview

    Answer: a   Key 1: R

5. When political candidates ask to interview groups of their constituents prior to an election, the interview is most likely to be which type?

    a. appraisal
    b. selection
    c. persuasive
    d. survey

    Answer: c   Key 1: R

6. A difference between conversation and an interview is:

    a. purpose
    b. length
    c. transactional nature of speaking/listening roles
    d. There is no difference.

    Answer: a   Key 1: R

Answer Key Code: R = Recall   C= Conceptual   A = Application   S = Synthesis

7. By asking a newspaper interviewer to allow you to see the article about you before it is printed, you are most likely trying to accomplish the interviewee role of:

   a. giving clear, detailed answers
   b. keeping on the subject
   c. correcting any misunderstandings
   d. covering your own agenda

   Answer: c   Key 1: A

8. All of the following are ways the interviewee can enhance the interview encounter EXCEPT:

   a. clarify the interviewer's goals
   b. clarify your own goals
   c. set the agenda
   d. prepare answers in advance

   Answer: c   Key 1: R

9. What type of question is the following?

   "Our company is very environmentally conscious. Do you think that's important?"

   a. hypothetical
   b. atopical
   c. leading
   d. neutral

   Answer: c   Key 1: A

10. In an interview it is good to use a secondary question when you want to:

    a. collect information from many respondents
    b. check a response that sounds inaccurate
    c. provoke or challenge an interviewee
    d. make the interviewee feel relaxed

    Answer: b   Key 1: R

11. If you are the interviewer and your intention is to maintain a fairly high degree of control over the interview, it would be advisable to:

    a. use many open questions
    b. use many closed questions
    c. use many neutral questions
    d. use many opinion questions

    Answer: b   Key 1: A

12. The type of questions which are phrased in such a way that they encourage the interviewee to answer in detail are known as:

    a. coptic questions
    b. leading questions
    c. open questions
    d. closed questions

    Answer: c   Key 1: A

13. By definition, all interviews:

    a.   are preconceived
    b.   have a serious purpose
    c.   are bipolar
    d.   all the above

Answer: d   Key 1: R

14. Probes in an interview include:

    a.   amplifying
    b.   repeating
    c.   silence
    d.   all the above

Answer: d   Key 1: R

15. Cynthia asks the job applicant, "How long were you employed at the Harris Brothers law firm?" Her question is an example of which of the following?

    a.   an open question
    b.   a closed question
    c.   a leading question
    d.   a secondary question

Answer: b   Key 1: A

TRUE/FALSE

16. A good interviewer is sometimes quiet.

Answer: T   Key 1: R
An interviewer can gather information by silence.

17. An interview must have at least one participant who has a preconceived purpose.

Answer: T   Key 1: R
By definition.

18. It is rarely a good idea to ask personal friends and contacts for help with your job search.

Answer: F   Key 1: A
A survey by the U.S. Department of Labor showed that 70 percent of the respondents learned about the job they held through contacts with people in their personal networks: friends, coworkers, relatives, and teachers.

19. If an interviewer wants to keep an open mind, she/he should enter an interview without a clear purpose.

Answer: F   Key 1: R
Interviewers and interviewees should always go into interviews with clear purposes in mind.

20. Performance appraisal interviews should use evaluative language.

Answer: F   Key 1: R
Descriptive language is most effective.

Answer Key Code: R = Recall   C= Conceptual   A = Application   S = Synthesis

21. The opening stage of an interview should preview the topics of the interview.

    Answer: T   Key 1: R
    This will help the interviewee know what to expect.

22. At a job interview the applicant should ask approximately half the questions.

    Answer: F   Key 1: R
    The applicant should have some questions, but the interviewer should control the interview.

23. Sincere pleasantries should only be exchanged in the opening stage of an interview.

    Answer: F   Key 1: R
    This is also appropriate in the closing stage.

24. The opposite of a leading question is a neutral question.

    Answer: T   Key 1: C
    A neutral question does not influence the interviewee whereas a leading question signals the desired response.

25. The phrase, "What if . . . ?" is often used in leading questions.

    Answer: F   Key 1: R
    This is used most in hypothetical questions.

26. It is considered pushy for an interviewee to write a thank you note after an employment interview.

    Answer: F   Key 1: R
    This is highly recommended.

SHORT ANSWER

27. There are several topics that are typically asked about in a job interview. Select three of them and for each one (1) explain why it is an important topic, (2) give an example of a question from this area, and (3) explain what you as an interviewee would want to communicate about this topic area.

    Answer: Key 1: S

28. List three things that are appropriate to do in the closing of a job interview.

    Answer: Key 1: R

29. Compare the purposes of selection and performance appraisal interviews. Explain what types of questions might be useful for each. Defend your position.

    Answer: Key 1: A

30. Explain the responsibilities of the interviewee during an interview. Illustrate with an example.

    Answer: Key 1: A

31. Explain the role of nonverbal communication in interviewing.

    Answer: Key 1: S

32. Can an interview move to a public speaking situation? Explain.

    Answer: Key 1: C

33. The following interview purposes are too broad to be helpful. Change each one into a specific content objective.

    a. Learn about the job of newspaper editor.
    b. Learn about how to use the school library.
    c. Learn about recreational opportunities in town.
    d. Learn how to do well in a specific course.

    Answer: Key 1: A

34. Discuss the role of self-disclosure in interviewing.

    Answer: Key 1: C

35. Your authors suggest that it is important to collect background information before an interview. Select one of the following topics and describe the information you would collect before the interview.

    #1 - An interview with a local police officer about the drug situation on campus
    #2 - An interview with a local winner of the state "Mother of the Year Award"

    Answer: Key 1: A

36. Write a brief hypothetical scenario of things an interviewer says in the opening stage of a selection interview.

    Answer: Key 1: A

37. Describe how an interviewer's "hidden goals" might influence the types of questions he/she would ask in a selection interview. Give examples.

    Answer: Key 1: A

MATCHING

38. Match the type of interview with the most likely purpose.

    ____ Increase employee productivity   A. Performance appraisal

    ____ Selling a product   B. Information gathering

    ____ Researching a speech topic   C. Persuasive

    ____ Helping a couple solve their financial   D. Counseling
           budget imbalance problems

    Answer: A, C, B, D   Key 1: R

39. Match the following types of interviews with the appropriate reason.

    ____ Selection interview   A. A market survey

    ____ Information gathering interview   B. Promotion

    ____ Problem and evaluation interview   C. Counseling

    ____ Persuasive interview   D. Selling services

    Answer: B, A, C, D   Key 1: R

Answer Key Code: R = Recall   C= Conceptual   A = Application   S = Synthesis

OTHER

40. Change each of the following closed questions into open questions.

    a. What was your major in college?
    b. Do you like to play golf?
    c. Have you read our last annual report?
    d. Does your company provide dental insurance?

    Answer: Key 1: A

GUIDE TO MEDIATED COMMUNICATION

MULTIPLE CHOICE

1. All of the following could be considered forms of mass communication EXCEPT:

    a. movies
    b. newspapers
    c. television
    d. public speeches

    Answer: d   Key 1: C

2. _____ determine what messages will be delivered to media consumers, how those messages will be constructed, and when they will be delivered.

    a. Informants
    b. Gatekeepers
    c. Knowledge consumers
    d. Marketers

    Answer: b   Key 1: R

3. According to the _____ theory, people who watch violent movies become violent.

    a. bullet
    b. two-step
    c. multistep
    d. social flow

    Answer: a   Key 1: R

4. _____ theory states that media effects occur in interaction with interpersonal communication.

    a. Bullet
    b. Two-step
    c. Multistep
    d. Social flow

    Answer: b   Key 1: R

5. _____ theory relies on the fact that opinion leaders greatly influence the message, and opinion leaders may have other opinion leaders that influence their opinions.

    a. Bullet
    b. Two-step
    c. Multistep
    d. Social flow

    Answer: c   Key 1: R

6. _____ theory is based on the assumption that people learn how to behave by observing others.

    a. Flow
    b. Diffusion of innovations
    c. Social learning
    d. Individual differences

    Answer: c   Key 1: R

Answer Key Code: R = Recall   C= Conceptual   A = Application   S = Synthesis

7. According to which theory would someone with a higher level of education be more susceptible to logical appeals?

    a. diffusion of innovations theory
    b. individual differences theory
    c. social learning theory
    d. flow theory

    Answer: b   Key 1: R

8. Which people in the diffusion of innovations theory are more likely to be opinion leaders?

    a. late majority
    b. early majority
    c. innovators
    d. early adopters

    Answer: d   Key 1: R

9. _____ theory suggests that the primary effect of television is to give heavy viewers a perception that the world is less safe and trustworthy and more violent than it really is.

    a. Flow
    b. Social learning
    c. Cultivation
    d. Agenda-setting

    Answer: c   Key 1: R

10. The theory that states that media messages that are driven home through redundancy and have profound effects over time is known as which theory?

    a. cultivation theory
    b. agenda-setting theory
    c. cumulative effects theory
    d. social learning theory

    Answer: c   Key 1: R

11. Mediated communication consists of:

    a. mass communication
    b. mediated interpersonal communication
    c. communication through converged media that are both mass and interpersonal in nature
    d. all the above

    Answer: d   Key 1: R

12. Which of the following is not the responsibility of a gatekeeper?

    a. They determine what messages will be delivered to media consumers.
    b. They determine what use the receiver will make of the message.
    c. They determine how messages will be constructed.
    d. They determined when messages will be delivered.

    Answer: b   Key 1: R

13. Which of the following is NOT a way that most people use media according to the uses and gratifications theory?

    a. surveillance
    b. passing time
    c. self improvement
    d. identity management

    Answer: c   Key 1: R

14. The theory that media do not tell us what to think but do tell us what to think about is called:

    a. uses and gratification theory
    b. agenda setting theory
    c. cultivation theory
    d. individual differences theory

    Answer: b   Key 1: R

TRUE/FALSE

15. The distinction between mass communication and interpersonal communication is much fuzzier today than in the past.

    Answer: T   Key 1: R
    The web resembles other forms of mass media, and it contains an interpersonal element as well, making the distinction more difficult.

16. Opinion leaders are also known as gatekeepers.

    Answer: F   Key 1: R
    Opinion leaders are people whose views are seen as credible, and gatekeepers are those who regulate the flow of communication.

17. Laggards are people who make careful, deliberate choices after frequent interaction with their peers and with opinion leaders.

    Answer: F   Key 1: R
    This would be the description of the early majority.

18. There is little or no interaction between senders and receivers when mass messages are aimed at large audiences.

    Answer: T   Key 1: R
    It is the size of the audience that restricts the interaction.

19. Mediated communication is any type of communication conveyed via some medium or face to face.

    Answer: F   Key 1: R
    Mediated communication cannot occur face-to-face.

20. The feedback component of mass communication is delayed or restricted.

    Answer: T   Key 1: R
    The feedback is a major difference between interpersonal communication and mass communication.

Answer Key Code: R = Recall   C= Conceptual   A = Application   S = Synthesis

21. Mediated communication cannot be interpersonal.

    Answer: F   Key 1: R
    Mediated communication that occurs via e-mail, telephone, or videotape, for example, is interpersonal.

22. The bullet theory implies that the media had direct and powerful effects, like a bullet entering a brain.

    Answer: T   Key 1: R
    This is the correct definition.

23. Uses and gratification theory of media effects claims the media tell us what to think about.

    Answer: F   Key 1: R
    That effect is called agenda setting.

24. Feminist/gender studies examine how media construct and perpetuate gender roles.

    Answer: T   Key 1: R
    They study how male/female roles are presented in mediated messages. ·

25. Marxist critics believe that the media help create a "false consciousness" within the wealthy class.

    Answer: F   Key 1: R
    The Marxist critics believe the false consciousness is created within the working/consuming class.

SHORT ANSWER

26. Explain the three ways in which mass communication differs from interpersonal, small group, and public communication.

    Answer: Key 1: R

27. Describe a live musical performance you attended and explain how and why the experience was different from listening to the same performance on CD or on television. How did the medium alter the experience?

    Answer: Key 1: A

28. Explain two ways in which the Web possesses characteristics of interpersonal communication.

    Answer: Key 1: R

29. What are at least two reasons to study mediated communication? How do those reasons seem to relate to you?

    Answer: Key 1: A

30. Explain why watching reruns of the TV show "America's Funniest Home Videos" is considered mass communication, but watching your own home videos is not.

    Answer: Key 1: S

31. Your text claims that most mass communication has delayed feedback. What would delay it?

    Answer: Key 1: S

32. Select a current issue of importance to you. What effect have the media had, viewed from an agenda setting theory perspective?

    Answer: Key 1: A

33. What role do the media play in society's values? What position do Cultural Studies take on this issue?

    Answer: Key 1: A

34. Explain uses and gratification theory. Be sure to include your own examples in your explanation.

    Answer: Key 1: A

35. What are the similarities of the bullet, two-step flow, and the multistep flow theories? Which is the most accurate with current research? Explain in detail.

    Answer: Key 1: A

MATCHING

36. Match the theory with the description.

    _____ Audience members imitate behavior   A. flow theory
          presented in the media.
                                                     B. social learning theory
    _____ The media teaches a common world
          view.   C. individual differences theory

    _____ Deals with the way media effects   D. cultivation theory
          traveled to the audience.
                                                     E. uses and gratification theory
    _____ Some types of people are more
          susceptible to some types of media   F. agenda setting theory
          messages.

    _____ The media tell us what to think about.

    _____ Views the audience as active
          consumers of media.

    Answer: B, D, A, C, F, E   Key 1: R

Answer Key Code: R = Recall   C= Conceptual   A = Application   S = Synthesis

CHAPTER 1 HUMAN COMMUNICATION: WHAT AND WHY

CHAPTER 1 SKELETON OUTLINE

This outline can be a helpful study tool to assist you in seeing the order and sequence of the chapter and the relationship of ideas. Use it to take notes as you read and/or to add concepts presented in lecture.

I.   Communication is the process of humans responding to symbolic behavior.

    A. Communication is human.

    B. Communication is a process.

        1.   continuous

        2.   ongoing

        3.   transactional

        4.   involves personal history contributing to your interpretation

    C. Communication is symbolic.

        1.   Symbols represent something.

        2.   Symbols are arbitrarily chosen and agreed upon.

II.   Types of communication

    A. Intrapersonal communication

    B. Dyadic/interpersonal communication

    C. Small group communication

    D. Public communication

    E. Mass communication

III. Communication functions to satisfy needs.

    A. Physical health needs

    B. Identity needs

    C. Social needs

    D. Practical needs

IV. Models of communication

    A. Linear model

        1.   one-way activity

        2.   sender, message, channel, receiver, and noise (external/physical, physiological, and psychological)

        3.   different environments

    B. Transactional model

        1.   simultaneous sending & receiving (feedback)

        2.   fluid, not static

3. relational, not individual

V. Communication competence

    A. Communication competence definition

        1. no one, ideal way

        2. situational

        3. relational

        4. can be learned

    B. Competent communicators have

        1. a wide range of behaviors rather than just a few

        2. the ability to choose the most appropriate behavior

        3. skill at performing behaviors

        4. empathy/perspective taking

        5. cognitive complexity

        6. self-monitoring ability

        7. commitment to the relationship

VI. Correcting common misconceptions

    A. Communication doesn't always require complete understanding.

    B. Communication is not always a good thing.

    C. No single person or event causes another's reaction.

    D. Communication will not solve all problems.

    E. Meanings are in people, not in words.

    F. Communication is not simple; it is complex.

    G. More communication is not always better

CHAPTER 1 KEY TERMS

This list of key terms corresponds to those in boldface in your text. In your own words write a definition and an original example of the word.

channel

communication

communication competence

coordination

decode

dyad

dyadic communication

encode

environment

feedback

interpersonal communication

intrapersonal communication

linear communication model

mass communication

mediated communication

message

noise

public communication

receiver

sender

small group communication

symbol

transactional communication model

Name _____

CHAPTER 1 ACTIVITY 1 COMMUNICATION MODELS & METAPHORS

Purpose:

1.   To think creatively about the transactional process of communication.
2.   To construct a model based on a metaphor that illustrates the communication process.

Instructions:

Read the example below. Then construct and explain your own metaphor of communication, taking into account the transactional nature and elements of the communication process.

Example: Draw or explain your metaphor model: <u>Communication is like the human body.</u>

Explanation: <u>The body has many systems: circulatory system, gastrointestinal system, skeletal system, nervous, cardiovascular, etc. Communication has verbal and nonverbal communication, intentional and unintentional. Like the human body, you can break it down and study certain parts, but what counts is that all are happening at once. A doctor who couldn't understand all the systems functioning together is not good at diagnosing or healing. A communicator who can't analyze the parts (verbal/nonverbal, content/relational, and intentional/unintentional) and also look at all the parts together is probably not competent either. If I'm injured, I expect a physician to be able to know which part to pay attention to, but also see the relationship of all systems. I may have a broken bone, but be losing blood, too. The doctor needs to prioritize and pay attention. Likewise, the competent communicator needs to see what elements of the transactional process might be causing a problem, and give attention there, while not neglecting other aspects.</u>

Where does the metaphor break down? <u>The metaphor isn't entirely accurate because the human body is physical; communication is relational, intangible. Communication may end in a different way than a physical body comes to an end.</u>

Your turn:

If working with others, brainstorm about metaphors for communication. Choose one metaphor to explain in detail. Use as many principles and elements of communication as you can in explaining how your metaphor works and where it breaks down. Here are ideas to start, but don't limit yourself. Use your imagination! Communication is like a football game, traffic patterns, the solar system, a gambling machine, the ecosystem.

Draw or insert a picture or drawing of your metaphor model:

Explanation:

Where does the metaphor break down?

Name _____

CHAPTER 1 ACTIVITY 2 MEETING NEEDS THROUGH COMMUNICATION

Purpose:

1. To classify communication behaviors with regard to what needs each meets.
2. To identify ways in which behaviors meet certain communication needs.

Instructions:

Using news story examples or your own examples, indicate how people meet different needs through communication. One example is provided.

Type of need met	Behavior	How did it meet this need?
Physical (health)		
Identity		
Social		
Pleasure		
Affection		
Inclusion	Asking a co-worker if I could go with her to an after-work gathering	I'm new, so I wanted to feel part of this group of people at work. Going with them to a social event may help me feel like part of the group.
Escape		
Relaxation		
Control		
Practical		

Complete the following:

Much of my communication is to meet _____ needs. I think this is because

Not much of my communication is for the purpose of meeting _____ needs.

I had the most difficulty thinking of an example of how communication meets

_____ needs.

Much of my behavior meets more than one need at once, for example

I spend the most time meeting _____ needs because

I spend the least time meeting _____ needs because

I would like to learn to spend more time meeting _____ needs by (doing)

Name _____

CHAPTER 1 ACTIVITY 3 PRINCIPLES OF COMMUNICATION

Purpose:

To identify and apply principles of communication.

Part One Instructions:

Using your own life and examples from current news media, give an example of each of the following:

Communication does not always require understanding.

Communication is not always a good thing.

No single person or event causes another's reaction.

Communication will not solve all problems.

Meanings are in people, not words.

Communication is not simple.

More communication is not always better.

Part Two Instructions:

For each principle listed below, think of other short examples (scenes from books or films, poetry, song lyrics) that illustrate these principles.

Meanings are in people, not words.

Communication is not simple.

More communication is not always better.

Communication will not solve all problems.

Communication is not always a good thing.

Part Three Instructions:

For each principle listed below, think of ways that pop culture, current events, and/or society at large imply the **opposite** of these is true. Why do you think it might be appealing to believe the opposite?

Example: Meanings rest in people, not words. <u>When lawyers, or others, state that something said was unequivocal, they fail to recognize that individuals attach their own meanings (decode) to messages (words). Lawyers often imply that the meaning is in words, not in people. In fact, the reverse is true.</u>

Communication does not always require understanding.

Communication is not simple.

More communication is not always better.

Communication will not solve all problems.

Communication is not always a good thing.

Communication is not simple.

No single person or event causes another's reaction.

Meanings rest in people, not words.

Name _____

CHAPTER 1 ACTIVITY 4 CHARACTERISTICS OF COMPETENT COMMUNICATORS

Purpose:

1. To evaluate your own communication behaviors with regard to characteristics of competent communicators.
2. To identify ways in which you can develop greater communication competence.

Instructions:

1. For each of the six items listed below, rate yourself from 1-5 using the scale below. You might want to ask a close friend to rate you also, as their perception may remind you of strengths you have
2. Then give an example of why you rated yourself as you did or of your thoughts or feelings about your rating. Describe what you think you can do to enhance your competence with regard to that factor.

> 1=I do not possess this characteristic to any degree.
> 2=I have seen this characteristic in myself on rare occasions.
> 3=About half the time, I think I display this characteristic.
> 4=Most of the time I think I act in accordance with this characteristic.
> 5=This is so much a part of me that I don't even think about it. I display this characteristic continuously in my interaction with others.

1. Competent communicators own a wide range of behaviors rather than just a few.

Self-rating: (Optional) Friend's rating:

Comments on, reasons for, or examples of why this rating was given:

Ways that I might become more competent with regard to this factor:

2. Competent communicators have the ability to choose the most appropriate behavior.

Self-rating: (Optional) Friend's rating:

Comments on, reasons for, or examples of why this rating was given:

Ways that I might become more competent with regard to this factor:

3.   Competent communicators have the skill at performing behaviors.

Self-rating: (Optional) Friend's rating:

Comments on, reasons for, or examples of why this rating was given:

Ways that I might become more competent with regard to this factor:

4.   Competent communicators demonstrate empathy and perspective taking.

Self-rating: (Optional) Friend's rating:

Comments on, reasons for, or examples of why this rating was given:

Ways that I might become more competent with regard to this factor:

5.   Competent communicators employ cognitive complexity.

Self-rating: (Optional) Friend's rating:

Comments on, reasons for, or examples of why this rating was given:

Ways that I might become more competent with regard to this factor:

6.   Competent communicators exercise self-monitoring.

Self-rating: (Optional) Friend's rating:

Comments on, reasons for, or examples of why this rating was given:

Ways that I might become more competent with regard to this factor:

Name _____

CHAPTER 1 ACTIVITY 5 EXPLORING THE WEB

Professional Communication Associations

The study of communication, like the study of any other academic subject, may seem overwhelming to a student who has just enrolled in a class. Five types of communication (intrapersonal, interpersonal, group, public, and mass) are described in Chapter One, yet there are many more facets to the communication discipline. One way to get an overview of the field of communication is to look at the web sites of professional organizations in communication.

Some of the major professional organizations are:

American Communication Association (ACA) www.americancomm.org
International Communication Association (ICA) www.icahdq.org
National Communication Association (NCA) www.natcom.org
World Communication Association (WCA) http://facstaff.uww.edu/wca/Home.htm

1. Go to the NCA web site. List ten or more communication categories by looking at the divisions and commissions. (Go to "About NCA" and the "Unit Affiliations" for a complete list.)

2. If you were to continue your study of communication, which divisions would you want to know more about? Why?

3. Are there any categories of communication that you would expect to find and don't? If so, which ones?

4. How closely are the types of communication discussed in your text reflected in the divisions of the NCA?

5. Which of these web sites (NCA, ICA, WCA, ACA) is most useful for beginning communication students? What part of these web sites is of particular help?

6. Can you find the web sites of other professional communication organizations? You might look for: Eastern Communication Association, Southern States Communication Association, Central States Communication Association, and Western States Communication Association. (Hint: From the Western States site at www.csufresno.edu/speechcomm/wscalink.htm you will be able to find the others, plus many state associations and other national associations.)

Name _____

CHAPTER 1 SELF TEST

MATCHING Part One Match each term listed on the left with its correct definition from the column on the right.

_____ 1. channel

_____ 2. communication

_____ 3. communication competence

_____ 4. decoding

_____ 5. dyadic communication

_____ 6. encoding

_____ 7. environment

_____ 8. external noise

_____ 9. feedback

_____ 10. inclusion

a. continuous, irreversible process in which persons are simultaneously sending and receiving messages

b. process in which receiver attaches meaning to message

c. a need to be involved in and a part of other groups

d. a response to another message

e. process of putting thoughts into symbols, which are frequently words

f. physical setting and personal perspectives involved in the communication process

g. medium through which a message passes

h. factors outside the communicators, such as blaring radios and hot temperatures, that interfere with accurate reception of a message

i. ability to maintain a relationship on terms acceptable to all parties

j. communication defined by the number of persons (involves two people)

MATCHING Part Two Match each term listed on the left with its correct definition from the column on the right.

_____ 11. intrapersonal communication

_____ 12. linear model

_____ 13. mass communication

_____ 14. messages

_____ 15. noise

_____ 16. physiological noise

_____ 17. sender

_____ 18. small group communication

_____ 19. social need

_____ 20. transactional model

a. the source of a message

b. external, physiological, and psychological distractions that interfere with a message

c. characterization of communication as a one-way event with messages going from sender to receiver

d. biological factors that interfere with accurate communication

e. communication that occurs within a single person

f. communication shown as simultaneous sending and receiving of messages in an ongoing, irreversible process

g. communication in which each person can actively participate with others in the group

h. symbolic behavior presented to a large audience, through a medium, with delayed or restricted feedback

i. planned and unplanned words and nonverbal behaviors that others attach meanings to

j. needs associated with interpersonal relationships

MULTIPLE CHOICE Choose the BEST response from those listed.

1. The way the term "communication" is used in this text

    a. includes all human, animal, and mechanical communication.
    b. includes communion, as used in a religious sense.
    c. includes radio and television programming.
    d. includes all of the above.
    e. includes none of the above.

2. "Communication is a process" means that

    a. communication has clear beginning and ending points.
    b. communication resembles still pictures more than motion pictures.
    c. communication is ongoing and continuous.
    d. communication consists of discrete and separate acts.
    e. all of the above

3. The same behavior in two different contexts may be perceived as competent in one setting and incompetent in another. This situation best illustrates the concept that communication competence

    a. involves choosing inappropriate behavior
    b. involves conflict.
    c. requires cognitive complexity.
    d. is situational.
    e. all of the above

4. Journaling (keeping a private journal in which you write down your feelings and thoughts with the intention that only you will read it) is an example of

    a. dyadic communication.
    b. intrapersonal communication.
    c. mass communication.
    d. interpersonal communication.
    e. public communication.

5. Which of these is dyadic communication?

    a. two sisters arguing
    b. a husband and wife making plans for the weekend
    b. a coach and player discussing last week's game
    c. an editor and reporter hammering out an outline for an article
    d. all of the above

6. An example of self-monitoring is

    a. videotaping your practice interview.
    b. carrying a checklist to remind you of some skills to practice.
    c. paying attention to the sound of your voice.
    d. watching others react to your joke telling.
    e. all of the above

7. When we say that communicators occupy different environments, we mean that

    a. one might be rich and one poor.
    b. one might be from China and one from the U.S.
    c. one might be retired with time on her hands, while one is rushing to meet family and career demands with never enough time.
    d. one has been at a company for 10 years and one has just been hired.
    e. All of the above represent differing environments.

8. A plane flying overhead and interfering with your conversation is an example of _____ noise.

    a. external
    b. physiological
    c. psychological
    d. all of the above
    e. none of the above

9. An instructor is lively and joking in a class in which students come prepared and always do more than the assigned work. The same instructor is strict and unyielding in a class that tries to slide by with minimal work and comes without having read assignments. Although this is the same instructor, the communication behavior illustrates which concept?

    a. All communication is equally effective and competent.
    b. Communication is linear.
    c. Communication is static.
    d. Communication is transactional and relational.
    e. none of the above

10. Symbols

    a. stand for something other than themselves.
    b. represent ideas, but not people, things or events.
    c. mean exactly the same thing to various people.
    d. are not arbitrary; all symbols have logical reasons for their existence.
    e. have nothing to do with verbal communication.

11. The instructor dislikes the music group pictured on your shirt. Her attitude toward the group and its impact on her attitude toward you is an example of _____noise.
    a. external
    b. physiological
    c. psychological
    d. all of the above
    e. none of the above

12. You have an auditory processing difficulty and cannot always understand directions when they are spoken too quickly. You experience _____ noise.

    a. external
    b. physiological
    c. psychological
    d. all of the above
    e. none of the above

13. Your friend asks to borrow your car. Recently, you've had car problems and have been bombarded by other friends for requests to use your car. You're not feeling well and just want to go home. You respond angrily to your friend's request, although on other occasions this particular friend has borrowed your car with no problems. Your reaction this time best illustrates which principle?

    a. Communication will not solve all problems.
    b. No single person or event causes a reaction.
    c. Communication does not always require understanding.
    d. More communication is not always better.
    e. Competent communicators don't yell.

14. Which statement is accurate regarding communication competence?

    a. It is situational.
    b. You either have it or you don't.
    c. For any situation, there is one ideal way to communicate.
    d. Competence requires meeting one goal at the expense of another.
    e. None of the above is true.

15. In most situations, competent communicators will

    a. be able to choose from a wide range of behaviors.
    b. demonstrate empathy.
    c. demonstrate skill at a chosen behavior.
    d. employ self-monitoring behaviors.
    e. all of the above

16. Which type of noise is represented by having a stuffy nose, allergy congestion, and a sore throat?

    a. physical
    b. external
    c. physiological
    d. psychological
    e. none of the above

17. This is which type of model? s→r   [s=sender r=receiver]

    a. linear
    b. transactional
    c. interpersonal
    d. all of the above
    e. none of the above

TRUE/FALSE Circle the T or F to indicate whether you believe the statement is true or false. If it is **true**, give a **reason** or an **example**. If it is false, **explain** what would make it true.

T F   1. According the text, there is little research to suggest a connection between communication skills and physical health.

T F   2. Linear models offer the best hope for understanding the complexity of communication.

T F   3. Some examples of computer-mediated communication such as e-mail and IMing illustrate that quality communication can occur on line.

T F   4. Mediated communication is always face-to-face.

T F   5. If you are very good at a particular communication skill, you should probably use that skill in most situations, rather than trying to use new skills for various contexts.

COMPLETION Fill in each of the blanks with a word from the lists provided. Choose the BEST word for each sentence. There are more words than you will use, but each word will be used only once.

message	feedback
control	noise
transactional	social

1. This C↔C (c=communicator) represents a/an _____ model of communication.

2. Anything that interferes with effective communication is called _____.

3. A/an _____ is any stimulus that other people create meaning from, for instance, your hair color.

4. A nod or smile in response to someone saying "hello" to you would be called

    _____.

5. A need to be with other people and have interpersonal relationships is identified in your text as a/an

    _____ need.

CHAPTER 1 ANSWERS TO SELF-TEST

MATCHING Part One

1. g	2. a	3. i	4. b	5. j
6. e	7. f	8. h	9. d	10. c

MATCHING Part Two

11. e	12. c	13. h	14. i	15. b
16. d	17. a	18. g	19. j	20. f

MULTIPLE CHOICE

1. e	2. c	3. d	4. b	5. e
6. e	7. e	8. a	9. d	10. a
11. c	12. b	13. b	14. a	15. e
16. c	17. a			

TRUE/FALSE

1. False	2. False	3. True	4. False	5. False

COMPLETION

1. transactional	2. noise	3. message
4. feedback	5. social	

Related Reading

"Shyness: The Behavior of Not Communicating" from (Chapter 3) <u>Communication: Apprehension, Avoidance, and Effectiveness</u>. 5th edition by Virginia P. Richmond and James C. McCroskey, 1998, Allyn and Bacon.

Preview

Who cannot identify with feeling shy at some point? If, as this chapter indicates, 80% of us at some point (possibly now) have considered ourselves shy, then most of us will find this article engaging. Virginia P. Richmond and James C. McCroskey are renowned communication scholars, researchers and writers. In this chapter from their book on communication apprehension, they delve into the concept of shyness and the communication implications of that behavior. You will see how choosing not to communicate verbally may result in your communicating to others messages that you may not intend. The scales in the book include an Introversion, a Shyness, and a Willingness to Communicate scale. Also included is a Personal Report of Communication Apprehension measure which gives you an overview of your level of apprehension in key areas addressed in this text: group discussion, interpersonal conversation, and public speaking situations. You will find these scales an interesting way to initiate your study of Communication. As you explore the correlation between communication and the nature and causes of shyness, the types of shy people and the measures of shyness, you may discover new ways to relate the material in the text to your individual needs.

Review

1. What kinds of comments (like those in paragraph three) do you think people make about you with regard to effectiveness of, amount of, and desire for communication?

2. How would you rate yourself on these continuums:

ineffective communicator	1	2	3	4	5	effective communicator
talks little	1	2	3	4	5	talks a lot
not very willing to communicate	1	2	3	4	5	willing to communicate

3. What do you think of the author's contention that it usually isn't talking too much that creates a negative impression but not having something deemed worthwhile to say?

4. How could you "translate" the concepts in this article into general advice for students with regard to appropriate classroom participation?

5. In what ways have your attempts to communicate been met with "inconsistent reinforcement"?

6. What do you think played a greater role in your learning to communicate: genetics, modeling, or reinforcement?

CHAPTER 2 PERCEPTION, THE SELF, AND COMMUNICATION

CHAPTER 2 SKELETON OUTLINE

This outline can be a helpful study tool to assist you in seeing the order and sequence of the chapter and the relationship of ideas. Use it to take notes as you read and/or to add concepts presented in lecture.

I. Perceiving others is an activity influenced by our own narratives, perceptual tendencies, situational factors, culture, and our ability and willingness to empathize.

    A. Narratives help us make sense of the world by telling our stories

        1. discussing events defines them

        2. making sense of stories is interactive

    B. Common perceptual tendencies

        1. judging ourselves more charitably

        2. being influenced by the most obvious stimuli

            a) intense

            b) repetitious

            c) contrasting

            d) motives

        3. clinging to first impressions

        4. assuming others are similar to us

        5. favoring negative impressions

        6. blaming the victims

    C. Situational factors

        1. relational satisfaction

        2. degree of involvement

        3. past experience

        4. expectations

        5. social roles

        6. knowledge

        7. self-concept

    D. Culture influences perception

        1. perceptual filter

        2. value placed on talk and silence

        3. differences between co-cultures

        4. geography

    E. Empathy is related to perception and can aid effective communication.

        1.   empathy

            a)   perspective taking

            b)   emotional dimension

            c)   concern

            d)   differs from sympathy which involves compassion, not identification

            e)   empathy exists from birth

            f)   genetic and environment

        2.   a three-part perception check helps discern perception's accuracy

            a)   description of behavior

            b)   two different but possible interpretations

            c)   request for clarification

            d)   congruent nonverbal behavior

II.   Self-concept influences perception of oneself

    A.   Self-concept and self-esteem (define)

    B.   Reflected appraisal by significant others

    C.   Culture, language, and values influence self-concept

        1.   speaking the same or different language as majority

        2.   collectivism and individualism influence values

            a)   collectivistic culture

            b)   individualistic culture

        3.   each culture emphasizes and rewards different behaviors and self-perceptions

    D.   Self-concept relates to personality and communication

        1.   personality (define)

        2.   contextual variations affect behavior, interpretation, personality, and communication

    E.   Self-fulfilling prophecies influence communication

        1.   what you tell yourself

        2.   what another person tells you

III. Identity management (impression management) is managing others' views of oneself

    A.   Public and private selves parallel presenting and perceived selves.

        1.   presenting self (define)

        2.   perceived self (define)

        3.   many behaviors are attempts to manage impressions (facework)

            a)   manage our own identity

            b)   reinforce others' identities

    B. Characteristics of identity management

        1. strive to construct multiple identities

        2. collaborative nature of identity management

        3. deliberate or unconscious

        4. differing degrees of identity management

    C. Reasons why we manage impressions

        1. social rules and social roles

        2. personal goals

    D. How we manage impressions

        1. face-to-face impression management

            a) manner

            b) appearance

            c) setting

        2. mediated impression management

            a) advantages

            b) disadvantages

    E. Impression management involves issues of honesty

        1. honest or dishonest

        2. choices of faces and impressions

CHAPTER 2 KEY TERMS

This list of key terms corresponds to those in boldface in your text. In your own words write a definition and an original example of the word.

empathy

face

facework

impression management

narratives

perceived self

perception checking

personality

presenting self

reflected appraisal

self-concept

self-esteem

self-fulfilling prophecy

self-serving bias

significant others

sympathy

Name _____

CHAPTER 2 ACTIVITY 1 PERCEPTUAL TENDENCIES

Purpose:

To classify specific instances of common perceptual tendencies.

Instructions:

1. Common perceptual tendencies often distort our perception of others. Being able to recognize when this is occurring can help improve communication. Read the following situational descriptions.
2. For each, identify which of the following perceptual tendencies is illustrated.

    1. judging ourselves more charitably than others, thus perceiving similar behavior from others and ourselves differently
    2. being influenced by what is most obvious, including stimuli that is intense, repetitious, contrasting, or related to our motives
    3. clinging to first impressions, even if they're wrong
    4. assuming others are similar to us in attitudes and motives
    5. favoring negative impressions over positive ones
    6. blaming innocent victims for their misfortunes

Example: A 13-year old is hit and killed by car speeding through a red light at 1:30 a.m. A person wonders aloud, "What in the world was she doing out at 1:30 in the morning? She should have been home."

Example: #6 We tend to blame victims, in this case the teen, and act like it is her fault, instead of blaming the driver for speeding and running a red light.

1. You are trying to pay attention to a friend who is talking to you, but you're worried about your child falling from the playground equipment.

2. A child brings home a report card with six A's and a D. The parents first want to know why the child is getting a D.

3. The story is told of woman sitting next to a man on an airplane. He said, "I just got out of prison for murdering my wife." "Oh," she replied, "then you're single."

4. A parent (who married at age 20), "My son is so young to be dating seriously. He's only twenty and not very mature and already talking marriage with his girlfriend."

5. You thought a new co-worker was trying to juggle the schedule to get the best days and time off at your expense. You later learn that he didn't know the procedure to sign up for scheduling, but you are still suspicious of the person.

6. A person is attacked and robbed in a particular neighborhood. Others comment, "He should have known better than to walk through that area."

7. You don't understand why a neighbor turned down a much better paying job just because she'd have to move to another city. You always love the excitement of moves and more money.

Add your own examples:

1.

2.

Name _____

CHAPTER 2 ACTIVITY 2 CULTURE AND PERCEPTION

Purpose:

1. To discover the ways in which culture influences our selection and perception.
2. To illustrate the variety of ways our interpretations are influenced by culture.

Instructions Part One:

Introduction: Perception and culture are closely related; culture teaches us how to perceive and strongly influences our selection of what to pay attention to, our interpretation of nonverbal behavior, and the value we place on talk and silence.

1. For each proverb write down your own impressions of what each proverb tells us about communication behaviors that are and are not valued. If you repeatedly heard this proverb, what would you select to pay attention to when communicating with someone? How would you interpret other's verbal and nonverbal behavior? How would exposure to this proverb and its cultural values influence the way you communicate with others?
2. Then, discuss with others what your impressions were, how similar or different they are, and whether these proverbs or similar ones were familiar to you.

Example: He who speaks does not know; he who knows does not speak. (Chinese). <u>Someone who hears this proverb would believe that the person who talks a lot doesn't really know much. The person with wisdom would be the silent one. A person would pay attention to a quiet person and ignore loud, boisterous, outgoing people, judging them to be ignorant.</u>

He who raises his voice first, loses. (Chinese)

The squeaky wheel gets the grease.

Loud thunder brings little rain. (Chinese) Contrast this proverb to the previous one.

Beauty is only skin deep.

Turn your face to the sun and the shadows fall behind you. (Maori)

Blood is thicker than water.

Life is a dance, not a race. (Irish)

You can catch more flies with honey than with vinegar.

Silence is golden; speech is silver.

All's well that ends well.

Cleanliness is next to godliness.

Order is half of life. (German)

The mouth maintains silence in order to hear the heart talk. (Belgian)

Nothing done with intelligence is done without speech. (Greek, from Isocrates)

The eyes are the windows to the soul.

Instructions Part Two

What proverbs are popular in your culture to remind members of appropriate verbal and nonverbal communication behaviors? List some proverbs or sayings you frequently heard while growing up and describe how they influence your perception and communication. If there are students in class or if you have friends who speak languages other than English, ask them to think of proverbs in other languages and try to translate and explain them for you.

Proverb:

Explanation and impact on communication:

Proverb:

Explanation and impact on communication:

Instructions Part Three

Discuss the proverbs below and determine if they reinforce collectivism or individualism. What behaviors would be rewarded? What behaviors would be rebuked?

The nail that stands out must be pounded down. (Japan)

The early bird gets the worm.

A single arrow is easily broken, but not a bunch. (Asian)

God helps those who help themselves.

Name _____

CHAPTER 2 ACTIVITY 3 PERCEPTION CHECKS

Purpose:

1. To become familiar with the parts of the perception check.
2. To develop competence in identifying contexts in which to use perception checks.
3. To develop skills in creating appropriate perception checks.

Instructions Part One:

1. Read each situation below and think about various perceptions of the event.
2. Create a three-part **perception check** to help you discern whether your perceptions are accurate. Write it in first person, as you would actually say it to the other person. Be sure to include
   1. a description of the behavior
   2. two possible, but different, interpretations of the behavior
   3. a request for clarification of how to interpret the behavior
3. Now, role play with a classmate. Practice delivering your perception check with the appropriate nonverbal delivery skills to reflect a sincere attempt to understand.
4. Finally, consider whether you actually would use a perception check in each situation. Why or why not?

1. For the last three evenings you've come home and found your neighbor's car (Apt. 2) parked in your space (marked Apt. 3).

Describe the behavior.

One interpretation

Second, different, but possible interpretation

Request for clarification

Nonverbal behaviors I would and wouldn't display

2. You wanted two pieces of tuna sushi, so you inquired how many come with an order. Your wait person tells you that two pieces come with one order. You asked for one order. Two orders (four pieces) are delivered to your table.

Describe the behavior.

One interpretation

Second, different, but possible interpretation

Request for clarification

Nonverbal behaviors I would and wouldn't display

3. Your and your spouse agreed not to write checks until after deposits are made. You go to the checkbook (joint account) and find a space left for a deposit but no amount written in. And below that, information about two checks was written out.

Describe the behavior.

One interpretation

Second, different, but possible interpretation

Request for clarification

Nonverbal behaviors I would and wouldn't display

4. A group of six of you and your friends eats at a restaurant. You noticed that the menu indicates that a 20% tip will automatically be added to groups of eight or more. When the bill comes, a 20% charge is added in.

Describe the behavior.

One interpretation

Second, different, but possible interpretation

Request for clarification

Nonverbal behaviors I would and wouldn't display

5. A certain bookstore gives a 10% discount to students. You show your ID for your purchase of a book on sale for $18.00. The clerk rings up $18.00 plus tax and tells you the total.

Describe the behavior.

One interpretation

Second, different, but possible interpretation

Request for clarification

Nonverbal behaviors I would and wouldn't display

6. You just started a new job. You know about a party Friday night at Joe's house because several other co-workers (not Joe) include you in conversations about the party as if you are invited. You never received an invitation, and you don't know if the invitations are just word of mouth and everyone understands that all co-workers are invited, or if only certain people are invited.

Describe the behavior.

One interpretation

Second, different, but possible interpretation

Request for clarification

Nonverbal behaviors I would and wouldn't display

Instructions Part Two:

1. Divide the situations (by number) into those you probably would use a perception check and those you wouldn't.
2. For each group, discuss the advantages and disadvantages and the probable results of using or not using perception checks.

Numbers of the situations in which I probably would use a perception check:

Advantages and probable results of using perception checks

Possible disadvantages

Numbers of the situations in which I probably would not use a perception check:

Disadvantages and probable results of using perception checks

Possible disadvantages

Name _____

CHAPTER 2 ACTIVITY 4 IDENTITY MANAGEMENT

Purpose:

1. To understand how identity management (impression management) is used to create or maintain a presenting self.
2. To practice creative thinking with regard to ways to manage impressions.

Instructions:

1. For each situation below, describe ways in which you have tried or would try to manage impressions.
2. For each situation tell which reason was behind the impression: following situational social rules or to meet personal goals such as appearing likeable, responsible, or competent.
3. Now go back to your description of what you did or would do and label the items to indicate which were accomplished through **manner** (words, nonverbal actions); **appearance** (clothing, make-up, hair); and **setting** (briefcase, car, type of furniture, music, color, computer).
4. After reflecting on the categories in #3, are there additional ways you could improve managing impressions?

Example: You just started a new job, and you have been invited to a new co-worker's home for a backyard barbecue.

What would you or did you do? __Probably wear something in denim, but nicer than just jeans and a tee shirt. Perhaps a blazer with jeans, so the blazer could be removed if others were more casual. I'd see if the host is introducing people. If not, I'd greet everyone and introduce myself to those I'd seen at work but didn't really know.__

Reason for managing impression: __I'd want to be polite and show respect by dressing appropriately, not so "dressed up" that it looked like I was showing off, not torn or dirty or such informal clothes that they'd think I didn't care. I'd want to create a friendly impression since I'm new at work.__

Ways in which impression management was done (label items manner, appearance, setting)

Additional ways you would manage impressions:

manner __smiles, moving around among people if that's what others are doing__

appearance __nothing real showy or revealing. Depending on the region of the country, I'd think about cowboy boots or shorts.__

setting __I'd ask if I should bring some food or drinks, as that's the custom some places.__

1.   Job interview (Identify the type of job):

What would you or did you do?

Reason for managing impression:

Ways in which impression management was done (label items manner, appearance, setting)

Additional ways you would manage impressions:

manner

appearance

setting

2.   First day of class and you want to create an impression of _____ .

What would you or did you do?

Reason for managing impression:

Ways in which impression management was done (label items manner, appearance, setting)

Additional ways you would manage impressions:

manner

appearance

setting

3.   Dinner with your boyfriend/girlfriend's family and you want them to think highly of you.

What would you or did you do?

Reason for managing impression:

Ways in which impression management was done (label items manner, appearance, setting)

Additional ways you would manage impressions:

manner

appearance

setting

4.   Appearing in court to seek dismissal of a traffic violation.

What would you or did you do?

Reason for managing impression:

Ways in which impression management was done (label items manner, appearance, setting)

Additional ways you would manage impressions:

manner

appearance

setting

5.   Challenge: You want to impress someone on the Internet whom you've never met. (I'd like to make this kind of impression: _____)

What would you or did you do?

Reason for managing impression:

Ways in which impression management was done (label items manner, appearance, setting)

Additional ways you would manage impressions:

manner

appearance

setting

Do any of the ways fit these categories? (manner, appearance, setting)

Besides those three, are there additional channels (not available in face-to-face) available to you on web pages? In chat rooms? In list-serve discussions?

In using the Internet channels, what are the advantages you gain in terms of impression management? What would you or did you do?

What disadvantages do you need to contend with?

Besides Internet channels, what other mediums or channels have you used that have presented you with distinct advantages or disadvantages in terms of managing impressions?

Name _____

CHAPTER 2 ACTIVITY 5 SELF-CONCEPT AND COMMUNICATION

Purpose:

To explore one's self-concept and the role of communication in forming self-concept and influencing perception.

Instructions:

Introduction: Perceiving the self involves understanding self-concept and its impact on communication. Self-concept is defined as the relatively stable set of perceptions we hold about our physical, social, and psychological traits.

1.   List several characteristics that are significant in your self-concept in the left column below. Try to choose some characteristics that are physical, emotional, psychological, and social.
2.   Describe in the center column the role of communication in forming this part of your self-concept.
3.   Then in the right column, describe some ways in which each characteristic affects how you communicate with others.

Describe or draw a trait that is part of your self-concept here:	What was communicated to you? How? How did communication play a role in your belief that this is the way you are? Did you learn these things about yourself directly/indirectly from others? from direct communication to you or others' feedback or reactions to you?	What do you communicate to others? How does this trait affect with whom you communicate? for what reasons you communicate? how you communicate with others? how much you communicate?
Example: I'm shy around new people and I'm not comfortable meeting new people.	When I was young, my older sister was always invited to talk to guests, and introduce them to others. I watched, but believed I wasn't good at this. Others probably paid more attention to my sister because she spoke with them.	Sometimes, I really have to talk myself into approaching new people, and I may not walk up to strangers and start a conversation. I'll wait for someone to start talking to me first.

Describe or draw a trait that is part of your self-concept here:	**What was communicated to you? How?** How did communication play a role in your believing yourself to be this way? Did you learn these things about yourself directly/indirectly from others? from direct communication to you or others' feedback or reactions to you?	**What do you communicate to others?** How does this trait affect with whom you communicate? for what reasons you communicate? how you communicate with others? how much you communicate?

Name _____

CHAPTER 2 ACTIVITY 6 EXPLORING THE WEB

Impression Management

Chapter 2 discusses various aspects of impression management. Read the following articles:

Miller, Hugh. "The Presentation of Self in Electronic Life: Goffman on the Internet." Retrieve from http://ess.ntu.ac.uk/miller/cyberpsych/goffman.htm.

Chandler, Daniel. "Personal Home Pages and the Construction of Identities on the Web." Retrieve from www.aber.ac.uk/media/Documents/short/webident.html.

Additionally, find annotations and links to many more articles at http://ess.ntu.ac.uk/miller/cyberpsych/.

If you have your own web page, answer the following questions with regard to your own home page. If not, use either your instructor's page or the page of a friend or famous person you admire.

I will use ____ my own site. ____ a friend's site ____ instructor's site ____ celebrity site

URL:

1. What evidence does Chandler cite to support his claim that home pages represent a blurring of private and public arenas?

2. Chandler refers to five elements present in the construction of web pages: <u>inclusion</u> of certain

   elements, _____ to particular elements,

   _____ of certain elements, _____ or borrowing of

   elements (by addition, deletion, substitution, or transposition), and

   _____ of the elements on a web page.

3. Describe how each of the five underlined elements in question 2 above relates to the person's web page you're analyzing.

   1.

   2.

   3.

   4.

   5.

4. Define *bricolage*. Explain Chandler's use of the term *bricolage* as it relates to the web page you're analyzing.

5. Analyze the content and form of the web page you are examining. What do you find appealing or unappealing about its content? About its form?

6. Does the page have any of these: guest book, e-mail capacity, chat link? What does the presence or absence of these contribute to the web-identity of the person?

Review these sites for more information about analyzing web pages and their design:

www.wilsonweb.com/articles/12design.htm

www.werbach.com/web/page_design.html

Read about "How Search Engines Rank Web Pages" at
www.searchenginewatch.com/webmasters/rank.html

Name _____

CHAPTER 2 SELF-TEST

MATCHING Match each term listed on the left with its correct definition from the column on the right.

_____ 1.   empathy

_____ 2.   face

_____ 3.   facework

_____ 4.   impression management

_____ 5.   narrative

_____ 6.   perceived self

_____ 7.   perception checking

_____ 8.   personality

_____ 9.   presenting self

_____ 10. reflected appraisal

_____ 11. self-concept

_____ 12. self-esteem

_____ 13. self-fulfilling prophecy

_____ 14. self-serving bias

_____ 15. significant other

_____ 16. sympathy

a. tendency to interpret and explain information in a way that casts oneself in the most favorable manner

b. person whose opinion is important enough to another person to strongly affect his or her self-concept

c. beliefs about oneself based on one's perception of how others regard you

d. story we tell that frames our perception of events

e. ability to project oneself into another's point of view, to experience their thoughts and feelings

f. a three-part method for verifying the accuracy of one's perception of another

g. feeling compassion or concern for another person

h. communication strategies used to influence others' views of oneself

i. the relatively stable set of perceptions a person has of himself or herself

j. the person a communicator believes, in candid moments, that he or she is

k. verbal and nonverbal behavior to create and maintain communicator's and others' public images

l. value or worth placed on one's self-concept

m. a relatively consistent set of traits a person exhibits across a variety of situations

n. a prediction or expectation of oneself that makes an outcome more likely to occur than would otherwise have been the case

o. another term for the presenting self

p. the socially approved identity that a communicator tries to present

MULTIPLE CHOICE Choose the BEST response from those listed.

1. Perception checks include all EXCEPT

    a. a description of behavior observed.
    b. a request for clarification.
    c. a statement of intent—how you will treat the person in the future.
    d. the use of objective words to describe behavior.
    e. appropriate nonverbal behaviors.

2. In her book, <u>First Ladies</u>, Margaret Truman writes of a letter that Jacqueline Kennedy Onassis wrote to Nancy Reagan following the attempted assassination of then-President Reagan. Onassis knew "better than any living former First Lady, the terror and grief and anguish such an experience evokes." It seems that Jackie communicated so well because she demonstrated

    a. empathy.
    b. facework.
    c. self-serving bias.
    d. sympathy.
    e. attribution.

3. When John's car is stolen after being left unlocked in front of his home, Mary said, "He should have known better. He should lock his car." When Mary's car was subsequently stolen after being left unlocked in front of her home, Mary said, "The police aren't doing their job protecting us. We should be safe in our own neighborhoods. They need to be tougher on crime." Mary's statements about the two thefts indicate which perceptual error?

    a. favoring negative impressions
    b. being influenced by the most obvious stimuli
    c. judging ourselves more charitably
    d. assuming others are similar to us
    e. clinging to first impressions

4. "When I see the crumbs all over the counter and dishes stacked in the sink, I don't know if you've got a big exam and have been too busy studying to clean up or if you have time but are hoping that I'll just clean up. What's the reason?" This is an example of a

    a. significant other.
    b. perceived self.
    c. perception check.
    d. reflected appraisal.
    e. self-serving bias.

5. As it is used in this text, a significant other is always someone

    a. with whom you have a romantic involvement.
    b. whose opinion matters to you.
    c. whom you have known since childhood.
    d. who holds the job you aspire to.
    e. whose reflected appraisal of you doesn't matter to you.

6. Two people speak Spanish as a first language and English as a second. With regard to this trait, one has been made fun of for her accent, was punished by teachers in elementary school for speaking Spanish, and feels inferior. Teachers and family always praised the other for speaking two languages. She is happy when co-workers call upon her to translate, and feels proud and accomplished at being bilingual. With regard to their self-concepts, this example illustrates

    a. that having the same traits results in the same or similar self-concepts.
    b. that self-concept consists not only of the traits we possess, but also of the significance we attach to them.
    c. that reflected appraisal helps to shape self-concept.
    d. both a and b
    e. both b and c

7. Maslow wrote, "If the only tool you have is a hammer, you tend to treat everything as if it were a nail." This statement illustrates the importance of

    a. attribution.
    b. perception.
    c. facework.
    d. perception checking.
    e. impression management.

8. The primary way we develop our self-concepts is through

    a. reflections during our solitude.
    b. interaction with others.
    c. religious beliefs.
    d. building defenses against unwanted experiences.
    e. None of the above really influences self-concept.

9. "Our thoughts not only reveal what we are; they predict what we will become." — Tozer. This quotation seems to be most closely related to the concept of

    a. sympathy.
    b. empathy.
    c. attribution.
    d. significant other.
    e. self-fulfilling prophecy.

10. The social science term "self-serving bias" is most closely related to which common perceptual error?

    a. judging ourselves more charitably
    b. being influenced by the most obvious stimuli
    c. clinging to first impressions
    d. assuming others are similar to us
    e. favoring negative impressions

11. "At Laguna Pueblo in New Mexico, 'Who is your mother?' is an important question. At Laguna, . . . your mother's identity is the key to your own identity. . . . every individual has a place within the universe—human and nonhuman—and that place is defined by clan membership." — P. G. Allen. This quotation is describing a/an _____ culture.

    a. nonverbal
    b. narrative
    c. individualist
    d. collectivist
    e. assertive

12. A child whose parents believe he is a great athlete buy him the best equipment, pay for special coaching and camps, and praise his efforts. He becomes a skilled athlete. That scenario is typical of which concept?

    a. sympathy
    b. empathy
    c. attribution
    d. significant other
    e. self-fulfilling prophecy

13. The perceptual error of being influenced by the most obvious stimuli refers to stimuli that is

    a. intense.
    b. repetitious.
    c. contrasting.
    d. in line with our motives.
    e. all of the above

14. In many Asian cultures being very talkative, speaking directly even when you disagree with a person, and not allowing much silence in a conversation would likely be regarded as

    a. a very positive sign of a cultured person.
    b. a sign of a very intelligent, knowledgeable person.
    c. both a and b
    d. someone who is insincere, lacking knowledge, impolite.
    e. a sign of belonging to the group.

15. Culture often influences people's perception of

    a. the amount of talk considered appropriate.
    b. the value placed on silence.
    c. whether direct disagreement is seen as positive or negative.
    d. whether eye contact is considered polite and respectful.
    e. all of the above

16. Practicing empathy appears to

    a. make communication more difficult between people.
    b. help persons see more possible reasons for another's behavior.
    c. help others be more tolerant of another.
    d. both b and c
    e. all of the above

17. Which of these is not one of the key types of communication we use to manage impressions?

    a. manner
    b. setting
    c. appearance
    d. All of these are types of communication we use to manage impressions.
    e. None of these are types of communication we use to manage impressions.

18. Which is likely an example of a self-fulfilling prophecy?

    a. A student performs poorly on a test after hearing the instructor refer to her as a "remedial" student.
    b. You tell your spouse that you don't want to go to his/her office party because you think his/her co-workers are snobs and you know you won't have a good time. You go and have a lousy time.
    c. An employee hears his supervisor say, "There's no way he/she will be able to handle the work without additional help." Although he/she had been doing this kind of work by himself for a long time, the employee feels unable to keep up now.
    d. All could be examples of self-fulfilling prophecy.
    e. None are likely examples of self-fulfilling prophecy.

19. "A man is hurt not so much by what happens, as by his opinion of what happens." — Montaigne. This statement reflects the concepts relating to the role of _____ in communication.

    a. perception
    b. self-concept
    c. impression management
    d. ethics
    e. significant others

TRUE/FALSE   Circle the T or F to indicate whether you believe the statement is true or false. If it is **true,** give a **reason** or an **example.** If it is false, **explain** what would make it true.

T F   1. Common perceptual errors often distort our perception of others, but have little impact on our communication with others.

T F   2. Culture teaches us how to perceive and strongly influences our interpretation of nonverbal behavior.

T F   3. Empathy and sympathy are essentially the same.

T F   4. A perception check is a way for you to get others to understand your point of view.

T   F   5.   Our behavior and our interpretation of behavior affect our communication.

COMPLETION Fill in each of the blanks with a word from the lists provided. Choose the BEST word for each sentence. There are more words than you will use, but each word will be used only once.

empathy   self-fulfilling prophecies

perception checks   culture

impression management   selective

reflected appraisal   sympathy

1.   Our perceptions of others are always _____.

2.   A valuable tool for understanding others is increased _____.

3.   To find out whether our interpretations of others' behaviors are accurate, we can use

_____.

4.   Deciding which face to display in public is the process of _____.

5.   Communication and _____ shape our self-concepts.

6.   Self-concepts may lead us to create _____, which result in our acting as if certain beliefs about ourselves were true and increasing the chances of the beliefs becoming true.

CHAPTER 2 ANSWERS TO SELF-TEST

MATCHING

1. e		2. o		3. k		4. h		5. d
6. j		7. f		8. m		9. p		10. c
11. i		12. l		13. n		14. a		15. b
16. g								

MULTIPLE CHOICE

1. c		2. a		3. c		4. c		5. b
6. e		7. b		8. b		9. e		10. a
11. d		12. e		13. e		14. d		15. e
16. d		17. d		18. d		19. a		

TRUE/FALSE

1. False	2. True	3. False	4. False	5. True

COMPLETION

1. selective	2. empathy	3. perception checks
4. impression management	5. culture	6. self-fulfilling prophecies

Related Reading

"White Privilege: Unpacking the Invisible Knapsack." by Peggy McIntosh. (Accessible at www.utoronto.ca/acc/events/peggy1.htm or at http://seamonkey.ed.asu.edu/~mcisaac/emc598ge/Unpacking.html) Copies or permission to copy available from Peggy McIntosh, Wellesley College, MA phone number: 617-283-2520.

Preview:

How has our perception of others been influenced by our culture and by our ability and willingness to empathize? Our text describes the key role culture and empathy play in our perception of and communication with others. This provocative article may influence your ideas of "privilege." If you are not Euroamerican, the article may reflect concepts you've been aware of and tried to articulate. If you are Euroamerican, you may not have given much thought to the unspoken or unacknowledged privileges that you've had in life. Consequently, it may be harder to empathize with others who have not had these privileges, especially since on the surface, they don't involve large sums of money, great give-aways, or other things that may come to mind when you hear the word "privilege." This reading may serve to help you see yourself and your privileges as others may see you. Author Peggy McIntosh delves beneath the surface and looks at the subtle advantages that "white" skin has bestowed on its bearers. Ms. McIntosh presents quite a challenge to readers.

Review:

1. If you are Euro-American, what is your initial reaction to the article? Does the article reflect ways in which you've perceived the privileges of others? Or do you see other more significant privileges not mentioned?

2. If you are not Euro-American, does the article reflect ways in which you've perceived the privileges of others? Or do you see other, more significant privileges not mentioned?

3. Why do you think the author uses the metaphor of a backpack to represent these privileges?

4. Has reading this article altered your perception of privilege? How?

5. Has the article made a difference in how you perceive yourself? In how you perceive others?

CHAPTER 3 LANGUAGE

CHAPTER 3 SKELETON OUTLINE

This outline can be a helpful study tool to assist you in seeing the order and sequence of the chapter and the relationship of ideas. Use it to take notes as you read and/or to add concepts presented in lecture.

I.   The nature of language

    A. Language is symbolic

        1. elements create symbols (words & other symbols)

        2. sign language is symbolic, linguistic

        3. Symbols are the way we experience the world

    B. Meanings are in people, not in words

        1. meanings are personal

        2. Ogden & Richards's Triangle of Meaning

    C. Language is rule-governed; understanding rules helps us understand each other.

        1. phonological rules

        2. syntactic rules

        3. semantic rules

        4. pragmatic rules

II. Power of language

    A. Language shapes attitudes.

        1. naming

        2. credibility

        3. status

        4. sexism & racism

    B. Language reflects attitudes.

        1. power

        2. affiliation

            a) convergence

            b) divergence

        3. attraction & interest

            a) demonstrative pronouns

            b) negation

            c) sequential placement

        4. responsibility

       a) "it" vs. "I" statements

       b) "you" vs. "I" statements

       c) "but" statements

       d) questions vs. statements

III. Troublesome language

    A. The language of misunderstandings

       1. equivocal words

       2. relative words

       3. slang and jargon

       4. overly abstract language

          a) abstraction ladder

             (1) low level abstractions are specific

             (2) high level abstractions are generalizations

                (a) useful as a short-cut

                (b) useful to avoid confrontations

                (c) problematic as stereotyping

                (d) problematic when confusing others

          b) behavioral descriptions avoid overly abstract language

             (1) identify specific, observable phenomenon

             (2) person(s) — who?

             (3) circumstances-- when and where?

             (4) observable behaviors — what?

    B. Disruptive language

       1. fact-opinion confusion

          a) factual statements can be verified

          b) opinion statements are beliefs

       2. fact-inference confusion

          a) fact

          b) inferential statements are conclusions from interpretations of evidence

       3. emotive language

    C. Evasive language

       1. euphemism

       2. equivocation

IV. Gender and language

    A. Content differences and similarities

    B. Reasons for communicating

    C. Conversational style

    D. Non-gender variables

        1. social philosophy

        2. occupation & social roles

        3. sex roles

V. Culture and language

    A. Cultures have diverse ideas of appropriate language styles.

        1. directness

            a) low-context cultures

            b) high-context cultures

        2. elaborate or succinct

            a) Arab elaborated style

            b) succinctness and silence valued

        3. formality and informality

    B. Language can shape our world view.

        1. linguistic determinism

        2. Whorf-Sapir hypothesis

        3. linguistic relativism

    C. Language shapes and reflects views in North American culture.

        1. surnames

        2. ethnic names

CHAPTER 3 KEY TERMS

This list of key terms corresponds to those in boldface in your text. In your own words write a definition and an original example of the word.

abstract language

abstraction ladder

behavioral description

convergence

divergence

emotive language

equivocal words

equivocation

euphemism

factual statement

high-context culture

inferential statement

jargon

language

linguistic determinism

linguistic relativism

low-context culture

opinion statement

phonological rules

pragmatic rules

relative rules

semantic rules

sex role

slang

symbol

syntactic rules

Whorf-Sapir hypothesis

Name _____

CHAPTER 3 ACTIVITY 1 POWERFUL/POWERLESS LANGUAGE

Purpose:

1. To expand understanding of powerless and powerful language
2. To use language which takes rather than avoids responsibility
3. To identify types of powerless language and language lacking in responsibility

Instructions Part One:

1. Read the sentences in the first chart. Identify the type of powerless language used by writing the type of language in the left column.
2. Then re-write the sentence in the right column expressing the idea in more powerful, but not rude or offensive language. See Table 3-1 in the textbook.

Type of language usage	Less Powerful	Rewrite using more powerful language
polite forms	Ms. Smith, I wanted to ask you about the assignment ma'am.	I wanted to ask about the assignment.
	There's probably a better way to do this, but let me explain.	
	It was really a good speech.	
	That was a good meeting, wasn't it?	
	I sort of wanted to leave early today.	

Instructions Part Two:

1. Read the sentences in the second chart.
2. Identify the type of language responsibility problem shown by writing the type of language in the left column. Then re-write the sentences with language that takes responsibility in the right column.

Type of language	Lacking responsibility	Rewrite using responsible language
You vs. I	You irritate me with your singing in the car.	I feel irritated when I'm driving and listening to your singing.
	There's no reason it won't work, but we don't have the money.	
	Do you think we could go to a Chinese restaurant rather than a pizza place?	
	It's not a good idea.	
	You really get me upset when you drive like that.	

Name _____

CHAPTER 3 ACTIVITY 2 SEXIST AND RELATIVE LANGUAGE

Purpose:

1. To expand understanding of sexist and relative language.
2. To use nonsexist language and non-relative words.

Instructions Part One:

1. In the first chart, identify the problem with the language on the left, and write it in the middle column.
2. Then think of other terms that could be substituted, and write them in the right column.

Sexist language	Problem	Rewrite using language which describes the function
waitress	Two people doing an identical job have different labels based on sex. Title should describe the job.	Server Wait person
mailman		
Master of ceremonies		
"peace on earth good will to men"		
In great matters men show themselves as they wish to be seen; in small matters, as they are. -Gamaliel Bradford		

Instructions Part Two:

Replace the relative word with a word that is specific and measurable.

Use relative words	Replace relative words
I'd like a small brownie.	Make mine no more than 1" square.
My dad is not very tall.	
I'll be back in a little while.	
Don't make your papers too long.	
I'm not a very good pitcher.	

Name _____

CHAPTER 3 ACTIVITY 3 BEHAVIORAL DESCRIPTIONS

Purpose:

To practice replacing abstract statements with behavioral descriptions.

Instructions Part One:

1. Read the following abstract statements.
2. Rewrite each using behavioral descriptions.

Example: You always get more help from the folks than I do.

Who is involved? __Mom__

In what circumstances? _One time, when you couldn't pay your tuition last semester_

What behaviors are involved?__ paying tuition for you_

Clearer statement: _Mom paid your tuition last semester._

Advantages or disadvantages to using the clearer statement: _In a discussion with my sister, it limits the scope of what sounds like an attack on her. There is something concrete for her to respond to. The scope of my resentment is narrowed. The "fact" is presented, rather than a vague statement._

Impact on you of having to think through the three questions: _I had to stop and think of what I really meant and what the "facts" were that I was basing my broad attack on. I had to ask myself what the problem really was and stop exaggerating it._

1. School is so easy for you.

Who is involved?

In what circumstances?

What behaviors are involved?

Clearer statement:

Advantages or disadvantages to using the clearer statement:

Impact on you of having to think through the three questions:

2.   The work load around here sure isn't fair.

Who is involved?

In what circumstances?

What behaviors are involved?

Clearer statement:

Advantages or disadvantages to using the clearer statement:

Impact on you of having to think through the three questions:

Part Two

1.   What do you have to do in order to change abstract statements to behavioral descriptions?

2.   What effect does this activity have on your thought process?

3.   What effect does this activity have on the time you take to talk to yourself? to express yourself?

4.   Predict what would happen if all abstract speech were converted to behavioral descriptions and other forms of more concrete, specific language. What would happen in personal relationships? government? classrooms? television shows?

Name _____

CHAPTER 3 ACTIVITY 4 FACTS AND INFERENCES

Purpose:

1. To distinguish between facts and inferences.
2. To rewrite inferences in a factual statement.

Instructions Part One:

1. Read the inferences below.
2. Re-write them to be factual statements. If you don't know the "facts" indicate what data you would need.

1. The U.S. is an educated society.

2. Family relationships on the Internet are better than face-to-face.

3. Everyone wants to have a meaningful job.

4. Businesses would be more productive if every one were bilingual.

5. Generation Y students are lazy and unproductive.

Instructions Part Two:

Replace the following opinions with factual statements that can be verified. Indicate what facts you would need if you don't know the facts.

1.   This is a better school than UM.

     <u>Tuition is $100 lower and the student/teacher ratio is 20% lower here than at UM.</u>

2.   Europe is a better place to live than the U.S.

3.   Communication courses are more valuable than physics courses.

4.   People in the U.S. have lousy marriages.

5.   Cuban food is less popular than Chinese food.

Name _____

CHAPTER 3 ACTIVITY 5 EXPLORING THE WEB

Machine Translation

In order to "test" the power of machine translation, go to http://babelfish.altavista.com/tr.

1. Write out a simple command in English. (Go to the store and buy some eggs. Pick up my laundry on the way home. Put the book on the desk.) Write it here:

2. Now, use the web translator to translate from English into French, German, or Portuguese or Italian. (Use the "translate from" button.) If you are fluent in one of those languages, see how their translation compares to yours. Once you have the translation, copy it and translate from that language back to English. Write the English retranslation here:

3. If the translation comes back differently (and even humorously) from your original English, speculate on what the difficulties were. It usually will not be exactly the same as your original. If it is exact, speculate why it would be.

4. Now try it with a more complex thought: your political ideas or your feelings about a complex issue. Go through the same steps as above. Example: "I like my mom" translated to Spanish as "Tengo gusto de mi mama" and back to English as "I have taste of my breast."

   Sentence typed in:

   English re-translated:

5. What did you predict would happen when the sentence is re-translated back into English? Why?

6. What properties of language account for some of the difficulties?

7. How would you assess the overall usefulness of a site like this to translate the homepage of your school?

8. Speculate about what might happen if government officials relied on machine translation.

What's in a name? John Wayne's real name was Marion Morrison. Discover the real names of politicians, actors, singers, and athletes at www.triv.net/html/Users9/u21596.shtml. Hypothesize about the reasons for the name changes with regard to this chapter's discussion of names and Chapter 2's discussion of identity management.

Just for fun Learn a bit about hieroglyphics and translate your name into hieroglyphics: www.quizland.com/hiero.htm.

For further exploration Using a search engine, find a site that will translate your name into Japanese, Chinese, Arabic, or another language that does not use the same alphabet English uses.
Web sites:

Name _____

CHAPTER 3 SELF TEST

MATCHING Set One Match each term listed on the left with its correct definition from the column on the right.

_____ 1. abstract language

_____ 2. abstraction ladder

_____ 3. behavioral description

_____ 4. convergence

_____ 5. divergence

_____ 6. emotive language

_____ 7. equivocal words

_____ 8. equivocation

_____ 9. euphemism

_____ 10. factual statement

_____ 11. high-context culture

_____ 12. inferential statement

_____ 13. jargon

_____ 14. language

a. language that is not specific or detailed

b. conclusion arrived at through interpretation of evidence

c. symbols, governed by rules, used to convey messages between persons

d. a list of terms or phrases ranging from more to less detail to describe an event or object

e. words with more than one commonly used dictionary definition

f. linguistic strategy in which speakers emphasize their commonality with others through use of a similar language style

g. words that convey the sender's attitude rather than objective description

h. an account that refers only to observable phenomena

i. vague statement that can be interpreted more than one way

j. pleasant-sounding term used in place of a less pleasant one

k. statement that can be verified as true or false

l. culture which avoids direct use of language; meaning is conveyed through context more than words

m. a linguistic strategy in which speakers emphasize differences between their style and others to create distance

n. language shared by professionals or others with a common interest, such as medical short hand, computer terms, or banking phrases

MATCHING Set Two Match each term listed on the left with its correct definition from the column on the right.

____ 15. linguistic determinism

____ 16. linguistic relativism

____ 17. low-context culture

____ 18. opinion statement

____ 19. phonological rules

____ 20. pragmatic rules

____ 21. relative language

____ 22. semantic rules

____ 23. syntactic rules

____ 24. sex role

____ 25. slang

____ 26. symbol

____ 27. Whorf-Sapir hypothesis

a. words used by a particular group to differentiate itself, possibly by geographical region or age

b. a culture that relies heavily on language to make message explicit

c. anything that is arbitrarily designated to stand for something else

d. a theory that a culture's world view is shaped and reflected by its language

e. a moderate form of the Whorf-Sapir linguistic theory which argues that language strongly influences (but doesn't totally shape) peoples' perceptions

f. statement based on the speaker's beliefs

g. linguistic rules governing how sounds are combined to form words

h. rules that govern everyday use of language

i. rules that govern the meaning of words

j. words that gain their meaning by comparison

k. social orientation that governs behavior

l. rules that govern ways symbols are arranged

m. the form of the Whorf-Sapir theory which states that the language used shapes the world view of its users

MULTIPLE CHOICE Choose the BEST response from those listed.

1. If a person says, "Pencil me to give the" instead of "Give the pencil to me," which kind of rule has most obviously been broken?

   a. phonological
   b. semantic
   c. syntactic
   d. pragmatic
   e. none of the above

2. Language

   a. is symbolic.
   b. is rule-governed.
   c. can shape attitudes.
   d. can reflect attitudes.
   e. all of the above

3. Using the same kind of language and language style as someone else can be a way to demonstrate _____ through convergence.

   a. power
   b. responsibility
   c. affiliation
   d. high-context
   e. divergence

4. The statements "You make me disgusted" or "You make me happy" demonstrate a lack of

   a. convergence.
   b. status.
   c. credibility.
   d. semantics.
   e. responsibility.

5. An instructor describes a particular book to a student and tells the student she thinks the student might enjoy it and tells him to "check it out." The student checks the book out of the library and brings it to class and tells the instructor it isn't a book he would enjoy. The instructor wonders why the student bothered to bring it from the library. The instructor used "check it out" to mean "see if you'd like it." The student thought "check it out" meant he was supposed to actually borrow the book from the library. This is an example of _____ language.

   a. jargon
   b. pragmatic
   c. equivocal
   d. non rule-governed
   e. denotative

6. Which of the following indicates a speaker's willingness to take responsibility for oneself?

   a. "it" statements [It's not ready yet.]
   b. "but" statements [I wanted to get the report done, but something came up.]
   c. "I" statements [I didn't finish the report.]
   d. questioning statements [Do you think its okay to finish the report later?']
   e. "you" statements [You made me miss the deadline for the report.]

7. In a study not quoted in your text, researchers found that teachers gave different grades to the same papers when told the papers were written by students with various different names. This seems to indicate that names have the power to

   a. create disruptions.
   b. shape people's attitudes and behaviors towards people unknown to them.
   c. reflect personality traits.
   d. avoid misunderstandings.
   e. demonstrate linguistic relativism.

8. Persons decide whether to call themselves Mexican-American, Hispanic, Latino/a, or Chicano/a, and others decide among Negro, Black, and African-American, and still others choose from Euroamerican, Anglo, and white. The conscious choice of a name demonstrates the use of _____ to both shape and reflect attitudes toward themselves.

    a. syntactic rules
    b. equivocation
    c. language
    d. stereotypes
    e. jargon

9. Which is true of men's speech, according to research cited in the text?

    a. It is used to accomplish tasks more than to build intimate relationships.
    b. It is used often to disclose vulnerabilities.
    c. It is used to diminish status differences.
    d. It is rarely used to exert control.
    e. all of the above

10. Communicators in a high-context culture are more likely to

    a. state feelings explicitly.
    b. use language to build harmony.
    c. ask for things they need directly.
    d. engage in confrontation.
    e. speak out about their needs.

11. "I don't want to interrupt, but if we could start the meeting now. . ." This is an example of

    a. sequential placement
    b. tag question
    c. a disclaimer
    d. stereotyping
    e. perception check

12. It is popular to use a variety of chilies for cooking. According to a recent Newsweek article, some of the most popular chiles have names like *prik khi nu* which translates from Thai as "rat-dropping chile" and *chile tecpin*, which means "flea chile." When stores and markets use the chic-sounding foreign name rather than a less pleasant translation, the foreign term acts as

    a. a relative word.
    b. an inference.
    c. a behavioral description.
    d. a succinct-style expression.
    e. a euphemism.

13. When you are unsure about what a person means by a statement, you could improve your understanding by using

    a. a relative term
    b. a perception check
    c. an inference
    d. a syntactic rule
    e. terms that are more abstract than the other person used

14. "Misunderstanding results when one person assumes that words mean the same thing to him or her as to all other persons." This is a paraphrase of which concept of language:

    a. Many words have similar meanings.
    b. Dictionaries are adequate for everyday language.
    c. Meanings are in people not in words.
    d. Gender influences our language style and content.
    e. Cultures have a preference for direct or indirect styles.

15. Which statement is least abstract (low level abstraction)?

    a. You're the best friend I've ever had.
    b. I think you've just been terrific.
    c. I appreciated your letting me borrow your car.
    d. You are so thoughtful.
    e. I appreciate your friendship.

MATCHING Set Three Match the following terms or phrases with the definitions.

    a. behavioral description   **d. low-context cultures**

    b. equivocal language   **e. opinions**

    c. high-context cultures

_____ 1. ambiguous language that has two or more equally plausible meanings

_____ 2. cultures that avoid direct use of language, relying more on nonverbal messages and context

_____ 3. an low-level abstraction that refers only to persons, contexts, and behaviors

_____ 4. cultures that use language abundantly and rely on words for explanation and clarity

_____ 5. beliefs about something that are not necessarily verifiable

MATCHING Set Four Match each situation with the type of language problem demonstrated.

    a. emotive language   **d. inference**

    b. relative word   **e. euphemism**

    c. equivocal language

_____ 6. After promising not to raise taxes, the administration requires that additional money be paid by each person buying gasoline. It insists that this is not a new tax, but a **"revenue enhancer."**

_____ 7. Your friend borrows your shirt and promises to return it **"soon."** You are angry because it is the end of the day and he has not returned it. He used "soon" to mean by the end of the week.

_____ 8. I refer to my roommate as **"interesting and exciting."** After meeting her you tell me that you thought she was **"rude and obnoxious."** Each of us has chosen _____.

_____ 9. She didn't call on me when I raised my hand so she must not like me.

_____ 10. A teacher tells a student about a book that might be helpful to the student. She tells the student to "check it out." The next day the student (dutifully) shows the instructor that she has checked out the book in her name. She doesn't think it will be helpful. The teacher didn't intend for her to sign out the book if it wasn't helpful. She used "check it out" to mean "see if it is of use."

TRUE/FALSE Circle the T or F to indicate whether you believe the statement is true or false. If it is **true**, give a **reason** or an **example**. If it is false, **explain** what would make it true.

T   F   1.   Our use of language rarely affects our credibility.

T   F   2.   Phonological rules are those that govern the way sounds combine to form words.

T   F   3.   Tag questions, intensifiers, and hedges are all types of powerful speech.

T   F   4.   Women's speech tends to differ in content but not in goals from men's speech.

T   F   5.   Stereotyping and confusing others are frequent results of overly abstract speech.

COMPLETION Fill in each of the blanks with a word from the lists provided. Choose the BEST word for each sentence. There are more words than you will use, but each word will be used only once.

negotiate meanings	**stop thinking**
accomplish tasks	**create misunderstanding**
influence perception	**nourish relationships**

1.   Men tend to use speech in order to _____.

2.   The idea that the language which members of a culture speak can _____ is called the Whorf-Sapir hypothesis.

3.   Women tend to use speech in order to _____.

4.   In order to have effective communication when statements are ambiguous it is necessary to

_____.

5.   Emotive and evasive language have the potential to _____.

CHAPTER 3 ANSWERS TO SELF TEST

MATCHING Set One

1. a	2. d	3. h	4. f	5. m
6. g	7. e	8. i	9. j	10. k
11. l	12. b	13. n	14. c	

MATCHING Set Two

15. m	16. e	17. b	18. f	19. g
20. h	21. j	22. i	23. l	24. k
25. a	26. c	27. d		

MULTIPLE CHOICE

1. c	2. e	3. c	4. e	5. c
6. d	7. b	8. c	9. a	10. b
11. c	12. e	13. b	14. c	15. c

MATCHING Set Three

1. b	2. c	3. a	4. d	5. e

MATCHING Set Four

6. e	7. b	8. a	9. d	10. c

TRUE/FALSE

1. False	2. True	3. False	4. False	5. True

COMPLETION

1. accomplish tasks
2. influence perception
3. nourish relationships
4. negotiate meanings
5. create misunderstanding

Related Reading

"Antioch College Sexual Offense Policy, 1992." www.ejhs.org/volume1/conseapa.htm

Preview

A "menace to spontaneous sex"? Or something that enables students to feel "more respected and more empowered"? The former is Newsweek's description of the media's reaction to the Antioch (Ohio) College Sexual Offense Policy, 1992. The latter is one co-ed's reaction. The policy was instituted as a way of addressing the delicate issue of appropriate sexual conduct and concerns particularly about acquaintance rape. The policy illustrates an attempt to use language--low-level abstractions and highly specific language--to grapple with issues of sexual conduct. The cornerstone of the 1992 policy was the need for "verbal consent at each new level of physical and/or sexual contact".

A 1996 revision based on accumulated experiences strengthens the policy. According to the 2002 catalog, "This policy has come from students with the support of faculty, staff, and administrators. It applies to every member of the Antioch Community. The "explicit consent" clause of the policy makes it distinctive in higher education, and helps mark Antioch as a pioneer in the arena of educating about sexual and human relations." (Retrieved from www.antioch-college.edu/Catalog/antioch_community.htm on January 4, 2005.)

As you read, look for ways in which the policy mandates the use of verbal language as well as ways the perceived need for the policy reflects principles in this chapter regarding the meaning of language, the power of language, and the language of misunderstandings.

Review

1. How does the policy reflect a belief in the power of language? What principles of language are reflected in this policy?

2. Do you think encouraging people to use more low-level abstractions more often while discussing their sexual desires will reduce acquaintance rape? Will following the policy make words less equivocal?

3. Would someone from a low-context or high-context culture be more comfortable with this policy? Why?

CHAPTER 4 LISTENING

CHAPTER 4 SKELETON OUTLINE

This outline can be a helpful study tool to assist you in seeing the order and sequence of the chapter and the relationship of ideas. Use it to take notes as you read and/or to add concepts presented in lecture.

I.   Misconceptions about listening

    A. Listening and hearing are different

        1.   hearing

        2.   listening

            a)   attending

            b)   understanding

            c)   responding

            d)   remembering

                (1)   rate of forgetting

                (2)   residual message

    B.   Listening is not a natural process

    C.   Listening requires effort

    D.   Listeners receive different messages

II. Overcoming challenges to effective listening

    A.   Faulty listening behaviors

        1.   pseudolistening

        2.   selective listening

        3.   defensive listening

        4.   ambushing

        5.   insulated listening

        6.   insensitive listening

        7.   stage hogging

    B.   Reasons for poor listening

        1.   effort

        2.   message overload

        3.   rapid thought

        4.   psychological noise

        5.   physical noise

        6.   hearing problems

        7.   faulty assumptions

      8. talking's apparent advantages

      9. cultural differences

     10. media influences

III. Personal listening styles

  A. Content-oriented

  B. People-oriented

  C. Action-oriented

  D. Time-oriented listening

IV. Informational listening

  A. Don't argue or judge prematurely

  B. Separate message and speaker

  C. Be opportunistic

  D. Look for key ideas

  E. Ask questions

      1. sincere questions

      2. counterfeit questions

          a) questions that make statements

          b) questions that carry hidden agendas

          c) questions that seek "correct" answers

          d) questions based on unchecked assumptions

  F. Paraphrase

      1. restating thoughts and feelings of speaker

      2. methods

          a) change wording

          b) offer an example

          c) reflect underlying theme

  G. Take notes

      1. don't wait too long before taking notes

      2. record only key ideas

      3. develop a note-taking format

V. Critical listening (Evaluative listening)

  A. Listen for information before evaluating

  B. Evaluate the speaker's credibility

      1. competence

2. impartiality

C. Examine the speaker's evidence and reasoning

    1. recent evidence

    2. enough evidence

    3. source of evidence

    4. interpretation of evidence

D. Examine emotional appeals

VI. Empathic listening

A. Advising

    1. requests not always clear

    2. advice not always best

    3. allows others to avoid responsibility

    4. before offering advice, make sure

        a) it is the correct advice

        b) it will be accepted

        c) you will not be blamed

B. Judging

    1. did the person request your judgment?

    2. is your judgment constructive?

C. Analyzing

    1. be tentative

    2. be reasonably correct

    3. be sure the other is receptive

    4. be well-motivated

D. Questioning

    1. don't ask for curiosity

    2. be sure questions are not confusing or distracting

    3. don't disguise suggestions or criticism as questions

E. Supporting

    1. be sure you're sincere

    2. be sure other can accept your support

F. Prompting

G. Paraphrasing thoughts and feelings

    1. helps speaker clarify problem

    2. catharsis for speaker

    3. listeners show involvement and concern

    4. helps listener understand thoughts and feelings

        a) problem's complexity

        b) adequate time and concern

        c) genuine interest

        d) withhold judgment

        e) proportion to other responses

H. When and how to help?

    1. situation

    2. other person

    3. yourself

CHAPTER 4 KEY TERMS

This list of key terms corresponds to those in boldface in your text. In your own words write a definition and an original example of the word.

action-oriented listeners

advising

ambushers

analyzing

attending

content-oriented listeners

counterfeit question

critical listening

defensive listening

empathic listening

hearing

informational listening

insensitive listeners

insulated listeners

judging

listening

paraphrasing

people-oriented listeners

prompting

pseudolistening

questioning

remembering

residual message

responding

selective listening

sincere question

stage hogs

supporting

time-oriented listeners

understanding

Name _____

CHAPTER 4 ACTIVITY 1 AN ANALYSIS OF POOR LISTENING

Purpose:

1. To analyze poor listening.
2. To identify ways to improve listening.

Instructions:

1. Choose one situation in which you listened poorly.
2. Answer the following questions to carefully analyze each factor that affected your listening.

AN EXAMPLE OF POOR LISTENING

Context Briefly describe where you were, who else was there, what was happening and why it was important to listen well, even though you didn't.

As a listener, I was not attending (paying attention to) the message because of interference of the following factors.

Describe your particular **needs** and how they adversely affected your listening.

Describe your particular **wants/desires** and how they adversely affected your listening.

Describe your particular **interests** and how they adversely affected your listening.

Describe your particular **attitudes** and how they adversely affected your listening.

Describe your particular **goals** and how they adversely affected your listening.

Describe your particular **past experiences** and how they adversely affected your listening.

Describe your particular **habits** and how they adversely affected your listening.

I was selectively listening for _____ and that affected my listening adversely because

     _____ I did not understand the syntax.

     _____ I did not understand the semantics.

     _____ I did not understand the pragmatics.

     _____ I did not exert effort to listen.

     _____ I was not motivated to listen.

     _____ The message was not clear to me.

     _____ The channel was not familiar to me.

My own responses were less than desirable because I: (check all those that apply)

     _____ lacked eye contact.

     _____ failed to lean forward.

     _____ didn't stop other activities to listen.

     _____ didn't turn toward speaker/turned away from speaker.

     _____ showed an inappropriate facial expression.

     _____ failed to use paraphrasing.

     _____ asked irrelevant or threatening questions.

Other problems were that:

_____ I was experiencing message overload because

_____ I used my spare time unwisely by

_____ there was too much psychological noise because

_____ there was too much physical noise such as

_____ I have a hearing problem which made this difficult

I bought into some of these faulty assumptions while listening:

_____ I assumed I'd heard this all before because

_____ I assumed the speaker was too simple because

_____ I assumed the speaker was too complex because

_____ I assumed the speaker was unimportant because

Summary What have you learned from this analysis that may help you prevent these listening problems in the future? If you were to give yourself one piece of advice, what would it be?

Name _____

CHAPTER 4 ACTIVITY 2 AN ANALYSIS OF GOOD LISTENING

Purpose:

1.   To analyze good listening.
2.   To identify strengths in listening.

Instructions:

1.   Choose one situation in which you listened well.
2.   Answer the following questions to analyze each area and tell how or why each factor affected your listening in a positive way.

Situation Briefly describe where you were, who else was there, what was happening, and why it was important to listen well.

As a listener, I was attending (paying attention to) the message.

Describe your particular **needs** and how they positively affected your listening.

Describe your particular **wants/desires** and how they positively affected your listening.

Describe your particular **interests** and how they positively affected your listening.

Describe your particular **attitudes** and how they positively affected your listening.

Describe your particular **goals** and how they positively affected your listening.

Describe your particular **past experiences** and how they positively affected your listening.

Describe your particular **habits** and how they positively affected your listening.

I was selectively listening for _____ and that affected my listening positively because

        ____ I understood the syntax.

        ____ I understood the semantics.

        ____ I understood the pragmatics.

        ____ I exerted effort to listen.

        ____ I was motivated to listen.

        ____ the message was clear to me.

        ____ the channel was familiar to me.

My own responses involved (check all those that apply)

        ____ eye contact.

        ____ leaning forward.

        ____ stopping other activities to listen.

        ____ turning toward the speaker.

        ____ showing an appropriate facial expression.

        ____ paraphrasing.

        ____ asking non-threatening questions.

I avoided message overload by

I used my spare time wisely by

I minimized psychological noise by

I minimized physical noise such as _____ by

I ____ do ____ do not have a hearing problem which made listening difficult.

I avoided these faulty assumptions while listening

    ____ Instead of thinking, "I heard this all before," I was thinking

_____ Instead of thinking, "The speaker is too simple," I was thinking

_____ Instead of thinking, "The speaker is too complex," I was thinking

_____ Instead of thinking, "The speaker is unimportant," I was thinking

Summary What have you learned from this analysis that you will use again in the future?

Describe, design, or draw a model or symbol that represents effective listening.

Name _____

CHAPTER 4 ACTIVITY 3 PARAPHRASING

Purpose:

To practice paraphrasing and observe the process of paraphrasing.

Instructions:

1. Choose two people to work with. Designate yourselves "A," "B," and "C."
2. "A" should choose one of the following quotations to discuss, preferably one which "A" feels strongly about. After reading the quotation, "A" begins by commenting and giving opinions and feelings about it. [At this time "C" is observing both "A" and "B" and filling out the Observer Form on the following page.]
3. "B" now paraphrases what "A" said to "A's" satisfaction before adding to the discussion. Then "B" expresses a feeling/opinion about that same quotation and "A" paraphrases before adding to the discussion. Except for "A's" first comment, no one speaks until the other person has paraphrased to the satisfaction of the person who made the comment.
4. After about five minutes of discussion, "C" reports his/her observations on the listening skills of "A" and "B."
5. Repeat the steps above with "B" starting a conversation, "C" listening and responding, and "A" observing. Then repeat the steps above with "C" starting a conversation, "A" listening and responding, and "B" observing.
6. When you have finished three rounds (two as listeners/one as observer), fill out the Analysis of Exercise individually. After you've finished, share your responses with each other.

Quotations to choose from:

The unused coat in your closet belongs to the man who needs it. - St. Basil

From what we get, we can make a living; what we give, however, makes a life. - Arthur Ashe

Happiness is having a large, loving, caring, close-knit family in another city. - George Burns

Patriotism is the willingness to kill and be killed for trivial reasons. - Bertrand Russell

Love does not consist in gazing at each other, but in looking outward together in the same direction. - Antoine de Saint-Exupery

There are two tragedies in life: not getting what you want and getting what you want.

Sometimes it's a little better to travel than to arrive. - Robert Pirsig (Zen and the Art of Motorcycle Maintenance)

Education is the ability to listen to almost anything without losing your temper or your self-confidence. - Robert Frost

There's a fine line between being on the leading edge and being in the lunatic fringe. - Frank Armstrong (Preparing for Tomorrow's Challenges)

Education is not filling a bucket but lighting a fire. - William Butler Yeats

The one who chooses the quotation will give his or her comments first. From then on, speak only after paraphrasing the other to his/her satisfaction.

OBSERVER FORM

As you observe both persons, try to comment on each of these factors:

Person's name

Did it appear that ____ effort was exerted? ____ there was motivation to listen?

Was there appropriate (check all those that apply)

        ____ eye contact?

        ____ forward lean?

        ____ lack of distracting behaviors (pencil tapping, foot tapping)?

        ____ body orientation (turned toward speaker)?

        ____ facial expression?

        ____ paraphrasing of facts?

        ____ paraphrasing of feelings?

        ____ asking non-threatening questions?

What would you say are this person's strength as a listener?

If you could make one comment on something for this listener to improve on, what would it be?

ANALYSIS OF EXERCISE

After your conversation, fill in the following:

1. What was your **initial** reaction to the exercise?

2. What nonverbal behaviors did you observe in yourself and your partner initially?

3. Did these change as time went on? How?

4. Describe the **effect** paraphrasing had on your conversation.

5. How did this conversation differ from other, more typical conversations? If you hadn't paraphrased, predict the direction and tone of the conversation that might have ensued.

6. What are some phrases you and your partner used to paraphrase?

7. How did you **feel** when your partner tried to paraphrase your answers and tried to understand what you were saying?

8. In what ways did your self-concept or your own perceptions influenced how you understood or misunderstood what your partner was saying? Explain.

9. How would you summarize what you learned from this exercise?

Name _____

CHAPTER 4 ACTIVITY 4 PARAPHRASING PRACTICE IN DYADS

Purpose:

To provide you an opportunity to practice and sharpen listening and paraphrasing skills. The goal of this assignment is **not** self-disclosure, assistance, or friendship, but rather a clearer understanding of the **process** and requirements of listening actively.

Setting:

Arrange to carry out the dyad interview in a place that is comfortable for you—cafeteria, outdoor tables. Focus on the interview and try to tune out distractions.

Time: 45-75 minutes.

Instructions:

1. Statements should be completed in the order in which they appear.

2. You may decline to answer any question; just say "pass."

3. Treat information with respect and confidentiality; **take no notes**, listen and paraphrase for better understanding.

Opening: First, one person completes statement one; then the second person completes the same statement. Do the same for statements 2 - 4. Alternate speaking and listening roles throughout the exercise.

1. One thing I like or dislike about my name is . . .

2. When we got this listening assignment I thought . . .

3. When we got this listening assignment I felt . . .

4. When I hear the word "listen" I think . . .

Body: From here on, one person will **complete** a statement and **expand** on it. The other person will listen and then **paraphrase**. Use your **own different words** to paraphrase what you think the other person is saying. Paraphrase both **thoughts and feelings**. The other person must either **verify** that he or she has been correctly paraphrased or **clarify** what the listener paraphrased so the "listener" can correctly paraphrase. The "listener" must correctly paraphrase to the satisfaction of the "speaker." **Switch roles** so each person completes and expands on the same statement before going on to the next.

5. The best role model of listening I've ever known is/was . . . because . . .

6. If you ask my friends, they'd say that in terms of listening I . . .

7. When someone is really listening to me, I know they are listening because. .

8. When someone really listens to me I feel . .

9. When someone isn't listening to me I feel . . .

10. When someone isn't really listening to me, I know they aren't listening because. .

11. I find it very difficult to listen when . . .

12. I find it very difficult to listen to . . .

13. I find it easy to listen when . . .

14. I find it easy to listen to. . .

Break: Now stop and talk about how you're doing. Then practice paraphrasing some more.

15. If parents really listened to children, I think the impact on families would be that . . .

16. If world leaders listened to each other, I think the world would . . .

17. If bosses really listened to employees, I would predict that . . .

18. If politicians really listened to constituents, I would predict that . . .

19. For me, the hardest thing (barrier) about listening to significant others is that . . .

20. I do/don't think that listening is related to academic success because . . .

> (Do you believe that students who get better grades are smarter?)
>
> (Do you believe that students who get better grades listen better?)
>
> (Do you believe that student success is dependent on listening ability or motivation?)

21. Listening courses should/should not be required in school because . . .

22. Listening courses should/should not be required of college instructors because . . .

23. In order to graduate, students should [not] demonstrate listening skills by . . .

24. Much of what I know and believe about listening I learned from. . .

Conclusion:

25.   When I think of how we've completed this exercise I think/feel . . .

Now, thank your partner, and individually and apart from each other fill out the response form.

RESPONSE FORM

After your conversation, fill in the following:

1. What was your **initial** reaction to the exercise?

2. What nonverbal behaviors did you observe in yourself and your partner initially?

3. Did these change as time went on? How?

4. Describe the **effect** paraphrasing had on your conversation?

5. How did this conversation differ from other, more typical conversations? If you hadn't paraphrased, predict the direction and tone of the conversation that might have ensued.

6. What are some phrases you and your partner used to paraphrase?

7. How did you **feel** when your partner tried to paraphrase your answers and tried to understand what you were saying?

8. Were there any ways that your self-concept or your own perception influenced how you understood or misunderstood what your partner was saying? Explain.

9. How would you summarize what you learned from this exercise?

Name _____

CHAPTER 4 ACTIVITY 5 LISTENING STYLES

Purpose:

1. To identify various listening styles.
2. To evaluate the advantages and disadvantages of each style in particular contexts.

Instructions:

1. Read each of the following scenarios.
2. Construct a response that represents each of the styles of listening.
3. Consider the consequences of each style by responding to the questions.

1. Your best friend is telling you about his/her concerns about the person he/she has been seeing for two years. They had always planned to marry after college, but now your friend says, "I'm just feeling like we never really dated anyone else seriously. I love Pat, but I wonder if we should see other people while we're still in college. I don't think we'll know if we're right for each other if we don't really know anyone else."

advising response

judging response

analyzing response

questioning response

supporting response

prompting response

paraphrasing response

As a listener, which types of responses do you think would harm your relationship with the person you are listening to? Why?

Which response do you think would be best? Why?

2. Two friends have been advised by their physician that they fit the profile of someone at higher than average risk for Hepatitis B. Their health plan won't pay for the vaccines (about $250). They are considering getting the vaccine, but are concerned about the cost. One says to you, "I know I'm in a high risk group, but I'm not sure there's much chance of getting it. I haven't really known anyone who has. What would you do?"

advising response

judging response

analyzing response

questioning response

supporting response

prompting response

paraphrasing response

As a listener, which types of responses do you think would harm your relationship with the person you are listening to? Why?

Which response do you think would be best? Why?

3. Your supervisor is considering allowing some employees (including you) to begin to experiment with flexible hours. She is discussing the idea with you and a few other employees before work one morning. She says, "I'd really like to have some of you try flex hours and see the impact on morale and productivity. I know some of you have concerns about transportation and child care, and others are trying to take classes and work. But if some are allowed to try flex hours and all aren't, it could create more hard feelings. I can't make it department wide without my district manager's okay, and he's not willing to try it. But I do have leeway to experiment on a small scale. I wonder what would be best."

advising response

judging response

analyzing response

questioning response

supporting response

prompting response

paraphrasing response

As a listener, which types of responses do you think would harm your relationship with the person you are listening to? Why?

Which response do you think would be best? Why?

4. A co-worker with whom you must coordinate projects says, "Ever since my brother was killed in that car accident, I just haven't felt like this job is important. I haven't felt that much of anything is important. I can't focus or concentrate very well, and nothing matters much. I'm sorry I've caused you to miss some deadlines, too."

advising response

judging response

analyzing response

questioning response

supporting response

prompting response

paraphrasing response

As a listener, which types of responses do you think would harm your relationship with the person you are listening to? Why?

Which response do you think would be best? Why?

Name _____

CHAPTER 4 ACTIVITY 6 EXPLORING THE WEB

Listening Competencies

The National Communication Association has outlined a set of listening competencies, or behaviors and listening skills, that are expected of students. Look at www.natcom.org/Instruction/assessment/collegecomp/college_competencies_table1.htm. Scroll down to II. Listening Competencies.

Compare and contrast the definition of listening given in your text with the definition in the paragraph at the beginning of the Listening Competencies.

1. What are the four competencies listed under "A. Attend with an open mind."

A.

B.

C.

D.

2. Do you think there are others that should be listed? Explain.

3. List the competencies associated with being able to listen with critical comprehension (A through J).

A.

B.

C.

D.

E.

F.

G.

H.

I.

J.

4. In your own words, what does competency J-1 mean?

5. What term used in your book for a type of listening parallels the term "literal comprehension" as used in these competencies?

6. What term used in your book parallels the NCA term "critical comprehension"?

7. Compare and contrast the competencies shown for literal and for critical comprehension.

8. How would you explain the fact that there are ten competencies under critical listening compared to only four under literal comprehension?

9. Now, look at the standards (numbers 13-15) for competent listeners in grades K-12 as defined by NCA. These are can be found at www.natcom.org/Instruction/new_page_1.htm. Do you think it is realistic for high school students to be able to have and demonstrate this knowledge? Why or why not?

10. For an interactive listening assessment, go to International Listening Leadership Institute at www.listeningleaders.com/LHProfile.html.

11. Randall S. Davis, experienced ESL instructor, has put together over 100 listening quizzes at various levels of difficulty. Test your listening skills by visiting *Randall's Cyber ESL Listening Lab* at www.esl-lab.com.

Name _____

CHAPTER 4 SELF TEST

MATCHING Part One Match each term listed on the left with its correct definition from the column on the right.

_____ 1. action-oriented listener

_____ 2. advising

_____ 3. ambushing

_____ 4. analyzing

_____ 5. attending

_____ 6. content-oriented listener

_____ 7. counterfeit question

_____ 8. critical listening

_____ 9. defensive listening

_____ 10. empathic listening

a. the process of focusing on certain stimuli from the environment

b. listening in which the goal is to judge the quality or accuracy of the speaker's remarks

c. response style in which the receiver reassures, comforts, or distracts the person seeking help

d. attempts to send a message disguised as a question

e. a helping style in which the listener offers an interpretation of a speaker's message

f. a listening style in which the receiver listens carefully to gather information to use in an attack on the speaker

g. a listener concerned most with the task at hand and least with emotional components

h. a listener most interested in the quality of messages, details, and analysis of the ideas

i. a helping response in which the receiver offers suggestions about how the speaker should deal with a problem

j. A student innocently asks what time it is. The instructor hears that as an attack. Instructor *hears* "This class is boring. Are we almost done?" The instructor is demonstrating ____.

MATCHING Part Two Match each term listed on the left with its correct definition from the column on the right.

_____ 11. hearing

_____ 12. informational listening

_____ 13. insensitive listening

_____ 14. insulated listening

_____ 15. judging

_____ 16. listening

_____ 17. paraphrasing

_____ 18. people-oriented listener

_____ 19. prompting

_____ 20. pseudolistening

a. a reaction in which the receiver evaluates the sender's message either favorably or unfavorably

b. listening style that uses silence and "uh-huh" or "hmmmm" to draw out more information from the speaker

c. the process wherein sound waves strike the eardrum and cause vibrations that are transmitted to the brain

d. feedback in which the receiver rewords the speaker's thoughts and feelings

e. process wherein the brain reconstructs electrochemical impulses generated by hearing into representations of the original sound and gives them meaning

f. listening in which the goal is to receive accurately the same thoughts the speaker is trying to convey

g. a listener who is most concerned with maintaining relationships

h. an imitation of true listening in which the receiver pretends to listen but has his/her mind elsewhere

i. listening in a way that misses hidden meanings and hears only the surface remarks; not attuned to nonverbal or vocal signals of feelings or indirectness

j. style in which the receiver ignores undesirable information

MATCHING Part Three Match each term listed on the left with its correct definition from the column on the right.

_____ 21. questioning

_____ 22. remembering

_____ 23. residual message

_____ 24. responding

_____ 25. selective listening

_____ 26. sincere question

_____ 27. stage hogging

_____ 28. supporting

_____ 29. time-oriented listener

_____ 30. understanding

a. a style of listening (helping) in which the receiver seeks additional information from the sender

b. a listening style in which the receiver is more concerned with making his or her own point than in understanding the speaker

c. agreeing, praising, offering to help, and reassuring are all types of _____ responses

d. a listener who is most concerned with efficiency and speed

e. giving observable feedback to the person you are listening to

f. the part of a message a receiver can recall after short- and long-term memory loss

g. process of making sense of a message

h. retaining information

i. a listening style in which the receiver responds only to messages that interest him or her

j. a type of question which genuinely seeks to understand the other, not to make a point

MULTIPLE CHOICE Choose the BEST response from those listed.

1. Of these activities, which one occupies a greater percentage of a typical person's day?

    a. listening
    b. writing
    c. speaking
    d. reading
    e. Most people spend an equal amount of time on each.

2. Research cited in your text shows listening to be a significant factor in maintaining

    a. marital relationships.
    b. family relationships.
    c. career success.
    d. persuasive skills.
    e. all of the above.

3. The stages of listening include all BUT

    a. attending.
    b. understanding.
    c. responding.
    d. activating.
    e. remembering.

4. Which is true?

    a. Listening and hearing are remarkably similar.
    b. Listening and hearing are exactly the same process.
    c. Listening is physical; hearing is psychological.
    d. It is possible to listen without hearing.
    e. It is possible to hear without listening.

5. Which is true?

    a. Listening is a natural process.
    b. Listening requires effort.
    c. All listeners receive the same message.
    d. All of the above are true.
    e. None of the above is true.

6. Nodding and smiling and pretending to listen is called

    a. selective listening.
    b. defensive listening.
    c. stage hogging.
    d. pseudolistening.
    e. insensitive listening.

7. John barely pays attention to Mike's office talk, until Mike starts to describe how many employees have been missing work recently. Then John really pays attention because he's been trying to prove to Mike how the new flex time policy will lead to more absenteeism. John then uses Mike's own words to attack Mike's liking of flex time. John is engaged in

    a. pseudolistening.
    b. insensitive listening.
    c. defensive listening.
    d. ambushing.
    e. critical listening.

8. Generally people speak between 100 and 140 words a minute, but are capable of understanding speech at _____ words per minute.

    a. 600
    b. 400
    c. 750
    d. 500
    e. 100

9. Listening is poor when

    a. we don't expend the effort.
    b. we experience message overload.
    c. we experience psychological noise.
    d. all of the above
    e. none of the above

10. Which of these is a faulty assumption discussed in your text?

    a. "I've heard this before."
    b. "This is too hard to understand."
    c. "This is too easy."
    d. "This is boring and not very important."
    e. All of these are faulty assumptions.

11. When listening for information, it is wise to

    a. make some quick judgements about the speaker, so you're not misled.
    b. tie the message and speaker together in your mind.
    c. be opportunistic by learning what you can from this speaker, even if you learn what not to do.
    d. listen for details rather than thesis.
    e. all of the above

12. Which of these is a sincere question?

    a. Can you help me understand why this is so difficult for you?
    b. Why are you acting so weird?
    c. Are you **finally** getting a promotion?
    d. Do you still have a weight problem?
    e. None of the above

13. Which is the best paraphrase of "I'm in such a rut; I'm unhappy with work and with my relationship. Seems like everything's the same day after day after day."

    a. Why don't you jazz up your life by doing something different?
    b. Sounds like you don't feel much excitement and like you're bored with the routine.
    c. Seems like your problem is that you haven't put yourself in any new situations lately.
    d. What are you unhappy with: not having a mate or not being promoted?
    e. All are equally good paraphrases.

14. When would you use critical listening?

    a. when your special friend is having a difficult time at work
    b. when you need to know what time a meeting is being held
    c. when you are the object of a sales pitch
    d. when a friend has lost a close election and is very upset
    e. All of these would be appropriate times for critical listening.

15. A fallacy is an error in

    a. listening.
    b. reasoning.
    c. speaking.
    d. advising.
    e. expressing.

TRUE/FALSE Circle the T or F to indicate whether you believe the statement is true or false. If it is **true**, give a **reason** or an **example**. If it is false, **explain** what would make it true.

T F 1. Examining emotional appeals is a part of empathic listening.

T F 2. Analyzing may create defensiveness in another.

T F 3. All questioning responses are confusing or distracting to a person with a problem.

T F 4. Supporting responses are always *perceived* as reassuring and encouraging.

T F 5. Paraphrasing involves restating both thoughts and feelings.

COMPLETION Fill in each of the blanks with a word from the lists provided. Choose the BEST word for each sentence. There are more words than you will use, but each word will be used only once.

understanding	**remembering**
listening	**attending**
responding	**hearing**

1. _____ is a physiological process; listening is psychological.

2. _____ to a message involves giving observable feedback to the speaker.

3. Individual needs, wants, and interests help determine whether you will be

    _____ to a message.

4. Making sense of a message is called _____ and requires understanding syntax and semantics.

5. The size of the residual message from any event has to do with the final step in the listening process,

    _____ .

CHAPTER 4 ANSWERS TO SELF TEST

MATCHING Set One

1. g	2. i	3. f	4. e	5. a
6. h	7. d	8. b	9. j	10. c

MATCHING Set Two

11. c	12. f	13. i	14. j	15. a
16. e	17. d	18. g	19. b	20. h

MATCHING Set Three

21. a	22. h	23. f	24. e	25. i
26. j	27. b	28. c	29. d	30. g

MULTIPLE CHOICE

1. a	2. e	3. d	4. e	5. b
6. d	7. d	8. a	9. d	10. e
11. c	12. a	13. b	14. c	15. b

TRUE/FALSE

1. False	2. True	3. False	4. False	5. True

COMPLETION

1. hearing	2. responding	3. attending
4. understanding	5. remembering	

Related Reading

"New Wineskins: A Lesson in Listening" by Deanna Wylie Mayer
(www.sojo.net/index.cfm?action=magazine.article&issue=soj9505&article=950553)
From Sojourners Magazine. May-June 1995. Vol. 24 No. 2. p. 37.

Preview

Barriers to authentic listening abound. Listening to one another on emotional topics is especially tough. This article advocates really listening, even when we may have an agenda or a desire to use someone else's story for our own purposes. Before reading this article, be up front with yourself about how your beliefs about abortion and women who have had abortions bias or present barriers for you when listening. What kind of speakers or writers are you ready and willing to listen to with an open mind? Which ones do you listen to defensively? Selectively? With insulation or ready to ambush? Can you set aside your own biases and avoid arguing or judging prematurely? Before reading, prepare yourself to listen to really understand the writer and to empathetically listen to "Jeanne's story," a story within the reading.

Review

1. Before re-telling Jeanne's story, the author cautions us not to "use" her story to support or negate positions we advocate or denounce, but to just listen. As both pro-choice and pro-life groups listen to a story like this one, what kind of listening might each group tend to use?

2. What kind of listening discussed in the text would be equivalent to what this author asks us to do, "just listening?"

3. What kind of listening does Jeanne imply that both pro-choice and pro-life groups have done in the past?

4. What other issues would you say are on a par with this one, in terms of being as emotional and as difficult for people to listen to each other?

5. Paraphrase the author's main point.

CHAPTER 5 NONVERBAL COMMUNICATION

CHAPTER 5 SKELETON OUTLINE

This outline can be a helpful study tool to assist you in seeing the order and sequence of the chapter and the relationship of ideas. Use it to take notes as you read and/or to add concepts presented in lecture.

I. Characteristics of nonverbal communication

    A. Nonverbal communication always exists in interpersonal communication

    B. Nonverbal behavior has communicative value.

        1. unintentional

        2. unconscious

    C. Nonverbal communication is primarily relational.

        1. identity management

        2. define relationships

        3. express attitudes and feelings

    D. Nonverbal communication is more ambiguous than verbal communication.

        1. some emotions are easier to decode than others

        2. some people are better at decoding nonverbal messages

        3. to understand nonverbal communication, consider

            a) context

            b) history of the relationship

            c) other's moods

            d) your feelings.

    E. Nonverbal communication is different from verbal communication.

    F. Nonverbal skills are important.

II. Influences on nonverbal communication

    A. Nonverbal communication is culture-bound

        1. gestures

        2. distances

        3. eye contact

        4. display rules

        5. some nonverbal communication is universal

    B. Gender influences nonverbal communication.

        1. physiological

        2. social

        3. status

      4. culture

      5. more similar than different

III. Functions of nonverbal communication

    A. Repeating (may use emblems)

    B. Substituting (may use emblems)

    C. Complementing (may use illustrators)

    D. Accenting

    E. Regulating

    F. Contradicting

    G. Deceiving

IV. Types of nonverbal communication

    A. Posture and gesture

      1. kinesics

      2. manipulators

    B. Face and eyes

      1. quantity and speed of expressions

      2. basic expressions and affect blends

    C. Voice (paralanguage)

      1. tone, speed, pitch, volume, pauses, disfluencies

      2. compliance, contradiction, perception

    D. Touch

      1. earliest contact

      2. need

      3. type of relationship

      4. type of touch

    E. Physical attractiveness

    F. Clothing

    G. Distance (proxemics)

      1. intimate distance

      2. personal distance

      3. social distance

      4. public distance

    H. Time (chronemics)

      1. status

2. culture

I. Territoriality (territory)

J. Environment

1. provides information (impression)

2. shapes interaction

CHAPTER 5 KEY TERMS

This list of key terms corresponds to those in boldface in your text. In your own words write a definition and an original example of the word.

affect blends

chronemics

disfluencies

emblems

illustrators

intimate distance

kinesics

manipulators

nonverbal communication

paralanguage

personal distance

proxemics

public distance

social distance

territory

Sketch or insert pictures of some emblems here:

Sketch or insert pictures of some facial expressions and affect blends here:

Name _____

CHAPTER 5 ACTIVITY 1 CATEGORIES OF NONVERBAL BEHAVIOR

Purpose:

To analyze and categorize nonverbal behaviors.

Instructions:

1. Select a paragraph from a news article.
2. Underline or highlight as many references as you can to different types of nonverbal communication.
3. Draw a line from the words (or number them) to the margin and write the words describing the **type** of nonverbal behavior in the margin: posture and gesture, face and eyes, voice, touch, physical attractiveness, clothing, distance, time, territoriality, or environment.

Example:

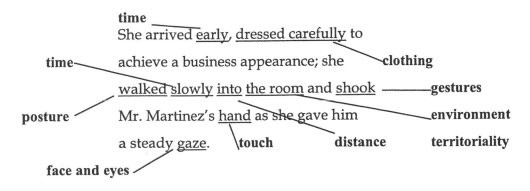

Your turn:

Insert two or three paragraphs from news articles that make references to nonverbal communication. Label each type of nonverbal communication referred to.

Name _____

CHAPTER 5 ACTIVITY 2 NONVERBAL IMPRESSION MANAGEMENT

Purpose:

To develop skills in using nonverbal communication to manage impressions and define relationships.

Instructions:

1. Read each situation. After reading it, describe as many nonverbal behaviors as you think are appropriate to help you manage the situation.
2. After recording your own thoughts, compare responses with your classmates.
3. Use as many **types** of nonverbal behavior as you deem appropriate: posture and gesture, face and eyes, voice, touch, physical attractiveness, clothing, distance, time, territoriality, or environment.

Part One Identity management

1. You want to be seen as a competent and conscientious person who is also outgoing and friendly at your new job with the State Taxation Department.

2. You left home after high school and now when you go back home you want your parents to see you as different from the rebellious high school student that you were. You want them to see you as a serious college student.

Part Two Defining the relationship

3.   You want to indicate to co-workers that you are warm and friendly, **and** that you are married and not available to date, flirt, or party.

4.   You want to indicate to a sister or brother that the days of competitive sibling rivalry are over and that now (age 23) you want a close, respectful relationship in which you see each other as individuals.

5.   You are extremely busy with school this semester but want your significant other/spouse to know how much you care about him/her even though you have little free time this semester.

Summary: What types of nonverbal behaviors do you tend to rely on the most to manage impressions?

How could channels that you don't frequently use assist you in impression management?

Name _____

CHAPTER 5 ACTIVITY 3 FUNCTIONS OF NONVERBAL COMMUNICATION

Purpose:

To identify the functions of nonverbal communication in context.

Instructions Part One:

For each scenario below, tell which function of communication is being illustrated: repeating, substituting, complementing, accenting, regulating, contradicting, or deceiving.

_____ 1. The teacher pointed to the letter "s" on the board each time she pronounced it for the first-graders.

_____ 2. The umpire shouted "safe" but made the sign for "out."

_____ 3. The parent looked at the child with a look that clearly told her the topic of "chicken guts" was off limits at the dinner table.

_____ 4. Each time the politician said the word "taxes" he pounded on the table.

_____ 5. Without saying a word, he just slipped his arm around her shoulders as if to tell the others that they were a couple.

_____ 6. First the instructor explained the karate form, then she demonstrated it.

_____ 7. The father did not want his children to be frightened in the storm, so he masked his own fear and wore a smile and confident look.

1. Are there some behaviors that might fulfill more than one function? Which ones?

2. Are functions always distinctly different or are there ways in which they overlap? Explain your answer.

Instructions Part Two:

For each function, think of two examples (from your life, from films or stories) that illustrate that function.

repeating

1.

2.

Substituting

1.

2.

complementing

1.

2.

accenting

1.

2.

regulating

1.

2.

contradicting

1.

2.

deceiving

1.

2.

Instructions Part Three:

Many cartoons are based on contradicting nonverbal behaviors. Insert a cartoon here to illustrate that.

Name _____

CHAPTER 5 ACTIVITY 4 PRACTICING NONVERBAL SKILLS

Purpose:

To illustrate the richness of nonverbal communication in conveying a variety of meanings.

Instructions:

1. Choose a partner.
2. Take turns saying the following sentences in each of the ways described.

1. Target person: your friend

Verbal message: I'd like to go with you this weekend.

Context: You frequently go away with each other, this is just routine, another weekend.

What nonverbal channels are used most distinctly to convey the message this way?

Context: You're hesitant. You've never gone with this friend on the weekend and you're suggesting it for the first time.

What nonverbal channels are used most distinctly to convey the message this way?

Context: Your friend is taking someone else with him/her, but you'd like to go. You wish you were the one invited to go with him/her.

What nonverbal channels are used most distinctly to convey the message this way?

2. Target person: your spouse or significant other

Verbal message: Do you want to go to the office party with me?

Context: I don't really want to go; I'm too tired, and I sure hope you don't want to go.

What nonverbal channels are used most distinctly to convey the message this way?

Context: I really want you to come with me because I'm excited about going.

What nonverbal channels are used most distinctly to convey the message this way?

Context: I have to go so I will, but I'm not excited about it. I'd like you to go with me so at least it isn't so miserable.

What nonverbal channels are used most distinctly to convey the message this way?

3.   **Target person: your boss**

Verbal message: Do you think I'll get a promotion this year?

Context: sincere honest request for information

What nonverbal channels are used most distinctly to convey the message this way?

Context: as if you're already convinced you won't, you're sad, disillusioned

What nonverbal channels are used most distinctly to convey the message this way?

Context: as if it's a big joke because you know for sure you won't (because you just did)

What nonverbal channels are used most distinctly to convey the message this way?

4.   **Target: your child**

Verbal message: Well, you're free to choose the college and the major you want.

Context: Parents clearly want to convey the message that if the child doesn't do as they suggest there will be consequences for the child.

What nonverbal channels are used most distinctly to convey the message this way?

Context: Parents sincerely believe their child will make the best choices and they want their child to make choices. They will respect their child and support whatever choices are made.

What nonverbal channels are used most distinctly to convey the message this way?

Context: Parents really don't care. They've been through this with two older children and just really don't care what decision the child makes. They're just resigned to having no input.

What nonverbal channels are used most distinctly to convey the message this way?

Debrief:

1.   Which situations were hardest for you to convey? Why?

2. Which were easiest? Why?

3. List three attitudes and feelings (besides those in the text) that are easy to express nonverbally.

    1.

    2.

    3.

4. List three ideas that are difficult to express nonverbally.

    1.

    2.

    3.

5. Give an example of a situation in which you think the nonverbal communication may be more important than the verbal and explain why.

6. Give an example of a situation in which you think the verbal communication may be more important than nonverbal and explain why.

Name _____

CHAPTER 5 ACTIVITY 5 EXPLORING THE WEB

Variety in Nonverbal Communication

1. Survey the table of contents of the latest issue of the <u>Journal of Nonverbal Behavior</u> at
    <u>www.kluweronline.com/issn/0191-5886/current</u>. Also visit The Nonverbal Communication Research
    Page (http://euphrates.wpunj.edu/faculty/wagnerk/webagogy/hecht.htm) and Ohio State's
    Nonverbal page (<u>www.lib.ohio-state.edu/gateway/bib/nonverbal.html</u>)

List at least four current topics in nonverbal research.

    1.

    2.

    3.

    4.

    5.

2. Trying to express emotion on-line is often done through the use of what is commonly called smileys
    or emoticons (keystrokes to represent facial expressions). Go to
    http://help.yahoo.com/help/us/mesg/use/use-38.html for an introduction to the use of smileys.

What categories of smileys do you find?

Look at any section on emotional smileys. What generalizations can you make about the parts of the face
frequently used in the attempt to express emotions on line?

Can you generalize about which kinds of emotions are and aren't commonly expressed in emoticons?

3. Deception is closely related to nonverbal communication. Look at the bibliography on deception
    found at http://cotton.uamont.edu/~roiger/biblio/decept.htmlx.

What is the year of the oldest piece of research you find?

What was the specific topic?

List the titles of at least five different journals in which deception research is published.

1.

2.

3.

4.

5.

6.

What inferences can you draw with regard to who is interested in research on deception?

4. Choose a particular topic of nonverbal communication that you would like to know more about. Where can you find more information on your topic?

What are the titles of articles and specific journals that might inform your search?

5. Look at the pictures and answer the questions in the on-line exercises in nonverbal communication found throughout the site at http://nonverbal.ucsc.edu/. State three things you learned from these on-screen examples.

1.

2.

3.

6. For further information on distances, nonverbal behaviors that affect interaction climates, and various meanings of gestures, go to www.cba.uni.edu/buscomm/nonverbal/body%20Language.htm. Note your findings here:

Name _____

CHAPTER 5 SELF TEST

MATCHING Match each term listed on the left with its correct definition from the column on the right.

____ 1. affect blends

____ 2. chronemics

____ 3. disfluency

____ 4. emblems

____ 5. illustrators

____ 6. intimate distance

____ 7. kinesics

____ 8. manipulators

____ 9. nonverbal communication

____ 10. paralanguage

____ 11. personal distance

____ 12. proxemics

____ 13. public distance

____ 14. social distance

____ 15. territory

a. messages expressed by other than linguistic means

b. nonlinguistic means of oral expression: rate, pitch, and tone

c. nonverbal behaviors that accompany and support verbal messages

d. deliberate nonverbal behaviors with precise meanings, known to members of a cultural group

e. a nonlinguistic verbalization such as um, er, and ah

f. the combination of two or more expressions, each showing a different emotion

g. one of Hall's four distance zones, extending outward from twelve feet

h. study of body movement, gesture, and posture

i. one of Hall's four distance zones, ranging from skin contact to eighteen inches

j. movements in which one part of the body fidgets with another part

k. one of Hall's distance zones, ranging from four to twelve feet

l. fixed space that an individual assumes some right to occupy

m. the study of how people and animals use space

n. the study of how humans use and structure time

o. one of Hall's distance zones, ranging from 18 inches to four feet.

MULTIPLE CHOICE Choose the BEST response from those listed.

1. Paralanguage refers to

    a. the words spoken.
    b. the various meanings in different languages.
    c. the vocal messages of pitch, rate, and loudness.
    d. languages passed on from parent to child.
    e. none of the above

2. With regard to touch, which is true?

   a. Babies have never died from lack of touch.
   b. Touch is related to physical functioning, but not mental functioning.
   c. Touch seems to decrease people's compliance with requests.
   d. In mainstream U.S. culture, men touch men more than men touch women.
   e. Touch can communicate various messages ranging from aggression to affection.

3. According to research cited in the text,

   a. physical attractiveness has social and economic advantages.
   b. preschoolers seemed to like unattractive children more than attractive ones.
   c. teachers rated unattractive students as more intelligent and friendly than attractive ones.
   d. persons in uniforms seem less likely to influence or persuade people to act in a certain ways.
   e. the longer we know someone, the more important that person's clothing is to our impressions of them.

4. The main point of the diversity reading in this chapter is that

   a. women have an advantage in having more styles available to them than men.
   b. men don't like women who dress like men.
   c. a woman is "marked" by the clothes she wears because she doesn't have the freedom of an "unmarked" style--it doesn't exist.
   d. men have a more difficult time blending in with their clothing--their type of suit always seems to draw attention.
   e. none of the above

5. According to Edward T. Hall, the distance at which most mainstream North American business is conducted is called

   a. intimate.
   b. personal.
   c. social.
   d. public.
   e. none of the above

6. Which of these is a chronemic message that indicates status?

   a. Bosses dress more formally than employees.
   b. A person conducting an interview is usually conveying a less rigid posture than the person being interviewed.
   c. Students sit far apart at library tables to indicate their wish to study, not converse.
   d. Employees are rarely late for appointments with their supervisors, although supervisors may be late without penalties.
   e. Taller job candidates are more often chosen for jobs.

7. Which is true?

   a. Environments influence the kind of communication that takes place there.
   b. A particular environment can communicate the type of relationship desired.
   c. Environments can be designed to increase or decrease interaction.
   d. all of the above
   e. none of the above

8. Which is NOT a principle of nonverbal communication?

    a. Communication occurs even when language is not used.
    b. It is possible not to communicate nonverbally.
    c. Nonverbal communication is ambiguous.
    d. Nonverbal communication is culture-bound.
    e. Nonverbal communication can serve various functions.

9. Which function of communication is illustrated when a person rolls his or her eyes while making a negative comment about another?

    a. substituting
    b. accenting
    c. regulating
    d. contradicting
    e. repeating

10. Which of these factors should be considered when trying to make sense out of ambiguous nonverbal behavior?

    a. context
    b. history of the relationship
    c. the other's mood
    d. your feelings
    e. all of the above

11. Marking your spot at a library or restaurant table by leaving a sweater and backpack illustrates a type of

    a. territory.
    b. chronemic.
    c. paralanguage.
    d. emblem.
    e. all of the above

12. One difference between verbal and nonverbal communication is that verbal communication is

    a. more multidimensional.
    b. usually continuous.
    c. more ambiguous.
    d. usually deliberate.
    e. has a stronger impact if verbal and nonverbal message conflict.

13. Smiling a lot to convince people you are friendly, nodding to appear interested, and dressing to look professional are all types of nonverbal behavior that could be used for

    a. identity management.
    b. defining the relationship.
    c. expressing attitudes and feelings.
    d. all of the above
    e. none of the above

14. Which of these statements almost always requires verbal communication and would be difficult to express nonverbally?

    a. I'm tired and bored.
    b. The party is exciting to me and I'm enjoying it.
    c. The recent budget fiasco could have been prevented by better statistical analysis.
    d. I'm confident about this opportunity to publicly address this group.
    e. I'm in love with you and want to be near you.

15. Silence

    a. has only one commonly accepted cultural meaning.
    b. can be used to convey very different meanings, depending on the context.
    c. rarely holds communication value or is given meaning by anyone.
    d. all of the above
    e. none of the above

TRUE/FALSE Circle the T or F to indicate whether you believe the statement is true or false. If it is **true,** give a **reason** or an **example**. If it is false, **explain** what would make it true.

T F 1. Some nonverbal messages are vocal.

T F 2. In trying to make sense out of nonverbal behavior, it is best to think of nonverbal behaviors as clues to check out rather than absolute facts.

T F 3. Most nonverbal messages are deliberate and intentional.

T F 4. Unlike verbal messages, which use many words at once, nonverbal communication utilizes only one channel at a time.

T F 5. Research indicates that when people perceive inconsistencies between verbal and nonverbal messages, they usually believe the nonverbal one.

COMPLETION Fill in each of the blanks with a word from the lists provided. Choose the BEST word for each sentence. There are more words than you will use, but each word will be used only once.

paralanguage   **proxemic**

chronemic   **kinesic**

emblem   **disfluency**

1. "It is not sufficient to know what one ought to say, but one must also know **how to say it**." — Aristotle. The boldface words refer to the nonverbal category called

    _____.

2. When a speaker says, "I, **uh,** I'm glad to, **uh,** be here," this is an example of a

    _____.

3. Walking back and forth in front of a group you are speaking to would be a

    _____ message.

4. Showing up three hours late for work is a type of _____ message.

5. Purposefully standing closer to the person you love to let others know you are at this party

    together is an example of a _____ message.

CHAPTER 5 ANSWERS TO SELF TEST

MATCHING

1.	f	2.	n	3.	e	4.	d	5.	c
6.	i	7.	h	8.	j	9.	a	10.	b
11.	o	12.	m	13.	g	14.	k	15.	l

MULTIPLE CHOICE

1.	c	2.	e	3.	a	4.	c	5.	c
6.	d	7.	d	8.	b	9.	b	10.	e
11.	a	12.	d	13.	d	14.	c	15.	b

TRUE/FALSE

1.	True	2.	True	3.	False	4.	False	5.	True

COMPLETION

1.	paralanguage	2.	disfluency	3.	kinesic
4.	chronemic	5.	proxemic		

Related Reading

"Don't Let Your Image Sabotage Your Career" by Sherry Maysonave
(Access through www.casualpower.com/about_us/news/innews58.htm.)

Preview

What impact does dress have on issues of credibility, status, power, and authority? This article looks at the importance of nonverbal behavior and dress at work and offers some advice.

Review

1. What ten pieces of advice does the author give for "powering up" your image at work?

2. What does the article mean by stating that your " Your image is the 'Home Page' of your personal web site and a web page of your company's site"? Do you agree?

3. Do you agree or disagree with the specific advice given in the article?

4. Speculate on the relationship of office dress and behavior and the rate of unemployment. Does office dress change as the job market grows tighter?

5. For an international view on what is considered conservative, formal or casual, read the article, "Dress for Success," (http://getcustoms.com/2004GTC/Articles/new003.html). Compare the two articles.

CHAPTER 6 UNDERSTANDING INTERPERSONAL RELATIONSHIPS

CHAPTER 6 SKELETON OUTLINE

This outline can be a helpful study tool to assist you in seeing the order and sequence of the chapter and the relationship of ideas. Use it to take notes as you read and/or to add concepts presented in lecture.

I.   Characteristics of interpersonal relationships

    A. Definitions: context vs. quality

        1. Contextually interpersonal, dyadic

        2. qualitatively interpersonal: impersonal vs. interpersonal

    B. Interpersonal communication on the internet

        1. Less face-to-face contact reported

        2. Internet enhances communication quantity and quality

    C. Content and relational messages

        1. content messages

        2. relational messages

            a) affinity

            b) respect

            c) immediacy

            d) control

            e) expressed nonverbally

    D. Metacommunication

        1. communication about communication

        2. benefits

            a) resolving conflicts

            b) reinforcing relationships

        3. risks of interpretation and analysis

II. Intimacy and distance

    A. Dimensions of intimacy

        1. physical

        2. intellectual

        3. emotional

        4. shared activities

    B. Male and female intimacy styles

        1. differences in expressing emotions

        2. differences in role of activity – expressing and creating intimacy

C. Cultural influences

    1. expectations and expression vary

    2. collectivist cultures' variations

III. Relational development and maintenance

    A. Developmental perspective show stages of relationships

        1. initiating

        2. experimenting

        3. intensifying

        4. integrating

        5. bonding

        6. differentiating

        7. circumscribing

        8. stagnating

        9. avoiding

        10. terminating

    B. Dialectical perspectives

        1. connection and autonomy (as in Desmond Morris' three stages)

            a) "Hold me tight"

            b) "Put me down"

            c) "Leave me alone"

        2. predictability and novelty

        3. openness and privacy

        4. eight strategies for coping with dialectical tensions

            a) denial

            b) disorientation

            c) selection

            d) alternation

            e) segmentation

            f) moderation

            g) reframing

            h) reaffirmation

    C. Characteristics of relational development and maintenance

        1. change

        2. movement to a new place

IV. Self-disclosure in interpersonal relationships involves information that is deliberate, significant, and unknown by others.

    A. Social penetration model

        1. breadth

        2. depth

    B. Johari window model

        1. open

        2. blind

        3. hidden

        4. unknown

    C. Characteristics of effective self-disclosure

        1. influenced by culture

            a) appropriateness varies

            b) definition varies

            c) norms vary

        2. usually occurs in dyads

        3. usually is symmetrical

        4. usually occurs incrementally

        5. relatively scarce

    D. Guidelines for appropriate self-disclosure

        1. Is the other person important to you?

        2. Is the risk of disclosing reasonable?

        3. Are the amount and type of disclosure appropriate?

        4. Is the disclosure relevant?

        5. Is the disclosure reciprocated?

        6. Will the effect be constructive?

        7. Is the disclosure clear and understandable?

    E. Alternatives to self-disclosure

        1. lies

        2. equivocation

        3. hinting

CHAPTER 6 KEY TERMS

This list of key terms corresponds to those in boldface in your text. In your own words write a definition and an original example of the word.

affinity

altruistic lies

breadth (of self-disclosure)

content messages

contextually interpersonal communication

control

depth (of self-disclosure)

developmental model

dialectical model (of relational maintenance)

dialectical tensions

equivocal language

immediacy

intimacy

Johari Window

metacommunication

qualitatively interpersonal communication

relational message

respect

self-disclosure

social penetration model

Name _____

CHAPTER 6 ACTIVITY 1 CONTENT AND RELATIONAL MESSAGES

Purpose:

To examine relational messages.

Instructions:

For each situation, describe the types of relational messages you think are conveyed: affinity, respect, immediacy, or control.

Example: Your out-of-town friends call and say, "We'll be passing through the night of the 22nd. We'd like to see you. Would it be convenient for us to visit, or stay, or would it be better if we stopped another time?"

What relational messages do you perceive?

The message seems high in respect because they care enough to call ahead, which shows respect for your schedule and life. It seems low in control because they aren't insisting on staying, thereby controlling your time.   There is affinity and immediacy (attraction and interest) because they express an interest in seeing each other.,. Assuming one could stay might send a more controlling message. I think there is affinity and caring for the others' schedule. Really close friends and family might have unspoken agreements and assumptions about always staying with each other that imply a higher level of affection.

1. A couple is discussing where to take their children and friends for pizza. The setting is loud and noisy. One parent says, "Okay, listen up. We're going to Pizza Hut. Jump in the car."

What relational messages do you perceive?

2. A new employee is on the job for the first day. As the lunch hour approaches, s/he says to the other employees in the area, "Well, where do we go for lunch?"

What relational messages do you perceive?

3.   Your sister calls and starts telling you about a family reunion she's planning for this next summer. Before you've indicated whether or not you'll be able to attend, she says, "Everyone will be so glad to see you. And we can do some humorous decorations and you're always good with games for the kids. This will be so much fun."

What relational messages do you perceive?

4.   A co-worker says she's noticed how well you relate to everyone at work and asks if you'd consider running for local union steward.

What relational messages do you perceive?

5.   Your roommate leaves you a note saying, "I was hoping you'd be home before I had to go to class. I borrowed your blue sweatshirt for the evening. All my clothes were still wet. I hope you don't mind."

What relational messages do you perceive?

Name _____

CHAPTER 6 ACTIVITY 2 SELF-DISCLOSURE

Purpose:

1. To understand the reasons for self-disclosure.
2. To distinguish between various purposes of self-disclosure.
3. To understand the relationship between our perception and other's disclosure.

Instructions Part One:

1. Use Table 6-1 in the text. For each scenario, think about the various purposes for which the person described would self-disclose. Given the situation, what do you consider to be the most likely purposes for self-disclosing?
2. Write down the reasons why you think a person in that situation is most likely to self-disclose. Put a * by the one which you consider to be **the single most likely** reason for self-disclosure by the person.
3. Share and compare your answers with your classmates.

1. Think about recent incidents when a political candidate disclosed personal information to the press. In what ways might the self-disclosure be related to these reasons:

catharsis

self-clarification

self-validation

reciprocity

impression management

relationship maintenance and enhancement

control

2. A person is troubled by the fact that his father spent time in a mental institution. When getting involved in a relationship, he doesn't want to share this information immediately (Hi! I'm John but before you get to know me you should know that . . .), but he feels he is withholding something significant if he goes with someone very long without sharing this information. In this case self-disclosure is likely for these reasons:

catharsis

self-clarification

self-validation

reciprocity

impression management

relationship maintenance and enhancement

control

3.   Reflect on your own self-disclosure. Think of an example you are comfortable sharing and is
     appropriate for class discussion. What was the context?

How was your disclosure related to each of these?
catharsis

self-clarification

self-validation

reciprocity

impression management

relationship maintenance and enhancement

control

Part Two

1. In what kinds of situations are you most aware of your own reasons for disclosure?

2. In what kinds of situations, is it more difficult to know your reasons for disclosing?

3. In personal relationships, how could you use a perception check (See Chapter 3: description, interpretation, request for feedback) to more accurately understand another's motives for disclosure?

Name _____

CHAPTER 6 ACTIVITY 3 RISKS AND REWARDS OF SELF-DISCLOSURE

Purpose:

To explore the risks and rewards of self-disclosure and its impact on relationships.

Instructions:

Read the following quotations and respond to each with your own thoughts and reactions.

1. "I can know only so much of myself as I have had the courage to confide to you. To the extent that I have hidden myself from you, the meaning of your love will be diminished. I will forever fear that you love only the part of me that I have let you know; and that if you knew the real me, all of me, you would not love me. Love follows upon knowledge, and so you can love me only to the extent that I let you know me." — John Powell, <u>The Secret of Staying in Love</u>, p. 131.

My first response to this quotation:

In your own words, what is this quotation saying about the impact of self-disclosure on relationships? about the risks of self-disclosure? about the rewards of self-disclosure?

Do you agree or disagree with what is expressed here? Why?

What statements in the text lead you to believe the authors would agree or disagree with this quotation?

2. "Most of us feel that others will not tolerate such emotional honesty [as disclosing feelings] in communication. We would rather defend our dishonesty on the grounds that it might hurt others, and having rationalized our phoniness into nobility, we settle for superficial relationships." — John Powell, The Secret of Staying in Love.

My first response to this quotation:

In your own words, what does Powell mean by "rationalized our phoniness into nobility"? If we choose not to self-disclose our feelings, are we being phony?

Do you agree or disagree with what is expressed here? Why?

3.   "There is a strong human temptation to judge people only in terms of these acts or masks [that we wear rather than disclosing]. It is all too rare that we are able to see through the sham and pretense of masks the insecure or wounded heart that is being camouflaged and protected from further injury. . . We fail to realize that masks are worn only as long as they are needed." — John Powell, Why Am I Afraid to Love? p. 54.

My first response to this quotation:

In your own words, what is this quotation saying about the need not to self-disclose if one is not comfortable doing so?

What "masks" do you see being worn most often?

Do you think they are worn because they need to be? Do you agree or disagree with what is expressed here? Why?

4. Jourard wrote, " . . . when you permit yourself to be known, you expose yourself not only to a lover's balm, but also to a hater's bombs. When he knows you, he knows just where to plant them for maximum effect."

My first response to this quotation:

In your own words, what does Jourard mean by "lover's balm" and "hater's bombs"?

Do you agree or disagree with what is expressed here? Why?

5. President Calvin Coolidge (Silent Cal) once said, "I have never been hurt by anything I didn't say."

My first response to this quotation:

Paraphrase the statement.

Do you agree or disagree with what is expressed here? Why?

6.   Reflect on your own self-disclosure:

When do you/have you disclosed largely for reasons of:

catharsis

self-clarification

self-validation

reciprocity

impression management

relationship maintenance and enhancement

control

Name _____

CHAPTER 6 ACTIVITY 4 STAGES OF RELATIONSHIPS

Purpose:

To understand the stages of relationships and correlate specific behaviors and words to stages of relationships.

Instructions:

1. Choose a relationship that has ended. Can you identify behaviors that fit the characteristics of each stage?
2. For each stage, list some behaviors that "prove" you were in that stage.

initiating

experimenting

intensifying

integrating

bonding

differentiating

circumscribing

stagnating

avoiding

terminating

If a relationship is in the stagnating stage and you don't want it to terminate, what would you recommend so that it moves into a "coming together" stage rather than a "coming apart" stage? (Ideas: Pick a new activity that neither of you has tried like line dancing, cross-country skiing, or bridge and learn it together and see how you like it.)

If you tried these suggestions, what stage would you be moving into?

Songs Reflect Relational Stages Many song lyrics describe stages of relationships. Find lyrics that describe each of the stages of relationships. Some titles are deceiving. For instance, "I Said I Loved You But I Lied" may sound like terminating, but the lyrics make clear that it is "more than love" that is felt, making it a better candidate as a description of bonding. You may find this easier to do in a small group brainstorming session, especially when it comes to recalling lyrics. Starters: Dance with My Father, Infatuation, My Prerogative, Fly Away with Me.

initiating

experimenting

intensifying

integrating

bonding

differentiating

circumscribing

stagnating

avoiding

terminating

Share your answers with classmates Do you think that any particular types of music [rap, R&B, hard rock, jazz, hip hop, Latin, rock, show tunes] tend to have greater numbers of songs that reflect particular stages of relationships? For instance, do rock songs tend to speak more of initiating or bonding? Do country songs tend to speak more of bonding or terminating? Do certain types of music tend to emphasize initiating? experimenting? Are there plenty of songs about all stages in all types of music? Speculate on these questions. (Scholarly journals have articles that look systematically at themes from music. You might enjoy reporting on this now, or as part of a speech later in the course.)

Name _____

CHAPTER 6 ACTIVITY 5 INTIMACY AND DISTANCE

Purpose:

To explore the relationship between intimacy and autonomy in relationships.

Instructions:

Read the following quotations and respond to each with your own thoughts and reactions.

1. "Each of us needs to establish our autonomy, or independence, and at the same time each of us desires intimacy with other people. We wish to be self-governing and independent individuals, but we also have a need to be a part of a group, to belong, to be needed by others, and to need them. We desire relational development and increased intimacy, but we are sometimes afraid of relationships developing too quickly. These seemingly conflicting goals exist in each of us." — Judy Pearson, Communication in the Family, p. 237.

My first response to this quotation:

In your own words, what is this quotation saying about everyone's needs? about time and intimacy?

Do you agree or disagree with what is expressed here? Why?

What words in the text lead you to believe the authors would agree or disagree with this quotation?

2. "For her, intimacy without words is small comfort most of the time. It's not that she needs always to talk, but it's important to her to know what's going on inside him if she's to feel close. And it's equally important for her to believe he cares about what's going on inside her." — Lillian B. Rubin, Intimate Strangers, p. 75.

My first response to this quotation:

In your own words, what is this quotation saying about gender differences regarding verbal and nonverbal expression of intimacy?

Do you agree or disagree with what is expressed here? Why?

What words in the text lead you to believe the authors would agree or disagree with this quotation?

3.   "Wife: I say that foreplay begins in the morning.
      Husband: It seems to me being sexual would make us closer, but she says it works the other way — if
      she felt closer, there'd be more sex." — Lillian B. Rubin, Intimate Strangers, p. 98.

My first response to this quotation:

In your own words, what is this quotation saying about the difference between talking and doing as paths to intimacy?

Do you agree or disagree with what is expressed here? Why?

What words in the text lead you to believe the authors would agree or disagree with this quotation?

4. "Being vulnerable in the presence of others--which we call intimacy — is closely related to maintaining commitment among family members. Family members reveal their vulnerabilities to one another, often with a sense of trust and usually with the hope that their vulnerabilities will not be used against them. For a family to live in the presence of each others' vulnerabilities and to stay intact, all members make an agreement (implicit or explicit) to maintain the family unit, at least at some minimum level." — Janet Yerby, Understanding Family Communication, p. 21.

My first response to this quotation:

In your own words, what is this quotation saying about intimacy in families?

Do you agree or disagree with what is expressed here? Why?

What words in the text lead you to believe the authors would agree or disagree with this quotation?

5.   "Most mothers receive more self-disclosure than fathers (Waterman 1979). Parents perceived as nurturing and supportive elicit more disclosure from children who find those encounters rewarding. College students are more likely to disclose more information more honestly to same-sex best friends than to either parent (Tardy, Hosman, and Bradac 1981)."
— Kathleen M. Galvin and Bernard J. Brommel, Family Communication, 4th ed., p. 124.

My first response to this quotation:

In your own words, what is this quotation saying about intimacy in families and changes over time?

In what ways does this quotation reflect or not reflect your experiences?

Name _____

CHAPTER 6 ACTIVITY 6 EXPLORING THE WEB

Self Disclosure and the Johari Window

The text discusses the Johari Window as a model of self-disclosure. Go to the following site: http://cotton.uamont.edu/~roiger/write/self-dis.html. Appendix J.1 at that site provides a self-assessment and scoring procedure that you can use to learn more about yourself with regard to self-disclosure levels and comfort. Complete this assessment.

1. What are the labels and definitions of each label given to the four quadrants of the chart?

    1.

    2.

    3.

    4.

2. The two columns you tally are "disclosure" and "feedback." What would you predict are the personality traits and behaviors of someone who scores high in the feedback area? Why?

3. What kinds of careers would you predict persons who score high in disclosure choose? Why?

4. What would be the characteristics that you would predict they would choose for mates? Why?

5. Answer the same questions (3 and 4) for low-disclosers.

6. The Relational Satisfaction Scale (http://cotton.uamont.edu/~roiger/write/satisfac.html) provides interesting insights into relationships. The Interpersonal Communication Competency Scale (http://cotton.uamont.edu/~roiger/write/competen.html) categorizes motivation, knowledge, and skill in interpersonal communication with subscales in adaptability, involvement, conversation management and empathy. Using the Interpersonal Solidarity Scale (http://cotton.uamont.edu/~roiger/write/solidari.html) and the Relational Intimacy Communication Scale (http://cotton.uamont.edu/~roiger/write/intimacy.html), present interesting perspectives for thinking about your relationships.

Name _____

CHAPTER 6 SELF TEST

MATCHING Part One Match each term listed on the left with its correct definition from the column on the right.

_____ 1. affinity

_____ 2. altruistic lie

_____ 3. breadth (of self-disclosure)

_____ 4. content message

_____ 5. contextually interpersonal communication

_____ 6. control

_____ 7. depth (of self-disclosure)

_____ 8. developmental model

_____ 9. dialectical model (of relational maintenance)

_____ 10. dialectical tensions

a. relational message of influence or power

b. model of relationship that emphasizes relational issues rather than stages

c. conflicting desires or goals in a relationship

d. interpersonal communication measured only by the number of people involved

e. a message that communicates information about the subject being discussed

f. relational message indicating liking

g. model of communication that looks at stages of relationships

h. information that is not truthful, but thought to be harmless for the person being spoken to

i. the intensity or profoundness of topics revealed to another

j. range of subjects and topics revealed to another

MATCHING Part Two Match each term listed on the left with its correct definition from the column on the right.

____ 11. equivocal language

____ 12. immediacy

____ 13. intimacy

____ 14. Johari Window

____ 15. metacommunication

____ 16. qualitatively interpersonal communication

____ 17. relational messages

____ 18. respect

____ 19. self-disclosure

____ 20. social penetration model

a. A model that describes the relationship between self-disclosure and self-awareness (blind, hidden areas)

b. messages (usually relational) that refer to other messages or communication

c. communication in which the parties consider one another as unique individuals rather than as objects

d. a vague statement that can be interpreted in more than one way

e. the process of deliberately revealing information about oneself that is significant and would not be known by others

f. a model by Altman and Taylor to describe two dimensions of self-disclosure

g. the message that expresses the feelings two parties have for each other or the way they view each other

h. relational message of interest and attraction

i. relational message of esteem and admiration

j. closeness developed through activity or emotional, physical, or intellectual bonding

MULTIPLE CHOICE Choose the BEST response from those listed.

1. Which of these is a **qualitative** definition of interpersonal communication?

   a. It involves two persons
   b. It occurs in dyads
   c. It involves each considering the other unique
   d. It is characterized as group or mass communication
   e. All of these are qualitative definitions.

2. The existence of dialectical tensions in relationships tends to contribute toward

   a. a tendency of absolute sequential movement through the stages of relationships.
   b. a tendency for back and forth movement across stages.
   c. a tendency to stagnate at one stage.
   d. all of the above
   e. none of the above

3. Which is true of stages of relationships according to Knapp?

   a. Relationships always exist in many stages at a time.
   b. Circumscribing does not involve total avoidance.
   c. Stagnating is usually followed by bonding.
   d. The stage after bonding is integrating.
   e. The goal of all relational development is to get to the final stage.

4. Self-disclosure is often gauged by two factors:

    a. depth and breadth
    b. high and low
    c. caring and respect
    d. significance and privacy
    e. stages and movement

5. You disclose to your parent the way you dumped your girl/boy friend in the hope that your parent will agree that you handled the situation well. This illustrates disclosure for which reason?

    a. catharsis
    b. self-clarification
    c. self-validation
    d. reciprocity
    e. none of the above

6. In the film <u>Breakfast Club</u>, a group of teens are together for detention. One girl, Allison, seemingly self-discloses her bizarre sexual activity in an effort to get another teen, Claire, to disclose her sexual activity. Self-disclosing about oneself in an effort to get information from someone else may work because of which characteristic of self-disclosure?

    a. Self-disclosure usually occurs in increments.
    b. Self-disclosure usually is reciprocal.
    c. Self-disclosure usually occurs in dyads.
    d. all of the above
    e. none of the above

7. Jourard wrote, " . . . when you permit yourself to be known, you expose yourself not only to a lover's balm, but also to a hater's bombs. When he knows you, he knows just where to plant them for maximum effect." This statement relates to risks of

    a. dialectical tensions.
    b. equivocation.
    c. self-fulfilling prophecy.
    d. self-disclosure.
    e. control.

8. Which is true of self-disclosure?

    a. It is viewed essentially the same way around the world.
    b. It rarely occurs incrementally.
    c. It is strongly influenced by culture.
    d. It usually occurs in large groups rather than dyads.
    e. none of the above

9. Which of these represents a type of dialectical tensions in relationships?

    a. connection and autonomy
    b. openness and privacy
    c. predictability and novelty
    d. all of these
    e. none of these

10. You say, "SHUT THE DOOR!" in a loud, commanding, angry tone of voice or you say, "Shut the door" with a softer voice, rising intonation to indicate a request. Which is true?

    a.   The content is essentially the same, but the relational message is different.
    b.   The content and relational messages are the same.
    c.   The relational message is essentially the same, but the content is different.
    d.   The content and relational messages are both different.
    e.   There is no relational message, but the content message is the same.

11. A comment like, "Let's talk about the way we talk to each other in front of my parents." is most obviously a type of

    a.   metacommunication.
    b.   self-disclosure.
    c.   impersonal communication.
    d.   dialectical tension.
    e.   contextual definition.

12. Intimacy can best be defined as

    a.   physical.
    b.   intellectual.
    c.   emotional.
    d.   shared activities.
    e.   all of the above

13. Which of these is NOT one of the guidelines your text suggests for gauging appropriate self-disclosure?

    a.   Is the disclosure as in-depth as you can make it?
    b.   Is the risk of disclosing reasonable?
    c.   Is the other person important to you?
    d.   Is the disclosure relevant?
    e.   Is the disclosure understandable?

14. The Johari Window is

    a.   a model of metacommunication.
    b.   a model of self-disclosure.
    c.   a model of relational stages.
    d.   a model of contextual communication.
    e.   none of the above

15. A Johari Window of someone who shares a lot of him or herself with another and knows another well would look like this:

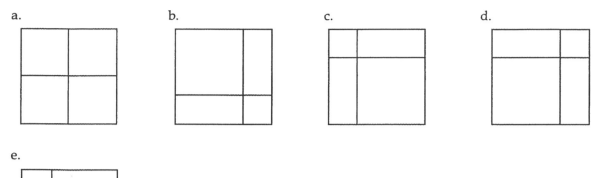

a.   b.   c.   d.

e.

MATCHING RELATIONAL STAGES Match each term listed on the left with the correct description of it from the column on the right.

A. differentiating

B. experimenting

C. intensifying

D. stagnating

E. circumscribing

_____ 1.   when partners begin to use more familiar forms of address and begin to talk about "us" and begin to express commitment, but still use communication strategies to "test" commitment

_____ 2.   a stage of dissolution in which partners don't totally avoid each other, but do withhold somewhat and display less interest and commitment

_____ 3.   a relationship stage that often occurs after bonding in which the partners express a need for increased privacy or autonomy

_____ 4.   a stage that results after a period of circumscribing in which there is no growth or joy in the relationship, although the couple may go through the motions they previously enjoyed

_____ 5.   a stage of "getting to know you" in which partners begin to find out whether they have shared interests, common goals, etc...

TRUE/FALSE Circle the T or F to indicate whether you believe the statement is true or false. If it is **true,** give a **reason** or an **example.** If it is false, **explain** what would make it true.

T   F   1.   Equivocation refers to the completely ethical behavior of telling "the truth, the whole truth and nothing but the truth."

T F   2. Compared to perception checks and listening, self-disclosure carries far fewer risks for the communicator.

T F   3. The Johari window is a model that is useful for looking at the relative amount of open, closed, hidden and blind areas in a relationship.

T F   4. Hinting is a type of indirect behavior that can seek to get a desired response from the other and/or save the other from embarrassment.

T F   5. Men are more likely to see talk as a way to build intimacy; women are more likely to want to use shared activity to create intimacy.

COMPLETION Fill in each of the blanks with a word from the lists provided. Choose the BEST word for each sentence. There are more words than you will use, but each word will be used only once.

metacommunication	**equivocal**
immediacy	**intimacy**
content	**relational**

1. Message which tell us whether we are liked, respected, or controlled are called

    _____ messages.

2. A relational message that conveys attraction and interest is said to involve

    _____.

3. _____ may arise from intellectual or emotional closeness.

4. Language that has two equally plausible meanings is termed _____.

5. Communication about communication is called _____.

CHAPTER 6 ANSWERS TO SELF-TEST

MATCHING Part One

1. f	2. h	3. j	4. e	5. d
6. a	7. i	8. g	9. b	10. c

MATCHING Part Two

11. d	12. h	13. j	14. a	15. b
16. c	17. g	18. i	19. e	20. f

MULTIPLE CHOICE

1. c	2. b	3. b	4. a	5. c
6. b	7. d	8. c	9. d	10. a
11. a	12. e	13. a	14. b	15. b

MATCHING RELATIONAL STAGES

1. c	2. e	3. a	4. d	5. b

TRUE/FALSE

1. False	2. False	3. True	4. True	5. False

COMPLETION

1. relational	2. immediacy	3. intimacy
4. equivocal	5. metacommunication	

Related Reading

"Can Women and Men Be Friends?" Chapter 15 from <u>Among Friends: Who We Like, Why We Like Them, and What We Do With Them</u> by Letty Cottin Pegrebin (1987) McGraw-Hill.

Preview

Long before and certainly ever since the film, *When Harry Met Sally*, one of the hottest topics of conversation has been "Can Women and Men be Friends?" This chapter by Letty Cottin Pogrebin addresses this question in the context of her larger subject, friends. The whole book is about friends: how we make them, why we keep them, and how friendships develop. This chapter parallels many themes from chapter six, including the importance of intimacy and distance, gender differences in intimacy, stages of and self-disclosure in relationships. Whether or not you agree with her, her analysis and summary of male/female friendships is fascinating and thought provoking.

Review

1. Can you think of any famous non-sexual friendships between men and women? Can you think of any (not so famous) from among your peers, family members, or acquaintances?

2. What did you find when you answered the questions at the beginning of the chapter? Were more of your answers the same sex as you or the opposite?

3. Do you agree that "male-female friendship is still the exception because equality — **social equality** — is still the exception?" (my boldface) Why or why not?

4. What is the author's "sociopolitical motive for wanting sex and friendship to remain distinct"? Do you agree that love and friendship can never be the same?

5. Paraphrase and respond to the summary or conclusion that Ms. Pogrebin presents.

CHAPTER 7 IMPROVING INTERPERSONAL RELATIONSHIPS

CHAPTER 7 SKELETON OUTLINE

This outline can be a helpful study tool to assist you in seeing the order and sequence of the chapter and the relationship of ideas. Use it to take notes as you read and/or to add concepts presented in lecture.

I.   Communication climates

    A. Confirming and disconfirming messages

        1. confirming responses

            a) recognition

            b) acknowledgement

            c) endorsement

        2. disconfirming responses

            a) disagreeing

            b) ignoring

            c) distancing

            d) a matter of perception

    B. Development of communication climates

        1. relational climates are formed verbally and nonverbally

        2. spirals reinforce climates

            a) escalatory conflict spirals

            b) de-escalatory conflict spirals

    C. Creating positive communication climates (Gibb categories)

        1. evaluation vs. description

            a) "you" language

            b) "I" language

         2. control vs. problem orientation

        3. strategy vs. spontaneity

        4. neutrality vs. empathy

        5. superiority vs. equality

        6. certainty vs. provisionalism

II.   Managing interpersonal conflict

    A. The nature of conflict

        1. expressed struggle

        2. perceived incompatible goals

        3. perceived scarce rewards, scarce rewards, and interference

      4.   interdependence

  B. Styles of expressing conflict

      1.   nonassertion

          a) avoidance

          b) accommodation

      2.   direct aggression

      3.   passive aggression "crazymaking"

          a) pseudo-accommodators

          b) guiltmakers

          c) jokers

          d) trivial tyrannizers

          e) withholders

      4.   indirect communication

          a) advantages

          b) disadvantages

      5.   assertion

  C. Characteristics of an assertive message

      1.   behavioral description

      2.   possible interpretation of behavior (may include perception check)

      3.   description of feelings

      4.   description of consequences

          a) what happens to you

          b) what happens to person spoken to

          c) what happens to others

      5.   statement of your intentions

          a) where you stand

          b) requests of others

          c) description of your future action plan

      6.   Guidelines

          a) use the order that works for you

          b) use your own style

          c) elements may be combined

          d) may need repetition or restatement

  D. Gender and conflict style

    1. differences begin in childhood

       a) boys

       b) girls

    2. differences continue as adults

       a) men

       b) women

E. Cultural influences on conflict

    1. individualistic or collectivist

    2. high- or low-context

    3. ethnicity

F. Methods of conflict resolution

    1. win-lose

       a) power

       b) situations for use

    2. lose-lose

    3. compromise

    4. win-win

       a) satisfy everyone's needs

       b) situations for use

G. Steps in win-win problem solving

    1. identify problem and needs

    2. make a date

    3. describe problem and needs

    4. partner checks back

    5. solicit partner's needs

    6. check your understanding of partner's needs

    7. negotiate a solution

       a) identify and define the conflict

       b) generate a quantity of solutions

       c) evaluate solutions

       d) decide on best solution

    8. follow up the solution

CHAPTER 7 KEY TERMS

This list of key terms corresponds to those in boldface in your text. In your own words write a definition and an original example of the word.

assertive

certainty

communication climate

compromise

confirming response

conflict

controlling message

crazymaking

de-escalatory conflict spiral

descriptive communication

direct aggression

disconfirming response

empathy

equality

escalatory conflict spiral

evaluative communication

Gibb categories

"I" language

indirect communication

lose–lose problem solving

neutrality

nonassertion

passive aggression

problem orientation

provisionalism

spiral

spontaneity

strategy

superiority

win–lose problem solving

win–win problem solving

"you" language

Name _____

CHAPTER 7 ACTIVITY 1 RELATIONAL CLIMATES

Purpose:

To investigate communication behaviors that can help create supportive climates.

Instructions:

1.   For each situation, write down in the middle column specific ways (verbal and nonverbal) that the person could behave to establish a confirming climate.
2.   For each, tell why that would create a positive climate for you. Write this in the right column.

Situation	Describe several behaviors that, if engaged in by the **person in boldface,** would create a confirming climate for you.	Explain **why** you think these behaviors would create a supportive climate for you.
You have done poorly on a test and wish to talk to the **instructor** about it after class.	The instructor could make eye contact with me and listen to my concerns. He/she could refrain from looking at the clock, and appearing hurried. Praise my effort and my taking time to come to the office.	By looking at and acknowledging me I'd feel valued. By being praised for taking time to come to the office, rather than hurried away, I'd feel appreciated.
You have just walked into a large room for a wedding reception. You know very few **people.**		
A new **supervisor** is taking over your work group and will meet employees for the first time.		

Situation	Describe several behaviors that, if engaged in by the **person in boldface**, would create a confirming climate for you.	Explain **why** you think these behaviors would create a supportive climate for you.
You are a patient at a new dental office and have arrived for your first visit. **[staff, hygienist, dentist]**		
You stop by to pick up a new classmate who isn't ready. The **roommates** answer the door.		
You have volunteered in a group home for at-risk teens and have arrived to meet the **director,** tour the home, and have an orientation.		

Name _____

CHAPTER 7 ACTIVITY 2 DEFENSIVE/SUPPORTIVE CLIMATES (GIBB)

Purpose:

To apply Gibb's categories to situations in order to analyze and improve communication.

Instructions:

For each item listed below, complete the forms as if you are the person speaking. Refer to the section in your text on **Creating Positive Communication Climates.**

1. Situation: You and your brother both have 2-year-old children. You were at the park watching them play (your child was barefoot), and your brother said to you, "I never let Grigori (his child) go barefoot. It's really a health hazard for children and there are so many risks. I always take time to put shoes on him before we play outside."

I would become defensive because I would perceive _____
(choose one or more Gibb category) on the part of my brother. Explain.

Alternative behavior based on Gibb categories: What could your brother have said or done differently?

2. Situation: A classmate looks over at your desk and says, "You still using spiral notebooks? I used those in high school."

I would become defensive because I would perceive _____
(choose one or more Gibb category) on the part of my brother. Explain.

Alternative behavior based on Gibb categories:

3. Situation: You've been invited to a party by a co-worker. You arrive and the co-worker looks at you and says, "Oh, hi. I didn't know if you'd come." He/she then goes over to other guests. You know no one there.

I would become defensive because I would perceive _____
(choose one or more Gibb category) on the part of my brother. Explain.

Alternative behavior based on Gibb categories:

4. Situation: You are at work and helping a client while two others wait for your help. Your supervisor comes out and says, "I'll see you in my office right now. We need to discuss your problems working with clients."

I would become defensive because I would perceive _____
(choose one or more Gibb category) on the part of my brother. Explain.

Alternative behavior based on Gibb categories:

Name _____

CHAPTER 7 ACTIVITY 3 PROBLEM SOLVING

Purpose:

To apply win-win problem solving.

Instructions:

1. Choose a conflict that you are comfortable addressing with someone. As a first practice, it is not advisable to take neither the biggest nor the most emotional conflict in your life. First try working out a more manageable conflict.
2. Plan how you would accomplish each step, then think carefully about your goals and the other person involved as you consider how to work through these steps.

Identify your problem and unmet needs. This stage involves much intrapersonal communication. Thinking about your needs necessitates giving a lot of thought to your underlying relational needs. Write out what you believe is the problem and what your unmet needs are.

Make a date. Consider timing. Is this a morning or an evening person? Are you watching nonverbals carefully? Has the other had time to think about this as you have? Will you suggest a time and a place free of distractions? What is your plan for making a date?

Describe your problem and needs. Write out some ways you could verbally describe your problem and needs in a way that does not create defensiveness.

Partner checks back. What could you say or do to encourage your partner's understanding of you?

Solicit partner's needs. What could you say or do to encourage your partner to express his/her needs?

Check your understanding. After your partner has spoken, how could you check if you've understood his/her needs correctly? [Although you can't write out exact words without hearing your partner, write out some guidelines for yourself.]

Negotiate a solution. Again, without specifics, you cannot do this in advance. List the four guidelines for negotiating that the text advises you to keep in mind.

Follow up the solution. Remember to build in a follow-up so that neither of you feels this is unchangeable or locked in. What could you say or do to encourage follow up?

As you look over your plan, what parts will be important for a successful solution? What potential pitfalls do you see?

Will you likely approach this person about this conflict? Why or why not?

Name _____

CHAPTER 7 ACTIVITY 4 WIN-WIN PROBLEM SOLVING

Purpose:

To apply win-win problem solving.

Instructions:

1. For each step of the win-win problem solving method, some possible statements to achieve that step are given. Read each one.
2. Which ones are keeping with the spirit of win-win? Which statements might sabotage the process? Which ones create defensiveness? a disconfirming climate? Which ones are better than others in the group? Why? Rate each statement and be prepared to tell why.
   1=excellent communication to achieve that goal
   2=not the best, but it could work
   3=poor communication, likely to create defensiveness or disconfirming climate.

Identify your problem and unmet needs.

A parent wanting a teen at home by curfew.

_____ I need to have you home at midnight.

_____ I need to know you respect my authority.

_____ I need to know that I can control you.

_____ I don't sleep until I know you are safe, and I need to get up early.

A roommate who frequently ends up cleaning up after others.

_____ I need to feel valued and appreciated when I do clean up after you.

_____ I need a clean room to bring my guests into.

_____ I want to be able to go to the refrigerator and find the food that belongs there and not have to look all around the house for it.

_____ I don't want to be taken for granted.

Make a date.

A couple is planning when to discuss whether or not their relationship will be exclusive.

_____ Let's talk it over on the way to the party.

_____ Can we talk about it Monday night?

_____ Let's go for a walk on the beach sometime.

_____ Let's talk Sunday at my mom's party.

Describe your problem and needs.

_____ You make me mad when you won't ask your friends to be quiet while I'm studying.

_____ I'd like to have a time set each night that I know your friends will be gone or at least be quiet. When I come home from the library to study and it's noisy here, I don't get anything done.

_____ You're always leaving books around and you're always asking to borrow my computer. Just show some respect.

Partner checks back.

_____   I've told you how it is for me, now you have to do the same.

_____   You'll ruin our chances of solving this if you don't put as much time and effort into this as I do.

_____   Can't you just quickly say what you need?

Solicit partner's needs.

_____   So what do you want, anyway?

_____   Do you have to have everything your way?

_____   I'd like to hear how you see the situation and what you need.

Check your understanding.

_____   I think you're telling me that . . . but I'm not sure.

_____   I don't see why you think like that. That's not the way it is.

_____   So you're saying that you'd rather . . . than . . . ?

Negotiate a solution.

_____   Let's think of as many ways as we can to solve this to both of our satisfactions.

_____   Can't we come up with something fast 'cause this discussing is driving me nuts.

_____   Let's just do SOMETHING. If it doesn't work, we can try again.

_____   I'm sick and tired of talking about it. Let's agree to something and be out of here.

Follow up on the solution.

_____   Okay, if this doesn't work let me know.

_____   If you're unhappy with this after six weeks, say something.

_____   Let's set a date for two weeks from now to see how this is working for us.

_____   Would you like to save our list of ideas, so if this doesn't work we can try another solution?

Summary What do the items marked with a "1" have in common? Identify at least four characteristics these responses have in common.

Name _____

CHAPTER 7 ACTIVITY 5 CONFLICT STYLES

Purpose:

1. To become aware of the choices of response styles in any conflict situation.
2. To consider the various consequences of different response styles.

Instructions:

1. Assume you are the person in the situations given. Look at the possible response styles and FIRST fill in the response style for the way you would be most likely to handle that conflict [or the way you actually did handle a similar one]. Put a * in front of that response style and write down the results or probable results for you and for the other(s) involved.
2. Then look at the list of other possible response styles. Think of an option you have for each style. Write down a response that is an example of that style and note the probable results for you and others. Do the same for each item.

1. Situation: You just bought a new backpack at a well-known sporting goods store. It was expensive and you anticipated it would last through your college years. The first day you used it the zipper broke.

Nonassertive response:

Probable results for you:

Probable results for other(s):

Directly aggressive response:

Probable results for you:

Probable results for other(s):

Passive aggressive response:

Probable results for you:

Probable results for other(s):

Indirect communication response:

Probable results for you:

Probable results for other(s):

Assertive response:

Probable results for you:

Probable results for other(s):

2.   Situation: A classmate doesn't have a working car. A few weeks ago you gave him/her a ride on your way home. You casually said, "If you need a ride sometime, call me." You were thinking of occasionally, maybe a few times in the semester. Now, the classmate has called three or four times a week to ask for rides to different places.

Nonassertive response:

Probable results for you:

Probable results for other(s):

Directly aggressive response:

Probable results for you:

Probable results for other(s):

Passive aggressive response:

Probable results for you:

Probable results for other(s):

Indirect communication response:

Probable results for you:

Probable results for other(s):

Assertive response:

Probable results for you:

Probable results for other(s):

3. Situation: An instructor continually places his/her hand on the back of your shirt as you work at the computer in class. You are uncomfortable with this.
   OR Describe a conflict situation that you or others have encountered:

Nonassertive response:

Probable results for you:

Probable results for other(s):

Directly aggressive response:

Probable results for you:

Probable results for other(s):

Passive aggressive response:

Probable results for you:

Probable results for other(s):

Indirect communication response:

Probable results for you:

Probable results for other(s):

Assertive response:

Probable results for you:

Probable results for other(s):

Name _____

CHAPTER 7 ACTIVITY 6 EXPLORING THE WEB

Resources for Improving Interpersonal Communication

1. At http://cotton.uamont.edu/~roiger/write/conflict.html you will find an activity that asks you to read 25 proverbs and score them with regard to their desirability as conflict strategies. Scoring gives you insight into your preferred conflict resolution style(s). Print out a copy of the activity. Complete the exercise and score yours according to the directions given. (Read carefully and be certain to do the math correctly.)

2. List the five conflict styles as shown in this assessment with your score for each:

Conflict style from assessment	Score	Identical category In text	Text doesn't have identical category, but this similar one

3. What is your predominant conflict style according to the assessment?

4   Evaluate this assessment. Do you think this instrument is a valid measure of your conflict style? Why or why not?

5. What is the impact of a self-assessment?

6. Predict what would happen if people closest to you completed the inventory about you.

7. Use a search engine and find at least four places that offer training, education, or consulting for improving interpersonal communication or dealing with conflict. Try key words like interpersonal communication or interpersonal conflict.

    List the name of the organization offering the training, their URL and a description of the type of training they offer.

Name of organization	Web site	Type of training offered

8. What kinds of **skills** seem to be advanced by these organizations as skills for dealing with conflict?

For dealing with relational issues?

Name _____

CHAPTER 7 SELF TEST

MATCHING Part One Match each term listed on the left with its correct definition from the column on the right.

_____ 1. assertive

_____ 2. certainty

_____ 3. communication climate

_____ 4. compromise

_____ 5. confirming response

_____ 6. conflict

_____ 7. controlling message

_____ 8. crazymaking

_____ 9. de-escalatory conflict spiral

_____ 10. descriptive communication

a. direct expression of needs, thoughts or feelings

b. an expressed struggle between at least two interdependent parties who perceive incompatible goals, scarce rewards, and interference from the other party in reaching their goals

c. messages that give an account of a speaker's position without evaluating others

d. a communication spiral in which the parties become less interdependent and less invested in the relationship

e. messages that dogmatically imply that one's own position is correct and that the other's ideas are not worth considering

f. the emotional tone of a relationship

g. an approach to conflict resolution in which both parties attain part of what they want and give up part of what they want

h. message in which sender tries to impose some sort of outcome on the receiver

i. passive aggressive messages sent in indirect ways that frustrate and confuse the recipient

j. a general category of responses that express caring and respect

MATCHING Part Two Match each term listed on the left with its correct definition from the column on the right.

____ 11. direct aggression

____ 12. disconfirming response

____ 13. empathy

____ 14. equality

____ 15. escalatory conflict spiral

____ 16. evaluative communication

____ 17. Gibb categories

____ 18. "I" language

____ 19. indirect communication

____ 20. lose–lose problem solving

a. messages in which the sender judges the receiver in some way

b. supportive communication that suggests others are of equivalent worth as a human beings

c. six sets of contrasting styles of behavior. One set describes a communication style likely to arouse defensiveness, the other set a style likely to reduce it

d. hinting at a message instead of expressing thoughts and feelings in a straight-forward way

e. messages that show a lack of regard for others or deny their value

f. communication behavior that attacks the position and dignity of another person

g. a communication spiral in which one attack leads to another

h. an approach to conflict resolution in which neither party achieves its goals

i. a direct way of speaking that describes one's feelings, thoughts, or needs without attacking or evaluating others

j. the ability to project oneself into another person's point of view, so as to experience their thoughts and feelings

MATCHING Part Three Match each term listed on the left with its correct definition from the column on the right.

____ 22. neutrality

____ 23. nonassertion

____ 24. passive aggression

____ 25. problem orientation

____ 26. provisionalism

____ 27. spiral

____ 28. spontaneity

____ 29. strategy

____ 30. superiority

____ 31. win–lose problem solving

____ 32. win–win problem solving

____ 33. "you" language

a. the inability or unwillingness to express thoughts or feelings when needed

b. reciprocal communication pattern in which each person's message reinforces the other's

c. language that evaluates or judges others

d. communication that expresses willingness to change or be open to other ideas; opposite of dogmatic

e. a defense-arousing style of communication in which a person states or implies that one is better than others

f. an approach to conflict in which one party reaches its goal at the expense of the other

g. supportive communication that is honest and makes no attempt to manipulate the receiver

h. a supportive style of communication in which communicators focus on working together to solve problems instead of imposing solutions on each other

i. defense-arousing style of communication in which the communicator tries to manipulate or trick or receiver

j. an approach to conflict in which parties work together to satisfy all their goals

k. defense-arousing behavior that expresses indifference

l. expressing hostility in an obscure way

MATCHING Gibb Opposites Match each defensive-provoking term listed on the left with the term that Gibb describes as being nearly its opposite.

____ 1. superiority	a. description
____ 2. control	b. empathy
____ 3. certainty	c. equality
____ 4. neutrality	d. provisionalism
____ 5. evaluation	e. spontaneity
____ 6. strategy	f. problem-orientation

MATCHING Assertive Message Elements Match each item on the bottom with the part of an assertive message (above) that it represents. They can be used more than once. The boldfaced part of the item is the part to pay attention to; the other is there for context.

a. **behavioral description**   d. **consequences**

b. **interpretation**   e. **intentions**

c. **feelings**

____ 1.   "When you came over without calling, . . .

____ 2.   . . . **I felt uncomfortable** because I don't have time for you."

____ 3.   Tonight I came home and found the kitchen clean, . . .

____ 4.   . . . so I have time to cook you a great dinner.

____ 5.   (When you say you love me), **I feel appreciated and loved.**

____ 6.   (When you called me "sweetie" in the office), **I thought you were trying to show your power over me.**

____ 7.   I think you're being rude.

____ 8.   I don't want you to ignore my sister anymore.

____ 9.   "When my sister is here and you don't say hello, . . .

____ 10.   . . . I have to apologize to her for your behavior."

MULTIPLE CHOICE Choose the BEST response from those listed.

1.   Which of these is NOT a confirming response?

    a. praise
    b. compliment
    c. pseudolistening
    d. acknowledging
    e. all of the above

2. A de-escalatory conflict spiral

    a. refers to a positive, nondestructive climate.
    b. involves intense fights.
    c. refers to less involvement and greater withdrawal.
    d. produces greater involvement in the relationship.
    e. none of the above

3. Spontaneity, as used by Gibb, is closest to

    a. spur-of-the-moment.
    b. unplanned.
    c. honesty.
    d. uncaring.
    e. fair.

4. Practicing the communication behaviors Gibb labels supportive, rather than those labeled defensive

    a. increases the chance of a constructive relationship.
    b. increases the chance of more positive relationship if it is already positive, but decreases the chances of a positive relationship if it is already defensive.
    c. increases the chances of you feeling better about yourself with regard to this relationship.
    d. both b and c
    e. both a and c

5. Neutrality, as used by Gibb, is closest to

    a. mean-spirited.
    b. unplanned.
    c. kind.
    d. indifferent.
    e. fair.

6. Accommodation and avoidance are both forms of

    a. assertion.
    b. nonassertion.
    c. crazymaking.
    d. passive aggression.
    e. direct aggression.

7. Crazymaking is synonymous with

    a. assertion.
    b. nonassertion.
    c. indirect communication.
    d. passive aggression.
    e. direct aggression.

8. Guiltmakers, jokers, trivial tyrannizers, and withholders are all engaged in behaviors called

    a. assertion.
    b. nonassertion.
    c. crazymaking.
    d. indirect communication.
    e. direct aggression.

9. Which is NOT true of assertive communication?

    a. It expresses feelings clearly and directly.
    b. It does not judge or dictate to others.
    c. It treats others with respect and dignity.
    d. It helps communicators maintain better feelings about themselves.
    e. It ensures communicators can always get what they want.

10. When using an assertive message, the text stresses that you

    a. put the message in the order given in the text.
    b. put intentions first so you're not seen as manipulative.
    c. choose the best order for your particular situation and goal.
    d. keep each element in a separate sentence.
    e. c and d

11. Most theorists believe that gender differences in conflict style stem from

    a. biology/heredity.
    b. parental influence.
    c. school and society.
    d. socialization.
    e. all but a

12. The conflict resolution method and assertive message skills taught in this chapter would work well when communicating

    a. in Asian cultures
    b. among Latin Americans
    c. in predominantly Euroamerican work environments
    d. all of the above
    e. none of the above

13. Which of these is NOT typical of a win-lose style?

    a. courts awarding sole custody to one parent, when both want custody of a child.
    b. the World Series or Super Bowl
    c. political elections
    d. job sharing/flex time
    e. all indicate a win-lose style

14. Susan needs to be at class from 6-9 pm. Demetri needs to be at a meeting from 6:30-8:30. They have only one car. If Demetri drops Susan off at class and picks her up, so both get to be where they need to be, and it works better for Susan not to have to park in a student parking lot far from the class, this solution could be called

   a. win-win.
   b. win-lose.
   c. compromise.
   d. lose-lose.
   e. none of the above

15. A person from a low-context culture

   a. will likely hint at a problem, rather than come right out and speak of it.
   b. will usually speak directly and assertively.
   c. will usually not say "no" right to another person's request.
   d. will not risk embarrassing the other person by direct talk.
   e. none of the above reflect a low-context cultural stance.

TRUE/FALSE Circle the T or F to indicate whether you believe the statement is true or false. If it is **true,** give a **reason** or an **example.** If it is false, **explain** what would make it true.

T   F   1.   In order for "expressed struggle" to exist, the struggle must be verbalized.

T   F   2.   A communication climate is determined by the amount of talk that exists in a relationship.

T   F   3.   Conflict exists when there is expressed struggle, interdependence, perceived incompatible goals, scarce rewards, and interference with goals.

T   F   4.   While culture and gender influence speech patterns, researchers have not found any gender or culture differences with regard to how persons view and handle conflict.

T   F   5.   Win-win is the most widely used method of conflict resolution in our society.

COMPLETION Fill in each of the blanks with a word from the lists provided. Choose the BEST word for each sentence. There are more words than you will use, but each word will be used only once.

valued   needs

neutrality   empathy

power   empowered

superiority

1. Communication climate is determined by the degree to which people feel they are

    _____.

2. _____ is the most distinguishing characteristic of win-lose problem solving.

3. In order to frame a conflict in such a way that a win-win solution is likely, it is necessary to

    think in terms of the _____ of each person.

4. "The worst sin toward our fellow creatures is not to hate them, but to be indifferent to them; that's the essence of inhumanity." This quotation by Shaw is closest to the Gibb category of

    _____.

5. In the age of e-mail, supercomputer power on the desktop, the Internet, and the raucous global village, attentiveness — a token of human kindness — is the greatest gift we can give someone."
    - Tom Peters, The Pursuit of WOW! This quotation is closest to what Gibb describes as

    _____.

CHAPTER 7 ANSWERS TO SELF-TEST

MATCHING Part One

1. a	2. e	3. f	4. g	5. j
6. b	7. h	8. i	9. d	10. c

MATCHING Part Two

11. f	12. e	13. j	14. b	15. g
16. a	17. c	18. i	19. d	20. h

MATCHING Part Three

21. k	22. a	23. l	24. h	25. d
26. b	27. g	28. i	29. e	30. f
31. j	32. c			

MATCHING Gibb Opposites

1. c	2. f	3. d	4. b	5. a
6. e				

MATCHING Assertive Message Elements

1. a	2. c	3. a	4. d	5. c
6. b	7. b	8. e	9. a	10. d

MULTIPLE CHOICE

1. c	2. c	3. c	4. e	5. d
6. b	7. d	8. c	9. e	10. c
11. d	12. c	13. d	14. a	15. b

TRUE/FALSE

1. False	2. False	3. True	4. False	5. False

COMPLETION

1. valued	2. power	3. needs
4. neutrality	5. empathy	

Related Reading

"When Black Women Talk with White Women: Why Dialogues are Difficult" by Marsha Houston from Our Voices: Essays in Culture, Ethnicity, and Communication: An Intercultural Anthology. 3rd edition. pp. 98-104. Alberto Gonzalez, Marsha Houston, and Victoria Chen, editors. 2000. Roxbury Publishing Company.

Preview

Chapter Seven takes a broad view of avenues to improve many different interpersonal relationships. This reading focuses more narrowly on a particular relationship: friendships between black and white women. Author Marsha Houston provides interesting correlations to previous chapters on the role of self-concept, perception, and language in sustaining or undermining friendships. Her advice in this article can be seen as a means of creating more confirming messages and more positive climates in black and white women's friendships, thus perhaps avoiding at least one type of interpersonal conflict. As you read, consider how your experiences or perceptions of black and white women influence your view of this author's analysis of the difficulties of dialogue between black and white women.

Review

1. Imagine this article written by a Euroamerican woman. Would any of the three pieces of advice be appropriate for Euroamerican women (or men) for interracial friendships? Why or why not?

2. The author states that she does not intend to give a "definitive or an exhaustive analysis" of interracial women's talk. Would you add anything to her understanding of the two reasons why black women often find conversations with white women unsatisfying and/or the three statements she suggests avoiding?

3. How do you think an article on interracial men's talk would be similar or different from this article?

4. Do your experiences validate or refute the author's conclusions?

CHAPTER 8 THE NATURE OF GROUPS

CHAPTER 8 SKELETON OUTLINE

This outline can be a helpful study tool to assist you in seeing the order and sequence of the chapter and the relationship of ideas. Use it to take notes as you read and/or to add concepts presented in lecture.

I.   What is a group?

    A. Interaction

    B. Interdependence

    C. Time

    D. Size

    E. Goals

II. Goals of groups and members

    A. Individual goals

        1. task-orientation

        2. social orientation

    B. Group goals

        1. relationship between group/individual goals

        2. hidden agenda

III. Types of groups

    A. Learning groups

    B. Growth groups

    C. Problem-solving groups

    D. Social groups

IV. Characteristics of groups

    A. Rules and norms

        1. rules

        2. norms

            a) social

            b) procedural

            c) task

            d) identify norms by looking at

                (1) habitual behaviors

                (2) punishment for violation

    B. Roles

        1. formal

2. informal

    a) task

    b) social/maintenance

    c) dysfunctional

3. role emergence

4. role problems and solutions

    a) under filled

    b) over filled

    c) role fixation

C. Patterns of interaction

1. mathematical

2. sociograms

3. physical arrangement

4. networks

    a) all-channel

    b) chain

    c) wheel

    d) gatekeeper

D. Decision-making methods vary and the most effective method depends on the type and importance of the decision and the time available.

1. consensus

2. majority control

3. expert opinion

4. minority control

5. authority rule

V. Cultural influences on group communication

A. Individualism vs. collectivism

1. individualistic orientation

2. collectivistic orientation

B. Power distance

1. Low power distance

2. High power distance

C. Uncertainty avoidance

1. Low uncertainty avoidance

2. High uncertainty avoidance

D. Task vs. social orientation

1. high task orientation

2. high social orientation

E. Short vs. long term orientation

1. short term orientation

2. long term orientation

CHAPTER 8 KEY TERMS

This list of key terms corresponds to those in boldface in your text. In your own words write a definition and an original example of the word.

all-channel network

chain network

collectivistic orientation

consensus

dysfunctional roles

formal roles

gatekeeper

group

group goals

growth groups

hidden agenda

individual goals

individualistic orientation

informal roles

learning group

norms

power distance

problem-solving groups

procedural norms

roles

rules

social groups

social norms

social orientation

social roles

sociogram

task norms

task orientation

task roles

uncertainty avoidance

wheel network

Name _____

CHAPTER 8 ACTIVITY 1 GROUP CHARACTERISTICS AND GOALS

Purpose:

To identify characteristics of groups you belong to.
To analyze goals for groups you have membership in.

Instructions:

1.   Choose three groups that you are a part of. Try to choose groups that fit in different categories (problem-solving, learning, growth, and social).
2.   Analyze each by filling in the information below.

Group 1 Name of group:

Describe the group's interaction over time. (nature and amount of interaction? over what period of time?) How are the members interdependent?

Describe the size of the group.

Describe your goals in the group by describing:
    a.   What are your individual task-oriented goals?

    b.   What are your individual social-oriented goals?

Describe the group goals and how you know these are the group goals.

Do you or others have hidden agendas that you are aware of? If so, how do they affect the group?

Do your individual goals and the group goals harmonize or is there conflict between the two sets of goals?

Into what category (learning, growth, problem-solving, or social) would you characterize this group? Explain why.

Group 2 Name of group:

Describe the group's interaction over time. (nature and amount of interaction? over what period of time?) How are the members interdependent?

Describe the size of the group.

Describe your goals in the group by describing:
   a.   What are your individual task-oriented goals?

   b.   What are your individual social-oriented goals?

Describe the group goals and how you know these are the group goals.

Do you or others have hidden agendas that you are aware of? If so, how do they affect the group?

Do your individual goals and the group goals harmonize or is there conflict between the two sets of goals?

Into what category (learning, growth, problem-solving, or social) would you characterize this group? Explain why.

Group 3 Name of group:

Describe the group's interaction over time. (nature and amount of interaction? over what period of time?) How are the members interdependent?

Describe the size of the group.

Describe your goals in the group by describing:
   a.   What are your individual task-oriented goals?

   b.   What are your individual social-oriented goals?

Describe the group goals and how you know these are the group goals.

Do you or others have hidden agendas that you are aware of? If so, how do they affect the group?

Do your individual goals and the group goals harmonize or is there conflict between the two sets of goals?

Into what category (learning, growth, problem-solving, or social) would you characterize this group? Explain why.

DISCUSSION/CONCLUSIONS

What do you think is the correlation between the type of group (learning, growth, problem-solving, social) and the presence or absence of hidden agendas? Do you think hidden agendas are more or less likely in certain groups?

Are your social goals different depending on the type of group you belong to?

Are there some groups you don't currently belong to but would like to? What groups would you join if you could?

Why?

Are there any groups that you belong to but would like to be out of? Why? Are those groups failing to meet needs of yours? Which ones?

What was the most productive group you were ever part of? What made it so? Try to identify the factors that contributed to its productivity. Was it at all related to group and individual goals?

What was the most ineffective group you were ever part of? Why was it so bad? Can you identify factors that made it ineffective? Was it related to group and individual goals?

Name _____

CHAPTER 8 ACTIVITY 2 GROUP NORMS AND RULES

Purpose:

1. To distinguish between rules and norm.
2. To identify norms through observing behavior.

Instructions:

Choose three groups you belong to. For each, you will focus on the rules and norms of the group. Try to describe behaviors. How are the members interdependent?

Example: Work group at a fast-food restaurant

List several explicit (written) rules of the group.	1) Show up on time or be docked pay. 2) Wear the uniform given to you. 3) Don't leave until clean-up is done, even if shift is over.
Describe a social norm.	1) Everyone says hi to everyone else when starting a shift 2) Another strong social norm is if a new female starts working, the guys see who she talks to the most. The others are not to try to date her or get close to her. They are not to flirt, etc. if she shows interest in someone else.
What behaviors in the group reinforce following the norm or punish violations of the norm?	1) If someone doesn't say "hi" to someone else, they usually shout to him/her, "Hey, what's the matter? You gonna say "hi" today or not? 2) Everyone will talk about you, "Hey, John's making his move" or tease you if you violate the norm.
Describe a procedural norm.	The procedural norm is pretty much by seniority. For jobs we're supposed to share, those who've been there longest say whether they'll do grill or window or drive-up, the rest take what's left by pecking order.
What behaviors reinforce following the norm or punish violations of the norm?	Everyone just follows this. If a new person says what they'd like before a "senior" speaks, everyone pretty much ignores them and listens to the next senior person.
Describe a task norm.	Problems among employees are handled one-to-one. Don't go to the manager for "minor" concerns.
What behaviors reinforce following the norm or punish violations of the norm?	If someone goes to the manager with a "minor" problem (they don't like their hours, they want a different shift) the others ostracize them. It's understood that you take what you get.

Group 1	Name of group:
List several explicit (written) rules of the group.	1) 2) 3)
Describe a social norm.	
What behaviors in the group reinforce following the norm or punish violations of the norm?	
Describe a procedural norm.	
What behaviors in the group reinforce following the norm or punish violations of the norm?	
Describe a task norm.	
What behaviors in the group reinforce following the norm or punish violations of the norm?	

Group 2	Name of group:
List several explicit (written) rules of the group.	1) 2) 3)
Describe a social norm.	
What behaviors in the group reinforce following the norm or punish violations of the norm?	
Describe a procedural norm.	
What behaviors in the group reinforce following the norm or punish violations of the norm?	
Describe a task norm.	
What behaviors in the group reinforce following the norm or punish violations of the norm?	

Group 3	Name of group:
List several explicit (written) rules of the group.	1) 2) 3)
Describe a social norm.	
What behaviors in the group reinforce following the norm or punish violations of the norm?	
Describe a procedural norm.	
What behaviors in the group reinforce following the norm or punish violations of the norm?	
Describe a task norm.	
What behaviors in the group reinforce following the norm or punish violations of the norm?	

CHAPTER 8 ACTIVITY 3 GROUP ROLES

Purpose:

1. To identify roles in groups.
2. To be able to describe behaviors characteristic of various roles.

Instructions:

1. Form groups of eight to ten. Half of the members should designate themselves as A's and half as B's. For the first discussion, A's will be group participants; B's will be observers. One B should take on the additional role of timekeeper. For the second discussion, roles will be switched.
2. Sit in "fish bowl" style, with the A's seated in a small circle as close to each other as possible, while B's surround that group so they can observe.
3. A's should choose one of the "Group Exercises" below. After 10 minutes one of the B's will inform them that their time is up.
4. During the discussion B's should use the observation forms and watch for evidence of different roles being performed by various group members. Jot down behaviors that seem to characterize various roles. Your job is to report **observations, not evaluations,** of group members and activities.
5. After the discussion, B's should report their observations to the whole group (A's and B's).
6. Discuss the questions at the bottom of this page as a whole group.

GROUP EXERCISES

1. Hypothetical situation: The instructor is willing to add between 1 and 50 points (out of 1,000) to students' grades for notable class participation this semester. Devise a plan to determine the number of participation points each student should receive. Your job is to come up with a plan to assign points, not to assign them. The plan should be a workable, fair plan that you can present to the instructor.

2. Money has been allocated for five new student support positions at your college. These are not instructor positions, but may be any type of support services. What student support services are most needed? Provide a plan for use of these funds.

3. Assume that this group is a student liaison committee to facilitate communication between students and administration. There is no additional money. Create a directive to the administration citing the three most significant things the administration could do to benefit students at no additional cost.

POST-OBSERVATION DISCUSSION QUESTIONS FOR THE WHOLE GROUP

1. Which roles did each person fill?

2. Which roles were not filled?

3. Which roles were competed for?

4. Why might group members see their own behaviors differently from each other?

5. Why might observers and group members "see" behaviors differently?

6. Was there any role fixation?

7. For participants: Which roles were you comfortable in? Did you have to stretch yourself to fulfill any roles that aren't part of your usual repertoire? Which ones?

8. What decision-making method(s) was used by the group?

OBSERVATION OF GROUP ROLES

TASK ROLES IN GROUPS	DESCRIBE BEHAVIORS HERE (verbal/nonverbal) (Include names of participants displaying behaviors)
1. **Initiator/contributor** (proposes ideas, solutions, suggestions)	
2. **Information seeker** (asks others for relevant information)	
3. **Information giver** (offers facts, relevant evidence)	
4. **Opinion giver** (states opinions and beliefs)	
5. **Opinion seeker** (asks others for opinions/beliefs)	
6. **Elaborator/clarifier** (expands ideas, shows how idea would work for group)	
7. **Coordinator** (clarifies relationships among contributions)	
8. **Diagnostician** (assesses group behavior, "We spend a lot of time . . .")	
9. **Orienter/Summarizer** (reviews and identifies themes in what's been said)	
10. **Energizer** (invigorates, enthuses group for task)	
11. **Procedure developer** (attends to seating, equipment)	
12. **Secretary** (keeps notes)	
13. **Evaluator/critic** (constructive analysis of accomplishment)	
Other comments	

SOCIAL/MAINTENANCE ROLES IN GROUPS	DESCRIBE BEHAVIORS HERE (verbal/nonverbal) (Include names of participants displaying behaviors)
1. **Supporter/encourager** (praises, accepts others, warmth and recognition freely given)	
2. **Harmonizer** (mediates interpersonal conflicts and reduces tensions among group members)	
3. **Tension reliever** (helps relieve anxiety and pressures in group)	
4. **Conciliator** (offers options if his/her ideas are creating conflict, maintains cohesion)	
5. **Gatekeeper** (keeps channels open; encourages interaction.)	
6. **Feeling expresser** (makes feelings/moods of group and self explicit)	
7. **Follower** (passive acceptance of group movement)	

DYSFUNCTIONAL ROLES

1. **Blocker** (prevents progress by raising objections constantly)	
2. **Aggressor** (aggressively questions others' motives or competence)	
3. **Deserter** (refuses to participate, take stand, or respond to others)	
4. **Dominator** (interrupts, monopolizes)	
5. **Recognition-seeker** (boasts, brags, and calls attention to self and accomplishments inappropriately)	
6. **Joker** (shows lack of involvement by clowning or joking in excess)	
7. **Cynic** (shoots down ideas, discounts chances for success)	

Source: "Functional Roles of Group Members" and "Dysfunctional Roles of Group Members" adapted from *Groups in Context: Leadership and Participation in Decision-Making Groups* by Gerald Wilson and Michael Hanna, pp. 144-46. © 1986. Reprinted by permission of McGraw-Hill.

INDIVIDUAL SUMMARY
Roles that I am most comfortable with in most groups:

Why are these roles comfortable for you?

Roles that I am least comfortable with:

Why are these roles uncomfortable for you?

What would it take for me to feel comfortable with some of these roles?

Roles I may compete for:

In what circumstances?

Decision-making method that I tend to gravitate toward:
Why?

Decision-making method I'm most comfortable with:
Decision-making method I'm least comfortable with:

Name _____

CHAPTER 8 ACTIVITY 4 GROUP DECISION-MAKING

Purpose:

To apply group decision-making skills.

Instructions Part One:

Read each scenario. For each, decide which decision-making method you would recommend and why.

Decision-making methods:

consensus   majority   expert   minority   authority

1. The budget for the (Speech) Communication Department has been increased. You are on a student committee to report to the department. Your task is to create and prioritize a list of items that, if funded, would best satisfy student needs.

Decision-making method recommended:

Reasons:

2. You are asked to serve on an ad hoc committee of the student government. Money has been allocated for grounds and physical plant improvements at your college. The committee is to decide what improvements in the physical environment would be most beneficial for students' academic, social, and safety needs. You are to prepare a concrete list of ideas and prioritize them for the student government.

Decision-making method recommended:

Reasons:

3. You are part of a campus organization that is going to sponsor a fund-raiser. The decision about what type of fund-raiser needs to be made.

Decision-making method recommended:

Reasons:

4. Your family is trying to decide what kind of party to give for your grandparent's 50th wedding anniversary.

Decision-making method recommended:

Reasons:

5. Most class members want to have lunch together after the 9-11 a.m. final.

Decision-making method recommended:

Reasons:

6. You work for a small company and they want to purchase a word processing/database software program that all employees will be using.

Decision-making method recommended:

Reasons:

7. You and your spouse are accepted into excellent, but different, graduate schools in different cities. You have two pre-schoolers and you both want to be together, but you also want to participate in these programs (2-3 years).

Decision-making method recommended:

Reasons:

Part Two:

Can you think of times or situations when you have used each of the types of decision-making described in the text? Write at least one example of each.

consensus

majority

expert

minority

authority

In what situations are you most comfortable with each type of decision-making?
consensus

majority

expert

minority

authority

Name _____

CHAPTER 8 ACTIVITY 5 EXPLORING THE WEB

1. Find the home page for the Center for Collaborative Organizations at www.workteams.unt.edu/. What is the purpose and mission of the Center?

2. From the "List of Links" on the homepage, go to Journal of Computer Mediated Communication (www.ascusc.org/jcmc/vol3/issue4) and from there to "Trust in Global Virtual Teams." After reading that article,
   a. Describe the challenges facing virtual teams.

   b. Summarize the methods used by the authors to study these challenges.

   c. What conclusions do the authors draw about communication behaviors that might contribute to trust in virtual teams?

3. Read David Gould's article "Leading Virtual Teams," at www.seanet.com/~daveg/ltv.htm. Summarize what you find. How does it compare or contrast with what your text expresses?

4. If you are working in a group and need tools for your group, look at www.intranets.com or http://groups.yahoo.com. Each offers a variety of methods to facilitate your virtual teamwork. List some of the tools and what they do here:

Name _____

CHAPTER 8 SELF TEST

MATCHING Part One Match each term listed on the left with its correct definition from the column on the right.

_____ 1. all-channel network

_____ 2. chain network

_____ 3. collectivistic orientation

_____ 4. consensus

_____ 5. dysfunctional roles

_____ 6. formal roles

_____ 7. gatekeeper

_____ 8. group

_____ 9. group goals

_____ 10. growth group

_____ 11. hidden agenda

a. network in which all parties have equal access to one another

b. person through whom information flows

c. small collection of individuals who interact over time to reach goals.

d. network in which information passes sequentially from one member to another

e. individual goals that group members are unwilling to reveal

f. decision-making method in which group members discuss an issue until they reach agreement

g. cultural orientation focusing on the group as a whole, rather than a concern by individuals for their own success

h. group which seeks no goal of its own, but to promote individual members' personal development

i. individual roles of group members that inhibit the group's effectiveness

j. objectives that a group collectively seeks to accomplish

k. officially recognized and labeled behaviors that are expected of persons in a group, such as secretary and manager

MATCHING Part Two Match each term listed on the left with its correct definition from the column on the right.

_____ 11. individual goals

_____ 12. individualistic orientation

_____ 13. informal roles

_____ 14. learning group

_____ 15. norms

_____ 16. power distance

_____ 17. problem-solving group

_____ 18. procedural norms

_____ 19. roles

_____ 20. rules

a. degree to which members are willing to accept a difference in status among members

b. norms that describe rules for the group's operations

c. member roles necessary for the group to accomplish its task-related goals

d. broad category of patterns of behavior expected of members

e. explicit, officially stated guidelines that govern what the group is supposed to do and how the members should behave

f. unofficial, but powerful set of standards for behavior in a group, often unstated

g. cultural orientation focusing on the value and welfare of individuals, as opposed to concern for the group as a whole

h. motives of separate group members that influence their behavior in the group

i. group whose goal is to expand their knowledge about some outside topic

j. task-related group whose goal is to resolve a mutual concern

MATCHING Part Three Match each term listed on the left with its correct definition from the column on the right.

_____ 21. social group

_____ 22. social norms

_____ 23. social orientation

_____ 24. social roles

_____ 25. sociogram

_____ 26. task norms

_____ 27. task orientation

_____ 28. task roles

_____ 29. uncertainty avoidance

_____ 30. wheel network

a. group orientation that makes meeting objectives a priority

b. patterns of behaviors which help the group accomplish its goals

c. shared beliefs, behaviors, and procedures that govern how a group operates

d. emotional roles concerned with maintaining harmonious personal relationships among group members

e. communication pattern in which a gatekeeper regulates the flow of information among other members

f. cultural tendency to seek stability and honor instead of welcoming risk and change

g. group whose goal is to meet the interaction needs (inclusion, control, affection) of members

h. graphic representation of group interaction patterns

i. group orientation that stresses harmonious relationships over work

j. beliefs and behaviors that govern the relationship of group members

MULTIPLE CHOICE Choose the BEST response from those listed.

1. Which is an essential part of the definition of a group?

    a. individuals who interact verbally
    b. individuals who interact face-to-face
    c. individuals who interact over time.
    d. individuals who number at least five.
    e. all of the above.

2. An investment group in which members join to understand and practice investing would be primarily a _____ group.

    a. learning
    b. growth
    c. problem-solving
    d. social
    e. none of the above

3. Group norms are best identified by

    a. observing the habits of members
    b. reading the by-laws
    c. noting how members are punished for behaviors
    d. both a and b
    e. both a and c

4. A problem that occurs in groups with regard to roles is

   a. an important informal role is not filled.
   b. several people vie for a particular role.
   c. a member(s) acts out a certain role when the situation doesn't require it.
   d. all of the above can be problems in groups.
   e. None of these is a problem with regard to groups and roles.

5. You can be a more valuable group member if you

   a. look for missing roles; figure out what's not being done.
   b. fill or encourage others to fill missing roles.
   c. avoid role fixation when it is not helpful or needed.
   d. avoid dysfunctional roles
   e. all of the above

6. One way to visually see who speaks to whom and how often is to construct a/an

   a. sociogram
   b. role research diagram
   c. chain network
   d. collectivistic culture
   e. decision-making paradigm

7. Which network is described in this scenario? Jane stays at her desk and by her phone most of the workday. When others leave, they usually tell her. When Marcy is trying to reach Juan, but Juan is away from his desk, Marcy asks Jane to give Juan a message when he returns. Since Jane can see the other desks and is frequently asked to relay messages, she is performing the role of

   a. chain network
   b. sociogram
   c. gatekeeper
   d. collectivistic orientation
   e. uncertainty avoider

8. Which network is represented in the following diagram?

   Driver---Dispatcher---Terminal manager----General manager

   a. wheel
   b. chain
   c. all-channel
   d. y-channel
   e. none of the above

9. In a wheel network, the gatekeeper

   a. may distort messages to the detriment of the group.
   b. may facilitate communication between members with strained relations.
   c. is usually easily available and accessible to all members.
   d. both b and c
   e. all of the above

10. The major drawback of decision by consensus is

    a. it's undemocratic.
    b. full participation in decision-making decreases commitment to support the decision.
    c. it is impossible to use expert opinion.
    d. it takes a great deal of time.
    e. members don't get as involved emotionally as with other methods.

11. A group decision by minority often refers to a decision by

    a. a group of rabble rousers.
    b. committee.
    c. a small group of external experts.
    d. autocratic leaders.
    e. none of the above

12. The best decision-making method depends on

    a. the culture.
    b. the importance of the decision.
    c. the amount of time available.
    d. the type of decision.
    e. all of the above.

13. Usually members of individualistic cultures

    a. produce and reward "stars."
    b. find consensus easy to achieve.
    c. see their primary loyalty to groups.
    d. are found in Asian and Latin American cultures.
    e. are indirect.

14. U.S. cultures tend to

    a. have a low power distance.
    b. have high uncertainty avoidance.
    c. be collectivistic.
    d. have high social orientation.
    e. none of the above

15. In a society with high power distance

    a. leaders are not readily accepted and respected.
    b. group members are not likely to feel they need a leader.
    c. group members expect leaders to act like equals to all.
    d. all of the above
    e. none of the above

16. Societies with low uncertainty avoidance

    a. are willing to take risks.
    b. accept change readily.
    c. see conflict as natural.
    d. all of the above
    e. none of the above

17. Advantage(s) of virtual groups include:

    a. status is leveled or less important among members.
    b. speed and ease of meeting.
    c. reduced costs.
    d. all of the above
    e. none of the above

MATCHING ROLES Match the roles below with their types (A, B, C). You will use the letters more than once.

____ 1. tension reliever		A. task role
____ 2. information seeker		B. social/maintenance role
____ 3. cynic		C. dysfunctional role
____ 4. blocker		
____ 5. gatekeeper		
____ 6. orienter/summarizer		
____ 7. elaborator/clarifier		
____ 8. feeling expresser		
____ 9. harmonizer		
____ 10. dominator		

TRUE/FALSE Circle the T or F to indicate whether you believe the statement is true or false. If it is **true,** give a **reason** or an **example**. If it is false, **explain** what would make it true.

T F   1. Any time you are surrounded by other people, you are part of at least one group.

T F   2. Majority rule decisions are usually of higher quality than any other kind of decision.

T F   3. A decision by consensus means a vote of 51% or more.

T F   4. Gatekeepers serve a vital communication function in a wheel network.

T F   5. Role fixation occurs when a person enacts the same role in groups whether or not it is a needed or functional for that context.

COMPLETION Fill in each of the blanks with a word from the lists provided. Choose the BEST word for each sentence. There are more words than you will use, but each word will be used only once.

formal roles	**informal roles**
social goals	**hidden agenda**
norms	**sociogram**

1. Officially recognized and labeled behaviors, such as secretary, are known as

    _____.

2. Tasks or behaviors clearly operating but rarely acknowledged are called _____.

3. Important reasons for group membership, but reasons not always stated or recognized by members are called _____.

4. An individual goal that is not made known to or shared with a group is a

    _____.

5. Unwritten rules that operate in groups are called _____.

CHAPTER 8 ANSWERS TO SELF TEST

MATCHING Part One

1. a	2. d	3. g	4. f	5. i
6. k	7. b	8. c	9. j	10. h
11. e				

MATCHING Part Two

11. h	12. g	13. c	14. i	15. f
16. a	17. j	18. b	19. d	20. e

MATCHING Part Three

21. g	22. j	23. i	24. d	25. h
26. c	27. a	28. b	29. f	30. e

MULTIPLE CHOICE

1. c	2. a	3. e	4. d	5. e
6. a	7. c	8. b	9. e	10. d
11. b	12. e	13. a	14. a	15. e
16. d	17. d			

MATCHING ROLES

1. B	2. A	3. C	4. C	5. B
6. A	7. A	8. B	9. B	10. C

TRUE/FALSE

1. False	2. False	3. False	4. True	5. True

COMPLETION

1. formal roles	2. informal roles	3. social goals
4. hidden agenda	5. norms	

Related Reading

"Fraternities and Rape on Campus" by Patricia Yancey Martin and Robert A. Hummer.
from Gender & Society, Vol. 3, No. 4, December 1989, pp. 457-573.

Preview

Groups can be powerful forces for good or for evil. What makes this article so pertinent to our chapter on the nature of groups is its exploration of the norms in fraternities and how adherence to these norms may perpetuate the exploitation and rape of women. This investigation into the group dynamics of fraternities shows that what may result are rules and roles that characterize patterns of interaction in which coercion in sexual relations with women is normative. Authors Patricia Yancey Martin and Robert A. Hummer contend that it is oversimplistic to conclude that fraternity members are more likely to rape because of peer pressure. Rather, they assert that the more complex process of communication within fraternities creates a view of women as commodities and thus creates a social context in which individuals are more likely to rape. The article is relevant to this chapter's discussion of group dynamics and patterns of interaction; however, articles about violence toward others are never an easy read and this one is no exception.

Review

1. According to the authors of this article, how might membership in a fraternity shape a person's self-concept and perception of others?

2. What evidence does the author's present to substantiate their claim that "fraternities are a physical and sociocultural context that encourages the sexual coercion of women"?

3. Do you believe the authors would argue that the group norms shape the individuals or that the individuals shape the group norms? Explain your answer.

4. Explain how the transactional process of communication and interaction shape our perception of and relationship with others, i.e., fraternity men and women.

5. Can you think of other groups in which cohesiveness may lead to similar violent problems? Should society play a role in re-shaping or destroying these groups?

More related research articles:

"Getting inside the house: The effectiveness of a rape prevention program for college fraternity men" by Tracy L Davis. Journal of College Student Development, Washington; Jan/Feb 2002; Vol. 43, Iss. 1; pg. 35, 16 pgs.

"Fraternities, athletic teams, and rape: Importance of identification with a risky group" by Stephen E. Humphrey. Journal of Interpersonal Violence, Beverly Hills; Dec 2000; Vol. 15, Iss. 12; pg. 1313, 10 pgs.

CHAPTER 9 SOLVING PROBLEMS IN GROUPS

CHAPTER 9 SKELETON OUTLINE

This outline can be a helpful study tool to assist you in seeing the order and sequence of the chapter and the relationship of ideas. Use it to take notes as you read and/or to add concepts presented in lecture.

I.   Problem-solving in groups: when and why

    A. Advantages of group problem-solving

        1. resources

        2. accuracy

        3. commitment (participative decision making)

    B. When to use group problem solving

        1. job

        2. interdependence

        3. multiple solutions

        4. potential disagreement

II. Group problem-solving formats

    A. Types of face-to-face problem solving groups

        1. buzz groups

        2. problem census

        3. focus group

        4. parliamentary procedure

        5. panel discussion

        6. symposium

        7. forum

    B. Computer-mediated groups

        1. types

            a) teleconferencing

            b) computer conferencing

        2. advantages

        3. disadvantages

III. Approaches and stages in problem-solving

    A. Structured problem-solving approach

        1. identify the problem/challenge

        2. analyze the problem

            a) create probative question

          b) gather information

          c) identify impelling & restraining forces/force field analysis

      3. develop creative solutions

          a) brainstorm

              (1) no criticism

              (2) freewheeling

              (3) quantity

              (4) combination

          b) nominal group technique

              (1) solo lists

              (2) round robin offering a solution but no evaluation

              (3) rank solutions

              (4) discussion

              (5) decision

    4. evaluate solutions

          a) desirability

          b) implementation

          c) disadvantages

    5. implementation

          a) tasks

          b) resources

          c) responsibilities

          d) emergencies

    6. follow up

          a) periodic evaluation

          b) revision as necessary

  B. Developmental stages in problem-solving groups

    1. orientation stage

    2. conflict stage

    3. emergence stage

    4. reinforcement stage

IV. Maintaining positive relationships

  A. Basic skills

  B. Building cohesiveness

      1. cohesiveness and productivity

      2. boosting cohesiveness

         a) shared/compatible goals

         b) progress toward goals

         c) shared norms and values

         d) lack of perceived internal threats

         e) interdependence

         f) outside threat

         g) mutual perceived attractiveness and friendship

         h) shared group experiences

V. Leadership and power in groups

    A. Power in groups

        1. types of power

           a) legitimate power (position)/nominal leader

           b) coercive power

           c) reward power

           d) expert power

           e) information power

           f) referent power

        2. characteristics of power

           a) group-centered

           b) distributed among members

           c) not either-or

    B. What makes leaders effective

        1. trait analysis

        2. leadership style

           a) communication style

              (1) authoritarian

              (2) democratic

              (3) laissez-faire

           b) Leadership Grid

              (1) production/task

              (2) concern for relationships

        3. situational approaches

a) changing circumstances

b) group readiness

VI. Overcoming dangers in group discussion

A. Information underload and overload

1. underload

2. overload

B. Unequal participation

1. advantages of participation

2. balance

3. encouraging participation

a) size

b) reinforcement

c) tasks

d) nominal group technique

4. discouraging unhelpful talk

a) withhold reinforcement

b) assert desire to hear from others

c) challenge relevancy

C. Pressure to conform

1. recognizing groupthink

2. reducing groupthink

CHAPTER 9 KEY TERMS

This list of key terms corresponds to those in boldface in your text. In your own words write a definition and an original example of the word.

authoritarian leadership style

brainstorming

buzz group

coercive power

cohesiveness

conflict stage

democratic leadership style

emergence stage

expert power

focus group

force field analysis

forum

groupthink

information overload

information power

information underload

laissez-faire leadership style

leader

Leadership Grid

legitimate power

nominal group technique

nominal leader

orientation stage

panel discussion

parliamentary procedure

participative decision making

power

probative question

problem census

referent power

reinforcement stage

reward power

situational leadership

symposium

trait theories of leadership

Name _____

CHAPTER 9 ACTIVITY 1 TYPES OF POWER

Purpose:

To analyze types of power in different groups.

Instructions:

1. For this exercise, you will first consider this class, then think of and list two other groups that you belong to. For each group (this class and two others), consider the different types of power that various persons in the group have.
2. In the middle column, explain **your** relative amount of each type of power.
3. In the right column describe who you believe has the most of each type of power.

Group: this class

Which people have some of this type of power? Why?	Discuss the relative amount of each type of power you have.	Who has the most of this type of power? Why?
Legitimate		
Coercive		
Reward		
Expert		
Information		
Referent		

Group:

Which people have some of this type of power? Why?	Discuss the relative amount of each type of power you have.	Who has the most of this type of power? Why?
Legitimate		
Coercive		
Reward		
Expert		
Information		
Referent		

Group:

Which people have some of this type of power? Why?	Discuss the relative amount of each type of power you have.	Who has the most of this type of power? Why?
Legitimate		
Coercive		
Reward		
Expert		
Information		
Referent		

Name _____

CHAPTER 9 ACTIVITY 2 ENHANCING POWER IN GROUPS

Purpose:

To describe ways to enhance one's power in groups.

Instructions:

1.   List four groups that you belong to.
2.   Using Table 9-3: Methods for Acquiring Power in Small Groups from the text, list some specific ways that you could enhance your various types of power in each of these groups.

Types of power:

    Legitimate power   **Expert power**

    Coercive power   **Referent power**

    Reward power   **Information power**

Example: Group I belong to: _____Investment group_____

What I could do to enhance my power in that group and why:

 I could be sure that I can attend all meetings (visibility) and have my stock reports ready (demonstrate knowledge and follow group norms). Those who don't show up or never do their stock reports for the group lose credibility (legitimate authority). I could read and study more than our investment magazine and go to the extra workshops on stock analysis and then share that information with the group (expert and information power). When it is my turn to report on a stock, I can have copies for everyone or a clear overhead so that my ideas are clearly presented (referent power).

1.   Group I belong to:

What I could do to enhance my power in that group and why:

2.   Group I belong to:

What I could do to enhance my power in that group and why:

3.   Group I belong to:

What I could do to enhance my power in that group and why:

4.   Group I belong to:

What I could do to enhance my power in that group and why:

Name _____

CHAPTER 9 ACTIVITY 3 COHESION IN GROUPS

Purpose:

To recognize ways of building cohesiveness in groups.

Instructions:

1. Read each of the items below. For each, decide which of the ways of building cohesion it most closely resembles. Some may be combinations of one or more.
2. Justify your answer.

Ways of building cohesion:

shared/compatible goals	**outside threat**
progress toward goals	**lack of perceived internal threats**
shared norms and values	**shared group experiences**
interdependence	**mutual perceived attractiveness and friendship**

1. A husband and wife are planning a budget so they can purchase a home.

Greater cohesion could result from this because it is

However, cohesion wouldn't necessarily result because

2. A group of students are banning together to prevent tuition hikes threatened by the Board of Regents.

Greater cohesion could result from this because it is

However, cohesion wouldn't necessarily result because

3. A group of cousins decides to go camping together.

Greater cohesion could result from this because it is

However, cohesion wouldn't necessarily result because

4.   A team went from all loses last year to 4-4 this year.

Greater cohesion could result from this because it is

However, cohesion wouldn't necessarily result because

5.   A group of students must work together and they will all get only one grade on their project.

Greater cohesion could result from this because it is

However, cohesion wouldn't necessarily result because

6.   A family goes on a vacation.

Greater cohesion could result from this because it is

However, cohesion wouldn't necessarily result because

7.   A group of families in a neighborhood decides to clear a vacant lot to create a place for their children to play sports.

Greater cohesion could result from this because it is

However, cohesion wouldn't necessarily result because

Name _____   _____

CHAPTER 9 ACTIVITY 4 GROUP COHESION CASE STUDY

Purpose:

To apply information about group cohesion.

Instructions:

Read the case study below and answer the questions.

> A group of business students decides to form an investment club to learn more about the stock market and investments, and to contribute small amounts of money ($10-25) each month to be invested as a group. Mark and Maria came up with the idea and recruit some other students — Dan, Jana, and Jin-Sook. They realize the optimal number for an investment group is 12-15, so each agrees to recruit two or three more persons. A meeting time is set, and the group discusses ways to get started. There are other organizations in town they can learn from. There are national organizations that you can affiliate with and use their materials, get their newsletters, etc.

1. What factors are already at work to promote cohesion?

2. At this point, if you were an advisor to the club, and you wanted to promote cohesiveness among group members, what four specific things would you recommend?

    1.

    2.

    3.

    4.

Your turn: If you want more cohesiveness in a group you belong to, what can you do? Choose one group and describe what you could do to promote cohesiveness.

Name _____

CHAPTER 9 ACTIVITY 5 EXPLORING THE WEB

Internet Resources: Virtual Teams

1. Read the article "Communication and Trust in Global Virtual Teams," from the <u>Journal of Computer Mediated Communication</u> at <u>www.ascusc.org/jcmc/vol3/issue4/jarvenpaa.html</u>
   Summarize the thesis of that article:

Where is this journal published?

2. What are some communication behaviors that would promote trust in global virtual teams?

3. Explore this site: <u>www.virtualteams.com</u>. What information and help is available for virtual teams?

Name _____

CHAPTER 9 SELF TEST

MATCHING Part One Match each term on the left with its correct definition from the column on the right.

_____ 1.   authoritarian leadership style

_____ 2.   brainstorming

_____ 3.   buzz groups

_____ 4.   coercive power

_____ 5.   cohesiveness

_____ 6.   conflict stage

_____ 7.   democratic leadership style

_____ 8.   emergence stage

_____ 9.   expert power

_____ 10. focus group

a. forces that cause members to feel part of a group and desire to remain in the group

b. group formed to conduct market or other research

c. A group stage in which members defend their positions and criticize other positions

d. creative way of generating a large number of ideas without criticism or ownership

e. style in which the designated leader used legitimate, coercive, and reward power to dictate the group's actions

f. ability to influence others by virtue of one's perceived superior skill

g. A group stage in which members move from conflict to solution

h. subgroups (of a group too large for effective discussion) that simultaneously discuss an issue.

i. A leadership style in which the leader invites a lot of group participation

j. influence over others by threat or unpleasant consequences

MATCHING Part Two Match each term on the left with its correct definition from the column on the right.

_____ 11. force field analysis

_____ 12. forum

_____ 13. group think

_____ 14. information overload

_____ 15. information power

_____ 16. information underload

_____ 17. laissez-faire leadership style

_____ 18. leader

_____ 19. leadership grid

_____ 20. legitimate power

a. a leader gives up the formal leader role, transforming the group into a loose collection of individuals

b. decline in efficiency that occurs when there is a shortage of information

c. Decline in efficiency that occurs when the complexity of information is too great to manage

d. ability to influence others by virtue of the otherwise obscure information one possesses

e. two-dimensional model that describes various combinations of a leader's concern with task-related and relational goals

f. discussion format in which audience members are invited to add their comments to those of official panelists

g. G method of problem analysis that identifies the forces contributing to resolution of the problem and the forces that inhibit its resolution

h. person identified by title as the leader of a group

i. ability to influence others due to your position

j. group's striving for unanimity that discourages realistic appraisals of alternatives

MATCHING Part Three Match each term on the left with its correct definition from the column on the right.

_____ 21. nominal group technique

_____ 22. nominal leader

_____ 23. orientation stage

_____ 24. panel discussion

_____ 25. parliamentary procedure

_____ 26. participative decision making

_____ 27. power

_____ 28. probative question

_____ 29. problem census

_____ 30. referent power

a. open question used to analyze a problem by encouraging exploratory thinking

b. ability to influence others by virtue of the degree to which one is liked or respected

c. person identified by title as group leader

d. one step in group development in which members become familiar with others' positions and tentatively state their own positions

e. a problem-solving method used to equalize participation in groups by having members put ideas on cards individually, then compiling them for a comprehensive look at an problem.

f. discussion format in which participants consider a topic conversationally, without formal procedural rules

g. problem-solving method in which specific rules govern the way issues may be discussed and decisions made

h. development of solutions with input by the people who will be affected

i. ability to influence others

j. a group procedure to allow persons to first work individually to get ideas out without criticism, then to rank the ideas, and then conduct a group discussion of top ideas.

MATCHING Part Four Match each term on the left with its correct definition from the column on the right.

_____ 31. Reinforcement stage

_____ 32. Reward power

_____ 33. Situational leadership

_____ 34 . Symposium

_____ 35. Trait theories of leadership

a. theory that states that the most effective leadership style varies according to leader-member relations, nominal leader's power, and task structure

b. belief that it is possible to identify leaders by personal characteristics (intelligence, appearance, sociability)

c. discussion format in which participants divide the topic to allow each to deliver in-depth information without interruptions

d. The step in group development in which members endorse the decision they've made.

e. ability to influence others by granting or promising of desirable consequences

MULTIPLE CHOICE Choose the BEST response from those listed.

1. Groups are often effective in problem-solving because they exhibit all of these EXCEPT

   a. greater resources.
   b. greater accuracy.
   c. greater commitment.
   d. greater speed.
   e. Groups have none of the above advantages.

2. Which question should be asked when trying to decide whether to use a group or individual approach to problem solving?

   a. Is the job beyond the capacity of one person?
   b. Are the individual's tasks interdependent?
   c. Is there more than one decision or solutions?
   d. Is there potential for disagreement?
   e. All of the above are valid questions to ask when deciding whether to use a group or individual approach.

3. Which type of problem-solving format is likely to use Robert's Rules of Order?

   a. parliamentary procedure
   b. panel discussion
   c. symposium
   d. forum
   e. Each of these typically follows Robert's Rules.

4. Which step is the first step in the structured problem-solving approach?

    a. analyze the problem
    b. develop creative solutions
    c. implement the plan
    d. identify the problem
    e. evaluate the solutions

5. Identifying specific tasks, determining necessary resources, defining individual responsibilities, and providing for emergencies are all part of which step of structured problem solving?

    a. analyze the problem
    b. develop creative solutions
    c. implement the plan
    d. identify the problem
    e. evaluate the solutions

6. Which of these is a probative question?

    a. Should we buy Macs or IBMs?
    b. What will we gain from new computer systems?
    c. Will the computers be paid for with cash or purchase orders?
    d. Resolved, that our company should purchase new computers.
    e. All of the above fall within the parameters of probative questions.

7. Probative questions and force field analysis are part of which step?

    a. analyze the problem
    b. develop creative solutions
    c. implement the plan
    d. identify the problem
    e. evaluate the solutions

8. Brainstorming guidelines include all of the following EXCEPT

    a. no criticism.
    b. encourage freewheeling.
    c. state your opposition clearly.
    d. seek quantity.
    e. combine and piggyback.

9. The difference between nominal group technique and brainstorming is that

    a. nominal groups allow members to work alone first.
    b. brainstorming allows criticism, nominal group doesn't.
    c. nominal groups seek quantity, brainstorming seeks quality.
    d. brainstorming involves ranking ideas; nominal groups don't rank.
    e. None of these is a difference.

10. Evaluating progress and revising the group's approach are part of which step?

    a. analyze the problem
    b. develop creative solutions
    c. implement the plan
    d. follow up on the solution
    e. evaluate the solutions

11. Which is true of the reinforcement stage of group problem-solving?
    a. Members take strong positions and defend them.
    b. Members are reluctant to take a stand.
    c. Members approach consensus and back off dogmatic positions.
    d. Members find reasons to endorse and support the decision.
    e. None of these describes the reinforcement stage.

12. Comments such as, "There are probably several ways we could approach this," and "I wonder what would happen if we tried a new computer system." are typical of which stage?

    a. orientation
    b. conflict
    c. emergence
    d. reinforcement
    e. These comments are typical of each stage.

13. There may be a lot of in-fighting within an organization, but when a perceived outside threat confronts the organization, the result is often

    a. organizational ineffectiveness.
    b. increased cohesiveness.
    c. decreased cohesiveness.
    d. contradictory feelings toward group leaders.
    e. none of the above

14. Which of these is true of power?

    a. Power is conferred by a group; it is not an individual possession.
    b. Power is distributed among group members; many members have different kinds of power.
    c. Power is usually a matter of degree, not an all or nothing proposition.
    d. All of these are true.
    e. None of these are true.

15. You like getting invited to the boss's office often and getting to spend time sharing ideas with her. The fact that she can grant this time may represent a type of

    a. coercive power.
    b. reward power.
    c. expert power.
    d. referent power.
    e. legitimate power.

16. Information overload

    a. contributes to the quality of group decisions by having more information.
    b. can be detrimental to a group.
    c. is less and less a problem for groups who gather research well.
    d. is usually less paralyzing to a group than information underload.
    e. is unheard of in today's information age.

17. Leadership is often examined in terms of

    a. trait analysis.
    b. leadership style.
    c. situational variables.
    d. all of the above
    e. none of the above

18. The Leadership Grid looks at the relationship between a leader's concern for

    a. referent and expert power issues.
    b. democratic and authoritarian issues.
    c. task and relational issues.
    d. cohesiveness and interdependence.
    e. none of the above

19. A leadership style that is laid back and not very involved is

    a. authoritarian.
    b. democratic.
    c. laissez-faire.
    d. trait analysis.
    e. none of the above

TRUE/FALSE Circle the T or F to indicate whether you believe the statement is true or false. If it is **true,** give a **reason** or an **example.** If it is false, **explain** what would make it true.

T F 1. In most cases, groups produce more and higher quality solutions to problems than do individuals working alone.

T F 2. In the emergence stage of problem solving, groups resolve their disagreements and solve their problem.

T F 3. Groupthink refers to the ideal level of cohesion.

T   F   4.   Participative decision-making often produces members less likely to accept solutions and less committed to the decision than non-participative decision-making.

T   F   5.   If there is more than one decision or solution, it is best not to have a group tackle the problem; groups do better with problems that have a single answer.

COMPLETION Fill in each of the blanks with a word from the lists provided. Choose the BEST word for each sentence. There are more words than you will use, but each word will be used only once.

group think	**laissez-faire**
nominal group technique	**power**
information underload	**force field analysis**
interdependent	

1.   Listing all of the items that would help and that would hinder a group in solving a problem is called

_____.

2.   A technique that works to get many people's ideas out in group problem-solving is called

_____.

3.   Excessive cohesiveness that often results in poor decision-making is called

_____.

4.   Group problem-solving works best if the members have tasks that are _____.

5.   In most groups, _____ is conferred by the group and distributed among its members.

CHAPTER 9 ANSWERS TO SELF TEST

MATCHING Set 1

1. e	2. d	3. h	4. j	5. a
6. c	7. i	8. g	9. f	10. b

MATCHING Set 2

11. g	12. f	13. j	14. c	15. d
16. b	17. a	18. h	19. e	20. i

MATCHING Set 3

21. j	22. c	23. d	24. f	25. g
26. h	27. i	28. a	29. e	30. b

MATCHING Set 4

31. d	32. e	33. a	34. c	35. b

MULTIPLE CHOICE

1. d	2. e	3. a	4. d	5. c
6. b	7. a	8. c	9. a	10. d
11. d	12. a	13. b	14. d	15. b
16. b	17. d	18. c	19. c	

TRUE/FALSE

1. True	2. True	3. False	4. False	5. False

COMPLETION

1. force field analysis
2. nominal group technique
3. groupthink
4. interdependent
5. power

Related Reading

"Twelve Step Recovery and PTSD" by Patience Mason from The Post-Traumatic Gazette Vol. 1 No. 3. September-October 1995. Published by Patience Press, P.O. Box 2757, High Springs, FL 32655 Available at www.patiencepress.com/samples/ptg3.pdf.

Preview

Look at any city's listing of self-help groups and you will find Alcoholics Anonymous, Al-Anon (for family and friends of Alcoholics), Overeater's Anonymous, and more. What these and many other self-help groups have in common is that they are Twelve-Step groups in which members recover from addiction or trauma by using a model based on the Twelve Steps of Alcoholics Anonymous. Recently, PTSD (Post-Traumatic Stress Disorder) groups have flourished to meet the needs of those who have endured and survived war, rape, and natural disasters. Since September 11, 2001, these groups are essential for many. In this article, Patience Mason, author of <u>Recovering From the War: A Woman's Guide to Helping Your Vietnam Veteran, Your Family, and Yourself</u>, and editor of <u>The Post-Traumatic Gazette</u>, a newsletter for friends, families, and therapists of trauma survivors, explains how Twelve-Step groups assist persons who want to recover. Groups are anonymous (using only first names), fluid (different people attend from meeting to meeting, often with a "core" of regulars who attend at a particular time and place), and self-governing. If you are familiar with or practice a Twelve-Step program, you'll probably feel at home with this reading. If you are unfamiliar with Twelve-Step groups, you may want to read the Twelve Steps (remembering that different groups substitute appropriate words for the word alcohol) before you read the article. As you read, strive to understand how Twelve-Step groups come to be so life changing and life saving for their members. Notice the unique nature of solving problems, distributing leadership, ensuring participation and building cohesiveness in Twelve-Step groups.

Review

1. What does the author say is the correlation between admitting powerless (as in the first step) and empowerment?

2. Compare and contrast the structured problem-solving approach in the text and the Twelve-Step approach to a person's particular problem.

3. Underline the words groups and meetings throughout the article. How does the author impress upon readers the importance of meetings to recovery?

4. What contradiction does the author point out in court-mandated attendance in groups and the only requirement for group membership?

5. How does the author's description of leadership distribution and member participation compare and contrast with the advice in the text book?

CHAPTER 10 CHOOSING AND DEVELOPING A TOPIC

CHAPTER 10 SKELETON OUTLINE

This outline can be a helpful study tool to assist you in seeing the order and sequence of the chapter and the relationship of ideas. Use it to take notes as you read and/or to add concepts presented in lecture.

I. Choosing a topic

    A. Look for a topic early

    B. Choose a topic of interest to you

II. Defining a purpose

    A. General purpose

        1. to entertain

        2. to inform

        3. to persuade

    B. Specific purpose

        1. purpose statement is receiver oriented

        2. purpose statement is specific

        3. purpose statement is realistic

    C. Thesis statement

        1. Is the central idea of the speech

        2. Is delivered to the audience

III. Analyzing the speaking situation

    A. Listeners (audience analysis & adapting to audience)

        1. audience type

            a) passersby

            b) captives

            c) volunteers

        2. audience purpose

        3. demographics

            a) number of people

            b) gender

            c) age

            d) group membership

            e) other factors

        4. attitudes, beliefs, values

            a) attitudes

           b) beliefs

           c) values

   B. Occasion

       1. time

           a) time relates to other internal and external events

           b) time available

       2. place

       3. audience expectation

IV. Gathering Information

   A. Internet research

       1. Searching web sites

       2. evaluating web sites

           a) credibility

           b) objectivity

           c) currency

   B. Library research

       1. library catalog

       2. reference works

       3. periodicals

       4. nonprint materials

       5. databases

       6. librarians

   C. Interviewing

   D. Personal observation

   E. Survey research

CHAPTER 10 KEY TERMS

This list of key terms corresponds to those in boldface in your text. In your own words write a definition and an original example of the word.

attitude

audience analysis

belief

database

demographics

general purpose

purpose statement

search string

specific purpose

survey research

thesis statement

value

Name _____

CHAPTER 10 ACTIVITY 1 SPEECH TOPICS

Purpose:

To explore interests and activities for possible speech topics.

Instructions:

Fill in the blanks below with as much information as you can.

What news stories in the past year have been of interest to you?

What are your favorite books?

What magazines do you read regularly?

What magazines interest you even if you do not find time to read them regularly?

What local events have fascinated you?

What makes your family interesting, unusual, or unique?

What travel experiences have you had?

What activities do you participate in regularly?

What activities would you like to participate in but time or cost prohibits you?

What volunteer or service learning experiences have you had?

What jobs have you had?

List all the hobbies you have, even if you don't have as much time for them as you'd like.

What other hobbies have you pursued and been active in in the past?

What spiritual beliefs do you hold?

What beliefs do you hold with great intensity? [vegetarianism, world population, anti-materialism, pro or anti-military, environmentalist]

What activities do you regularly engage in? [Think of the mundane as well as the special: grocery shopping, car repairs, fitness center]

What awards have you ever received?

What probably makes you different from almost everyone in the class?

What common interests do you think you have with most everyone else in the class?

What experiences have you had as a teen or child that many people didn't have?

Now, look over your lists. Which of these topics could become speech topics? List at least five potential topics.

      to inform   to persuade   to entertain

It might be helpful to show your answers and your lists to a few classmates. Ask them to put a star beside topics they would like to hear you speak on.

Name _____

CHAPTER 10 ACTIVITY 2 GENERAL PURPOSES, PURPOSE STATEMENTS, AND THESIS STATEMENTS

Purpose:

To ascertain the correlation between general purposes, purpose statements, and thesis statements.

Instructions:

1.   For each purpose statement, tell the general purpose of the speech [inform, persuade, entertain].
2.   Then, construct a possible thesis for that speech.

1.   After hearing my speech, audience members will be able to describe five characteristics of the U.S. federal income tax.

This purpose statement is probably for a speech to _____.

A possible thesis statement would be:

2.   After hearing my speech on the top four reasons to participate in karaoke singing, the audience will join me in a sing-a-long.

This purpose statement is probably for a speech to _____.

A possible thesis statement would be:

3.   At the conclusion of my speech on the importance of corresponding with government officials, at least 15 audience members will pick up envelopes addressed to their Congressional representatives and write each a letter.

This purpose statement is probably for a speech to _____.

A possible thesis statement would be:

4.   After my presentation, audience members will understand four ways to be kind to the environment and be able to recite and explain the phrase: "Reuse, reduce, make do, go without."

This purpose statement is probably for a speech to _____.

A possible thesis statement would be:

5. Throughout my speech, I want my audience to laugh often and loudly and know that we Swedes have a sense of humor.

This purpose statement is probably for a speech to _____.

A possible thesis statement would be:

6. By the end of the week after hearing my speech, at least 50% will go to human resources and sign up for disability insurance.

This purpose statement is probably for a speech to _____.

A possible thesis statement would be:

7. After hearing my speech on what a mill levy is, students will be able to define a mill levy and explain the importance of the mill levy to their own education.

This purpose statement is probably for a speech to _____.

A possible thesis statement would be:

8. After hearing my speech on the need for bone marrow donors to be registered in the national registry, all students will be able to describe the need and use for bone marrow and at least five will pick up registry forms and information.

This purpose statement is probably for a speech to _____.

A possible thesis statement would be:

Name: _____

CHAPTER 10 ACTIVITY 3 PURPOSE & THESIS STATEMENTS

Purpose:

To identify well and poorly written purpose statements.

Instructions Part One:

1.   For each of these purpose statements, tell whether it is
         A = a well-stated purpose statement
         B = not receiver-oriented
         C = not specific enough
         D = not realistic
2.   Rewrite any purpose statements that you marked b, c, or d, and correct the problem.

_____ 1.   At the conclusion of my speech, each member of the audience will purchase a package of Intergalactic Cheesecake.

_____ 2.   When I finish speaking, audience members will be better informed about Tae Bo workouts.

_____ 3.   At the end of my speech, the audience will know something about fat content of foods.

_____ 4.   When my presentation concludes, audience members will be able to cite five reasons for not allowing military recruiters in the high schools.

_____ 5.   At the conclusion of my speech, 50% of the audience given an exit survey will indicate that they plan to vote for my candidate.

_____ 6.   At the conclusion of my speech, a lot of the audience will prefer the idea of adoption rather than abortion.

_____ 7.   After my presentation, 60% of the students will be able to list at least three arguments for and three arguments against interracial adoption.

_____ 8.   By the time I finish speaking, audience members will be able to identify five sources of support for families who have a member with Alzheimer's disease.

Instructions Part Two:

For each of these outlines, write a possible thesis statement.

Example:

Topic: Economic well-being

Major points: I.   pay off credit cards
                      II. participate in company retirement plans
                      III. create cash reserves

Possible thesis: <u>Ensure your economic well-being by paying off credit cards, joining retirement plans, and creating a cash reserve.</u>

1. Topic: Martial arts training

Major points: I.   mental benefits
                     II. physical benefits
                     III. safety benefits

Possible thesis:

2. Topic: Child care dilemmas

Major points: I.   costs for parents
                     II. trust and safety for child
                     III. location and transportation

Possible thesis:

3. Topic: Aromatherapy
Major points: I.   definition
                     II. possible advantages
                     III. possible disadvantages

Possible thesis:

4. Topic: Levels of political action

Major points: I.   vote
                       II. letters to representatives
                       III. run for office

Possible thesis:

5. Topic: Investment strategies for college students

Major points: I.   stocks
                       II. bonds
                       III. mutual funds

Possible thesis:

6. Topic: Taking your general electives at community colleges

Major points: I.   lower cost
                       II. smaller classes (individual attention)
                       III. transferability

Possible thesis:

7. Topic: Tattooing around the world

Major points: I.   Historical records of tattoos
                       II. Reasons for tattoos
                       III. Methods of tattooing

Possible thesis:

8. Topic: Service learning on college campuses
Major points: I.   origin
                       II. benefits for students
                       III. benefits for community

Possible thesis:

Name: _____

(Group) CHAPTER 10 ACTIVITY 4 DEMOGRAPHIC ANALYSIS

Purpose:

1. To investigate the demographics of this class as part of an audience analysis.
2. To complete a demographic survey.

Instructions:

1. Complete the following information.
2. Share and tabulate the information as a class or turn in the pages to one group or individual who agrees to tabulate the information and report it to the whole class.
3. Use the "CLASS DEMOGRAPHICS: TALLY SHEET" at the end of this exercise to fill in the results. You will use this information again for an exercise in Chapter 12.

_____ Male   _____ Female

Age category: ____ 18-24   ____ 25-30   ____ 31-40   ____ 41-50   ____ over 50

Year in school: ____ first year   ____ sophomore   ____ junior   ____ senior

____ already have a four-year degree, just taking the course

Major:

Ethnic background:

Group membership: List groups that you belong to that are important to you, including, but not limited to, fraternities/sororities, honor societies, religious groups, and athletic groups.

Group name/type   Group name/type

Group name/type   Group name/type

Primary reason for taking the class:

____ It is required for my major or degree.

____ I needed something at this time.

____ I needed it to prepare for/advance in my career.

____ It looked interesting.

____ Other :

CLASS DEMOGRAPHICS: TALLY SHEET

Numbers: The class consists of a total of

_____ students, _____ instructors, _____ teaching assistants.

Gender: The class consists of _____ males and _____ females.

Age: The class consists of the following number of students in each age category (put the number in front of each category):

_____ 18-24   _____ 25-30   _____ 31-40   _____ 41-50   _____ over 50

Year in school: _____ first year   _____ sophomore   _____ junior   _____ senior

_____ already have a four-year degree, just taking the course

Major: List major categories and lump those with few students together under "other."

Major: _____ Number

Major: _____ Number

Major: _____ Number

Major: _____ Number

Major: _____ Number

Other: _____ Number

Ethnic background:

Ethnic background: _____ Number

Ethnic background: _____ Number

Ethnic background: _____ Number

Ethnic background: _____ Number

Ethnic background: _____ Number

Groups:

Group name/type: _____ Number

Group name/type: _____ Number

Group name/type: _____ Number

Group name/type: _____ Number

Group name/type: _____ Number

Group name/type: _____ Number

Primary reasons for taking this class:

_____ major/degree   _____ time   _____ career   _____ interest   _____ other

SUMMARY

What general conclusions have you drawn about this audience?

How will these affect your selection and preparation of a speech topic?

Name: _____

CHAPTER 10 ACTIVITY 5 EXPLORING THE WEB

Purpose:

To compare search engines and evaluate web sites.

Instructions:

1. After reading the descriptions of the major search engines in Chapter 10, choose four of them. Select a potential speech topic, search the topic, and compare the results.

Topic:

Search engine used	Number of hits	Value of sites, remarks

2. **Evaluating web sites** Your text walks you through the process of evaluating web sites. Choose three sites with different domains (.com, .gov, .org, .edu) that you found for a potential topic. Answer the following for each site:

Site 1:

<u>Credibility:</u>

Can you tell who wrote the page?

If so, who?

Are the authors' credentials listed? _____ If so, what are they?

Do the credentials qualify them to write this document?

Is there a way to contact the pages' authors? _____ If so, how? E-mail? Phone? Address?

What institution publishes the document?

<u>Objectivity:</u>

Looking at the domain part of the address, identify whether the site is a commercial, government, organizational, or educational site (usually identifiable by .com, .gov, .org, or .edu). What type of site is it?

What biases may exist because of this?

Looking at the authors' credentials, what biases might exist?

<u>Currency</u>

Can you tell when the page was produced? _____ When?

When was it last updated?

As you try the links from the page, how many or what percent work?

How many or what percent are dead?

Site 2:

<u>Credibility:</u>

Can you tell who wrote the page?

If so, who?

Are the authors' credentials listed? _____ If so, what are they?

Do the credentials qualify them to write this document?

Is there a way to contact the pages' authors? _____ If so, how? E-mail? Phone? Address?

What institution publishes the document?

<u>Objectivity:</u>

Looking at the domain part of the address, identify whether the site is a commercial, government, organizational, or educational site (usually identifiable by .com, .gov, .org, or .edu). What type of site is it?

What biases may exist because of this?

Looking at the authors' credentials, what biases might exist?

<u>Currency</u>

Can you tell when the page was produced? _____ When?

When was it last updated?

As you try the links from the page, how many or what percent work?

How many or what percent are dead?

Site 3:

<u>Credibility:</u>

Can you tell who wrote the page?

If so, who?

Are the authors' credentials listed? _____ If so, what are they?

Do the credentials qualify them to write this document?

Is there a way to contact the pages' authors? _____ If so, how? E-mail? Phone? Address?

What institution publishes the document?

<u>Objectivity</u>:

Looking at the domain part of the address, identify whether the site is a commercial, government, organizational, or educational site (usually identifiable by .com, .gov, .org, or .edu). What type of site is it?

What biases may exist because of this?

Looking at the authors' credentials, what biases might exist?

<u>Currency</u>

Can you tell when the page was produced? _____ When?

When was it last updated?

As you try the links from the page, how many or what percent work?

How many or what percent are dead?

Name: _____

CHAPTER 10 SELF TEST

MATCHING Match each term on the left with its correct definition from the column on the right.

_____ 1.   attitude

_____ 2.   audience analysis

_____ 3.   belief

_____ 4.   database

_____ 5.   demographics

_____ 6.   general purpose

_____ 7.   purpose statement

_____ 8.   specific purpose

_____ 9.   string search

_____ 10. survey research

_____ 11. thesis statement

_____ 12. value

a.   a technique for electronic searches in which several words are put together with precise linking words

b.   a complete sentence describing the central idea of a speech

c.   the precise effect that the speaker wants to have on an audience, expressed in the form of a purpose statement

d.   a consideration of characteristics including the type, goals, demographics, beliefs, attitudes, and values of listeners

e.   one of three basic ways a speaker seeks to affect an audience: to entertain, inform, or persuade

f.   audience characteristics that can be analyzed statistically, such as age, gender, education, group membership, and so on

g.   a deeply rooted belief about a concept's inherent worth

h.   an underlying conviction about the truth of an idea, often based on cultural training

i.   information gathering in which the response of a sample of a population are collected to disclose information about the larger group

j.   a computerized collection of information that can be searched in a variety of ways to locate information

k.   predisposition to respond to an idea, person, or thing favorably or unfavorably

l.   a complete sentence that describes precisely what a speaker wants to accomplish

MULTIPLE CHOICE Choose the BEST response from those listed.

1. When choosing a topic for a speech, your text suggests it is best to

    a. choose a topic about which you know nothing so your topic will be fresh.
    b. choose a topic which you are not really interested in so you empathize with the audience and develop their interest.
    c. delay your choice as long as possible so that you spend as much time as you can searching for a good topic.
    d. choose a topic that interests you so you can make it interesting for others.
    e. choose a topic you've already written an essay on so you can just present the essay.

2. Which is NOT a general purpose?

    a. to inform
    b. to persuade
    c. to review
    d. to entertain
    e. All are general purposes.

3. Which is true of a general speech purpose?

    a. Most speeches have ONLY ONE purpose.
    b. Purposes are interrelated and cumulative.
    c. The general purpose is expressed in a purpose statement.
    d. The general purpose is the same as a specific purpose.
    e. All of the above are true.

4. Which is an effective purpose statement?

    a. The purpose of my speech is to inform.
    b. After my speech, the audience will be able to list four reasons why young people join gangs.
    c. My purpose is to inform you about crime and persuade you to stay out of gangs.
    d. The purpose is to inform the audience about crime.
    e. I want to tell my audience about the purpose of the Patriot Act.

5. An effective purpose statement

    a. is realistic.
    b. is specific.
    c. is receiver-oriented.
    d. does all of the above.
    e. does none of the above.

6. Which is the best thesis statement?

    a. Changing the way we fund campaigns will benefit candidates and voters.
    b. Adapting to a new CEO is like changing a tire.
    c. College students. In my audience will know how to use a search engine.
    d. After my speech the officers (audience) will be able to distinguish a bribery overture from innocent small talk.
    e. I want to tell the audience about radial keratotomy surgery.

7. Passerbys, captives, and volunteers refer to

    a. types of audiences.
    b. types of general purposes.
    c. types of speakers.
    d. types of occasions.
    e. types of specific purposes.

8. With regard to audience purpose, it is generally reasonable to say

    a. all members are always there for the same purpose.
    b. there may be a variety of purposes for listening within an audience.
    c. gender is generally the best predictor of purpose.
    d. audience demographics have no correlation to audience purpose.
    e. None of these is true.

9. Which of these is **not** a demographic factor?

    a. number of people
    b. age
    c. speech purpose
    d. gender
    e. group memberships

10. A predisposition to respond to something in a favorable or unfavorable way is a/an

    a. belief.
    b. demographic.
    c. attitude.
    d. purpose.
    e. value.

11. Your text cites five values shared by most U.S. Americans. Which is **not** one of them?

    a. good citizenship
    b. materialism
    c. tolerance of political views
    d. individualism
    e. work ethic

12. When considering time as part of an audience analysis, a speaker should include which of these?

    a. consider how much time you have been allotted or assigned
    b. consider what world or local events might be occurring the same day as your speech
    c. consider whether it is morning or after lunch, beginning or end of some shared segment of time (semester, retreat), or national or religious holiday
    d. All of these are valid time considerations.
    e. None of these is what is meant by considering time as part of audience analysis.

13. "The group I will be speaking to is composed of mostly Euroamerican, middle-class males who have been successful in business. Most are middle-aged and college-educated." Those statements are typical of statements from

   a. a specific purpose.
   b. a general purpose.
   c. an audience analysis.
   d. a speaker analysis.
   e. a thesis statement.

14. Which of these could be used for research for a speech?

   a. database
   b. search engine
   c. web site
   d. periodical
   e. all of the above

15. Reviewing your interests is a good step to take when

   a. analyzing the audience.
   b. analyzing the speaking situation.
   c. choosing a topic.
   d. organizing your speech.
   e. It is not helpful for any of these tasks.

TRUE/FALSE Circle the T or F to indicate whether you believe the statement is true or false. If it is **true,** give a **reason** or an **example.** If it is false, **explain** what would make it true.

T F 1. Personal experience should never be used for research for a speech.

T F 2. If your speech is very good, there is no need to consider what other speakers may say before you or what recent events the audience may be concerned with.

T F 3. Research for a speech is not limited to books and articles; it may include several non-print sources.

T F 4. A good specific purpose statement will be oriented toward the listeners.

T F 5. A thesis statement is purposefully vague.

COMPLETION Fill in each of the blanks with a word from the lists provided. Choose the BEST word for each sentence. There are more words than you will use, but each word will be used only once.

actions	entertain
persuade	interview
time	audience
attitudes	analyze

1. You can often make an inference about audience _____ by identifying their beliefs and values.

2. In preparing a speech, the speaker should analyze the _____ and the occasion.

3. _____, place, and audience expectation are three key elements of audience analysis.

4. A non-print research source for a speech is a/an _____.

5. An after-dinner speech probably has as its primary purpose to _____.

CHAPTER 10 ANSWERS TO SELF TEST

MATCHING

1.	k	2.	d	3.	h	4.	j	5.	f
6.	e	7.	l	8.	c	9.	a	10.	i
11.	b	12.	g						

MULTIPLE CHOICE

1.	d	2.	c	3.	b	4.	b	5.	d
6.	a	7.	a	8.	b	9.	c	10.	c
11.	b	12.	d	13.	c	14.	e	15.	c

TRUE/FALSE

1.	False	2.	False	3.	True	4.	True	5.	False

COMPLETION

1.	attitudes	2.	audience	3.	time
4.	interview	5.	entertain		

Related Reading

President George W. Bush, "Address to a Joint Session of Congress and the American People" presented September 20, 2001 at the U.S. Capitol and carried on live television. Retrieve from www.whitehouse.gov/news/releases/2001/09/20010920-8.html.

Preview

The unprecedented events of September 11, 2001 created unique needs and opportunities for public addresses by government leaders at many levels. President Bush needed to present the right tone, the right message, and the right attitude in his presentation. As you read this address, consider the nature of the audience that night: the Congress, the U.S. population, and the rest of the world.

Review

1. Although the topic may seem self-evident, within the broad topic of the events of September 11, how did the president narrow the topic?

2. What audiences was President Bush speaking to? Can you point to any lines that indicate he is directly addressing one of the many audiences?

3. Do you remember where you were on this occasion? Did you listen to this speech? By radio? Television? What do you think were the greatest needs of this occasion?

4. How successful do you think the President was in accomplishing his goals?

5. State the general purpose, the specific purpose, and the thesis statement of this speech.

CHAPTER 11 ORGANIZATION AND SUPPORT

CHAPTER 11 SKELETON OUTLINE

This outline can be a helpful study tool to assist you in seeing the order and sequence of the chapter and the relationship of ideas. Use it to take notes as you read and/or to add concepts presented in lecture.

I.   Structuring the speech

    A. Working outlines

    B. Formal outlines

    C. Speaking notes

II. Principles of outlining

    A. Standard symbols

    B. Standard format

    C. Rule of division

    D. Rule of parallel wording

III. Organizing in logical order

    A. Time patterns and climax patterns

    B. Space patterns

    C. Topic patterns

    D. Problem–solution patterns

    E. Cause–effect patterns

    F. Motivated sequence

        1. attention step

        2. need step

        3. satisfaction step

        4. visualization step

        5. action step

IV. Using transitions

    A. Internal previews and reviews

    B. Functions

        1. how introduction relates to body

        2. how one main point relates to next main point

        3. how supporting points relate to main point

        4. how subpoints relate to points they are a part of

V.   Beginning and ending the speech

    A. Introduction

      1.   capture attention

          a)   refer to audience

          b)   refer to occasion

          c)   refer to relationship of audience and subject

          d)   refer to something familiar

          e)   cite startling fact or opinion

          f)   ask a question

          g)   tell an anecdote

          h)   use a quotation

          i)   tell a joke

      2.   preview main points

      3.   set the mood and tone

      4.   demonstrate topic's importance

   B. Conclusion

      1.   functions

          a)   review thesis (summary statement)

          b)   review main points

          c)   provide memorable final remark

      2.   mistakes to avoid

          a)   ending abruptly

          b)   rambling

          c)   introducing new points

          d)   apologizing

VI. Supporting Material

   A. Functions

      1.   to clarify

      2.   to add interest

      3.   to make memorable

      4.   to prove

   B. Types

      1.   definitions

      2.   examples

          a)   factual

          b)   hypothetical

      3.   statistics

        4.   analogies/comparison–contrast

        5.   anecdotes

        6.   quotations/testimonies

   C. Styles of support

        1.   narration

        2.   citation

VII. Using visual aids

   A. Types

        1.   objects and models

        2.   diagrams

        3.   word and number charts

        4.   pie charts

        5.   bar and column charts

        6.   line charts

   B. Media for presentation

        1.   chalkboard, white board, polymer marking surface

        2.   flip pad/poster board

        3.   handout

        4.   projector

        5.   other electronic media

   C. Rules for use

        1.   simplicity

        2.   size

        3.   attractiveness

        4.   appropriateness

        5.   reliability

CHAPTER 11 KEY TERMS

This list of key terms corresponds to those in boldface in your text. In your own words write a definition and an original example of the word.

analogies

anecdote

bar chart

basic speech structure

cause-effect patterns

citation

climax pattern

column charts

conclusion (of a speech)

diagram

example

formal outline

hypothetical examples

introduction (of a speech)

line chart

models

motivated sequence

narration

number chart

pie chart

problem-solution pattern

space pattern

statistics

testimony

time pattern

topic pattern

transitions

visual aids

word chart

working outline

Name _____

CHAPTER 11 ACTIVITY 1 PARALLEL WORDING AND FORMAT

Purpose:

To practice parallel wording for outlines.

Instructions Part One:

Rewrite each of the following main points in a parallel fashion.

Example:

> The family of the 21st century will probably have experienced divorce.
>
> Twenty-first-century families may have children through increased fertility technology.
>
> More families in the next century will be interracial.

Rewritten in parallel form:

Twenty-first-century families will likely be divided by divorce.

Twenty-first-century families will likely be expanded by fertility technology.

Twenty-first-century families will likely be enriched by interracial connections.

1. You should never leave your car doors unlocked.

    Be sure to carry a flashlight and flares.

    Don't ever travel without adequate pre-trip maintenance to your vehicle.

Rewritten in parallel form:

2. Future goals for humankind should be to end warfare and violence.

    To survive, the world needs to understand and build a global community to prevent famine.

    The environment is the greatest concern of this century.

Rewritten in parallel form:

3. Education must include fluency in several languages.

    Without computer skills, there is no point in other education.

    The whole point of any education is to learn how to learn.

Rewritten in parallel form:

Instructions Part Two:

1. Read the sentences below and figure out which is the thesis statement.
2. Write that sentence on the line indicated.
3. Now, put the remaining sentences in correct outline form.

Community agencies gain stronger connections with college resources and personnel.

Service Learning benefits faculty and classrooms.

Service Learning benefits students, the community, and faculty.

Students discover the correlation between theory and practice.

Service Learning benefits students academically and personally.

Students return to the classroom and provide faculty and other students with real-life examples.

Service Learning benefits community agencies.

Students bring enthusiasm, talents, and hours of service to agencies.

Faculty members become aware of new areas for research and societal connections to academic areas.

Students develop networks for personal interests and possible career choices.

Thesis statement:

Outline:

Name _____

CHAPTER 11 ACTIVITY 2 LOGICAL ORDER

Purpose:

To practice various outline forms.

Instructions Part One:

Using "my life" as the topic (or pick someone else's life that you are familiar with, either a public figure or other individual you are familiar with), show a thesis statement and three or four main points for each of the following types of outlines.

Example:
Space pattern

      Thesis: <u>I've lived in several parts of the country, and learned something from each one.</u>

    I.   <u>In Texas, I learned country dance and the secret of barbecue.</u>

    II.   <u>In Maine, I learned to sail and appreciate sunrises.</u>

    III. <u>In Minnesota, I learned to make rosettes and canoe the boundary waters.</u>

Time pattern

    Thesis:

    I.

    II.

    III.

Space pattern

    Thesis:

    I.

    II.

    III.

Topic pattern

    Thesis:

    I.

    II.

    III.

Instructions Part Two:

Choose your city, your university, or another city or university you are familiar with and show a thesis and main points for these types of outlines.

Problem–solution

    Thesis:

    I.

    II.

    III.

Cause–effect

    Thesis:

    I.

    II.

    III.

Name _____

CHAPTER 11 ACTIVITY 3 INTRODUCTIONS

Purpose:

To identify various types of introductory techniques.

Instructions:

1. Read each of the introductory statements below.
2. For each, identify the type of introductory technique being used.
3. Write the type of technique on the line. If you think the statement is a combination of two techniques, write both on the line.

Techniques:

Refer to the audience

Refer to the relationship between audience and subject

Refer to something familiar to the audience

Cite a startling fact or opinion

Ask a question

Tell an anecdote

Use a quotation

Tell a joke

1. "If I were an American and you were an American audience, I would probably begin my speech with a joke. If I were Japanese speaking to a Japanese audience, I would probably begin with an apology. Since I am neither American nor Japanese, I will begin with an apology for not telling a joke." — R. Moran

Introductory technique:

2. Today is a very special day in the lives of these young people seated before us. It is a day they will always refer to as their graduation day.

Introductory technique:

3. William Butler Yeats said, "Education is not filling a bucket but lighting a fire." These words give us much to ponder tonight as we debate the future of this educational institution.

Introductory technique:

4. The number one fear of most Americans is public speaking! That's right. In surveys of U.S. Americans, the fear of public speaking even ranked above the fear of dying.

Introductory technique:

5. As I begin my after-dinner speech tonight, I'd like to ask: How many of you know the fat content or number of grams of fat in the meal we just ate together?

Introductory technique:

6. On September 11, 2001, the world mourned for the 3,000 people killed in the terrorist attacks on our country. That same day, over 30,000 people died of preventable causes. These 30,000 people didn't have 24-hour television coverage to talk about the causes of their deaths. They weren't the subject of statements by powerful political figures. Donors didn't spring into action to meet their needs. That day and every day since, 30,000 children die of diseases for which we have vaccinations and hunger.

Introductory technique:

Name _____

CHAPTER 11 ACTIVITY 4 SUPPORTING MATERIALS

Purpose:

To identify and classify types of supporting materials.

Instructions Part One:

Match each selection with its correct label.

examples   analogies

descriptions   anecdotes

definitions   statistics

_____ 1. $35 provides clean water for 40 refugees. $100 provides antibiotics for 40 wounded children. $500 provides 1,000 people with emergency sanitation materials.

_____ 2.   Sleeping sickness is transmitted from person to person by the tsetse fly with devastating effects. Once infected, victims become feverish and weak and their thinking is distorted. They are literally overcome by sleep, losing all control over sleeping and waking cycles. Eventually, sleep turns into coma, coma to death.

_____ 3.   Doctors Without Borders responds to natural disasters. In November 1995, North Korea was hit with severe floods followed closely by subzero weather. Doctors Without Borders provided emergency medical supplies and care, supplementary nutrition, and health kits. In Pakistan and Bangladesh, similar assistance was provided.

_____ 4.   Sleeping sickness is like a silent killer.

_____ 5.   When the Blizzard of '96 struck the east coast, Dr. Evan Lee couldn't get to work at his Boston hospital. Not because of the snow — but because he was in Uganda, eradicating the deadly "sleeping sickness" as a Doctors Without Borders volunteer.

_____ 6.   Yellow fever is a lethal, mosquito-borne virus that causes death by massive bleeding from the eyes, nose, mouth, bladder, and other organs.

[Information from the Doctors Without Borders/Medecins Sans Frontieres Newsletter, March 1996.]

Instructions Part Two:

For each of the following, determine what types of supporting material you would need and give reasons for your choices.

1. A speech to persuade classmates to give to your favorite charity.

Types of supporting material I'd want to use:

Reasons:

2. A speech to explain differences between Van Gogh's and Rembrandt's styles.

Types of supporting material I'd want to use:

Reasons:

3. A speech to describe the advantages and disadvantages of using computers to create sets for films rather than constructing life-size sets.

Types of supporting material I'd want to use:

Reasons:

4. A speech to convince classmates to listen to your favorite type of music.

Types of supporting material I'd want to use:

Reasons:

5. A speech to help classmates understand the different types of vegetarian lifestyles.

Types of supporting material I'd want to use:

Reasons:

6. A speech to help classmates understand the prerequisites for medical school.

Types of supporting material I'd want to use:

Reasons:

Name: _____

CHAPTER 11 ACTIVITY 5 VISUALS

Purpose:

To practice constructing various types of visuals.

Instructions Part One:

1. Use the information gathered in the demographic survey in Chapter 10, Activity 4 in this manual.
2. Take some of that information and create each of the following in a way that would be useful for a visual aid for a speech.
3. To see a variety of pie, column and bar charts related to workplace injuries and illness go to www.bls.gov/iif/oshwc/osh/os/osch0026.pdf

Make a bar chart to show the number of males and females in your class.

Make a column chart to show the number of students in each age category.

Make either a bar or column chart to show the number of students classified as first year, sophomore, etc.

Make a word chart to show the majors of students in the class.

Make a pie chart showing the primary reasons students take this class.

Instructions Part Two:

Use the following information to create a line graph.

Announced layoffs from major corporations (Newsweek, February 26, 1996):

AT&T 1/96: 40,000
Boeing 2/93: 28,000
Chemical/Chase Manhattan 8/95: 12,000
Delta Air Lines 4/94: 15,000
Digital Equipment 5/94: 20,000
GTE 1/94: 17,000
IBM 7/93: 60,000
Nynex 1/94: 16,800
Sears 1/93: 50,000

Thousands of people laid off

1992   1996

Instructions Part Three:

Create your own visual. You are writing a speech to convince the audience that every dollar counts when donated to Doctors Without Borders (www.doctorswithoutborders.org). Decide on the best type of visual aid to convey the following information and create it.

$35 supplies a basic suture kit to repair minor shrapnel wounds

$70 provides clean water for 85 refugees a day

$100 provides antibiotics to treat nearly 40 wounded children

$250 supplies 175 days of high-protein food for malnourished children

$500 brings emergency medical supplies to aid 2,500 refugees for a month

Name: _____

CHAPTER 11 ACTIVITY 6 EXPLORING THE WEB

Using the Web to Analyze Supporting Material

Part One

Using one or more speeches found at the Great American Speeches (www.pbs.org/greatspeeches/) or History Channel (www.historychannel.com/speeches/) or Doctor's Without Borders (www.doctorswithoutborders.org/publications/speeches), find at least two examples of each type of supporting material listed below. Note the speaker and write the example on the lines provided.

1. Definitions:

    1.

    2.

    3.

2. Examples:

    1.

    2.

    3.

3. Analogies:

    1.

    2.

    3.

4. Anecdotes:

    1.

    2.

    3.

Part Two

Now, use one of the following sites to find statistics for a speech to inform the audience about the increasing diversity of the United States. Then write several sentences to show how you would translate the statistics into clear lines of a speech.

Fedstats: www.fedstats.gov

Census Bureau: www.census.gov

Bureau of Labor Statistics: http://stats.bls.gov/

Part Three

Choose a topic for an informative speech. (Use the topic you are actually giving a speech on in this class if possible.) Find two quotations that could be used for support, introduction, or conclusion using Bartlett's (www.bartleby.com/100). Write the quotations and authors below.

Topic:

Quotations:

    1.

    2.

Name: _____

CHAPTER 11 SELF TEST

MATCHING Part One Match each term on the left with its correct definition from the column on the right.

_____ 1. analogy

_____ 2. anecdote

_____ 3. bar chart

_____ 4. basic speech structure

_____ 5. cause–effect pattern

_____ 6. citation

_____ 7. climax pattern

_____ 8. column chart

_____ 9. conclusion (of a speech)

_____ 10. diagram

a. a style of presenting information without story or narration, just the facts

b. a brief story used to illustrate or support a point in a speech

c. line drawing that shows important components of an object

d. visual aid that compares two or more values by showing them as elongated horizontal rectangles

e. final structural unit of a speech which reviews main points and motivates audience to act or remember

f. visual aid that compares two or more values by showing them as elongated vertical rectangles

g. a division of a speech into introduction, body, and conclusion

h. speech organizing plan that demonstrates how one or more events result in another event

i. extended comparison that can be used as supporting material in a speech

j. a type of time pattern in which the arrangement of events builds suspense

MATCHING Part Two Match each term on the left with its correct definition from the column on the right.

_____ 11. example

_____ 12. formal outline

_____ 13. hypothetical example

_____ 14. introduction (of a speech)

_____ 15. line chart

_____ 16. model

_____ 17. Motivated Sequence

_____ 18. narration

_____ 19. number chart

_____ 20. pie chart

a. consistent format and set of symbols used to identify the structure of ideas

b. visual depictions of important statistics

c. a specific case used to demonstrate a general idea

d. visual aid consisting of a grid that maps out the direction of a trend by plotting a series of points

e. scaled representations of an object

f. visual aid that divides a circle into wedges, representing percentages of the whole

g. presentation of speech support material as a story

h. a type of problem-solution organizational pattern that includes attention, need, satisfaction, visualization and action steps.

i. example that asks an audience to imagine an object or event

j. first part of a speech which gets attention and previews main points

MATCHING Part Three Match each term on the left with its correct definition from the column on the right.

_____ 21. problem-solution pattern

_____ 22. space pattern

_____ 23. statistics

_____ 24. testimony

_____ 25. time pattern

_____ 26. topic pattern

_____ 27. transition

_____ 28. visual aid

_____ 29. word chart

_____ 30. working outline

a. numbers arranged to show how a fact or principle is true for a large number of cases

b. visual depictions of key facts

c. organizational pattern that describes an unsatisfactory state of affairs and then proposes a plan to remedy the problem

d. pattern of speech organization based on location

e. pattern of speech organization according to chronology

f. supporting material that proves or illustrates a point by citing an authoritative source

g. organizing scheme that arranges points according to logical types or categories

h. phrase that connects ideas in a speech by showing how one relates to the other

i. a tool used to build your speech, showing your constantly changing arrangement of ideas

j. general category of devices to show how things look, relate, or work

MULTIPLE CHOICE . Choose the BEST response from those listed

1. Which is a correct use of formal outline symbols?

a.	b.	c.	d.
I.	A.	I.	I.
A.	I.	a.	A.
B.	II.	b.	1.
II.	B.	II.	2.
A.	I.	a.	B.
B.	C.	b.	II.
a.	I.	III.	A.
b.	2.		B.

2. Healthy foods **need not be** tasteless.
Healthy foods **need not be** dull.
Healthy foods **need not be** costly.

The boldfaced parts of the above sentences illustrate the rule of

a. division.
b. parallel wording.
c. logical order.
d. chronological order.
e. none of the above

3. The climactic pattern tends to

    a. move the audience to action.
    b. overcome the effects of an anticlimactic introduction.
    c. create suspense.
    d. create the illusion of being ethical.
    e. all of the above

4. Which is NOT a function of a transition?

    a. support and explain main points
    b. show how the introduction correlates to the body
    c. make the correlation of the main point to the subpoint
    d. show how the supporting materials relate to the points they support
    e. make the connection of the main points to each other clear

5. Which of these is a transition?

    a. Tonight, I'd like to talk with you about the crime rate in our city.
    b. In addition to a rise in property crime, we're also seeing an increase in violent crime.
    c. Crime can be defined as any act which violates an established law.
    d. Imagine yourself coming home and finding your apartment ransacked, your computer and DVD player gone, and your windows smashed.
    e. So, follow these guidelines and protect yourself from crime!

6. Which of these is NOT an appropriate way to begin a speech?

    a. refer to the audience
    b. refer to the occasion
    c. cite a startling fact or opinion
    d. ask a question
    e. apologize for any upcoming errors

7. Which of these is NOT an appropriate concluding technique?

    a. use strong, memorable words
    b. restate the thesis
    c. review main points
    d. relate the subpoints to the main points
    e. All of these are a part of the conclusion.

8. According to your text, which of these is NOT a function of supporting material?

    a. to present new points
    b. to clarify points
    c. to make points interesting
    d. to make points memorable
    e. to prove a point

9. This quotation relates to the skill it takes to create which part of a speech? "A speech is like a love affair. Any fool can start it, but to end it requires considerable skill." — Lord Mancroft

    a. transition
    b. introduction
    c. body
    d. conclusion
    e. support material

10. The boldfaced part of Henry David Thoreau's remark, "The basic trick is to choose the right words and **put them in the right order**," relates most closely to the purpose of

    a. organizational patterns.
    b. supporting material.
    c. introductions.
    d. conclusions.
    e. definitions.

11. The best way to write effective transitions is to

    a. tell an anecdote.
    b. use a quotation.
    c. tell a joke.
    d. have good supporting material for the transition.
    e. show a connection or correlation between parts.

12. Which of these is NOT a type of supporting material?

    a. examples
    b. definitions
    c. statistics
    d. quotations
    e. organization

13. Which of these is an analogy?

    a. Each dollar spent for education saves the state money in the long run.
    b. Four thousand dollars was spent on education for each $8,000 that was spent on prisons.
    c. Spending money on prisons instead of education is like spending money to cure diseases that we could prevent.
    d. Dollar for dollar and dime for dime, we decrease the decency of our democracy.
    e. Imagine yourself in a prison cell instead of in a college classroom.

14. Visual aids can help the audience because they can show

    a. how things work.
    b. how things look.
    c. how things relate.
    d. all of the above
    e. none of the above

15. Which item gives correct advice about using visual aids?

   a. If you're going to use them, make them complex so they're worth the time and energy of both you and your audience.

   b. Keep them small so you can easily transport them and you won't have to worry about overwhelming yourself with visuals.

   c. Always use complete sentences on visuals; phrases alone aren't enough.

   d. Be sure the visual aid is directly related to your speech; a visual aid that is remotely related should not be used.

   e. Look at your visual aid when you display it and continue looking at it as you speak so your audience will follow your lead and look at it too.

MATCHING III (Motivated Sequence) Below is a short speech following the steps of the motivated sequence. Match the labels of the motivated sequence with the part that fulfills that purpose.

need   **attention**

action   **visualization**

satisfaction

_____ 1. If someone offered you a place to play in the sand and the sun, a place to relax and warm up, would you take it?

_____ 2. I know many of you are like me and feeling like it is necessary to get away from it all. You require a place to warm up for a while and a time and a place to give your brain a break from exams.

_____ 3. Good news! Student services and the credit union have teamed up just for you. During winter break, they are offering a four-day Caribbean adventure at a price even a student can afford.

_____ 4. Picture yourself on a cruise to the Bahamas, soaking up sun while your classmates shovel snow from their cars. Writing papers and taking exams will be far from your mind.

_____ 5. Sign up now for the student rates offered by the credit union on this cruise of a lifetime.

TRUE/FALSE Circle the T or F to indicate whether you believe the statement is true or false. If it is **true**, give a **reason** or an **example**. If it is false, **explain** what would make it true.

T   F   1. An outline contains main ideas and shows how they relate to each other and to the thesis.

T   F   2. Basic speech structure refers to chronological, problem–solution, topical, and cause–effect.

T   F   3. One purpose of a formal outline is to show the specific purpose of the speech.

T   F   4. The motivated sequence is a variation of the chronological outline pattern.

T   F   5. Statistics are a type of transition.

COMPLETION Fill in each of the blanks with a word from the lists provided. Choose the BEST word for each sentence.

statistics	hypothetical
description	transition
quotation	diagram
analogy	working outline

1. A/an _____uses word pictures so an audience can visualize an idea.

2. To say that one idea is like another idea is to use a/an _____.

3. When it isn't just someone's ideas you want to cite, but the entire memorable way she or he said it, you would choose to use a/an _____.

4. To make an idea more specific by making it numerical, it is best to support the idea by _____.

5. If an audience is asked to imagine something, rather than be told a true story, the example is _____.

CHAPTER 11 ANSWERS TO SELF TEST

MATCHING Part One

1. i	2. b	3. d	4. g	5. h
6. a	7. j	8. f	9. e	10. c

MATCHING Part Two

11. c	12. a	13. i	14. j	15. d
16. e	17. h	18. g	19. b	20. f

MATCHING Part Three

21. c	22. d	23. a	24. f	25. e
26. g	27. h	28. j	29. b	30. i

MULTIPLE CHOICE

1. d	2. b	3. c	4. a	5. b
6. e	7. d	8. a	9. d	10. a
11. e	12. e	13. c	14. d	15. d

MATCHING (Motivated Sequence)

1. attention	2. need	3. satisfaction
4. visualization	5. action	

TRUE/FALSE

1. True	2. False	3. False	4. False	5. False

COMPLETION

1. description	2. analogy	3. quotation
4. statistics	5. hypothetical	

Related Reading

Hill, Julie. "The Audience: Changing demographics. Changing faces . . . facing change." *Presentations.* November 1, 2000. (Retrieved January 4, 2005 from www.presentations.com/presentations/search/search_display.jsp?vnu_content_id=1105053. You may need to search from the www.presentations.com home page.)

Preview

Chapter 10 introduces the idea that speakers need to analyze their audiences and adapt presentations to them. Chapter 11 stresses the importance of using visual aids well. This reading follows up on these notions with more specific considerations for the speaker with regard to adapting visual aids to audience expectations.

Review

1. The author states (in the fifth paragraph) that over half of the job growth predicted for the next eight years will be in professions that require presentation skills. As you look at the professions listed, explain how presentations might be a big part of these professions.

2. What are the most important ways the author believes "powerful young people" will influence the requirements for the types of visual aids used in presentations?

3. The author claims that resistance to PowerPoint is greatest in academia, saying some university professors consider computer presentations "the devil incarnate." In your college experience, is there a correlation between the age of the professor and his or her use of PowerPoint?

4. Since audiences are not always homogeneous with regard to age, what advise is given for speaking to audiences of various generations?

5. Write a one-sentence paraphrase of the author's main point regarding the role of respect between audiences and speakers.

CHAPTER 12 PRESENTING YOUR MESSAGE

CHAPTER 12 SKELETON OUTLINE

This outline can be a helpful study tool to assist you in seeing the order and sequence of the chapter and the relationship of ideas. Use it to take notes as you read and/or to add concepts presented in lecture.

I.   Dealing with stage fright

    A. Facilitative and debilitative stage fright

    B. Debilitative stage fright sources

        1. previous negative experience

        2. irrational thinking (fallacies)

            a) catastrophic failure

            b) perfection

            c) approval

            d) overgeneralization

    C. Overcoming Debilitative Stage Fright

        1. Use nervousness to your advantage.

        2. Be rational about your fears.

        3. Maintain a receiver orientation

        4. Keep a positive attitude.

            a) Use positive statements

            b) Use visualization.

        5. Be prepared.

II.   Types of delivery

    A. Extemporaneous

        1. definition

        2. advantages/uses

        3. disadvantages

    B. Impromptu

        1. definition

        2. advantages/uses

        3. disadvantages

        4. points to remember

            a) use time

            b) be original

        c) observe and respond

        d) positive attitude

        e) brevity

  C. Manuscript

    1. definition

    2. advantages/uses

    3. disadvantages

    4. points to remember

        a) note differences from written messages

        b) use short paragraphs

        c) type appropriately

        d) paper details

        e) rehearse

        f) time, speed, ideas

  D. Memorized

    1. definition

    2. advantages/uses

    3. disadvantages

    4. important guideline: practice

III. Practicing the speech

  A. Talk through your speech

  B. Tape record your speech

  C. Present to people

  D. Present in context

IV. Guidelines for delivery

  A. Visual aspects

    1. appearance

    2. movement

        a) voluntary can replace involuntary

        b) contact with all

    3. posture

    4. facial expression

    5. eye contact

      B. Auditory aspects

          1. volume

          2. rate

          3. pitch

          4. articulation

              a) deletion

              b) substitution

              c) addition

              d) slurring

V. Offering constructive criticism

      A. Be positive

      B. Be substantive

CHAPTER 12 KEY TERMS

This list of key terms corresponds to those in boldface in your text. In your own words write a definition and an original example of the word.

addition

articulation

debilitative stage fright

deletion

extemporaneous speech

facilitative stage fright

fallacy of approval

fallacy of catastrophic failure

fallacy of overgeneralization

fallacy of perfection

impromptu speech

irrational thinking

manuscript speech

memorized speech

pitch

rate

slurring

substitution

visualization

Name _____

CHAPTER 12 ACTIVITY 1 DELIVERY STYLES

Purpose:

To distinguish among delivery styles and determine which style is best suited to a specific situation.

Instructions:

Read each situation and decide which delivery style would work best in the situation. Give your reasons based on information in the text.

Delivery styles:

memorized   impromptu

manuscript   extemporaneous

1.   Each student in your World History class is assigned a topic and must give a five-minute talk to explain and illustrate the concept for the rest of the class.

Preferred delivery style:

Reasons:

2.   You are a member of a campus transitional mentoring group, helping to mentor high school seniors and encourage them to attend college. You are asked to speak to various student organizations on campus to encourage their members to become mentors to high school students.

Preferred delivery style:

Reasons:

3.   The local radio station has asked you to present a one-minute public service announcement about an upcoming campus concert. It must be exactly one minute.

Preferred delivery style:

Reasons:

4. You are attending a meeting at work and there is discussion of switching to a new software program. Most people have not used the program, but are favorably impressed by the salesperson and inclined to switch. You used the program in your previous job with disastrous results and you want to share your experience and information to avoid what you think would be a costly mistake. The decision will be made at this meeting.

Preferred delivery style:

Reasons:

5. You are one of six finalists for a job that requires you to train customer service representatives. All six are being called back before the selection committee and asked to make a four-minute presentation on what customer service means in this particular position.

Preferred delivery style:

Reasons:

6. Your college is putting together a video collage of all student organizations to be shown to the community to help ease some tensions between the city and the college. Each group has a chance to film a two-minute message. You are asked to be the "speaker" for the two minutes for an organization you belong to.

Preferred delivery style:

Reasons:

Name _____

CHAPTER 12 ACTIVITY 2 VOCAL DELIVERY

Purpose:

To practice auditory aspects of delivery.

Instructions Part One:

1. Choose several paragraphs from three different news stories, one about an exciting event, one about a sad event, and one about a routine event.
2. Read each paragraph with the appropriate vocalics.
3. Then experiment with using a different emotional tone for each story; read the sad story with excitement, the exciting story with boredom, etc.
4. Answer the following questions:

What did you notice about these aspects of delivery as you tried to convey different tones?

Your volume?

Your pitch?

Your rate?

Your pauses?

Instructions Part Two:

1. Try to enact each scene below, using ONLY the word "mom" or "sis" or "grandma." Listen to yourself and record what you think is happening with your auditory aspects of delivery.
2. With a partner, practice saying the word "mom" as if you were saying it in these settings. Listen to your partner and record your observations. Then switch roles. Do these in random order and see if you can guess each situation, based on vocal characteristics.

1. You come home and are very excited about getting a new job, making the team, or some other big event. You can't wait to tell mom. How would you say "mom" as you burst in the house to tell her?

What did you notice about:

volume?

pitch?

rate?

2. You are really angry with your mom. She has just given you some news that you didn't like (told you she can't pay your tuition anymore, can't loan you her car tonight, can't make it to some event you were counting on her being at). You are frustrated and angry at this change of events. How would you say "mom"?

What did you notice about:

volume?

pitch?

rate?

3. You are scared. You just did something pretty awful that involves your mom and now you need to tell her (you dented her car, broke or ruined something of hers you had borrowed). You are scared and apprehensive, but you need to tell her. You approach her and say "mom."

What did you notice about:

volume?

pitch?

rate?

4. You are a two-year-old (or a twenty-two-year-old) and you are whining about not getting something you want. You want mom to buy something for you and she won't. You whine "mom."

What did you notice about:

volume?

pitch?

rate?

Variations:

1. Four students line up in the back of the room and each enacts one scenario. Without looking at them, can you identify which one is enacting which scene?

2. Instead of the word "mom," choose nonsense syllables or a word out of context (try "helicopter" or "picture frame"). Use these words in the same scenarios to listen for changes in auditory aspects of delivery.

Questions to consider:

1. Compared to others, I consider my volume to be (louder, softer, more varied, less varied) than others. The implications this has for speech delivery are:

2. Compared to others, I consider my rate to be (faster, slower, more varied, less varied) than others. The implications this has for speech delivery are:

3. Compared to others, I consider my pitch to be (higher, lower, more varied, less varied) than others. The implications this has for speech delivery are:

With regard to articulation, I know I have a tendency toward

□   deletion in words such as _____

□   substitution in words such as _____

□   addition in words such as _____

□   slurring in words such as _____

See text for examples of these common errors. Compare your lists with those of your classmates.

Name _____

CHAPTER 12 ACTIVITY 3 REWRITING IRRATIONAL FALLACIES

Purpose:

To become skilled at rewriting irrational fallacies.

Instructions:

1.   For each item of self-talk below, identify the type of fallacy it represents.
2.   Then rewrite the statements to demonstrate more reasonable and rational ideas that a speaker could say to himself or herself.

Fallacies:

fallacy of approval   fallacy of overgeneralization

fallacy of catastrophic failure   fallacy of perfection

1.   I just know I'll blow it. I'll likely start off bad and then never be able to get the delivery going.

Irrational fallacy:

Rewrite, using more rational thoughts:

2.   My visuals just aren't as good as Melissa's. The coloring isn't quite right, and one of my bar graphs is off-center.

Irrational fallacy:

Rewrite, using more rational thoughts:

3.   I'll probably get a dry mouth and turn red. It'll be obvious to everyone that I'm nervous and scared.

Irrational fallacy:

Rewrite, using more rational thoughts:

4.   I always blow it when something is real important — like the time I used the wrong name when introducing my boss.

Irrational fallacy:

Rewrite, using more rational thoughts:

5.   Tim probably won't like the PowerPoint and Jose won't like some of the sources I cite.

Irrational fallacy:

Rewrite, using more rational thoughts:

6.   Every time I get up in front of people I make a fool of myself. My ears always turn bright red.

Irrational fallacy:

Rewrite, using more rational thoughts:

7.   I'll probably bomb this speech. Then I won't have enough points for a "C." If I don't get a "C," I'll flunk out of school and never get an education.

Irrational fallacy:

Rewrite, using more rational thoughts:

8.   I never say what I want to in front of others. I always blow these opportunities.

Irrational fallacy:

Rewrite, using more rational thoughts:

Name _____

CHAPTER 12 ACTIVITY 4 CRITIQUING CLASSMATES

Purpose:

To consider the purpose and improve the process of critiquing classmates.

Instructions:

1. Read the paragraph below about critiquing your classmates.
2. Respond to the paragraph by answering the questions at the end.

In Chapter 7, you read about Jack Gibb's understanding of characteristics which promotes a defensive or a supportive climate. In critiquing your classmates, you will want to try to be perceived as supportive, which means being perceived as descriptive rather than evaluative, with empathy not neutrality, equality not superiority, spontaneous not manipulative, provisional not certain, and problem-oriented not controlling. Remember, there is less defensiveness when a person believes the evaluation given is appropriate for the context. When students are placed in the role of critiquing their classmates, there may be some discomfort with the role. However, the term critic need not have a negative connotation. You can be of help to your classmates, helping them focus on strengths as well as areas that could be improved. Often, describing what you saw and felt is helpful. Try to remember these guidelines:

1. Accent the praiseworthy and positive.

    Often speakers are so full of self-criticism for what they wish they'd done, should have done, didn't do, or did poorly, that they don't immediately see their strong points.

    Try using:

    I appreciated the way you . . .
    I liked your ability to . . .
    I think . . . is one of your real strengths as a speaker.
    You seemed relaxed as you spoke to us.
    Your introduction made me want to hear more.

2. Use I-language, which is descriptive, not evaluative.

    Tell what you actually observed, what information you took in through your senses. Sometimes description, not evaluation, is all that is needed. If you do evaluate, be sure to describe first so the person knows what you are referring to.

"I" LANGUAGE/DESCRIPTIVE	"YOU" LANGUAGE/EVALUATIVE
I couldn't hear you. I had no trouble hearing you.	You were/weren't loud enough.
I saw you speak from several different places.	You moved too much.
I felt upset when you used the word "girl" to refer to your secretary.	You were demeaning to women.
I was unclear about your main point.	You didn't make your points clear.
I could see your note cards being tapped and shuffled over and over.	You kept messing with your notes.
I felt offended by your comment on women.	You offended all women.

Try using:

I felt . . .
From my point of view . . .
I couldn't . . . (see, hear, understand, etc.)
It seemed to me . . .
My reaction was . . .

Your turn

1. What do you especially agree or disagree with from this section of the text?

2. What are some other guidelines or standards that you think should apply to classmates critiquing each other?

3. What do you especially appreciate from a classmate/critic?

4. What do you especially want a classmate/critic NOT to do?

5. Do you want different things from a classmate in an oral critique (given to the whole class) than in a written critique given privately only to you? Explain.

Discuss your answers with your classmates and find your areas of agreement.

Name _____

CHAPTER 12 ACTIVITY 5 EXPLORING THE WEB

Listening to Auditory Aspects of Famous Speeches

Go to The History Channel's speech archives at www.historychannel.com/speeches/speeches.html. Choose four speeches (from over 100 listed) that will give you a mixture of ethnicity, gender, decade, region, and nationality. Listen to each speech and describe the auditory characteristics of the speaker. Notice how the speaker uses volume, rate, pitch, and articulation. From what you hear, how do these characteristics impact the effectiveness of the speaker?

1.   Name of speaker:

Occasion/topic:

How does the speaker use

volume?

rate?

pitch?

articulation?

Note examples of deletion, substitution, addition, slurring, or accents or dialects. What impact did they have on credibility? Intelligibility? If you were able to watch the speech on video, also comment on the speaker's appearance, movement, posture, facial expression and eye contact.

2.   Name of speaker:

Occasion/topic:

How does the speaker use

volume?

rate?

pitch?

articulation?

Note examples of deletion, substitution, addition, slurring, or accents or dialects. What impact did they have on credibility? Intelligibility? If you were able to watch the speech on video, also comment on the speaker's appearance, movement, posture, facial expression and eye contact.

3.   Name of speaker:

Occasion/topic:

How does the speaker use

volume?

rate?

pitch?

articulation?

Note examples of deletion, substitution, addition, slurring, or accents or dialects. What impact did they have on credibility? Intelligibility? If you were able to watch the speech on video, also comment on the speaker's appearance, movement, posture, facial expression and eye contact.

4.   Name of speaker:

Occasion/topic:

How does the speaker use

volume?

rate?

pitch?

articulation?

Note examples of deletion, substitution, addition, slurring, or accents or dialects. What impact did they have on credibility? Intelligibility? If you were able to watch the speech on video, also comment on the speaker's appearance, movement, posture, facial expression and eye contact.

Name: _____

CHAPTER 12 SELF TEST

MATCHING Part One Match each term listed on the left with its correct definition from the column on the right.

_____ 1. addition

_____ 2. articulation

_____ 3. debilitative stage fright

_____ 4. deletion

_____ 5. extemporaneous speech

_____ 6. facilitative stage fright

_____ 7. fallacy of approval

_____ 8. fallacy of catastrophic failure

_____ 9. fallacy of overgeneralization

_____ 10. fallacy of perfection

a. the irrational belief that the worst possible outcome will probably occur

b. the irrational belief that a worthwhile communicator should be able to handle every situation with complete confidence and skill

c. the irrational belief that it is vital to win the sanction or endorsement of virtually every person a communicator deals with

d. an articulation error of leaving out sounds of words

e. a speech that is planned in advance but presented in a direct, conversational manner

f. irrational beliefs in (usually negative) conclusions based on limited evidence or communicators exaggerating their shortcomings

g. intense level of anxiety about speaking before an audience, resulting in poor performance

h. a moderate level of anxiety about speaking before an audience that helps improve performance

i. an articulation error of putting in extra parts to words

j. the process of pronouncing words distinctly and carefully

MATCHING Part Two Match each term listed on the left with its correct definition from the column on the right.

_____ 11. impromptu speech

_____ 12. irrational thinking

_____ 13. manuscript speech

_____ 14. memorized speech

_____ 15. pitch

_____ 16. rate

_____ 17. slurring

_____ 18. substitution

_____ 19. visualization

a. the articulation error that involves replacing part of a word with an incorrect sound

b. a speech learned and delivered by rote without a written text or note cards

c. the highness or lowness of one's voice

d. a speech given "off the top of one's head" without advance preparation

e. the articulation error that involves overlapping the end of one word with the beginning of the next

f. broad category of beliefs that have no basis in reality or logic; one source of debilitative stage fright

g. a technique for self-improvement that involves picturing in successful completion of a task in your mind

h. a speech that is read word-for-word from a prepared text

i. the speed at which a speaker utters words

MULTIPLE CHOICE Choose the BEST response from those listed.

1. A certain candidate remarked that his only three mistakes in his first political speech were that he read it, read it poorly, and it wasn't worth reading. Chances are he used which type of delivery?

   a. impromptu
   b. manuscript
   c. memorized
   d. extemporaneous
   e. none of the above

2. Which of these describes extemporaneous delivery?

   a. It is off the cuff with no preparation.
   b. It is carefully prepared and rehearsed word for word.
   c. It is carefully prepared, then presented conversationally.
   d. It is read from a teleprompter.
   e. It is spontaneous and uses no notes.

3. Which delivery style is generally accepted as the most appropriate and effective for the college classroom?

   a. impromptu
   b. manuscript
   c. memorized
   d. extemporaneous
   e. All work equally well in the average college classroom.

4. If you need to be grammatically precise, keep an exact time limit, or have your speech be part of a legal record, the best delivery style would be

    a. impromptu.
    b. manuscript.
    c. memorized.
    d. extemporaneous.
    e. All would work equally well.

5. If you need to give a memorized speech, the single most important piece of advice is:

    a. practice.
    b. type the manuscript to practice from.
    c. use elaborate rather than succinct language.
    d. make the delivery more formal than the speech.
    e. All of the above are significant pieces of advice.

6. In using a manuscript delivery, all of the following guidelines are presented in your text EXCEPT:

    a. use longer paragraphs so you don't seem choppy and disjointed.
    b. rehearse until you can read whole lines without looking at the manuscript.
    c. vary your speed.
    d. type the manuscript and underline words you want to emphasize.
    e. use stiff paper that won't blow away or crumple easily.

7. You have been asked to give a quick reaction to a speaker at a small committee meeting. Which style would you use?

    a. impromptu
    b. manuscript
    c. memorized
    d. extemporaneous
    e. All would work equally well.

8. Movement as a part of delivery enables you to

    a. replace involuntary actions with voluntary ones.
    b. involve more members of the audience in the action zone.
    c. add emphasis to your message.
    d. all of the above
    e. none of the above

9. Which of these is NOT a method suggested by your text as a good way to practice for your speech?

    a. Silently think through the speech without really vocalizing it.
    b. talk through the speech
    c. practice in the room you'll actually use
    d. practice in front of a small group of friends
    e. tape record the speech

10. Maintaining eye contact with your audience usually

    a. convinces audience members that you are interested in them.
    b. overwhelms or intimidates audience members.
    c. helps you do a "reality check" regarding how the audience perceives you.
    d. both b and c
    e. both a and c

11. As you speed up or become louder, your pitch tends to

    a. vary greatly.
    b. rise.
    c. fall.
    d. rise when you speed up, fall when you become louder.
    e. fall when you speed up, rise when you become louder.

12. The most important thing for a speaker to remember when considering volume, rate, and pitch is to

    a. use variety and use them for emphasis.
    b. keep them low, slow, and low, respectively.
    c. keep them all as high as possible.
    d. concentrate on volume; rate and pitch will fall in place.
    e. None of the above represents sound advice.

13. Addition, substitution, slurring, and deletion are all types of problems with

    a. volume.
    b. emphasis.
    c. articulation.
    d. visual aspects of delivery.
    e. movement.

14. With regard to facilitative stage fright,

    a. it doesn't exist.
    b. it is far more common than debilitative stage fright.
    c. it can be used to aid your speech delivery.
    d. it can help you perform at your top capacity.
    e. both c and d

15. Debilitative stage fright is frequently caused by

    a. irrational thinking.
    b. previous negative experience.
    c. rationality and receiver-orientation.
    d. both a and b
    e. both b and c

MATCHING Part Two (Fallacies) Match each fallacy with the label for that type of debilitative and irrational thinking. One will be used more than once.

catastrophic failure   perfection
approval   overgeneralization

_____ 1. I sure messed up my visual aids; that one slide was upside down. [Four different visuals were used.]

_____ 2. If I can't get an A on this speech, I'm just a complete failure.

_____ 3. The instructor probably won't like my topic and I'll probably get a D for the course. If I get a D for the course, I'll never graduate. If I never graduate. . .

_____ 4. [After one of five jokes wasn't laughed at] The audience never laughs at my jokes.

_____ 5. Everyone just has to like my speech. I can't stand the thought of even one person in the class thinking I did a poor job.

TRUE/FALSE Circle the T or F to indicate whether you believe the statement is true or false. If it is **true**, give a **reason** or an **example**. If it is false, **explain** what would make it true.

T   F   1. When asked to respond to a classmate's speech, begin by giving suggestions for improvement and follow with very general remarks.

T   F   2. Saying "goin'" or "runnin'" instead of "going" and "running" are examples of substitution.

T   F   3. Receiver-orientation refers to concentrating on the audience rather than on yourself.

T   F   4. If you expect your speech to be perfect and keep telling yourself it has to be, you are likely to experience facilitative stage fright.

T   F   5. Practice your speech by actually talking through the whole thing, not just saying, "I'll give some examples here," but speaking through the examples.

COMPLETION Fill in each of the blanks with a word from the lists provided. Choose the BEST word for each sentence. There are more words than you will use, but each word will be used only once.

auditory   visual

impromptu   rational

fallacy   memorized

preparation   the audience

1. A/an _____ is a type of irrational thinking.

2. Being asked to give an immediate response to another student's speech is an example of a type of _____ speech you will likely make in this class.

3. The best way to avoid debilitative stage fright from fallacies is to replace those thoughts with _____ thinking.

4. _____ is the most important key to controlling speech anxiety.

5. Posture, movement, and eye contact are all part of the _____ aspects of delivery.

CHAPTER 12 ANSWERS TO SELF-TEST

MATCHING Part One

1. i	2. j	3. g	4. d	5. e
6. h	7. c	8. a	9. f	10. b

MATCHING Part Two

11. d	12. f	13. h	14. b	15. c
16. i	17. e	18. a	19. g	

MULTIPLE CHOICE

1. b	2. c	3. d	4. b	5. a
6. a	7. a	8. d	9. a	10. e
11. b	12. a	13. c	14. e	15. d

MATCHING Part Two (Fallacies)

1. overgeneralization
2. perfection
3. catastrophic failure
4. overgeneralization
5. approval

TRUE/FALSE

1. False	2. False	3. True	4. False	5. True

COMPLETION

1. fallacy
2. impromptu
3. rational
4. preparation
5. visual

Related Reading

"Learn how to manage preshow jitters." Dana Bristol-Smith. *Presentations*. April 1, 2001. Retrieve from www.presentations.com/presentations/search/search_display.jsp?vnu_content_id=1105027.

Preview

Stage fright. Communication apprehension. CA. Presentation paranoia. It goes by a number of names, and most of us can recall at least one attack of it. However, as Chapter 12 points out, stage fright can be debilitative or facilitative. The author of this article adds to the information and advice presented in this chapter and provides anecdotes that we can identify with and advice that we can heed.

Review

1. What experiences have you had that parallel or top the author's experience as described in the opening paragraphs of this article?

2. According to the author, how are conversations and presentations similar?

3. List all of the physical symptoms of stage fright mentioned in the article and add to the list if you can.

4. Do your experiences lead you to agree or disagree with the author's ideas about smiling and its physiological effects?

5. Summarize the author's advice and compare and contrast it with that in the text.

CHAPTER 13 INFORMATIVE SPEAKING

CHAPTER 13 SKELETON OUTLINE

This outline can be a helpful study tool to assist you in seeing the order and sequence of the chapter and the relationship of ideas. Use it to take notes as you read and/or to add concepts presented in lecture.

I.   Types of informative speaking

    A. Content

        1.   objects

        2.   processes

        3.   events

        4.   concepts

    B. Purpose

        1.   descriptions

        2.   explanations

        3.   instructions

II.   Informative vs. persuasive topics

    A. Informative topics tend to be noncontroversial.

    B. Informative speaking is not intended to change audience attitudes.

III. Techniques of informative speaking

    A. Define a specific informative purpose.

        1.   informative purpose statement

        2.   clear thesis

    B. Create information hunger by emphasizing physical, identity, social, and practical needs.

    C. Make it easy to listen.

        1.   limit information

        2.   use familiar to lead to unfamiliar

        3.   use simple to lead to complex

    D. Emphasize important points.

        1.   repetition

        2.   signposts

    E. Use a clear organization.

        1.   introduction

        2.   body (organize, use internal summary, review and transitions)

        3.   conclusion

    F. Use supporting material effectively.

    G. Use clear, simple language.

      1.   precise, simple vocabulary

      2.   simple syntax

H. Generate audience involvement.

      1.   personalize your speech

      2.   use audience participation

      3.   ask for volunteers

      4.   conduct a question-and-answer period

         a)   focus on substance

         b)   paraphrase

         c)   avoid defensiveness

         d)   answer briefly

CHAPTER 13 KEY TERMS

This list of key terms corresponds to those in boldface in your text. In your own words write a definition and an original example of the word.

audience involvement

audience participation

description

explanations

information anxiety

information hunger

information overload

informative purpose statement

instructions

knowledge

signposts

vocal citations

Name _____

CHAPTER 13 ACTIVITY 1 CREATING INFORMATION HUNGER

Purpose:

To illustrate ways to create information hunger.

Instructions:

For each speech being prepared, list ways you could create information hunger by appealing to the physical, identity, social, or practical needs of that audience.

1. You are speaking to a high-risk group about the rising incidence of Hepatitis B. What needs would you appeal to? How?

2. You are speaking to a group of high school students about the risks of teen pregnancy. What needs would you appeal to? How?

3. You are speaking to co-workers about the changes in health care providers. What needs would you appeal to? How?

4. You are speaking to a group of expectant parents about how the choice of names for a child affects him/her for life. What needs would you appeal to? How?

5. You are speaking to a low-risk group about the rising incidence of AIDS. What needs would you appeal to? How?

6. You are speaking to an incoming group of first-year students about identity theft. What needs would you appeal to? How?

7. You are speaking to middle school (junior high) students on starting early to think about scholarship opportunities. What needs would you appeal to? How?

8. You are speaking to foreign students about the medical care/medical insurance situation in the United States. What needs would you appeal to? How?

9. You are speaking to members of a community group about your travel to a recent convention they financed for you. What needs would you appeal to? How?

10. You are speaking to employees about the need to be aware of what behaviors constitute sexual harassment. What needs would you appeal to? How?

11. You are speaking to a group of students about the new registration procedures being implemented. What needs would you appeal to? How?

Name _____

CHAPTER 13 ACTIVITY 2 CRITIQUE SHEET

Purpose:

To critique an informative speech.

Instructions:

1. Review the information on critiquing a classmate from Activity 4 in Chapter 12.
2. Then, as directed by your instructor, fill in this sheet while listening to a classmate's speech or public videotaped speech. Try to use specific details.

Speaker's name: Topic:

1. In my opinion, the strengths of the introduction were

2. In my opinion, the introduction would be better if

3. It seemed to me that the speech was/was not clearly organized because

4. What I liked about the visual aids and supporting material was

5. What I think would improve the visual aids and supporting material is

6. I think the strong points of the delivery were

7. I think the delivery would be improved by

8. I think the best thing about the conclusion was

9. I think the conclusion would be improved by

10. Overall, what I liked best about the presentation was

Name _____

CHAPTER 13 ACTIVITY 3 ANALYZING A SPEECH

Purpose:

To analyze a speaker from outside class.

Instructions:

Arrange to listen to an outside speaker on campus or in the community. Fill in the following.

Speaker's name:

Location of speech:

Occasion:

Topic or title:

1. Describe the intended audience: (Was this for a particular group or club? open to the public? for profit?)

2. Was there a clear introduction? What technique was used? Did it get attention and preview the speech?

3. Was the speech clearly organized? Could you follow the main points? Could you always tell the main idea? What type of outline was used?

4. What types of support were used? Did the speaker use varied and appropriate forms of support?

5. Were there previews, transitions, and internal summaries? What kind? How effective were they?

6. Did the delivery enhance the speech or detract from it? What was especially good about the delivery? What would improve it?

7. Was there a clear conclusion? What technique was used? Did the conclusion review the key points and clearly bring the speech to a close?"

8. Other overall impressions or comments:

Name _____

CHAPTER 13 ACTIVITY 4 PRACTICING DELIVERY

Purpose:

To review a video of one's own speech to become aware of strengths and weaknesses in delivery.

Instructions:

1. Videotape yourself giving a speech.
2. Watch the whole video with sound, then watch a part of the video without sound and fill out the following.

1. My first reactions to seeing myself on this video were

2. While watching myself without the sound, I noticed this about my

    eye contact

    hands/gestures

    movement

    facial expression

3. The four things that I think I did well are:
    a.

    b.

    c.

    d.

4. I could improve my presentation for this audience if I would

Name _____

CHAPTER 13 ACTIVITY 5 EXPLORING THE WEB

Analyzing an Informative Speech

Choose a speech from any of the Web sites listed in Chapter 13. Gifts of Speech is a particularly good site to explore: www.giftsofspeech.org. Here you can choose a speech of interest to you from over 200 speeches by a variety of influential women. The following speech found there is recommended for this exercise: Address to the People of Prague, "Obecni Dum — A Moment of Celebration and of Dedication," by Madeleine Albright, July 14, 1997.

1. What is the informative purpose?

2. What is the thesis?

3. In this speech, what technique is used in the introduction?

4. How does the speaker create information hunger?

5. What needs (physical, identity, social, and practical needs) are used to create information hunger?

6. Give an example of how the speaker limits information.

7. Give an example of how the speaker uses something familiar to lead to something unfamiliar.

8. Give an example of the speaker using something simple to lead to something more complex.

9. How does the speaker emphasize important points?

10. Can you find an example of the speaker using repetition?

11. Can you find an example of the speaker using signposts?

12. Give examples of internal summaries, reviews, and transitions:
    a. internal summaries

    b. reviews

13. What transitions are used? Are they effective? Why or why not?

Name: _____

CHAPTER 13 SELF TEST

MATCHING Set One Match each term listed on the left with its correct definition from the column on the right.

_____ 1. audience involvement

_____ 2. description

_____ 3. explanation

_____ 4. information hunger

_____ 5. information anxiety

_____ 6. signpost

a. audience desire to learn information created by the speaker

b. a type of speech that builds a detailed word picture of the topic

c. psychological stress or confusion resulting from the amount of information available to a person

d. a type of informative speech that clarifies the topic, often by answering the question *why?*

e. phrase that emphasizes the importance of upcoming material in a speech

f. broad category of methods to encourage audience members to actively participate in some part of the speech process

MATCHING Set Two Match each term listed on the left with its correct definition from the column on the right.

_____ 1. knowledge

_____ 2. vocal citations

_____ 3. informative purpose statement

_____ 4. instruction

_____ 5. information overload

_____ 6. audience participation

a. method in which listeners (audience) actively become involved and do something during a speech

b. a statement that stresses knowledge and/or ability, rather than action or change of behavior

c. tension or anxiety resulting from overwhelming amount of information

d. a type of informative speech that teaches the audience how to do something

e. the result of making sense of information

f. speaker's explanation of the sources of his/her information

MULTIPLE CHOICE Choose the BEST response from those listed.

1. Which is true of an informative speech?

    a. It tends to change the audience's attitudes.
    b. It tries to move the audience to action.
    c. It tries to sway the audience's opinions.
    d. It tends to be noncontroversial.
    e. It is very persuasive.

2. Speeches which explain "how to" do something are called

    a. instructions.
    b. descriptions.
    c. explanations.
    d. events.
    e. objects.

3. You can create information hunger by

    a. responding to general needs of the audience.
    b. responding to specific needs of the audience.
    c. responding to self-actualization needs of the audience.
    d. all of the above
    e. none of the above

4. A speech on how to have more friends and meet people readily appeals most to

    a. physical needs.
    b. safety needs.
    c. social needs.
    d. esteem needs.
    e. self-actualization needs.

5. In order to make it easy for the audience to listen, a speaker should

    a. present as much information as possible to keep the audience interested.
    b. present only unfamiliar information; audiences will be bored with the familiar.
    c. use simple information to build up understanding of complex information.
    d. all of the above
    e. none of the above

6. One way to create emphasis in your speech is to stress important points through

    a. repetition.
    b. use of signposts.
    c. a clear introduction.
    d. paraphrasing confusing questions.
    e. both a and b

7. Detailed descriptions, examples, statistics, and definitions are important types of

    a. introductory materials.
    b. supporting materials.
    c. transition materials.
    d. concluding materials.
    e. none of the above

8.   With regard to the use of language, the following advice was given in the text:

    a.   use a complex vocabulary to show your competence.
    b.   try to choose words that are obscure.
    c.   use precise and simple words to convey thoughts.
    d.   use jargon to demonstrate your expertise, especially to outsiders.
    e.   use unusual, little-known words to spice up your speech.

9.   Which of these is a way to encourage audience involvement in your speech?

    a.   audience participation
    b.   use of volunteers from the audience
    c.   question-and-answer sessions
    d.   all of the above
    e.   None of the above encourages true audience involvement.

10.   Which of these does not demonstrate audience involvement?

    a.   In a speech about skin tone, ask audience members to pinch their elbow skin, and explain how to judge skin tone from the number of seconds it takes for the skin to "pop" back.
    b.   In a speech about blindness, ask audience members to close their eyes for twenty seconds.
    c.   In a speech about self-concept, ask members of the audience to write down their five "best" traits.
    d.   All of these represent examples of audience involvement.
    e.   None of these is an appropriate use of audience involvement.

11.   When conducting a question-and-answer session, the following guidelines are appropriate EXCEPT:

    a.   listen for the substance or big idea of the question.
    b.   paraphrase confusing questions before answering.
    c.   if the questioner is attacking you personally, use a subtle attack rather than give a defensive answer.
    d.   answer as briefly as possible.
    e.   avoid defensive reactions by responding to the substance.

12.   Speeches to inform are often classified according to purpose or

    a.   description.
    b.   content.
    c.   technique.
    d.   all of the above
    e.   none of the above

13.   "We've been talking about ways to enhance our effectiveness at work. Now here's the real important thing to remember . . ." Those words represent

    a.   a signpost.
    b.   audience involvement.
    c.   format.
    d.   repetition.
    e.   supporting material.

14. During a question-and-answer session, you are asked, "So what about those layoff rumors?" A paraphrase would be

   a. There is no truth to those rumors.
   b. I'll need to let my supervisor address that concern.
   c. Are you asking me to comment on whether or not I know if there is truth to the rumors?
   d. The rumors surface every time we bring out a new product line because people fear the loss of their jobs. What's your concern?
   e. All of these represent different types of paraphrases.

15. A speech about racism in the United States would be classified by content as a speech about

   a. an object.
   b. a process.
   c. an event.
   d. a concept.
   e. an instruction.

TRUE/FALSE Circle the T or F to indicate whether you believe the statement is true or false. If it is **true**, give a **reason** or an **example**. If it is false, **explain** what would make it true.

T   F   1.   One job of the audience is to create information hunger.

T   F   2.   An important characteristic of a speech is that it should use more formal, complex language than either writing or conversation.

T   F   3.   A good, specific, informative purpose will state what results the speaker wants.

T   F   4.   There is only one way to generate audience involvement in a speech.

T   F   5.   Repetition is inappropriate in a speech because it leads to redundancy and bores the audience.

COMPLETION Fill in each of the blanks with a word from the lists provided. Choose the BEST word for each sentence. There are more words than you will use, but each word will be used only once.

needs	volunteers
instruction	contents
purposes	descriptions
signposts	knowledge

1. A speech that shows the audience how to do something is a speech of _____.

2. Asking for _____ is a way to generate audience involvement.

3. A speaker can create information hunger by appealing to listeners' _____.

4. One way a speaker can emphasize important points for the audience is to use

   _____.

5. Descriptions, explanations, and instructions are all ways to classify informative speeches according to

   _____.

6. A good informational speech can reduce information overload for the audience by turning

   information into _____.

CHAPTER 13 ANSWERS TO SELF TEST

MATCHING Set One

1. f   2. b   3. d   4. a   5. c   6. e

MATCHING Set Two

1. e   2. f   3. b   4. d   5. c   6. a

MULTIPLE CHOICE

1. d   2. a   3. d   4. c   5. c

6. e   7. b   8. c   9. d   10. d

11. c   12. b   13. a   14. c   15. d

TRUE/FALSE

1. False   2. False   3. True   4. False   5. False

COMPLETION

1. instruction   2. volunteers   3. needs

4. signposts   5. purposes   6. knowledge

Related Reading

"The Reason Why We Sing: Understanding Traditional African American Preaching," by Janice D. Hamlet, *Our Voices: Essays in Culture, Ethnicity, and Communication: An Intercultural Anthology*, 3rd edition. Edited by Alberto Gonzalez, Marsha Houston, and Victoria Chen (Los Angeles: Roxbury Publishing Company, 2000).

Preview

Chapter 13 presents eight techniques for effective informative speaking, including emphasizing important points, making the words easy to listen to and generating audience involvement. Janice D. Hamlet explains the unique features of African American preaching. As you read, compare the points in Chapter 13 with the essential characteristics of and requirements for effective presentations of this type described in the article.

Review

1. What are four characteristics of African American preaching style that the author explains?

2. What supporting materials would carry weight with these audiences and perhaps not with others?

3. Which techniques of speaking presented in your text are discussed in this article?

4. Why is interaction (call and response) important for both the speaker and the listeners?

5. What speakers or speeches do you recall that demonstrated the characteristics described in this article?

CHAPTER 14 PERSUASIVE SPEAKING

CHAPTER 14 SKELETON OUTLINE

This outline can be a helpful study tool to assist you in seeing the order and sequence of the chapter and the relationship of ideas. Use it to take notes as you read and/or to add concepts presented in lecture.

I.   Characteristics of persuasion

    A. Persuasion is not coercive.

    B. Persuasion is usually incremental (explained by social judgment theory).

        1. anchor

        2. latitudes of acceptance

        3. latitudes of rejection

        4. latitudes of noncommitment

    C. Persuasion is interactive.

    D. Persuasion can be ethical.

        1. definition: ethical persuasion

        2. unethical persuasion (Table 14-1)

        3. disadvantage of unethical communication

II.   Categorizing types of persuasion

    A. By proposition

        1. fact

        2. value

        3. policy

    B. By desired outcome

        1. convincing

            a) reinforce

            b) begin to shift/consider the possibility

        2. actuating

            a) adoption

            b) discontinuance

    C. By directness of approach

        1. direct persuasion

        2. indirect persuasion

III. Creating the persuasive message

    A. Set clear, persuasive purpose

B. Structure the message

    1. describe the problem

        a) nature

        b) effect on audience

    2. describe the solution

        a) workability

        b) advantages

    3. describe desired audience response

        a) what can audience do?

        b) what are rewards?

    4. adapting the model persuasive structure

C. Use solid evidence

    1. support claim (including emotional evidence)

    2. cite sources

        a) credentials

        b) currency

D. Avoid fallacies

    1. attack on the person (ad hominem)

    2. reduction to the absurd (reductio ad absurdum)

    3. either-or

    4. false cause (post hoc ergo propter hoc)

    5. appeal to authority (argumentum ad verecundiam)

    6. bandwagon appeal (argumentum ad populum)

IV. Adapting to the audience (target audience)

A. Establish common ground

B. Organize for expected response

C. Neutralize potential hostility

    1. show understanding

    2. use appropriate humor

V. Build credibility

A. Credibility is based on perception, not objective

    1. initial

    2. derived

3.   terminal

B.   Three "Cs"

1.   competence

2.   character

3.   charisma

CHAPTER 14 KEY TERMS

This list of key terms corresponds to those in boldface in your text. In your own words write a definition and an original example of the word.

actuate

ad hominem fallacy

anchor

argumentum ad populum fallacy

argumentum ad verecundiam fallacy

convince

credibility

direct persuasion

either-or fallacy

emotional evidence

ethical persuasion

evidence

fallacy

indirect persuasion

latitude of acceptance

latitude of noncommitment

latitude of rejection

Motivated Sequence

persuasion

post hoc fallacy

proposition of fact

proposition of policy

proposition of value

reductio ad absurdum fallacy

social judgment theory

target audience

Name: _____

CHAPTER 14 ACTIVITY 1 LATITUDES

Purpose:

To differentiate between latitudes of acceptance, noncommitment, and rejection.

Instructions:

Assume that each of the statements below represents an anchor position for your audience. For each of the anchors below, write statements which would likely fall within the audience's latitudes of acceptance, noncommitment, and rejection.

Example:

Anchor: Capital punishment is wrong because it may be mistaken identity.

Views within their latitude of acceptance:

  The state taking a life is wrong.

  Taking life is wrong.

Views within their latitude of noncommitment:

  If someone confesses freely and wants the death penalty, it might be okay.

Views within their latitude of rejection:

  An eye for an eye, a tooth for a tooth.

  If someone commits murder, it is okay for the state to take his/her life.

1. Anchor: Minorities are treated fairly in juvenile justice systems.

Views within their latitude of acceptance:

Views within their latitude of noncommitment:

Views within their latitude of rejection:

2. Anchor: National health **care,** not just health insurance, is every person's right.

Views within their latitude of acceptance:

Views within their latitude of noncommitment:

Views within their latitude of rejection:

3.   Anchor: Alcoholism is a disease that can be treated if a person wants treatment.
Views within their latitude of acceptance:

Views within their latitude of noncommitment:

Views within their latitude of rejection:

4.   Anchor: Fighting terrorism with excessive military force creates more terrorists.
Views within their latitude of acceptance:

Views within their latitude of noncommitment:

Views within their latitude of rejection:

5.   Anchor. Write an anchor statement:

Views within their latitude of acceptance:

Views within their latitude of noncommitment:

Views within their latitude of rejection:

6.   Anchor. Write an anchor statement:

Views within their latitude of acceptance:

Views within their latitude of noncommitment:

Views within their latitude of rejection:

Name: _____

CHAPTER 14 ACTIVITY 2 FACT, VALUE, OR POLICY

Purposes:

1. To construct propositions of fact, value, and policy.
2. To demonstrate that any topic may lead to one of three types of propositions.

Instructions:

1. Choose four of these topics or create your own.
2. For each topic, create a proposition of fact, of value, and of policy ON THE SAME TOPIC.

airport security	changing the electoral college system	saving the environment	delinquent dads/child support
stem cell research		vegetarian lifestyle	
body piercing	judging the Olympics	funding for Olympic athletes	world AIDS crisis
honor classes			part-time students
funding presidential campaigns	sentencing juveniles in adult court	banning fraternities and sororities on campus	

Example:

Topic: ___E-mail_____

Proposition of fact: _____E-mail is not private._____

Proposition of value: ___It is ethical to use the office e-mail system for private business.___

Proposition of policy: _The United States should institute national laws regulating privacy in use of e-mail._____

1. Topic:

Proposition of fact:

Proposition of value:

Proposition of policy:

2. Topic:

Proposition of fact:

Proposition of value:

Proposition of policy:

3. Topic:

Proposition of fact:

Proposition of value:

Proposition of policy:

4. Topic:

Proposition of fact:

Proposition of value:

Proposition of policy:

5. Topic:

Proposition of fact:

Proposition of value:

Proposition of policy:

Name: _____

CHAPTER 14 ACTIVITY 3 CRITIQUE SHEET

Purpose:

To critique a speech of a classmate or public figure (video).

Instructions:

While listening to the speech, fill in the critique sheet.

Speaker's name: Topic:

1. In my opinion, the strengths of the introduction were

2. The speaker did/did not establish common ground with the audience by

3. It seemed to me that the speech was/was not clearly organized because

4. What I liked about the visual aids and supporting material was

5. What I think would improve the visual aids and supporting material is

6. An effective persuasive strategy and logical and emotional appeals were/were not evident by

7. The speaker did/did not establish credibility by

8. I think the strong points of the delivery were

9. I think delivery would be improved by

10. I think the best thing about the conclusion was

11. Strengths and weaknesses of the conclusion:

12. Overall, what I liked best about the presentation was

Name: _____

CHAPTER 14 ACTIVITY 4 SELF-CRITIQUE

Purpose:

To review a video of your own speech to become aware of strengths and weaknesses.

Instructions:

1.   Videotape yourself as you give a speech.
2.   Watch the whole video with sound, then watch a part of the video without sound and fill out the following.

1.   My first reactions to seeing myself on this video were

2.   While watching myself without the sound, I noticed this about my

eye contact

hands/gestures

movement

facial expression

3.   The four things that I think I did well are:
     a.

     b.

     c.

     d.

4.   Ways I could improve my presentation for this audience:

Name: _____

CHAPTER 14 ACTIVITY 5 EXPLORING THE WEB

Analyzing Speeches by Types of Propositions, Fallacies, and Audience Adaptation

1. Choose a topic of interest to you from The Douglass Archive at http://douglassarchives.org/. Read the speech and record the following:

Speech title:

Speaker: Date:

Topic:

Type of proposition (fact, value, policy):

Main proposition of speech (in the words of the speech or paraphrased):

Can you find examples of any of these fallacies?

    attack on the person (ad hominem)

    reduction to the absurd (reductio ad absurdum)

    either/or

    false cause (post hoc ergo propter hoc)

    appeal to authority (argumentum ad verecundiam)

    bandwagon appeal (argumentum ad populum)

2. Peruse *The Congressional Record*, at <u>www.gpoaccess.gov/crecord/index.html</u> , and choose a speech, preferably one by your senator or representative. Read the speech and record the following:

Speaker: Date:

Topic:

Speeches to Congress are often to persuade. Describe or quote from the speech to illustrate how the speaker performed any of the following methods of adapting to the audience.

Establishing common ground

Organizing for expected response

Adapting to hostile audience by showing understanding

Adapting to hostile audience by the use of appropriate humor

Name: _____

CHAPTER 14 SELF TEST

MATCHING Part One Match each term listed on the left with its correct definition from the column on the right.

____ 1.   actuate

____ 2.   anchor

____ 3.   convince

____ 4.   credibility

____ 5.   direct persuasion

____ 6.   emotional evidence

____ 7.   ethical persuasion

____ 8.   evidence

____ 9.   fallacy

____ 10. indirect persuasion

a.   a pre-existing opinion held by the object of your persuasion

b.   material used to prove a point

c.   a speech goal that aims at changing audience's thinking

d.   persuasion not dependent on false or misleading information

e.   persuasion which disguises or de-emphasizes a speaker's persuasive purpose

f.   persuasion that attempts to move a person to action

g.   evidence that arouses strong feelings in the audience

h.   an error in logic

i.   believability of a speaker or other information source

j.   persuasion that does not try to hide a persuasive purpose

MATCHING Part Two Match each term listed on the left with its correct definition from the column on the right.

_____ 11. latitude of acceptance

_____ 12. latitude of noncommitment

_____ 13. latitude of rejection

_____ 14. motivated sequence

_____ 15. persuasion

_____ 16. proposition of fact

_____ 17. proposition of policy

_____ 18. proposition of value

_____ 19. social judgment theory

_____ 20. target audience

a. that part of an audience that must be influenced in order to achieve a persuasive goal

b. in social judgment theory, statements that a person would not care strongly about one way or another

c. explanation of attitude change that posits opinions will change in small increments only when the target opinions lie in the receiver's latitudes of acceptance and noncommitment

d. persuasive plan that seeks to move an audience to immediate action

e. claim in which there are two or more sides of conflicting verifiable evidence

f. claim involving the worth of an idea, a person, or an object

g. in social judgment theory, statements that a person would not reject

h. in social judgment theory, statements that a person would not accept

i. claim that involves adopting or rejecting a specific course of action

j. the communication act of motivating a person to change a particular belief, attitude, value, or behavior

MULTIPLE CHOICE Choose the BEST response from those listed.

1. Which of these is true of persuasion?

    a. It is coercive.
    b. It is usually incremental.
    c. It is linear or one-way.
    d. It is unethical.
    e. all of the above

2. Following the thinking of social judgment theory, a speaker who is trying to persuade an audience will do best to appeal to propositions within the audience's

    a. anchor.
    b. latitude of acceptance.
    c. latitude of noncommitment.
    d. latitude of rejection.
    e. none of the above

3. Persuasive speakers who adhere to the principles of social judgment theory tend to

   a. seek realistic, if modest, goals from the audience's latitude of noncommitment.
   b. seek to move audiences to accept positions now in their latitude of rejection.
   c. seek to widen an audience's latitude of noncommitment.
   d. all of the above
   e. none of the above

4. Ethical persuasion, as defined by the text, is

   a. in the best interest of the audience.
   b. not dependent on false or misleading information.
   c. an honest attempt to change an audience's attitude or behavior.
   d. all of the above
   e. none of the above

5. Which of these is unethical communication behavior as defined by the text?

   a. insincerity
   b. withholding information
   c. plagiarism
   d. relaying false information
   e. all of the above

6. "Suicide bombing is immoral." This is a proposition of

   a. fact.
   b. value.
   c. policy.
   d. agency.
   e. none of the above

7. A speech that tries to get an audience to begin buying only low-carb foods is what type?

   a. convincing
   b. discontinuance
   c. adoption
   d. all of the above
   e. none of the above

8. Indirect persuasion would be most appropriate when

   a. talking to a group of nonsmokers about the dangers of smoking.
   b. talking to a group of Republicans about the merits of a Democratic proposal.
   c. talking to students who are in class on time about the importance of promptness over tardiness.
   d. talking to a group of teachers about the value of education.
   e. All of the above are equally germane occasions for using indirect persuasion.

9. The purpose statement for a speech to convince will usually stress an attitude; a purpose statement for a speech to actuate will stress a/an

   a. behavior.
   b. evidence.
   c. attitude.
   d. thought.
   e. Any of the above are equally appropriate for a purpose statement of a speech to actuate.

10. Assume these are three possible parts of an outline:

    I.   Describe the problem
    II.   Describe the solution
    III.   Describe the desired audience response

    A speech to actuate would most appropriately include

    a. I only.
    b. I and II only.
    c. I, II, and III.
    d. I and III only.
    e. II and III only.

11. In describing a proposed solution, which question(s) must a speaker be sure to answer?

    a. What will it cost?
    b. Will it work?
    c. What are the advantages?
    d. a and b
    e. b and c

12. A first step in adapting to most audiences is to

    a. establish common ground.
    b. organize your material with your toughest area of disagreement first.
    c. use humor.
    d. demonstrate how your view supersedes their view.
    e. use inductive reasoning.

13. Which of these represents the least biased citation?

    a. The current tax rate for those with $60,000–$80,000 taxable incomes—from the current IRS tax form
    b. Statistics on Chicago being one of the safest cities to live in—from a 1963 survey
    c. Information to convince you of the health benefits of milk—from the Wisconsin Dairy Association
    d. Your Republican senator's voting record published by the Young Republicans
    e. Your Republican senator's voting record published by the Young Democrats

14. The three C's of credibility described by your text are

    a. creation, completion, coordination.
    b. co-existence, cooperation, completion.
    c. competition, coordination, completion.
    d. competence, character, and charisma.
    e. collaboration, co-ordination, character.

MATCHING Part Three (Propositions) Match the label of the type of proposition with the items that are examples of that type of proposition. You will use some words more than once.

| | fact | value | policy |

_____ 1. The mayor did not violate campaign-spending laws.

_____ 2. The United States should continue to be involved in NATO.

_____ 3. It is better to kill animals for research than allow humans to suffer.

_____ 4. Children's interests should come ahead of adult interests when deciding cases of dispute between biological, surrogate, or adoptive parents.

_____ 5. The United States has a higher rate of crime than any other industrialized democracy.

_____ 6. The United States should institute national health insurance.

_____ 7. There was less bloodshed in Iraq after U.S. intervention.

_____ 8. College students should get credit for volunteer work in the community.

_____ 9. College students who work at jobs up to 20 hours a week have higher grade point averages than do those who don't work at jobs at all.

_____ 10. Internships are better preparation for careers than senior seminars.

TRUE/FALSE Circle the T or F to indicate whether you believe the statement is true or false. If it is **true,** give a **reason** or an **example.** If it is false, **explain** what would make it true.

T   F   1. Persuasion and ethics are unrelated.

T   F   2. Propositions of fact usually try to convince the audience what should be done.

T   F   3. When you are quoting the source of an interview or from a book, cite the source's credentials.

T   F   4. Emotional evidence is usually not convincing or credible in a speech to persuade.

T   F   5. A proposition of policy tries to convince the audience to believe something is true.

MATCHING Part Four (Fallacies) Match each description with the name of the fallacy described.

____ 1. either/or fallacy

____ 2. post hoc fallacy

____ 3. argumentum ad verecundiam fallacy

____ 4. reductio ad absurdum fallacy

____ 5. ad hominem fallacy

____ 6. argumentum ad populum fallacy

a. fallacious argument that attacks the integrity of a person to weaken his or her position, or argument that appeals to feelings rather than reason

b. fallacious reasoning that tries to support a belief by relying on the testimony of someone who is not an authority on the issue being argued

c. fallacious reasoning that mistakenly assumes that one event causes another because they occur sequentially

d. fallacious reasoning that unfairly attacks an argument by extending it to such extreme lengths that it looks ridiculous

e. fallacious reasoning based on the dubious notion that because many people favor an idea, you should too

f. fallacious reasoning that reduces complex issues to only two alternatives

MATCHING Part Five (Fallacious Arguments) Match each argument with the name of the fallacy that describes it. Some fallacies will have more than one argument.

____ 1. either/or fallacy

____ 2. post hoc fallacy

____ 3. reductio ad absurdum fallacy

____ 4. ad hominem fallacy

____ 5. argumentum ad populum fallacy

____ 6. argumentum ad verecundiam fallacy

a. There are only two kinds of instructors: those that make you think and those that prevent you from thinking.

b. In arguing a case in front of a jury, Abe Lincoln is said to have noticed that his opponent was wearing a new style shirt which buttoned up the back, a style viewed as "city slicker" shirts by the folks in Illinois. He supposedly said to the jury, "I am sure you will not be influenced by this gentleman's pretended knowledge of the law. Why, he doesn't even know which side of his shirt ought to be in front."

c. We need to try using Brand X. Ten thousand satisfied customers can't be wrong.

d. Because our professor says it is so, this is the way it is.

e. We never had problems with lawsuits before we started affirmative action. It's those affirmative action hires that create such a legal logjam.

f. Should we finance new parking lots for high school students? No. Next we'll be financing everything from babysitters to haircuts to make life easier for high school students.

g. We can either support the good old ways of teaching or turn our schools over to new age gurus and yogis.

h. We can't listen to someone who is an ex-con and a confessed criminal tell us how to restore values to our teens.

CHAPTER 14 ANSWERS TO SELF-TEST

MATCHING Part One

1. f	2. a	3. c	4. i	5. j
6. g	7. d	8. b	9. h	10. e

MATCHING Part Two

11. g	12. b	13. h	14. d	15. j
16. e	17. i	18. f	19. c	20. a

MULTIPLE CHOICE

1. b	2. c	3. a	4. d	5. e
6. b	7. c	8. b	9. a	10. c
11. e	12. a	13. a	14. d	

MATCHING Part Three (Propositions)

1. fact	2. policy	3. value	4. policy	5. fact
6. policy	7. fact	8. policy	9. fact	10. value

TRUE/FALSE

1. False	2. False	3. True	4. False	5. False

MATCHING Part Four (Fallacies)

1. f	2. c	3. b	4. d	5. a
6. e				

MATCHING Part Five (Fallacious Arguments)

1. a & g	2. e	3. f	4. b & h	5. c
6. d				

Related Reading

"Cultural Variations in Persuasion," by Myron W. Lustig and Jolene Koester, <u>Intercultural Competence: Interpersonal Communication across Cultures</u>, 4th ed. (Allyn & Bacon, 2002) pp. 243-253

Preview

Persuasion, as Chapter 14 illustrates, hinges on one's perception of reasoning, evidence, logic, and credibility. An easy mistake for speakers to make is to assume that what is reasonable and logical to them is also reasonable and logical to everyone else. It just isn't so, as Myron W. Lustig and Jolene Koester illustrate in this excerpt from their book, <u>Intercultural Competence</u>. With fascinating intercultural examples, they describe particular approaches to preferred choices of reason, logic, and evidence across cultures. What is often called common sense might better be called culture sense. You will find this information applicable as you strive to adapt to the audience, choose evidence, use reasoning, and establish your credibility in a way that is pertinent to the cultural context you are speaking in.

Review

1. Can you think of situations where stories provide the strongest evidence?

2. Describe how various cultures place different values on physical evidence and testimony.

3. Distinguish among the key characteristics of quasilogical style, presentation style, and analogical style. Which style are you most likely to be persuaded by?

4. Besides the Jesse Jackson example in the reading, can you think of other examples where audience and speaker styles clashed?

5. How can the information in this reading help you prepare and present your persuasive messages?